19

39

157

161

239

12

FRANKLIN OF PHILADELPHIA

Franklin

OF PHILADELPHIA

ESMOND WRIGHT

THE BELKNAP PRESS OF
HARVARD UNIVERSITY PRESS
CAMBRIDGE, MASSACHUSETTS
AND LONDON, ENGLAND
1986

UXORI
PULCHERRIMAE LITTERIS DEDITAE
HORUM STUDIORUM PER TOT ANNOS
SEMPER COMITI

PREFACE

*A*ny biographer of Benjamin Franklin faces many problems. One is the problem of scale: Franklin lived for eighty-four years; he was born poor in Cotton Mather's Boston and died as a man of eminence and distinction seven years after the independence of the United States was won. His story is thus a major part of colonial history, of the history of Britain and France in the eighteenth century, of the revolutionary ideas that swept North America, and of the formative years in the shaping of the new republic. This was, in Carl Van Doren's words, "a great and wise man moving through great and troubling events." So long and rich a life raises also the problem of consistency, for the boy of sixteen, for all his precociousness, learned a lot by the time he was eighty-four. Efforts to give consistency to his ideas or to his views on morality and religion are imperiled by the many experiences and challenges he encountered. He was, first and last, versatile, adaptable, adept at swimming with tides.

Another difficulty is that Franklin's career has been studied exhaustively, probed in every detail, and repeatedly chronicled, notably by Carl Van Doren in a big biography published in 1938 and by a host of lesser biographers and specialists before and since. Any biographer of Franklin also faces the rivalry with his subject's own prose, so clean and spare and polished, and carrying so much urbanity and irony that it is always more tempting to quote Franklin directly than to comment. Why listen to an organ grinder with a monkey like this on display? Or, as Poor Richard put it in January 1735: "Bad Commentators spoil the best of books/So God sends meat (they say), the devil cooks." Part of the merit of Van Doren's study lay precisely in the fact that he allowed the master largely to speak for himself; he set out avowedly to write a complete life as Franklin might have written it

had he ever finished his own famous *Autobiography*, which reached
only to 1757 with later addenda.

Another, not the least daunting, difficulty today is the sheer volume
of primary material available. From Yale University Press, under the
superb editing first of Leonard Labaree and now of William Willcox
and their teams, come the *Papers of Benjamin Franklin*. Growing approximately at the rate of one volume each year, these are gradually
offering a total canvas of the Franklin years with all the surviving
letters written by or to Franklin (he had in his lifetime more than four
thousand correspondents), and with a matching mass of scholarly
headnotes on all the topics of controversy. The Yale edition obviously
replaces the workmanlike but patchier edition of Franklin's writings
edited seventy years ago by A. H. Smyth and the various editions that
preceded Smyth.

Each age brings to bear on the writing of history its own questions,
as well as its own skills and its own enriched material. Editions of
correspondence, however impeccably done, are no substitute for biography. And biography, like history, demands endless rewriting. For
our era brings with it its own problems, its own opportunities and
viewpoints. It is an age of anxiety and uncertainty, of cynicism and
disillusion. It publishes the papers of great men, but it has little faith
that greatness exists. The American story has ceased to be one of
effortless progress. It has seen the presidency and vice-presidency imperiled by ambition, conspiracy, corruption, and—most of all—na-
ïveté. Revolution, rare in 1776, is now a constant feature of the contemporary scene abroad. There is no faith in absolutes, whether
social, political or moral, and there is a preference for means, taking
us only a little way, rather than for ends. These characteristics of the
age may make Franklin, already one of the most human of mortals,
even more engaging and even more understandable than in the past.
Much that he had to say makes him the most modern-minded of all
the Founding Fathers: in scientific experiment; in his faith in federalism; in his views on population growth; in his native curiosity sharpened by diligence; in his remarkable balance and moderation of political judgment. Few today would, I believe, write of him in the
disparaging fashion of D. H. Lawrence, painting him as a paper Yankee; we who have suffered from politicians' unbridled and undisci-
plined slogans have less sympathy for the similar and equally flatulent
extravagances of *littérateurs* or of debunkers. Only now has it be-

come possible to see the rounded man as he was, and to assess him, good or ill, virtuous or backsliding, warts and all.

He played many parts, and often contemporaneously, and in doing so sometimes played for effect, and sometimes overdramatized, but one part of him stayed always single, amused and sardonic. This is a rational man who only just curbed his animal nature, affable but scholarly—who we might feel would have taken to our own times, as to his own, and got on—in his word "swimmingly." For today we have learned to appreciate—as few in previous generations did—that to survive is itself to conquer, that in a world of turmoil there can be—despite the homilies of *Poor Richard*—few constants even of the spirit, that in adaptation is strength, and that if at the end it is possible to say—preferably with a wink and a grin—*J'ai vécu,* then that itself is triumph.

I was first led to an interest in Benjamin Franklin when, forty years ago, I held a Harkness Fellowship at the University of Virginia, where I was studying his two great compatriots Washington and Jefferson. I first wrote on him at A. L. Rowse's invitation in 1966, in a short study for his Teach Yourself History library, and at Arthur Wang's invitation in 1968, in editing a compilation, *Benjamin Franklin: A Profile.* The present book owes much to the kindness of the two editors of the Franklin *Papers,* Leonard Labaree and William Willcox, who have made my visits to Yale at once congenial and fruitful; to the assistance of Jonathan Dull, Claude-Anne Lopez, and Catherine Prelinger at Yale; to the generosity of Professor Robin Winks, the Master, and the Fellows of Berkeley College for their hospitality to the visitor; to the support and interest of Dr. Whitfield Bell of the American Philosophical Society; and to the University of London, the British Academy, the Wolfson Foundation, the Idlewild and Leverhulme Trusts, and the American Philosophical Society for assistance with travel and research grants.

I am grateful to a number of friends who kindly read portions of the script as it was being written: Dr. Ann Condon of the University of New Brunswick, Professor Peter Marshall of Manchester University, Willard Randall of Pennsylvania and Princeton, and Dr. Richard Simmons of the University of Birmingham. They rescued me from a number of errors and omissions, though for those that defied their scrutiny, I accept, of course, full responsibility, as I do for those perversities of interpretation which remain. The work could not have been completed without the generous and efficient help of a succession of secretaries at the Institute of United States Studies in London, prominent among them Marion Piper, Sharon Gunde, Susan Blake, and Eileen Rivers, and without the expert bibliographical knowledge of Alison Cowden. I am also grateful for the secretarial assistance of Brenda Owens and Beryl Anderson, and for the skill and vigilance of Aida Donald, Elizabeth Suttell, and Camille Smith at Harvard University Press. As a guest of the Rockefeller Foundation, I was privileged to complete the writing of the book in the idyllic setting of the Villa Serbelloni on Lake Como.

CONTENTS

ILLUSTRATIONS

Frontispiece
Benjamin Franklin, 1778, by Joseph Siffred Duplessis.
    Courtesy of the Metropolitan Museum of Art, bequest of Michael
    Friedsam, 1931, the Friedsam Collection.

Following page 66

Bonner, Map of Boston, 1722.
    Courtesy of the Map Division, New York Public Library, Astor, Lenox
    and Tilden Foundations.

Benjamin Franklin, ca. 1746, by Robert Feke.
    Courtesy of the Fogg Art Museum, Harvard University, bequest of
    Dr. John Collins Warren, 1856.

Deborah Franklin, usually attributed to Matthew Pratt, but in fact by
Benjamin Wilson, 1766.
    Courtesy of the American Philosophical Society.

Mrs. Richard Bache (Sarah Franklin), by John Hoppner.
    Courtesy of the Metropolitan Museum of Art, Wolfe Fund, 1901,
    Catharine Lorillard Wolfe Collection.

Join, or Die. *Pennsylvania Gazette,* 1754.
    Courtesy of the New-York Historical Society.

William Temple Franklin, 1790, by John Trumbull.
    Courtesy of the Yale University Art Gallery.

A Northwest View of the State House in Philadelphia, 1778, by Charles
Willson Peale.
    Courtesy of the New-York Historical Society.

Benjamin Franklin, 1785, by Charles Willson Peale.
    Courtesy of the Pennsylvania Academy of the Fine Arts, Joseph and
    Sarah Harrison Collection.

The Library and Surgeon's Hall on Fifth Street, by William Birch.
    Courtesy of the Historical Society of Pennsylvania.

CHRONOLOGY

1706   Born in Boston; baptized at Old South Church.

1718   Printer's apprentice to brother James.

1722   "Silence Dogood" essays published anonymously in *New England Courant*.

1723   Runs away to Philadelphia.

1724–26   In England; works as a printer.

1725   Writes and prints *A Dissertation on Liberty and Necessity, Pleasure and Pain*.

1726   Returns to Philadelphia.

1727   Forms the Junto.

1728   Opens his own printing office.

1730   Becomes sole owner of the *Pennsylvania Gazette*. Appointed printer to the Pennsylvania Assembly. Marries Deborah Read.

1731   Founds first circulating library in America. Begins publishing *Poor Richard: An Almanack* (continued annually until 1758).

1736   Appointed clerk of the Assembly. Founds Union Fire Company.

1737   Appointed postmaster of Philadelphia. (Elected to Assembly.)

1742–44   Public enterprises: invents the Franklin stove, proposes the University of Pennsylvania, establishes the American Philosophical Society, organizes defense on frontier.

1747   First writes of his electrical experiments. Writes *Plain Truth*. Organizes first militia in Pennsylvania.

1748   Retires from active business. Elected to the Philadelphia Common Council.

1749   Grand Master of the Pennsylvania Masons.

1751   *Experiments and Observations on Electricity* published in London. Pennsylvania Hospital chartered. Elected to

Pennsylvania Assembly; reelected annually until 1764. Writes *Observations Concerning the Increase of Mankind*.

1752 Founds the first American fire insurance company.

1753 Receives honorary M.A.'s from Harvard and Yale, and Copley Medal of the Royal Society. Appointed deputy postmaster general of North America.

1754 Aids General Braddock in defending Pennsylvania against Indian attacks.

1756 Elected Fellow of the Royal Society. Appointed postmaster general of the colonies.

1757 Goes to London as agent for Pennsylvania Assembly, to plead the cause against the Proprietors. Writes *The Way to Wealth*.

1759 Receives honorary LL.D. degree from University of St. Andrews. Meets David Hume and Lord Kames.

1760 Writes *Interest of Great Britain Considered*. Secures Privy Council approval of taxation of proprietary estates in Pennsylvania.

1762 Receives honorary D.C.L. degree from Oxford. Returns to Philadelphia.

1763 Tours northern colonies to inspect post offices.

1764 Defeated in Assembly elections. Returns to London as agent for Pennsylvania.

1765 Works for repeal of Stamp Act; writes many anonymous pieces for the London press.

1766 Examined on the Stamp Act before the House of Commons.

1767 Becomes agent for Georgia.

1768 Writes *Causes of American Discontents before 1768*.

1769 Elected president of the American Philosophical Society (reelected annually all his life). Becomes agent for New Jersey.

1770 Newspaper propaganda campaign against Townshend duties; duties repealed, except on tea. Petitions for grant of land in the West. Becomes agent for Massachusetts.

1771 Begins *Autobiography*.

1772 Elected to French Academy of Sciences.

1774 Hutchinson letters affair. Attacked before Privy Council; dismissed as deputy postmaster general. Coercive acts passed; begins final negotiations to preserve the British Empire.

1775 Returns to America. Elected to Continental Congress and Pennsylvania Committee of Safety; active in support of war measures. Submits Articles of Confederation of United Colonies.

1776 Helps draft and signs Declaration of Independence. Presides at Pennsylvania Constitutional Convention. Sails for France as an American commissioner.

1777 Lionized by Parisian society and French intellectuals.

1778 Negotiates and signs treaty of alliance with France.

1779 Appointed minister to France.

1781 Appointed a commissioner to negotiate peace.

1782 With John Adams and John Jay, negotiates treaty of peace with Great Britain. Writes *Information to Those Who Would Remove to America.*

1784 Negotiates treaties of commerce with Prussia and other European nations. Resumes *Autobiography.*

1785 Returns to Philadelphia. Elected president of Pennsylvania Society for Promoting the Abolition of Slavery. Delegate to the Constitutional Convention.

1789 Finishes last section of *Autobiography.*

1790 April 17: dies in Philadelphia, at age 84.

FRANKLIN OF PHILADELPHIA

1

A TRADESMAN IN THE
AGE OF REASON

To his contemporaries, American and European, Benjamin Franklin was the greatest figure America had yet produced. He was publisher and printer, essayist and author, successful businessman and successful "general," internationally known scientist and philologist, politician and diplomat, Fellow of the Royal Society because of his contributions to the "fluid" theory of electricity, Doctor of Laws of Oxford and St. Andrews, moralist and sage. Yet in all the parts he played in a long and active career that ran from Cotton Mather's Boston to Washington's presidency, he remained very much himself: insatiably curious, a racy writer with an ear for the forceful phrase, earthy, detached, and free from illusion. In his origins, his range, and above all his success, Franklin seemed to be the living answer to the famous question asked by Hector St. John de Crèvecoeur in 1782: "What then *is* the American, this new man?" Goethe in his youth was fascinated by Franklin. Lord Kames described him as "a man who makes a great figure in the learned world: and who would make a greater figure for benevolence and candor, were virtue as much regarded in this declining age as knowledge." Some of his own compatriots bracketed him with Washington.[1]

Honest, splenetic John Adams took a different view. He wrote, rather spitefully, to Benjamin Rush: "The history of our Revolution will be one continued lie from one end to the other. The essence of the whole will be that Dr. Franklin's electrical rod smote the earth and out sprang General Washington. That Franklin electrified him with his rod, and thenceforward these two conducted all the policy, negotiations, legislatures, and war." Adams admitted Franklin's genius, original, sagacious and inventive, but could not see where his excellence lay as legislator or politician or negotiator. "From day to day he sat in silence at the Continental Congress, a great part of his time fast asleep in his chair," and in France he was too self-indulgent to attend regularly to the business of the embassy. Many in America agreed with Adams's strictures. To Loyalists, both before and after 1776, and to their historians, he was simply a traitor, as to his one-time ally Joseph Galloway and to Henry Hulton, who called him "this arch-traitor! This most atrocious of men!" William Cobbett, at the time a bitter Federalist pamphleteer in Philadelphia, referred to Franklin seven years after his death as "a crafty and lecherous old hypocrite . . . whose very statue seems to gloat on the wenches as they walk the State House yard."[2]

Mark Twain poured scorn on Franklin's "stove, and his military aspirations, his unseemly endeavor to make himself conspicuous when he entered Philadelphia, and his flying his kite and fooling away his time in all sorts of such ways when he ought to have been foraging for soap-fat, or constructing candles." Nathaniel Hawthorne complained that Poor Richard's proverbs were "all about getting money or saving it," and Herman Melville saw Franklin as full of platitudes, obtrusive advice, and mock friendliness, possessed of a bookkeeper's mind, and altogether of that race of men who were "keen observers of the main chance; prudent courtiers; practical magicians in linsey-woolsey." To Carlyle, searching for heroes and the heroic born of tumult, Franklin was simply too rational a man—or at least presented to the world a lowbrow image. D. H. Lawrence's view of him is well known:

Middle-sized, sturdy, snuff-colored Doctor Franklin, one of the soundest citizens that ever trod or "used venery" . . . The soul of man is a dark vast forest, with wild life in it. Think of Benjamin fencing it off! . . . He made himself a list of virtues, which he trotted inside like a grey nag in a paddock . . . I do not like him . . . I can't stand Benjamin [because] he tries to take away my wholeness and my dark forest, my freedom.[3]

Charles Angoff added a touch of acid to the portrait: Franklin was "a cheap and shabby soul":

Franklin represented the least praiseworthy qualities of the inhabitants of the New World: miserliness, fanatical practicality, and lack of interest in what are usually known as spiritual things. Babbittry was not a new thing in

America, but he made a religion of it, and by his tremendous success with it he grafted it upon the American people so securely that the national genius is still suffering from it. He extolled the virtues of honesty, industry, chastity, cleanliness, and temperance—all excellent things. But it never occurred to him that with these alone life is not worth a fool's second thought. Philosophy, poetry, and the arts spring from different sources . . . Not a word about nobility, not a word about honor, not a word about grandeur of soul, not a word about charity of mind! Carlyle called Franklin the father of all the Yankees. That was a libel against the tribe, for the Yankees have produced Thoreau, Hawthorne, and Emily Dickinson. It would be more accurate to call Franklin the father of all the Kiwanians.[4]

*   *   *

Yet Franklin's success was striking. Born with no advantages, he became wealthy and esteemed; accepted into Old World society, he yet helped to procure the independence of his own country, and to manufacture for it an alliance with France that contributed to American victory in 1783; self-educated, he became a lion in the literary world of Paris and reached, as he put it, "some degree of reputation in the World"; and he acted as conciliator-at-large and Founding Father Extraordinary in the debates over the Constitution at Philadelphia in 1787. His services are clear enough. What is it that disturbs his critics?

The man was complaisant. Jefferson never forgot the adage Franklin taught him: "Never contradict anybody"; Franklin came to live by an aversion to contention. He unquestionably had force of character, versatility, at times originality and daring. But did he not lack in science, in politics, and in life a quality hard to define—passion, vision, penetration, that elusive and intense quality which transforms capacity into genius? Was the immense persuasiveness not based on a studious avoidance of dogmatic positions? The world is not changed by prudent men, or by humorists, or by men lacking *gravitas*. Franklin might well be described as a great man marred by his own common sense, limited by his own sense of humor, denied in the end a place in Valhalla by the very carefully manufactured controls over his own inclinations that made him so much and so successfully a man of his own times.

Moreover, his rationalism and his curiosity about all external phenomena, his accuracy and sharpness of observation, were so much greater because of his almost total lack of aesthetic response. The assiduous letter-writer left no descriptions of scenery, of nature, or of buildings; traveling in Scotland thirteen years after Culloden, he made no reference to the Jacobites and mentioned not a mountain. So with the Lake District. His intuitions were intellectual. He sought to make his Book of Common Prayer "reasonable." As Sainte-Beuve noted, the man who seemed so truly to understand the parables of the Gospel was out of his depth with Job and David. He did not like obscurities, or words from the clouds. He required that the universe be capable of comprehension, and by the human mind. Man for him was an animal who made tools, built stoves, and cured smoky chimneys. He worked in the light. He sought heat and comfort, cleanliness—and sanity. Lawrence's affirmation "my soul is a dark forest" would to Franklin have been nonsense. His rationalism might take the form of an irritating moral arithmetic, but it was at least lucid and clear. This was a cool man, a man the twentieth century can appreciate even more than did the eighteenth.[5]

If Franklin lacked a strong aesthetic sense, so for that matter did Washington and Adams. Indeed, the father of his country was much more limited in mind, none too literate, equally marked by ambition for fame and by calculation, certainly no more a man of passion than Franklin. And if there was passion in young Thomas Jefferson is that not seen today—as it was by his contemporaries—as a topic for amusement, or even for contempt? Perhaps it is only now, in the cynical but scholarly, ultrasophisticated and lavishly documented perspective of our post-Vietnam, post-Watergate and post-illusionist world that we can see the men of the eighteenth century as they truly were: not "great" except insofar as the combination of their qualities and the events of their day conspired to make their lives fortunate; and aware, as were the Romans, of the play of *fortuna* throughout history, recognizing, in the memorable words of H. A. L. Fisher, "the free play of the contingent and the unforeseen." They were intensely curious, very human, and conscious, as events unfolded, that to them and their age an immense and unexpected opportunity had been given.[6]

Franklin's lack of aesthetic and passionate responses reflected late seventeenth-century Boston. Scientific speculation and activity rather than poetry or evangelism were features of Harvard; even in religion a note of tolerance, of sectarianism and diversity was already apparent; Tillotson's sermons were recommended reading by Brattle and

Leverett, the Third Church clearly was more liberal than the First or the Second. Later, Addison's *Spectator,* as later still the writings of Voltaire, circulated widely. It was not surprising that a young journalist, hearing the topics of debate and sharing the sharp iconoclasm of his elders in the trade, should conclude that right behavior and a certain decent charity toward one's neighbors mattered more than theological hair-splitting. Linked to this view was the fortifying reflection that this world's goods and this world's jobs were not inherently wicked but signs of God's approval. Godliness was hard to distinguish from good citizenship. "What is serving God?" Franklin asked toward the end of his life, and answered, "It is doing good to man." To the assiduous Calvinist, material reward was but the manifestation of God's grace abounding.[7]

This liberation of the spirit was suited to Franklin's spirit of inquiry. The visible world was open now to secular explanations: lightning was produced not by God's wrath but by natural forces to be understood, explained, and controlled. Knowledge was a goal in itself, a rational understanding of the universe blessed in this world as in the next. And knowledge was to be put to use. Franklin refused to patent the stove, as he refused to patent the lightning conductor he perfected after challenging Olympus by floating a kite up into a thundercloud.

If there is in Franklin much that irritated Carlyle and Lawrence, there is even more to disturb the Puritans. He ran away from home, and he had an illegitimate son. He never lost his interest in women. If, unlike John Adams, he was never vain, he was certainly not untouched by flattery, in Philadelphia or in France. He remained a racy and roguish figure to the end, and rarely chose to hide his indiscretions. His correspondence is rich in letters to and from younger women, his *amitiés amoureuses,* in which he plays a role that suggests more than the avuncular. The language is risqué and daringly suggestive, equally for the young and virginal Catharine Ray of Rhode Island, whom he met in 1755, and for the experienced widow Mme Helvétius in Paris. Probably it was the words and not the deeds that were bold. He may well have thought this style was required of him in the Paris salons—but he could hardly have thought it required in Rhode Island.

Franklin's pieces of half-jocular, semiautobiographical prose angered Lawrence and Puritans alike. It was with his common sense that

Lawrence took issue; in particular the absence of passion and of deep primeval drives, not merely sexual, which in Lawrence's eyes were the essence of the human spirit. John Keats had a similar reaction: Franklin was "a philosophical Quaker full of mean and thrifty maxims." For Puritans they were anathema.[8]

*   *   *

Yet the form of Franklin's *Autobiography,* like the self-scrutiny of his "The Art of Virtue," was in the Puritan tradition. The *Autobiography* records his rise "from the poverty and obscurity in which I was born and bred to a state of affluence and some degree of reputation in the world." Its purpose was to serve as model, so that others might profit by the example. It was due to the "kind providence" of God "which led me to the means I used and gave them success." In the Puritan creed, humility, piety, and success were not deemed to be contradictory but interrelated, cause and effect. The central theme of Cotton Mather's *Essays to Do Good* is personal salvation through good works. There are explicit functions for ministers and teachers, lawyers and physicians. But the greatest opportunity awaits the man of wealth, for divine approval and its material rewards do not diminish one's obligations to society: "Honor the Lord with thy substance; so shall thy barns be filled with plenty . . . Obscure mechanics and husbandmen have risen to estates, of which once they had not the most distant expectation."[9]

For an industrious and ambitious Boston apprentice, no tune could be more appealing. The way to God, it seemed, was also the way to wealth. Luck is of no account. What matters is hard work. "Diligence is the Mother of good luck," as Poor Richard was to put it (February 1736), and as he also said, "God gives all things to industry. He that hath a trade hath an estate" (January 1742). In 1784, in a letter to Cotton Mather's son Samuel, Franklin acknowledged his indebtedness to the elder Mather's *Essays to Do Good.* Those *Essays* had given him "such a turn of thinking, as to have an influence on my conduct through life, for I have always set a greater value on the character of a *doer of good,* than on any other kind of reputation; and if I have been, as you seem to think, a useful citizen, the public owes the advantage of it to that book."[10]

This most secular of men thus considered himself a direct descendant of the Puritans. Franklin and Cotton Mather had more in common than a taste for moral precepts and an addiction to sermonizing. They shared an interest in reform and self-improvement, a perennial taste for chastisement, of others and of themselves, a foreknowledge that sin would keep breaking out, a morbid streak of self-analysis. The editor in Franklin seemed often to be speaking from a lectern, even if most of the time the sermon he preached was a witty and worldly one.

Moreover, he preached not from pulpits but in print. So he was storyteller and raconteur, tantalizer and tease, and not afraid of tall tales and spice, ribaldry and irreverence. He could on social occasions become Franklin the Wizard. Who but a Merlin would have dared to harness the malignant forces in thunderstorms to a riverside picnic, and provide "a turkey killed for our dinner by the electrical shock before a fire kindled by the electrical bottle"? When the guest of Lord Shelburne on a stormy day in 1772, he boasted that he could quiet the waters in the river. He walked 200 paces from his companions and made some sweeping passes over the water with his bamboo cane. The stream became as smooth as a mirror. Franklin then revealed that the artifice lay in his scientific knowledge: concealed in a hollow joint in the cane was enough oil to do the trick. In the country-house circle it was helpful to be Franklin the Magician.[11]

Franklin learned early that a smile and a twinkle in the prose made it readable, and humor became one of his weapons. At times it was spicy and colloquial, at others biblical and rhetorical, anecdotal at one moment and satirical the next, always honed to sparkle and to pierce. It may well have been as carefully cultivated as much else in his character. It responded clearly to his leather-apron vigor. He was not trusted to draft the Declaration of Independence, it has often been said, lest he put a joke in it.

Another lesson he learned early, and in Boston, was his low-key, conciliatory style of argument. A famous passage in the *Autobiography* describes his discovery of the socratic method:

I was charmed with it, adopted it, dropped my abrupt contradiction and positive argumentation, and put on the humble enquirer and doubter . . . I found this method safest for myself and very embarrassing to those against whom I used it; therefore I took a delight in it, practised it continually, and grew very artful and expert in drawing people, even of superior knowledge, into concessions, the consequences of which they did not foresee, entangling them in difficulties out of which they could not extricate themselves, and so obtaining victories that neither myself nor my cause always deserved. I continued this method some few years, but gradually left it, retaining only the habit of expressing myself in terms of modest diffidence; never using, when I advanced anything that may possibly be disputed, the words *certainly, undoubtedly,* or any others that give the air of positiveness to an opinion; but rather say, *I conceive or I apprehend a thing to be so and so; it appears to me,* or *I should think it so or so,* for such and such reasons; or *I imagine it to be so;* or *it is so, if I am not mistaken.* This habit, I believe, has been of great advantage to me when I have had occasion to inculcate my opinions, and persuade men into measures that I have been from time to time engaged in promoting . . .[12]

*   *   *

The shrewd and frugal, cautious and canny features that Lawrence and Carlyle disliked in Franklin came out of the clash in him of the Puritan with the permissive and urban man. What the nineteenth-century romantics criticized was less Franklin than Boston, and the Yankee efforts at discipline and control that mattered in disciplining a frontier or the turbulent spirit in men. Eighteenth-century America bred political freedom, but in practical matters it bred also caution and patience, judgment and discretion, tolerance and finesse, and it was on these qualities that successful careers were built. Americans then strove as much for self-restraint and self-mastery as for self-government. Witness the career of Washington on the one hand and his concern with what he called his "honor"; witness the observations of Paine and Jefferson on the other. However divided on matters of political interpretation they might be, all would have shared a common respect for the qualities of discipline and balance; all recognized in their own natures how their instincts had to be curbed by reason.

When Franklin devised Poor Richard and used him as a vehicle of exhortation and advice, and when from time to time he revealed how hard self-control was for himself, his readers knew what he meant. He was a practical man, writing for other practical men. Franklin recognized that natural instincts should, indeed must, be harnessed if a reputation was to be made and merited. And this, the self-reliance that originated as a frontier gospel, became the key doctrine of American transcendentalism. Franklin's disciple is Emerson, as Carlyle saw; if Emerson rejected Franklin's man because he lacked all trace of the heroic, Poor Richard nevertheless lives on, with sanctity added to sanctimoniousness, in the pages of Emerson's *Journals.* The middle-class morality that Lawrence pilloried but that is still at the vital roots of American prosperity and is reflected in its industry, its native shrewdness, its frugality, its practicality, can be said to have found its first prophet in Benjamin Franklin, though no one would have appreciated Lawrence's pride in virility more than Franklin. He confessed with gusto that he practiced the frugality he preached just as long as poverty forced him to, and not a moment longer.

*   *   *

Franklin himself is his own creation. He made books, and he made news—and his books and news "made" Franklin. Here is a man who talks to us apparently so frankly about himself while increasingly obscuring himself behind the public images, that at intervals we do not know what is fact and what is fiction. All is told in a limpid, deceptively simple prose, and we are even told how the style is achieved. Here is a career built at once, and often contradictorily, on moral precepts and on endless self-revelation. It is done always with a twinkle, with a sunny humor; and always, behind all the chat, with a touch of reserve.

He built a reputation, or at least an image. As Charles Coleman Sellers has demonstrated, of his contemporaries no one sat so often for a portrait—protest though he might—as did Franklin. Franklin himself realized early in his career that one source of successful salesmanship was his own reputation:

In order to secure my credit and character as a tradesman, I took care not only to be in *reality* industrious and frugal, but to avoid all *appearances* of the contrary. I dressed plain and was seen at no places of idle diversion. I never went out a fishing or shooting; a book, indeed, sometimes debauched me from my work, but that was seldom, snug and gave no scandal . . . Thus being esteemed an industrious, thriving young man, and paying duly for what I bought . . . I went on swimmingly.[13]

If this sounds like the wiliness of Mr. Pepys in the language of Mr. Pooter, it could be paralleled by similar, if less frank, reflections in the papers of many a contemporary, George Washington included. In a sense all the revolutionaries were self-made men, and some of them in making their reputations made a Revolution. The Yankee virtues triumphed not at Appomattox but at Yorktown.

Franklin, then, was a child of Boston, of Puritanism, and of the

Enlightenment: skeptical but uncynical, uncommitted but endlessly curious, and with confidence in reason, freedom, and humanity. There was amusement and detachment, but there was an eagerness for fame and for evidence of the approval of men—and women. The driving ambition, the hunger for work, the capacity—very striking in a journalist who made his mark by his skill in handling the public prints and public issues—for keeping confidences, all these came early. So did the manufacture of personae, from Silence Dogood to Poor Richard, ultimately to Benevolus, FB, and a host of pseudonyms. He became aware that his own carefully contrived persona would be durable. In particular it fitted like a glove what was looked for in Europe: to the Paris of the Enlightenment came a homespun genius, able to be both rural philosopher and scientist yet with much sophistication of manner. He played the part of the Natural Man to perfection, and it allowed him to be suitably impressed by all that was subtle, old-world and complicated in Western Europe.

*   *   *

Is there another, a more real, man behind the myriad personae? Since so many of the letters, pamphlets, squibs, and tracts are meant for audiences, and their bulk is daunting, how does one find the man himself—if he does exist independently of his images of himself, like a manipulator of the strings to his own puppet marionettes. Behind the plain, smug, and rounded face, with its cold eyes made bland by spectacles, the thin tight lips and the high domed forehead of the scholar, behind the easy manner and the all-too-ready quips and aphorisms, was there a "real" Franklin?

The analogy and the question are misplaced. While there was detachment of manner and emotion there could also be a genuine degree of engagement: in Philadelphia's welfare and urban growth; in the scientific experiments and the lifetime curiosity about natural forces; in the campaign against the Proprietors, which clearly produced a real sense of crusade; in his role as agent and—for too short a time—in his efforts to preserve that "noble china vase, the British Empire"[14] and in his role as diplomat in Paris. This was no Edward Bancroft, exploiting two causes with neither of which was he involved except for pay. Franklin became the parts he played, even if some of them were inconsistent and contradictory.

It is true that one does detect in a few of the letters another, and perhaps a more real Franklin, and—notably in the years of tension in Philadelphia in 1764 and in London from 1768 to 1775—a touch of savage bitterness. Nor can one escape noticing, amid all the words, the remoteness of the central figure, the absence of physical descriptions of people or places, and the striking lack of malicious gossip, even about obvious enemies. In the last of his London years there was, of course, a fear that his correspondence was read by government agents, as almost certainly it was. But, this said, for one concerned with winning the approval of posterity, total candor is lacking. What we know about the real man also includes the bitter anger in his youth toward his brother James and the wish to outdo him; the indulgence of sexual appetites at least until his marriage; the hunger for social acceptance; the ambition; the pride in his obvious success; and the facility, not to say guile, in dealing with critics and opponents. This could be an intriguing and a cajoling man. Perhaps one should add to this roster in the end his bitterness toward Britain, which, after his years of effort at conciliation, was all too thoroughly justified. What shines through in the man, however, and makes him come to life is the sharp native intelligence, the brightness of a mind enjoying itself in all the varied experiences that come to it as challenges, a mind that was sure that reason would prevail, that problems were for solving, that answers did exist. If the searches and the enjoyment could lead to useful results, that was good. If the results should lead also to a profit, so much the better.

Moreover, in sharp contrast with John Adams, there is little evidence of envy or of jealousy, and curiously little of vanity. Did not Poor Richard say "He that falls in love with himself will have no rivals"; yet the *Autobiography* is surely among the most modest of memoirs. Even discounting the fact that the major part of it ends in 1757 before the public career really begins, there is no vainglory, and the tale is told in dry and homespun fashion, with a simplicity that is at once disarming and deceptive.

Carl Van Doren said of Franklin that he was less a single personality than a committee, "a harmonious human multitude." If Mr. Worldly Wiseman was here, so were Mr. Legality and Mr. Civility. In one who had built his career and his fortune on selling words in print, the concern with fame and reputation was inevitable. For him it did not come easily or as a reflection of his landed status, as to Washington, or from practice in the law courts; it had to be earned, and the publicist could hardly earn it without stepping down into the forum and the marketplace. It is no accident that the Poor Richard Club of Philadelphia saluted Franklin's 250th birthday in 1956 by producing a tract with the title *Benjamin Franklin, Patron Saint of Advertising*. Franklin recommended his improved stove to the readers of his newspaper with the seductive claim that it would benefit the complexion and beauty of womenfolk. Reputation mattered, and was made by advertisement.[15]

Franklin was made for conciliation and diplomacy, for the winning of friends. His diplomatic services were not confined to his years abroad. If as colonial agent he worked for compromise, he worked for it all his life. Standing at the bar of the House, he told the Commons in 1766 that "every assembly on the American continent, and every member in every assembly" had denied Parliament's authority to pass the Stamp Act. As deputy postmaster general of North America he was himself an example of emerging colonial unity. As plain broad-shouldered Ben Franklin, self-taught and practical, he was the embodiment of the colonial protest, "the ultimate Whig." In the France of 1776 his qualities were held in high regard: to Vergennes he was an instrument of French imperial revenge on Britain; to the Encyclopedists and Physiocrats a natural man from a republican wilderness; to bluestockings a rustic philosopher with civilized tastes, an approving eye for the ladies, and a neat democratic wit. To all, Franklin was proof of republican simplicity and virtue; he was "The American, this new man." The fur cap, worn to hide his eczema, was mistaken for a badge of the frontier. Since he was cast in the role of wise and simple philosopher, he played the part. He could be Solon and Silenus, gallant and Gallic, to suit all tastes, and not least his own.

If he fought for colonial rights and understanding in London in 1776, he was still fighting for tolerance in 1787. The speech that James Wilson delivered for him on the last day of the Constitutional Convention—he himself was too old and infirm to stand—was the product of long experience and expressed that reasonableness which the twentieth century as well as the eighteenth might regard as the closest approximation that finite man can make to wisdom. He appealed to his colleagues among the Founding Fathers who opposed the Constitution to doubt with himself a little of their own infallibility. "I consent, Sir, to this Constitution, because I expect no better, and because I am not sure that it is not the best. The opinions I have had of its errors I sacrifice to the public good. I have never whisper'd a syllable of them abroad. Within these walls they were born, and here they shall die." [16]

*   *   *

What makes Franklin so compelling to study and so original is his almost total freedom from the limits of his own environment. He made the whole western world his own parish. Born poor in colonial Boston, he was at ease in Quaker Philadelphia, in royal London, and in elegant Paris; as much at home in St. Andrews as in Passy, or in Bethlehem and Easton on the Pennsylvania wilderness frontier. The reason is clear. He was far in advance of his time, not merely as editor turned scientist turned statesman, or from the prescience of so much of his writing, but because one is aware of his own awareness of challenges and of the immense potential of the human mind when left free to speculate, to question, and to experiment. One is always in a state of delight in reading Franklin's prose because of his skill in communicating his own enjoyment of the world when a lively mind is let loose in it. His was a free and a probing spirit, at home in the marketplace of ideas and inventions in an age of reason; and he knew no frontiers. Four months before his death he wrote to his English friend David Hartley, "God grant that not only the Love of Liberty but a thorough Knowledge of the Rights of Man may pervade all the Nations of the Earth so that a Philosopher may set his foot anywhere on its surface and say 'This is my country.'" [17]

2

A CITY UPON A HILL

*B*enjamin Franklin was born on Milk Street, just across the way from the Old South Church, on January 6, 1705 (Old Style), January 17, 1706 (New Style). His birthplace no longer stands, and commercial traffic now jostles the Freedom Trail. The house had two rooms on each of two floors, with a cellar and a garret. Only one room had a fireplace or any light. Breakfast was usually bread and milk or milk with cornmeal mush; dinner was some kind of meat, often a stew from the kitchen pot, or soup, perhaps with pickles or vegetables, and a pudding. Knives were few, and there were no forks.

Benjamin was the tenth, and the youngest son, of the seventeen children of Josiah Franklin. He recalled: "I remember 13 sitting at one time at this table, who all grew up to be men and women, and married." His older brother Ebenezer had been, at sixteen months, "drowned in a tub of suds," as Samuel Sewall noted in his diary.[1] Benjamin was the youngest son of the youngest son for five generations; and as he was the tenth son and born on a Sunday, his father, a church member in full communion of the Old South Church, "a Visible Saint," saw in him his titheling for the church. It was a curiously misplaced plan for one who was to become one of the most secular-minded of men.

Josiah Franklin had migrated from Banbury in Oxfordshire to Boston in 1683; the family roots, as Benjamin was later to trace them, were frankly and proudly plebeian—farmers, small landholders, blacksmiths, dyers, and "leather-apron men"—and went deep into Northamptonshire and Protestant soil. Josiah Franklin, though he had been apprenticed as a dyer, was, when Benjamin was born, a tallow-chandler and soap-boiler at the sign of the Blue Ball in Milk Street. When the boy was three, Josiah was sufficiently prosperous to supply the town with candles for the watch, enough to cost a pound. And three years later he bought, for £320, a new house at the corner of Union and Hanover streets, to which the family and the shop were moved. Though the son was to move out of his father's world, there was not a little of Josiah in Benjamin—intelligent, industrious, and independent. He recalled his father in his *Autobiography:*

He had an excellent constitution of body, was of middle stature, but well set, and very strong; he was ingenious, could draw prettily, was skilled a little in music, and had a clear, pleasing voice, so that when he played psalm tunes on his violin and sung withal, as he sometimes did in an evening after the business of the day was over, it was extremely agreeable to hear. He had a mechanical genius too, and, on occasion, was very handy in the use of other tradesmen's tools; but his great excellence lay in a sound understanding and solid judgment in prudential matters, both in private and public affairs . . . At his table he liked to have, as often as he could, some sensible friend or neighbor to converse with, and always took care to start some ingenious or useful topic for discourse, which might tend to improve the minds of his children. By this means he turned our attention to what was good, just, and prudent in the conduct of life.[2]

About his mother Franklin says little. Abiah Folger, Josiah Franklin's second wife, had been born on Nantucket. She was the daughter of Peter Folger, teacher and surveyor, weaver and miller, and interpreter for Indians; a writer of homespun verse, Folger had shown himself in his *A Looking-Glass for the Times* a critic of the persecutions of Baptists and Quakers that marred the story of the Bay Colony. Abiah's mother, Mary Morrill, had been an indentured servant whom Peter Folger bought for £20 and later married. Through his mother's family Benjamin had contacts with the Nantucket whalers and was aware of a world of trade and salt water far beyond the ordered confines of Puritan Boston. Abiah Folger was "a discreet and virtuous woman"; the phrase is Benjamin's, inscribed on her tombstone; of her he tells us little else. She was clearly robust—and prolific. Five children from Josiah's first marriage were still alive when Abiah married him; ten more followed, six boys and four girls over the next twenty-two years, and not one a troubled birth. She lived to the age of eighty-four, Josiah to eighty-seven; Benjamin inherited their sturdiness. But for her, presumably, there could be little but the chores.

*   *   *

Boston in 1706 was ceasing to be the tidy and planned city of the Saints of John Winthrop's noble vision. It was the largest town in North America and certainly—not least in its own eyes—the most important. Andrew Burnaby, visiting it in 1760, likened it to a thriving English town. In his map of 1722, Captain John Bonner already claimed for it "near 12,000" people, with "42 streets, 36 lanes and 22 alleys" and "houses near 3,000, 1,000 Brick, the rest Timber." The streets were crooked and irregular, paved with cobblestones, with open gutters in the middle; pigs served as collectors of garbage, and geese wandered off the Common. The houses were a maze of crowded, timbered tenements, all tiny, most of them firetraps—Boston had had eight great fires in the previous eighty years, and six outbreaks of smallpox. Families were large and lived public lives; privacy was impossible, so much so that it was rarely mentioned. Everyone knew everyone else's business.[3]

The city was all but an island, linked to the mainland by a mile-long neck of scrub and mudflats over which, in high tides or winter storms, the sea swept. North Boston, north of the Long Wharf and cut off by the Mill Creek (now Blackstone Street), was doubly a peninsula. The Common gave the city grace, and around it stood noble brick houses. Approached from the sea and guarded by Governor's Island and Castle Island, Boston rose like an amphitheater crowned with its three hills—Fort, Beacon and Copp's—and eleven steeples. A Revere engraving dated 1770 shows it to advantage, with eight big ships riding at anchor. The Long Wharf ran out to sea for half a mile, and the largest ship afloat could berth there whatever the tide. Around the wharves were the rope walks and cordwainers' shops, the taverns and tenements of a thriving community. The city lived by trade with the West Indies and by building ships. It exported codfish and barrel staves, salt pork, salt beef, and hard pine; it imported sugar and molasses, wine and slaves. One item of its own manufacture—rum—was at once solace and currency up and down the seaboard. Trade between New England, the West Indies, and Africa was funneled through Boston, and the city drew a rich dividend.

By 1706 Boston was moving out of its early generations of high Puritanism. Ten years earlier, Judge Sewall had stood in his pew in the meetinghouse to hear the reading of his confession of contrition for his share in the witchcraft delusion of 1692. The liberal Brattle Street Church, with its striking deviations from the principles of the Cambridge Platform, had been organized in 1699 by a group of wealthy Boston merchants. Morality rather than piety was being stressed, and in the train of prosperity secularism was creeping in. Afraid of water—the most frequent uses to which it was put, it has been said, were for transport and for drowning—Bostonians lavishly consumed beer, ale, applejack, and rum. Not only drunkenness but also dancing and games of chance were evident; the French wars brought sailors and rowdies to the waterfront, and crime and prostitution followed; wars against Catholic France allowed Guy Fawkes Day, or Pope's Day, to be celebrated overlustily; and in the clashes of North End with South End the Boston mob was born. In the charter granted in 1691, after the overthrow of Governor Andros, the nonconformist elements were no longer disfranchised. Although not a democratic state, since it insisted on a sharp property qualification for the suffrage, the Massachusetts of Franklin's youth was in social, as in political, character no longer an oligarchy of the spiritual elect.

Despite its small size, Boston in 1706 was the largest city and busiest port in the colonies, just ahead of, though soon to be outstripped by, Philadelphia. Nothing so much became part of the bone and sinew of Benjamin Franklin as the conviction that trade was a virtue, a source of wealth and power and prestige. Commerce and trade and the Puritan gospel of work were effectively destroying whatever class barriers a new world and its expanding and demanding frontier had ever permitted. John Hull, the goldsmith, started life as a blacksmith's son; his widow, Mary, married William Phips, a ship's carpenter who became wealthy in shipbuilding and trade (and the discovery and recapture of sunken treasure) to end up as Sir William and a rather unskillful royal governor of Massachusetts. Nathaniel Hancock, the shoemaker of Cambridge, was the grandfather of the Thomas Hancock who so prospered by trade, naval contracts, and smuggling that he could build the family home on Beacon Hill and fill it with furniture and a good library of volumes, "well bound with gilt edges," bought in London. Thomas's nephew and heir was to be the first signer of the Declaration of Independence.

*   *   *

Franklin's interest in reading—"I do not remember when I could not read"—encouraged his father to plan for him a career in the church. Accordingly at the age of eight he was sent to Boston Grammar School (now Boston Latin School), but he stayed less than a year for sound reasons of economy and prudence on his father's part: "from a view of the expense of a College education . . . and the mean living many so educated were afterwards able to obtain." A further year followed at the school of "a then famous man, Mr. George Brownell . . . I acquired fair writing pretty soon, but I failed in the arithmetic, and made no progress in it."[4] At ten he went into the shop to help his father; his formal schooling had lasted less than two years. For all practical purposes, Benjamin Franklin, like George Washington, was self-taught.

"I was employed in cutting wick for the candles, filling the dipping mold and the molds for cast candles, attending the shop, going on errands, etc. . . . I disliked the trade, and had a strong inclination for the sea."[5] His brother Josiah had already run away to sea, and Benjamin, who spent his spare time on the waterfront and was already a strong swimmer and skilled in managing boats, seemed likely to follow. Accordingly his father sought an apprenticeship for him in a trade. He was twelve and fond of books; his brother James, nine years his elder, had conveniently just returned from London where he had served an apprenticeship as a printer. Now master printer James got young brother Benjamin as his apprentice, undertaking to provide board and lodging in return for £10 and a promise of nine years of service; and Benjamin began the career in printing and journalism that he never completely abandoned, and in which he always took pride. He used his job, over the years, to educate himself, to make money, and to give the world news, including, necessarily perhaps, his own views. The line between the two in eighteenth-century and colonial journalism was always elusive; and when news was short, which was often, views had to be found, or invented, to replace or embroider it. Journalism was, in Franklin's day, the career before all others that offered opportunity to enterprise and imagination. His pen, he came to realize, was his chosen and carefully polished weapon, at once a rapier with which to wound and a key to unlock all doors.

The printing business grew slowly in a small town already well supplied with five printers and two newspapers, the *Boston News Letter* and the *Boston Gazette*. In 1719 the brothers secured the contract to print the *Boston Gazette*. When they lost it after forty numbers, they decided to start a newspaper of their own, and the *New England Courant* made its appearance in August 1721.

Meanwhile, Benjamin read voraciously: "all the little Money that came into my Hands was ever laid out in Books." The first book to which he refers in the *Autobiography* is Bunyan's *Pilgrim's Progress*. He was so "pleas'd" with it that he bought Bunyan's works in separate little volumes. The idiom and the style, the characters and their rich qualities and dramatic abodes—Mr. Worldly Wiseman and Mr. Legality, Mr. Obstinate and Mr. Pliable, the Delectable Mountains, Vanity Fair, the Valley of Humiliation—the theme of life as an odyssey of trials and temptations and triumphs: all left a permanent imprint. He sold his volumes of Bunyan in turn to buy Burton's *Historical Collections*, a ragbag miscellany of history and biography, travel and fiction; he read (and lamented the time wasted on) his father's books "of polemic divinity"; he read and valued Plutarch's *Lives* and, not least, Defoe's *Essay on Projects* and Cotton Mather's *Essays to Do Good*. He progressed to Locke's *Essay Concerning Human Understanding* and Xenophon's *Memorabilia*. If Locke influenced his political opinions—with consequences only gradually appearing— and Defoe much influenced his style, Cotton Mather, both as mentor and as subject for satire, had the deepest immediate impact.

Franklin took to arguing in would-be socratic style with his friend John Collins, and to putting his arguments into writing. His chance discovery of the third volume of the *Spectator* led him to train himself in frank imitation of its style:

I took some of the tales and turned them into verse; and, after a time, when I had pretty well forgotten the prose, turned them back again. I also sometimes jumbled my collections of hints into confusion, and after some weeks endeavored to reduce them into the best order, before I began to form the full sentences and compleat the paper. This was to teach me method in the arrangement of thoughts. By comparing my work afterwards with the original, I discovered many faults and amended them; but I sometimes had the pleasure of fancying that, in certain particulars of small import, I had been lucky enough to improve the method or the language, and this encouraged me to think I might possibly in time come to be a tolerable English writer, of which I was extreamly ambitious. My time for these exercises and for reading was at night, after work or before it began in the morning, or on Sundays, when I contrived to be in the printing-house alone, evading as much as I could the common attendance on public worship which my father used to exact on me when I was under his care, and which indeed I still thought a duty, though I could not, as it seemed to me, afford time to practise it.[6]

This sedulous self-training of the mind demanded a self-discipline that never came easily, nights of study after days at the press or in the streets. Whatever the note of impiety, idleness was still a waste of God's precious time, to use the Puritan phrase. In diligent application lay the way to wealth. And also in diligent self-examination, which, when recorded for the eyes of others, could sound vain, sanctimonious, and smug, a chronicling of temptations resisted, of trials attempted—and of unhappy errata, as Franklin called them, of judgment. Always let your conscience be your guide—or almost always. Impressed by Thomas Tryon's *The Way to Wealth*, Franklin became a vegetarian, as much to save the money spent on meals and the time spent consuming them as to produce "that greater clearness of head and quicker apprehension which usually attend temperance in eating and drinking." This process of self-analysis and self-exposure, so richly documented in his *Autobiography*, led him indeed to curb even his proneness to dialectic: "Persons of good sense, I have since observed, seldom fall into it, except lawyers, university men and men of all sorts that have been bred at Edinborough." He must, he told himself, cultivate a speech of "modest diffidence."[7]

This was decisively not the tone of the *New England Courant*. This new venture in Boston journalism, a single sheet printed in two columns on each side, was, like its two rivals, a weekly. Unlike them, however, it lacked the support of authority: to ensure survival a colonial newspaper needed the backing of the government and was usually published by the postmaster, who could give his sheet the news that reached him through the mails, and who had the privilege of using the mails for the distribution of his paper. Lacking patronage and quick access to the news from London, an independent journal was vulnerable. The *Courant* did attract some lively, if not always enlightened, spirits, such as Oxford-educated bookseller-apothecary John Checkley and Edinburgh-trained physician William Douglass. They called themselves "Honest Wags." They capitalized on their lack of access to foreign news and, instead of stale bits of London gossip, produced local news of their own, and briskly stimulated local controversy. Every feature of the local Establishment—the magistrates, the clergy, Harvard College—was considered fair game. They poured scorn on the practice of inoculation against smallpox, which had been tried when the epidemic of 1721 infected six thousand people and brought death to hundreds. Cotton Mather championed inoculation from his pulpit and circulated a paper asking the Boston doctors to give it a trial. Dr. Zabdiel Boylston was the only one who responded. When his experiment on his own children and servants was successful, others came to him for immunization. He treated 241, of whom only 6 died. But many saw this practice as dangerous, even wicked. Mather and Boylston were attacked by the mob, and a bomb was thrown into Mather's study. The town, thundered Mather, had become a hell upon earth, possessed by Satan. To James Franklin, Mather's role in the Salem witch trials had not given him a reputation for enlightenment, and he conducted a rough newspaper war against inoculation. In turn Mather denounced the paper as "notorious" and "scandalous," "full freighted with nonsense, unmanliness, profaneness, immorality, arrogance, calumnies, lies, contradictions and what not."[8]

Editor James Franklin then wisely tried to shift his ground, and his pages burgeoned with letters to the editor from Abigail Afterwit and Timothy Turnstone, from Tom Penshallow, Tom Trim, and Ichabod Henroost, from Fanny Mournful, Harry Meanwell, and Homespun Jack, Philanthropus and Hypercarpus: the pens of editor and friends busy behind a host of disguises. The change of front and the versatility of his contributions availed him little. In June 1722 the General Court ordered his arrest for publishing a satiric news item implying that the authorities were casual in dealing with piracy. With brother James in jail, the sixteen-year-old apprentice took over and carried on. When James offended again, in January 1723, charging that "hypocritical pretenders to religion" were worse for a commonwealth than those who were "openly profane," his paper was banned. The *Courant* then appeared with Benjamin in the guise of publisher and editor. To deceive the authorities, his indenture as an apprentice was returned to him and signed as fully discharged; but to guarantee his service to his brother, another was secretly substituted. The paper continued to appear as if edited by him until its demise in 1726.

The new editor announced a new policy: "diversion and merriment," "pieces of pleasancy and mirth," "to entertain the town with the most comical and diverting incidents of humane life . . . Nor shall we be wanting to fill up these papers with a grateful interspersion of more serious morals which may be drawn from the most ludicrous and odd parts of life." Among the early pieces of his own writing came a foretaste of democracy:

Adam was never called Master Adam; we never read of Noah Esquire, Lot Knight and Baronet, nor the Right Honorable Abraham, Viscount Mesopotamia, Baron of Canaan. No, no, they were plain men, honest country graziers, that took care of their families and their flocks. Moses was a great prophet and Aaron a priest of the Lord; but we never read of the Reverend Moses nor the Right Reverend Father in God, Aaron, by Divine Providence Lord Archbishop of Israel. Thou never sawest Madam Rebecca in the Bible, my Lady Rachel; nor Mary, though a princess of the blood, after the death of Joseph called the Princess Dowager of Nazareth. No, plain Rebecca, Rachel, Mary, or the Widow Mary or the like. It was no incivility then to mention their naked names as they were expressed.[9]

This was not the first appearance of Benjamin Franklin in print. He had, at twelve or thirteen, written two ballads: "The Lighthouse Tragedy" and a sailor's song on the death of Blackbeard the pirate. He wrote them, set them in type, printed them, and sold them on the streets—"wretched stuff," he said later, "in the Grub-street ballad style."[10]

In April 1722, when he was sixteen, he had attempted a *Spectator*-like essay, which he had copied out in a disguised hand, signed "Silence Dogood," and slipped under the door of his brother's shop. To his delight it was printed and more were publicly requested. They could be delivered at the printing house "or at the Blue Ball in Union Street, and no Questions shall be ask'd of the Bearer." Accordingly, between April and October 1722 came further adventures of this fictitious but forthright lady. The widow of a rural clergyman, she had robust opinions on a range of subjects, notably drunkenness:

It argues some shame in the drunkards themselves that they have invented numberless words and phrases to cover their folly, whose proper significations are harmless or have no signification at all. They are seldom known to be *drunk*, though they are very often *boozey, cogey, tipsey, fox'd, merry, mellow, fuddled, groatable, confoundedly cut, see two moons; are among the Philistines, in a very good humor, see the sun,* or, *the sun has shone upon them;* they *clip the King's English,* are *almost froze, feverish, in their altitudes, pretty well enter'd* etc.[11]

She was equally outspoken on the night life of Boston, the rich and their dissolute ways, the foolery and immodesty of hoop petticoats, the poor quality of New England poetry, and the still poorer quality of Harvard College. Silence Dogood was obviously derivative: an unpolished *Spectator* bred on the Yankee frontier, a piece of genial satire of the inflated pieties of the Mathers. The archetypal figure of the homely and often anonymous sage, full of wise saws, would keep recurring in Franklin's writing over the next sixty years. It proved to be a useful disguise—if disguise it ever was. For one whose trade was words this was a rich apprenticeship: it taught the merits of a plain style and of irony as a weapon.

But it was also an apprenticeship that Benjamin Franklin resented. He had often quarreled with his brother, and from time to time they had come to blows. Proud of his talents, he now bitterly disliked the secret indenture. When he tried to break it, James had him banned from working at other printing houses in Boston. Benjamin was also worried lest jail become his fate if he followed too outspokenly in his brother's footsteps. There was clearly a risk in giving "our Rulers some Rubs." So he sold some of his books and sailed away secretly to New York, in September 1723, in quest of work from William Bradford. Finding none there, he was directed on to Philadelphia, to Bradford's son Andrew. He crossed the bay in a boat for Perth Amboy, walked across New Jersey to Burlington—fifty miles in the rain—and then went by boat down the Delaware to Philadelphia. For all his apparent tolerance and malleability, in the wish to attain both fortune and fame, there was in Benjamin Franklin a deep Puritan-rooted iron in the soul. He was bland and affable in manner, but he was very much his own man. He would never sell his pride to keep his comfort; and, like Silence Dogood, he did not intend to wrap his Talent in a Napkin.

*   *   *

If the child was father of the man, what was the impact on him of his slender formal schooling, and of the early Boston years? Oliver Wendell Holmes, Sr., thought that Franklin's native city deserved credit for giving his life its distinctive impetus. He called Franklin "a Bostonian who dwelt awhile in Philadelphia." But Dr. S. Weir Mitchell, that very proper Philadelphian better known in his own day than in history, said that it was only after breathing the tolerant air of Philadelphia that Franklin began to live. According to Mitchell, Franklin "was born in Philadelphia—at the age of 17." It is a view that does little credit to Puritanism or to Franklin.[12]

There would seem to be three lessons Franklin never forgot. First, he was born when the Salem witchcraft trials were still a vivid and ugly memory in Boston, as a boy he heard Cotton and Increase Mather preach, and he read and studied carefully Cotton Mather's *Essays to Do Good.* Even if he moved away to the Quaker City, to a pew in Anglican Christ Church and ultimately to deism, he was in spirit never far away from his father's house, and he continued to pay his subscription in Philadelphia to the Presbyterian church. The imprint of Puritanism on Franklin was deep and binding. The cadences of his mature prose style as well as the homilies of Poor Richard, his moral earnestness and his diligence, his addiction to anecdote and parable, the self-scrutiny into what made virtue and vice, the tales of a pilgrimage through trial to grace—all these bear witness to his regular reading not only of the Bible and the catechism, but of Bunyan and the *New England Primer.* ("Have Communion with few. Be intimate with One. Deal justly with all. Speak Evil of None.") He never outgrew the addiction to adages and precepts, the popular gift of thinking in proverbs and of speaking in parables, the skill as preacher turned soothsayer; part of his own fortune was due to the appeal of Poor Richard, and to his capacity to raid and annex other people's *bon mots.* But in all their wit and salty humor, the proverbs and parables were instructional precepts, messages from a lay pulpit. The theology might get lost in the action, as it did with Bunyan, and good works might come to matter more than the doctrine of the elect, but life was earnest and serious, and success in it always seemed a mark of God's approval. Franklin began as a moralist, concerned with good conduct. Virtue was—at least thus far—a sufficient guide to the good life: "Without virtue men can have no happiness in this world." It might be its own reward, but it seemed, fortunately, to bring material dividends too. Franklin believed from the beginning that Calvinism and capitalism were twins.

Moreover, virtue to Franklin, as to the century in general, was robust and positive. It derived from the Latin *vir,* "man." In *Busy-Body* no. 3 Franklin asserted, "Virtue alone is sufficient to make a man Great Glorious and Happy." One of the first "little" pieces he wrote in Philadelphia was in the form of a socratic dialogue in which he sought to establish that whatever might be his abilities, a vicious man could not properly be called a Man of Sense. He followed this, a week later, with another: "Self-Denial not the essence of virtue." Were it so, then the naturally temperate man would not be virtuous. Franklin was struggling with some fundamental philosophical and religious issues, and he did not come to his central, rational position easily. When he did, he emphasized good sense and moderation—and the merit of habit. "Self-denial is neither good nor bad but as 'tis apply'd . . . he who does a foolish, indecent or wicked thing merely because 'tis contrary to his Inclination (As some mad Enthusiasts I have read of, who run about naked, under the notion of taking up the Cross) is not practising the reasonable Science and Virtue, but is lunatic." Moreover, it was more important to instruct in the art of virtue, to suggest methods of being, as well as doing, good, than to indulge in metaphysics.[13]

Secondly, theology was for Franklin—as in a measure for Cotton Mather—primarily works rather than faith, or works as the language of doctrine. Mather's *Essays to Do Good* and, even more, Defoe's *Essay upon Projects* were basic texts. Defoe proposed many of the practical and rational innovations that Franklin was later to attempt in Philadelphia. To serve mankind was to honor God. Defoe brought forward plans to reform banking laws, to provide pensions for the aged, to care for lunatics, to institute insurance schemes against accidents and fire hazards, to launch a military academy and schools for women. The proposals for insurance for widows and seamen recur in Silence Dogood. Defoe especially admired the Roman roads of England, and saw the Romans as "the Pattern of the whole World for Improvement and Increase of Arts and Learning, Civilizing and Methodizing Nations." We do not have to look far to find the mentor of Franklin's role as first citizen of Philadelphia. It is all here in Defoe, in his practicality, his quest for rational solutions for specific problems (to Defoe Reason was "First Monarch of the World"), his sense of the Enlightenment made civic and tangible. Indeed Defoe came to life in Philadelphia in a way he never did in London.[14]

The pen was not Franklin's only instrument, as it was Defoe's. Franklin organized his Junto and made this his civic instrument. In all his correspondence, however, dotted with practical proposals and fertile with projects, there is no statement of social intent, no Rousseauist or Voltairean credo, certainly no treatise à la Kant or Marx, no universalizing, and very little taste for theory or for absolutes. "Well done," in his own words, "is better than well said." Franklin was first and last the journalist, the pamphleteer, and the active man of affairs.

This second lesson was to be reinforced in Philadelphia, for in the Quakers the humanitarian strain was preeminent. "True Godliness don't turn Men out into the World," William Penn had written in *No Cross, No Crown*, "but enables them to live better in it and excites their Endeavours to mend it." Quakerism found the line hard to draw between the honor of God and the good of mankind. Franklin was keen to know and to put his knowledge to public use. And his inventions were practical: useful articles to warm the home or to avert lightning, to pave streets and to light them. What he did not invent he perfected—and advertised. The goal was never speculation for its own sake but action, cures for smoky chimneys or whatever other ills could rationally be cured.

Another influence that should not be underrated is that of Plutarch. The time Franklin devoted to reading *The Parallel Lives of the Noble Greeks and Romans* was, he wrote in the *Autobiography*, "spent to great Advantage." From Plutarch he learned, along with a grounding in classical history, the importance of good citizenship. Plutarch was a "teacher" like any Puritan pastor. What mattered to him was less issues and causes than what men made of their talents and of their own opportunities. Action, courage, and service to the commonwealth were even more important to Plutarch than to the Puritans.

The third legacy of Franklin's early years was a zest and spirit that may have been due to the self-imposed discipline of his reading or to his own buoyancy and impudence. What was the source of his endless curiosity, his sustained and creative drive? The habits of work, the acceptance of effort, the need for industry, the importance of cooperation and of community action were all deep in him; they came as much from his Puritan roots as from his own utilitarian ethic. But they came too from an inner personal compulsion to make a mark in the world, a drive for fame as much as for fortune. He was by nature a rebel against the established order—as his father had been before him. He ran away from Boston to Philadelphia, and then, again, ran away from Philadelphia. He was in no awe of his brother, whom he was contracted to serve as apprentice, nor of those religious and political interests which protected state and steeple and which could curb his newspapers. Politics as such mattered little to him as yet.

The component strands that went to fashion the boy who was the father of the man included the sturdy independence, industry, and integrity of his father, the literary addictions of his uncle Benjamin, and the stubbornness, the energy, and the quest for justice that drove his grandfather Folger of Nantucket. There was the impact, twice each Sunday and many a Thursday evening, of addresses from pulpit and lectern; the prolix and pun-addicted prose of Cotton Mather, the busybody zeal of Judge Sewall, his father's friend; the disputatiousness and liveliness of the Honest Wags of his brother's printshop; the preachment of virtue and the evidence of vice along the waterfront; the controversies over Quakers and Anabaptists. If he never shared the intensity or the emotional zeal of the Puritans, he never lost the traces of their sententiousness. Nor did he ever abandon their faith in reason, in exposition and discussion as key parts of religious intellectual analysis, their belief that ignorance itself was the most deadly of all the sins. For alongside orthodoxy and emotion, Cotton Mather also had open scientific curiosity and a knowledge of the classics; his library of three thousand titles was the largest in the colonies; and his own authorship was prolific. The mastery of books as tools and weapons was not the least important aspect of Boston's legacy to Franklin.

There was, too, the location of the Bible commonwealth in a wilderness, or on an inhospitable and rocky island off its shore. This was a society not yet noted for tolerance; independent-minded men and women had been regularly executed or banished, and even highly respected men could lose their jobs over differences of opinion, as had Henry Dunster, first president of Harvard College. The lords brethren were as ruthless as the lords bishop. To go into exile for one's convictions was no novelty, and, to paraphrase J. N. Figgis (though he wrote with reference to Britain, not New England), political liberty in the modern world was "the residuary legatee" of ecclesiastical animosities. This philosophy of politics could not be separated from a religious imperative that was intensely individualist, ethical, and combative. The Puritans' location on their bleak shore called for self-reliance and adaptability, respect for family and neighbor as well as for God, the need for trial, experiment, and knowledge, an open and nonaristocratic attitude of mind, and a balance of individualism and gregariousness. Franklin was unafraid of dissent and rebellion, and had no experience of servility. This was not yet, however, for all its lack of stratification, a democratic society, of either church or state.

Those who owned the covenant were the elect of God, destined for salvation; those whom God blessed with wealth of land or property were the political elite. They alone spoke the language of Canaan. "The best part is always the least," wrote John Winthrop, "and of that part the wiser part is always the lesser." John Cotton put it starkly: "Democracy, I do not conceyve that ever God did ordeyne as a fitt government eyther for Church or Commonwealth. If the people be governors, who shall be governed?"[15]

The young man who left his native city in 1723 did not yet challenge this doctrine. He was a product of a Puritan commonwealth, and all that he wrote and campaigned for was suffused with its spirit. Like many another young man, he found it hard to live up to its stern code. But there was more than this. In the liberalism of the Old South Church, in the excitement of the printing trade, and in his restless mind, a new spirit was stirring. Franklin was to be as much a product of the frontier, of the bustle and zest of the Boston waterfront and of Philadelphia's Market Street, as he was of the dream of a city upon a hill.

3

JOURNEYMAN PRINTER

"I was in my working dress, my best clothes being to come round by sea. I was dirty from my journey; my pockets were stuff'd out with shirts and stockings, and I knew no soul nor where to look for lodging. I was fatigued with travelling, rowing, and want of rest, I was very hungry; and my whole stock of cash consisted of a Dutch dollar, and about a shilling in copper. The latter I gave the people of the boat for my passage, who at first refus'd it, on account of my rowing, but I insisted on their taking it. A man being sometimes more generous when he has but a little money than when he has plenty, perhaps thro' fear of being thought to have but little.

"Then I walked up the street, gazing about till near the market-house I met a boy with bread. I had many a meal on bread, and, inquiring where he got it, I went immediately to the baker's he directed me to, in Second-street, and ask'd for biscuit, intending such as we had in Boston; but they, it seems, were not made in Philadelphia. Then I asked for a three-penny loaf, and was told they had none such. So not considering or knowing the difference of money, and the great cheapness nor the names of his bread, I bad him give me three-penny worth of any sort. He gave me, accordingly, three great puffy rolls. I was surpriz'd at the quantity but took it, and, having no room in my pockets, walk'd off with a roll under each arm, and eating the other. Thus I went up Market-street as far as Fourth-street, passing by the door of Mr. Read, my future wife's father; when she, standing at the door, saw me, and thought I made, as I certainly did, a most awkward, ridiculous appearance." [1]

The story of Franklin's arrival in Philadelphia in 1723 as he tells it in his *Autobiography* is one of the most familiar episodes in American history. Tired from his journey, he followed the crowd into their plain meeting house, devoid of pulpit and of altar, and, after looking around and hearing nothing said, fell fast asleep.

*   *   *

The Quaker city on the tongue of land between the Delaware and the Schuylkill was less than half a century old, but it almost matched Boston in population. The "greene countrie towne" of William Penn's planning had grown fast. From the first, Penn was as good a salesman as he was an organizer of government: his pamphlets in German and English, not to mention those of his Welsh lieutenants, encouraged many immigrants. His Frame of Government was attractive, providing for free education, the promotion of arts and sciences, full toleration in religion, free election of representatives, and trial by jury in open court. He sought to bring in the wealthy: 5,000 acres for £100, plus an extra 50 acres for every indentured servant. He also attracted the poor but enterprising: families could buy 500 acres and pay for them in installments over a period of years, as did Thomas Paschall, the Bristol pewterer. Of 275 homes in the Middle Ward (bounded by Arch, Walnut, Front, and Seventh streets), 47 belonged to shopkeepers and almost all the rest to artisans, including coopers, carpenters, cordwainers, merchants, a boatbuilder, and a ropemaker. As Gottlieb Mittelberger reported in 1754, "Pennsylvania is heaven for farmers, paradise for artisans and hell for officials and preachers." The city of brotherly love was from the first a city for tradesmen, craftsmen, and family homesteaders, for leather-apron men, for men of thrift, enterprise, and prudence—for men, in fact, like Benjamin Franklin.[2]

In 1683 the learned and public-spirited Lutheran Francis Daniel Pastorius, as much a Founder as Penn himself, led to Pennsylvania the Mennonites from Frankfurt and Crefeld who were to make Germantown noted for its flax and its handicrafts. His group included a doctor of medicine with eight children, an apothecary, a mason, a glassblower, a wheelwright, a cabinetmaker, a cooper, a cobbler, and a tailor, as well as farmers and seamstresses. And they came to work. "His opus," Pastorius said, "hic labor est." The first settlers lived in dugouts gouged from the banks of the Delaware. "Better a dug-out than a dungeon," they said, "better a cave than a loathsome prison." But within a year six hundred houses were built, and Samuel Powel had laid the basis of a fortune in house building. He also built, in 1709, the first brick-covered market; a second market was built in

1720. By 1723 Philadelphia was thriving, with a bustling mile-long waterfront and crowded wharves.[3]

The proprietary colony was austere in manner and Quaker-dominated, but, though it was only a generation old, the waves of Germans, Welsh, Scots, and Irish were already changing its character. In 1755 the Reverend William Smith, provost of the College of Philadelphia, believed that no less than half of the colony's population was German, one-fifth Presbyterian, and only one-fifth Quaker. James Logan, Penn's first secretary, feared that in the end Pennsylvania would become a German colony.

Germantown was a unique community with German-speaking schools, newspapers, and shops, and with some elegant country homes for those Philadelphia merchants lucky enough to escape the summer heat. For those less successful there were the almshouse and the debtor's prison—the latter a model of its kind, built the year before Franklin's arrival. But if they were thrifty and hard-working—and more fortunate—they could move up in the world: this was an open society. It was all but classless, but already polyglot, with clear ethnic communities. Even its Germans were mixed: Mennonites and Moravians, Lutherans and Catholics, Schwenkfelders from Silesia and Dunkers from Westphalia. All, however, spoke Deutsch, and thus became to all the rest "Pennsylvania Dutch."

Immigration was only half the picture: even more striking was the natural increase of population. Thus Hannah Milner, who died near Philadelphia in 1769 at the ripe age of 100 years and 10 months, had 14 children, 82 grandchildren, and 110 great grandchildren. A table of births and deaths of a Lutheran congregation of Philadelphia, covering the period between 1774 and 1787, showed the proportion of births to deaths as 2.15 to 1.

*   *   *

Philadelphia, still heavily Quaker in spirit, was, like Boston, coming to be irked by the paternal restraints of its founding fathers, and in its case by the persistent absence of its proprietors, now turned remote, autocratic, and high Anglican. For full tolerance in creed did not mean full liberty in conduct; although there was no civil ban on extravagance and frivolity, the Quaker Yearly Meeting tried to be an effective censor of laxity in morals or behavior. Dr. Alexander Hamilton in 1744 said he had never visited "a place so populous where the *gout* for public gay diversions prevailed so little."[4] But if "rude and riotous" sports, including gambling and the theater, were banned, the city was already strong in the number of its clubs, taverns, and grogshops, and appropriately convivial. In the October 1728 election it consumed 4,500 gallons of beer; and the rum importation for that year, as Franklin was to reveal in a "surprising tho' authentick" account in the *Gazette*, totaled 212,450 gallons, worth £25,000. "Cyder Royal," new cider fermented with applejack, was a favorite tipple in the Red Lion in Elbow Lane, the Pewter Platter off Market Street, or the Crooked Billet by Chestnut Street Wharf. By 1752 it was estimated that there were at least 120 taverns, 14 rum distilleries—and only 12 churches.

In exchange for its major imports of rum and molasses and a vast quantity of manufactured goods, Philadelphia exported grain and lumber, beef, pork and horses, furs, and tobacco to other colonies, the West Indies, and Britain. As many as a hundred merchantmen, with barges and shallops, might crowd the river. By 1723 the houses on Front Street had balconies overlooking the Delaware, and were coming to be furnished with imported luxuries. It would be another four years before the new and ornate Christ Church was begun, and another decade and much argument before the State House, birthplace of a nation, was slowly to rise. "The dear old folks, most of whom are dead, may have spoken to their children a good deal about plainness," wrote Christopher Sauer, the German Quietist leader, in 1724. "It is still noticeable in the clothes, except that the material is very costly, or is even velvet." Homemade leather and homespun were still general, but there was rich color in women's dress, and powdered wigs, broadcloth coats, and knee breeches were coming to be the fashion for men. The city had its hazards: streets were unpaved and ill-lit; disease and epidemics—yellow fever, "the bilious plague," "the epidemic pleurisy"—were regular visitors; and flies, mosquitoes, and other insects were a legend. The only public edifice of note was the Court House on the High (now Market) Street. Life revolved round Market Street and the twenty wharves on the river. When in 1732 the Assembly approved Andrew Hamilton's plans for the State House, they located it on Chestnut Street between Fifth and Sixth streets. Half a mile from the river, it was seen as on the city's outskirts.

Philadelphia was the transit point for a steady immigrant traffic moving through to the West, to the mountains and the forks of the

Ohio, or southwest into the Shenandoah and the valleys and the pied-
mont country of Virginia and the Carolinas. The Great Philadelphia
Wagon Road to Lancaster and York counties was a major artery, not
only for Germans but also for Scotch-Irish. Pennsylvania was also the
breadbasket colony, rich in wheat and corn, hemp and flax, cattle and
hogs, timber and bar-iron, almost able to be self-supporting, trading
favorably with a New England that lacked almost all these products.
It was beginning to turn also to manufacture. Iron and steel were
made, although the latter product was not developed; shipbuilding
and textiles were becoming important.

That Philadelphia developed so quickly was in part due to the
Quaker tradition. Penn's colony was tolerant, as Boston was not. It
was set up as a "holy experiment," an asylum for the persecuted. The
Philadelphia tax list of 1769 reveals that the Quakers constituted only
one in seven of the population but half of those who paid taxes in
excess of a hundred pounds. Of the seventeen wealthiest citizens, only
five were non-Quakers, and one of these, William Shippen, owed the
basis of his fortune to his Quaker grandfathers. As they prospered,
some residents moved from the Quaker Meeting to the fashionable
Christ Church and the Anglican Establishment, as did the Penns
themselves. "One might be a Christian in any Church," it was said,
"but one could not be a gentleman outside the Church of England."
But the Friends never quite abandoned the Quaker spirit: diligence
and thrift, plain and frugal living, discreet pride in business success,
enterprise, and faith in freedom. The conspicuous enjoyment of
wealth and of leisure were never quite respectable. Respectability
counted almost as much as reward to the Quakers, and Godfearing
seemed to be synonymous with moneymaking.

Quakers in Pennsylvania, unlike those in Britain, were free to play
a part in politics. It was a free society—much more so than Massachusetts—but not remotely a democracy. Political control was divided between absentee proprietors, the Penns, and the local oligarchy of merchants and landowners who dominated the council. As a
printer, Franklin would need these as patrons. They were prompt to
recognize talent, and this was a world in which talent could rise
quickly. Sir William Keith spotted Franklin early. So did James Logan,
a mathematician and classical scholar as well as a Founder and an
Establishment figure, who gave Franklin and his friends the use of his
library. Logan described Franklin to an English friend in 1750 as "an

extraordinary man in most respects—one of singular good judgment, but of equal modesty." For Franklin Philadelphia was a congenial place: man and setting could hardly have been more aptly matched.[5]

*   *   *

Franklin did not find employment with Andrew Bradford but did with Bradford's rival Samuel Keimer, who had an "old shatter'd press, and one small, worn-out font of English." He thought neither printer well qualified: "Bradford had not been bred to it, and was very illiterate; and Keimer, tho' something of a scholar, was a mere compositor, knowing nothing of presswork." Keimer was an eccentric, full of fads and fancies, with a Mosaic beard. Franklin found him "an odd fish; ignorant of common life, fond of rudely opposing receiv'd opinions, slovenly to extreme dirtiness, enthusiastic in some points of religion, and a little knavish withal." In fact Keimer's major—perhaps his sole—contribution to American history went unnoticed by Franklin. He reprinted in penny numbers "every Fourth Day of the Week" throughout 1724 Trenchard's and Gordon's *The Independent Whig*, the first periodical other than a newspaper to be published in the American colonies. No doubt he printed it because of its criticisms of high church principles. Its true merit, however, lay in its political stance: along with the same authors' *Cato's Letters*, it did as much as, if not more than, the writings of John Locke to prepare the ground for the political ideas of independence.[6]

Franklin lodged at Mrs. Read's, next door to Keimer's printshop, made a number of friends and some money, and lived "very agreeably." But one of these friends, no less a figure than Sir William Keith, the eccentric governor of the province, proved to be one of his errata. The governor heard of Franklin through Franklin's brother-in-law Robert Holmes, and called on him. "I was not a little surprised, and Keimer star'd like a pig poison'd." Sir William proposed that Franklin's father should set him up in a printing house and promised to procure for him the colony's printing business and that of Delaware (the lower counties) also. Franklin returned to Boston—a voyage that took two weeks—in order to lay the governor's proposal before his father, only to find his father cannily skeptical about it; he took the opportunity also to show off his new clothes, his watch, and his wealth to his former printing associates and his brother. "He receiv'd me not frankly, look'd me all over, and turn'd to his work again."[7]

When Franklin's father refused to set him up in business, Sir William promised to do so himself. He suggested that Franklin should go to England with an inventory of what he would need as a printer, and he promised to furnish the necessary letters of credit and of introduction to his friends. On November 5, 1724, the *London Hope*, with Franklin and his friend James Ralph aboard, sailed for England. They reached London on Christmas Eve. Only then did Franklin find that the governor, too busy to see him before he sailed, had not included any letters of credit for him in the ship's mail. Too late he discovered Sir William's true character—"to be liberal of promises which he never meant to keep. Yet unsolicited as he was by me, how could I think his generous offers insincere? I believ'd him one of the best men in the world." Another erratum went into the ledger of his account of himself to himself. And not the only one: Ralph had no intention of returning to Philadelphia—he was simply running away from his wife and children—and in London he managed to live on Franklin's earnings and, from the same happy source, to keep a mistress.

Sir William's reputation has suffered from Franklin's account of this episode. Like all who crossed Franklin's path, the governor was to be lost in the shadows cast by the bright searchlight that played on Franklin. His plans for Franklin may have been dependent on a favorable outcome of his struggles with the proprietors in London, when the exact succession to the title of proprietor was in dispute after William Penn's death. Had Franklin not existed, or been lost to history, Sir William might have won a different fame. He might, as his own biographer contends, have been extolled "as the only Proprietary Governor who championed the rights of the People. That his words were not always true, that his debts were not always paid, that his treatment of the Penn family, or of his successor or of James Logan was not always fair, would never have interfered." Even Franklin's verdict was somewhat kind: Sir William, he said in retrospect, "wished to please everybody, and having little to give, he gave expectations." [8]

Franklin's first sojourn in London lasted eighteen months. He took lodgings for 3s. 6d. a week in Little Britain, Aldersgate, near St. Paul's; then at 6 Duke Street (now Sardinia Street). He was employed as a printer, first at Samuel Palmer's printing house in Bartholomew Close, then at James Watt's larger firm in Wild's Court near Lincoln's Inn Fields. He claimed that his friend Ralph had kept him poor—but this was far from the whole truth. After Ralph left London to teach at a school in Berkshire—"where he taught reading and writing to ten or a dozen boys, at 6d each per week"—Franklin became fond of the company of Ralph's mistress: "Being at this time under no Religious Restraint, and presuming upon my Importance to her, I attempted Familiarities (another Erratum) which she repuls'd with a proper Resentment and acquainted him with my Behavior. This made a Breach between us."[9] It also allowed Ralph to cancel his debts to Franklin. Ralph remained in London to become a minor dramatist and a political writer in the employ of Bubb Dodington and of Frederick, Prince of Wales. He was so skillful a propagandist that the Pelham ministry was induced to pay him £300 a year not to write, since he favored the Opposition. The breach between the two friends was not permanent; when Franklin returned to London in 1757, he employed Ralph to see *An Historical Review of the Constitution and Government of Pennsylvania* through the press.[10]

*   *   *

Franklin did not return to Philadelphia until October 11, 1726. He returned with Thomas Denham, the Quaker merchant who had befriended him on the voyage out, who was half-owner of the *Berkshire* and advanced him £10 for his passage home. Denham opened a store in Philadelphia and employed Franklin as his clerk at a salary of £50 a year. "I attended the business diligently, studied accounts and grew, in a little time, expert at selling." But on Denham's sudden death in 1727 the store went to his executors, and Franklin returned to his trade, becoming Keimer's foreman at the printing press. In 1728 he left Keimer to form a partnership with Hugh Meredith—a Welsh Pennsylvanian, "honest and sensible" but "seldom sober"—a partnership in which Meredith's father provided the capital, Franklin provided the industry and skill, and Meredith drank the profits. In 1729 he and Meredith bought the *Pennsylvania Gazette,* which Keimer had founded the year before and which had failed to prosper, thanks in part to Franklin's writing his *Busy-Body Papers* for Andrew Bradford's rival *American Weekly Mercury,* thereby, and deliberately, reducing Keimer's circulation. In 1730, with funds provided by his friends Robert Grace and William Coleman, Franklin bought Meredith out and became sole proprietor of both printing press and newspaper. Keimer's business declined and he moved to Barbados, where he died a poor and unappreciated figure.[11]

Franklin wrote a pamphlet in a popular cause, the advocacy of a paper currency. There was much that was of interest in this tract: "The riches of a country are to be valued by the quantity of labour its inhabitants are able to purchase, not by the quantity of gold and silver they possess . . . Trade in general being nothing else but the exchange of labour for labour, the value of things is . . . most justly measured by labour . . . As bills issued upon money security are money so bills issued upon land are in effect coined land." The true measure, in other words, of all value was labor. For Pennsylvania, however, wealth lay not only in labor but in land. Increasing population would strengthen trade and manufactures, so that the future lay with land and commerce. An interest-bearing currency backed by land mortgages was Franklin's objective. That it would be inflationary—in fact it was simply printed money—and that it was unpopular with rich men and moneylenders, land speculators and lawyers, did not deter him. Nor did it deter the Assembly, which, converted reluctantly by his arguments, gave him the contract to print money—"a very profitable Jobb and a great help to me." He secured also the printing of the laws of the colony, and of the lower counties (Delaware). Franklin's sole competitor in Philadelphia was now Bradford, who was old, rich, and easy, but who kept the post office and thus had a certain advantage in hard news, and using the carriers to distribute only his own newspaper, the *Mercury*. But at the age of twenty-four, Franklin was the most active master printer and publisher in the most thriving city in North America. As it prospered, so did he. Rarely were stage and actor so well attuned.[12]

*   *   *

The city, as well as the printing shop, was already his stage. In 1727 on his return from London the Junto, or the Club of the Leather Aprons, was formed, a group of like-minded friends who, in a quest for self-improvement, read and discussed papers on "history, morality, poetry, physic, travel, mechanics and arts." It was part mutual aid society, part social fraternity, part academy. Its organization was modeled on Mather's neighborhood Benefit Societies, but it was touched also by Masonic principles: it was intended to be secret and exclusive. The questions the members set themselves included "queries on any point of Morals, Politics or Natural Philosophy," but the real motivation was self-improvement, the "wish to do good" that would also bring them advantages, or even profit. The topics discussed were real and immediate:

Have you lately heard how any rich man, here or elsewhere, got his estate? What unhappy effects of intemperance have you lately observed or heard? of imprudence? of passion? or of any other vice or folly? Is there any man whose friendship you want, and which the Junto, or any of them, can procure for you? Have you lately observed any encroachment on the just liberties of the people? What new story have you lately heard of any citizen thriving well, and by what means? Do you think of anything at present, in which the Junto may be serviceable to mankind, to their country, or to themselves?

Their range was wide, even ambitious: "all philosophical Experiments that let Light into the Nature of Things, tend to increase the Power of Man over Matter and multiply the Conveniences or Pleasures of Life." Between these queries there was, however, a pause "while one might fill and drink a glass of wine." [13]

The members of the Junto were drawn from silversmiths and glaziers, from printers like Franklin, shoemakers like William Parsons, ironmasters like Robert Grace, clerks like William Coleman, joiners like William Maugridge, and surveyors like Nicholas Scull. They had to declare that they loved mankind in general, "of what profession or religion soever." Their meetings fed Franklin with material for his newspaper and his press, and through the *Gazette* they became a nursery and a forcing house of reform. To facilitate their discussions the members temporarily pooled their individual collections of books. This not being adequate, plans were made in 1731 to establish a circulating library. It began with 50 subscribers, enlarged to 100 in 1742. Books were ordered from London through Peter Collinson, the Quaker botanist. Of their first list in 1732, not one was a work of religion or theology. As Edwin Wolf has pointed out, of the 375 titles listed in the 1741 catalog there were 114 in history, 69 in literature, 65 in science, and only 38 in theology and 33 in philosophy. Almost all the titles were English, and there were more titles by Locke than by any other author: "Locke's economic and humanitarian interests and his liberal views, his thoughts on education, toleration in a broad sense, the constitution of Carolina, currency reform and state responsibility for the poor approached from the view point of scientific psychology were a major influence on the thinking and government of the British Colonies, and later of the independent nation which evolved from them." This was the first subscription library in America, and it was soon being copied up and down the North Atlantic coast. "Reading became fashionable," Franklin wrote; he taught himself to read French, Spanish, and Italian, and he revived his elementary knowledge of Latin. And one Junto spawned others, though not as many as Franklin would have liked.[14]

Self-improvement led inevitably to the improvement of city and state. What the Philadelphia Junto inculcated was the art of civic virtue, a code of municipal improvement for Philadelphia. The successful editor and publicist became ipso facto advocate, fundraiser, and philanthropist. From Franklin and this group came a number of projects for civic improvement. A city police force—a "sufficient" watch—was set up in 1745, and the Union Fire Company in 1736, with Boston's as model. The various fire companies were organized into "the Philadelphia Contributionship": in essence, the first fire insurance company in America. As its first president, Franklin set premiums and payments for fire insurance. Plans were drawn up for the paving and the improved cleaning and lighting of Philadelphia streets. In February 1750 the Assembly provided for a board of six wardens, meeting each November, to "erect, put up and fix" as many lights as they felt necessary, and to enter into contracts with lamplighters. In September 1751 newly installed whale-oil lamps were lit for the first time. Franklin devised the four-sided ventilated lamp, which he said was much easier to clean than the closed globe John Clifton used in his brick house on Second Street. A forty-shilling fine failed, however, to protect the new lamps from vandals; a young man paid that amount for heaving an apple at one. By 1779 a reward of forty dollars was posted by the Clerk of the Wardens for the capture of "some evil disposed persons, who have yet been undiscovered" in a spree where "many of the public lamps . . . have been wickedly and wantonly broke and otherwise damaged, and the cups and oils taken out."

The American Philosophical Society was founded in 1744, the city hospital in 1751, and, in the same year, the Academy for the Education of Youth out of which grew, though transformed into a more conservative and classical institution than Franklin had planned, the University of Pennsylvania. The college was to be the most liberal institution of higher learning in the colonies; alongside the classics and religious subjects, it offered courses in science, agriculture, history, government, and modern languages. The purpose was as much civic as personal. As he wrote in his pamphlet *Proposals Relating to the Education of Youth in Pennsylvania* (October 1749):

> With the whole should be constantly inculcated that *Benignity of Mind,* which shows itself in *searching for* and seizing every Opportunity to *serve* and to *oblige;* and is the Foundation of what is called GOOD BREEDING; highly useful to the Possessor and most agreeable to all.
>
> The idea of what is *true Merit* should also be often presented to Youth, explain'd and impress'd on the Minds, as consisting in an *Inclination* joined with an *Ability* to serve Mankind, one's Country, Friends and Family; which Ability is (with the Blessing of God) to be acquir'd or greatly increas'd by *true* Learning; and should indeed be the great *Aim* and *End* of all Learning.
>
> . . . it would be well if [students] could be taught *every Thing* that is useful, and *every Thing* that is ornamental: But Art is long, and their Time is short. It is therefore propos'd that they learn those things that are likely to be *most useful* and *most ornamental,* Regard being had to the several Professions for which they are intended.

He recommended the teaching also of penmanship, drawing, arithmetic, geometry, and astronomy, and even a little "gardening, planting, grafting and inoculating." His special plea, however, was for teaching the English language by studying "our best writers . . . Tillotson, Addison, Pope, Algernon Sidney, Cato's Letters etc., should be Classicks; the Stiles principally to be cultivated, being the *clear* and the *concise.*"[15]

The purpose of the study of history, ancient and modern, was particularly that the pupils should learn its moral lessons: "the general natural Tendency of Reading good History, must be, to fix in the Minds of Youth deep Impressions of the Beauty and Usefulness of Virtue of all Kinds, Publick Spirit, Fortitude, etc." History would also demonstrate the "wonderful Effects of Oratory, in governing, turning and leading great Bodies of Mankind, Armies, Cities, Nations," and show "the Advantage of a Religious Character among private Persons; the Mischiefs of Superstition, etc. and the Excellency of the CHRISTIAN RELIGION above all others ancient or modern." For Franklin the purpose of the study of history was more than merely the inculcation of moral and civic duty. He urged the study of customs and trends in all the lands and societies known to man, and of natural history, "which would not only be delightful to Youth . . . but afterwards [be] of great Use to them, whether they are Merchants, Handicrafts, or Divines." Natural history would lead readily to a study of farming: "the Improvement of Agriculture being useful to all, and Skill in it no Disparagement to any." Commercial history would also be useful to all students and would lead to an interest in machines. Utility for Franklin was never forgotten.

*   *   *

On September 1, 1730, Franklin "took to wife" Deborah Read, the daughter of his first landlady, who had seen the tall, barrel-chested, and handsome lad struggling with his three rolls of bread seven years before. He had "made some courtship" of her before sailing for London, but any thought of marriage had been abandoned, partly because of the long voyage and the separation ahead, and partly because her mother thought them too young. During his stay in London Franklin had written her one letter, "and that was to let her know I was not likely soon to return." Miss Read thereupon married a potter, John Rogers, who already had a wife, and who in turn deserted her. "I piti'd poor Miss Read's unfortunate situation, who was generally dejected, seldom cheerful, and avoided company. I considered my giddiness and inconstancy when in London as in a great degree the cause of her unhappiness, tho' the mother was good enough to think the fault more her own than mine, as she had prevented our marrying before I went thither, and persuaded the other match in my absence." Since Rogers was presumed to be still alive, though nothing was known of him, the marriage was a common-law union, without a ceremony or any record at Christ Church, which Deborah attended. There was also the fear that a second husband might be responsible for the debts of the first—unless, as the law quaintly held, the bride was married in her chemise on the king's highway! "She proved," Franklin said, "a good and faithful helpmate, assisted me much by attending the shop, we throve together, and have ever mutually endeavour'd to make each other happy. Thus I corrected that great erratum as well as I could." [16]

The prudential and ironic tone of Franklin's writing, healthily deflationary as it is for most public occasions, becomes flat, cool, and unexciting when he has to take stock of private emotion. For one who wrote so much, he could be irritatingly unrevealing when he chose.

The emotional, the aesthetic, the spiritual never came easily to him. His account was, of course, written with the retrospective urbanity of forty years of happy wedlock, and after many years of separation from his wife. He made no pretense to a grand passion for Deborah, or indeed for any woman (or perhaps for any cause, including independence?). He married, he confesses, partly from "sympathy" for Deborah, though in the context it sounds disturbingly like "pity," and partly because that "hard-to-be-governed" passion of youth was carrying him into intrigues with "low women," "attended with some expense and great inconvenience besides a continual risque to my health by a distemper which of all things I dreaded, though by great good luck I escaped it." Franklin's *Autobiography* has become famous as a story of the progress of *l'homme moyen sensuel*.

The *Autobiography* fails to give an accurate picture of the marriage. Its account stops at 1757, when Franklin's letters to Debby begin in abundance. The letters reveal a rich and happy relationship: the correspondence rarely touches on public affairs, in which she was little versed, but it certainly gives evidence of a deep and mutual affection. Even when a letter is tantalizingly incomplete, there can be no denying its warmth.

I have made your compliments to Mrs Stevenson. She is indeed very obliging, takes great care of my health, and is very diligent when I am any way indispos'd; but yet I have a thousand times wish'd you with me, and my little Sally with her ready hands and feet to do, and go and come, and get what I wanted. There is a great difference in sickness between being nurs'd with that tender attention, which proceeds from sincere love; and . . .[17]

Debby never shared in his intellectual tastes or his social activities. She clearly had little education; her letters reveal her as all but illiterate: "a breste of vele," "Liberrey," "shues," "necklis," snow "two deep to go a Slaying." Yet she carried her devotion further than perhaps he was capable of doing. She brought William, Benjamin's illegitimate son, into their home to live with them—a remarkably generous act. The child had already been conceived at the time of the marriage, and there are those who contend that Franklin always understated William's age to hide his illegitimate origins. Yet in his own lifetime William was described as illegitimate. We will never know who William's mother was. Franklin's Pennsylvanian enemies thirty years later said it was Barbara, a maidservant in his home. One likely explanation, bearing in mind that the marriage took place in September 1730 and that William Franklin's date of birth was later given as "c. 1731," is that the mother was indeed Deborah herself, but that because of the risk of Rogers's return, it seemed wise to have the child appear to be Franklin's by an unknown woman. At any rate the child was acknowledged and brought into Deborah's home. As to the charge that relations were not cordial between Deborah and William, the only evidence occurs in the diary of Daniel Fisher, who was staying in the Franklin household in 1755, and to whom Deborah described William as "the greatest villain upon earth." She used, he said, "the foulest terms I ever heard from a gentlewoman." But although she is known to have been easily angered there is no other critical reference, and apparently no reference at all to William's illegitimacy. This single unkind reference to him by her hardly seems proof of illegitimacy.[18]

It was certainly Deborah's industry and frugality in tending the shop during Franklin's increasingly long absences that made his public career possible. "We kept no idle servants, our table was plain and simple." As Poor Richard said in February 1744, "He that hath not got a Wife, is not yet a Compleat Man." If she had a turbulent temper as the clerk who lodged in the Franklin home said she had, it never showed itself in any open criticism. Franklin relates an anecdote that gives us a glimpse of their relationship:

My Breakfast was a long time Bread and Milk (no Tea) and I ate it out of a twopenny earthen Porringer with a Pewter Spoon. But mark how Luxury will enter Families, and make a Progress, in spite of Principle. Being call'd one Morning to Breakfast, I found it in a China Bowl with a Spoon of Silver. They had been bought for me without my Knowledge by my Wife and had cost her the enormous Sum of three and twenty shillings, for which she had no other Excuse or Apology to make but that she thought her Husband deserv'd a Silver Spoon and China Bowl as well as any of his Neighbours.[19]

Of Deborah's last eighteen years, her husband spent fifteen absent from her in England, to which she never showed any wish to move. The decade of separation, and his years of fame, brought coolness and negligence on his part and for her an increasing loneliness and sense of loss. There were only two children besides William: Francis Folger Franklin, born in 1732, who died of smallpox when he was four, and whom his father recalled thirty-six years later as "my son

Franky . . . whom I have seldom since seen equalled in everything and whom to this day I cannot think of without a sigh"; and Sarah (Sally), born in 1743, who became the prop of her father's later years and outlived him. It was a tiny ménage for a fertile age—and for one of the Franklin families, usually strikingly fecund. Shortly before Deborah's death, her husband complained in a letter to her, "it is now nine long months since I received a line from my dear Debbie." She was in fact in great pain and unable to write, and he did not know. She died in December 1774, six months before he returned home.

If, as seems likely, Franklin is the author of the manuscript in the archives of the American Philosophical Society entitled "I sing my plain Country Joan," he left his own warm tribute. It had been said in 1742, probably in the Junto, or jokingly perhaps over a mug of beer in the Indian Queen, that married men often saluted their mistresses, rarely their wives.

> Of their Chloes and Phillisses Poets may prate
>   I sing my plain Country Joan
> Now twelve Years my Wife, still the Joy of my Life
>   Blest Day that I made her my own,
>   My dear Friends
>   Blest Day that I made her my own.
> Some faults have we all, and so may my Joan
>   But then they're exceedingly small;
> And now I'm grown used to them, So like my own
>   I scarcely can see them at all.
>   My dear Friends . . .[20]

*   *   *

Franklin's worldly-wise qualities emerge sharply in his writing in these early years. While employed at Palmer's in London in typesetting the second edition of William Wollaston's *Religion of Nature Delineated,* he attempted a refutation of it in a pamphlet, *A Dissertation on Liberty and Necessity, Pleasure and Pain.* In this work he allowed a denial of deism to lead him logically to a position of moral anarchy. If God was all wisdom and all goodness, did it not follow that there could be no distinction between virtue and vice? Men did what they must, and could not be praised or blamed for their behavior. They were moved to action only by one of two forces: to avoid pain or to have pleasure. If logic was the only guide, "Vice and Virtue," Franklin said, were "empty distinctions." Since God was infinitely wise, "all is right," and evil could not be the result of an all-wise and all-powerful God. For a young unattached man in London these were heady doctrines. One hundred copies of the pamphlet were printed. Later Franklin thought the tract one of his errata and came to doubt the adequacy of following such "metaphysical reasoning." A materialistic doctrine might indeed be true, but it was not very useful. He thought the tract might have an "ill tendency," and he burned all the copies he could find. He missed two, which survive as youthful evidence of the inadequacy of logic as sole guide in ethics. "I grew convinced," he says in the *Autobiography,* "that truth, sincerity and integrity, in dealings between man and man, were of the utmost importance to the felicity of life." It was by the most circuitous of routes that he made a slow return to the Puritan code; whatever its limitations in private life, it was to remain his business ethic.[21]

On the voyage home in 1726 he had drawn up his plan "for regulating my future conduct in life." "It is the more remarkable," he wrote in the *Autobiography* nearly fifty years later, "as being formed when I was so young, yet being pretty faithfully adhered to quite thro' to old age."

I have never fixed a regular design in life; by which means it has been a confused variety of different scenes. I am now entering upon a new one: let me, therefore, make some resolutions, and form some scheme of action, that henceforth I may live in all respects like a rational creature.

1. It is necessary for me to be extremely frugal for some time, till I have paid what I owe.

2. To endeavour to speak truth in every instance; to give nobody expectations that are not likely to be answered, but aim at sincerity in every word and action—the most amiable excellence in a rational being.

3. To apply myself industriously to whatever business I take in hand, and not divert my mind from my business by any foolish project of growing suddenly rich; for industry and patience are the surest means of plenty.

4. I resolve to speak ill of no man whatever, not even in a matter of truth; but rather by some means excuse the faults I hear charged upon others, and upon proper occasions speak all the good I know of every body.

It was not enough to vow to be frugal, sincere, and industrious; the virtues must be taught by a self-probing analysis that was in origin part Puritan and part Quaker but in result constituted a humanist guide to virtue; virtue, as he was to put it later, was an art to be practiced and perfected. He drew up a list of virtues, allotted a week to the practice of each in turn, and marked down in a diary the measure of success achieved in each. He began with twelve virtues, but finding himself accused by a Quaker friend of being smug about his merits, he added a thirteenth: humility. The course thus lasted thirteen weeks, and four courses covered the year. Little black spots were entered on his pages for every fault.

1. TEMPERANCE—Eat not to dullness; drink not to elevation.
2. SILENCE—Speak not but what may benefit others or yourself; avoid trifling conversation.
3. ORDER—Let all your things have their places; let each part of your business have its time.
4. RESOLUTION—Resolve to perform what you ought; perform without fail what you resolve.
5. FRUGALITY—Make no expense but to do good to others or yourself; i.e., waste nothing.
6. INDUSTRY—Lose no time; be always employ'd in something useful; cut off all unnecessary actions.
7. SINCERITY—Use no hurtful deceit; think innocently and justly, and, if you speak, speak accordingly.
8. JUSTICE—Wrong none by doing injuries, or omitting the benefits that are your duty.
9. MODERATION—Avoid extreme; forbear resenting injuries so much as you think they deserve.
10. CLEANLINESS—Tolerate no uncleanliness in body, clothes or habitation.
11. TRANQUILLITY—Be not disturbed at trifles, or at accidents common or unavoidable.
12. CHASTITY—Rarely use venery but for health or offspring, never to dulness, weakness, or the injury of your own or another's peace or reputation.
13. HUMILITY—Imitate Jesus and Socrates.

He was surprised at the number of faults this searching moral inventory uncovered, and he did take, in spite of point 13, a smug pride at "seeing them diminish." He hoped at some time in the future to compile a code of the "Art of Virtue," and to enlist all men of goodwill across the world in a society to promote it, to which he gave the name "The Society of the Free and Easy": "There seems to me at present to be great occasion for raising a United Party for Virtue, by forming the virtuous and good men of all nations into a regular body, to be governed by suitable good and wise rules, which good and wise men may probably be more unanimous in their obedience to, than common people are to common laws."[22]

This "Art of Virtue" has again a Masonic cast, a socialized religion devoid of ritual and with only headings to serve as dogma. It is not to the modern taste. It is easy to contrast the real ways in Franklin's world with this series of pious preachments, and to pour scorn on the conflict between them. D. H. Lawrence—not necessarily a superior model—was vehemently critical of virtue 12, or rather of Franklin's primarily therapeutic attitude to sex. Other critics, drawing on the references in the Franklin correspondence to the ladies of the salons, have seen him as at least a hypocrite or, worse, a lecher. The blame in part attaches to Franklin, in that he was ready to show his affection for young women—who clearly reciprocated it—and to use words like "wife" and "daughter" in a teasing fashion. Some of the references were risqué, even bawdy, and there was an openness of manner, a willingness to sound daring, a love of hoaxes, that some of his contemporaries found shocking. In the world of Boswell and Fielding much of this was unsurprising. In sober fact, in Franklin's long and varied private life, there is no hard evidence—William's birth perhaps apart—of any serious dereliction from his own strict Puritan code.

It was clear now, nevertheless, that art was being substituted for faith. There was Puritan soul-searching here, of a laborious kind, and there was a rational and realistic view of human weakness and capacity to err. But there was none of the agonizing and breast-beating sense of sin, damnation, and hellfire that tormented the Puritan spirit. Since man's faith was weak, notably his faith in prayer and revelation, he must be taught and trained in the art of virtue. It was, however, to be a "reasonable science of virtue," for a reasonable man in a reasonable age. But even this rational religion and primitive deism were not based on "metaphysical reasonings," to which Franklin was as alien as he was to mysticism itself. In religion as in morals—as later in science and politics—observation, experiment, and trial rather than deductive reasoning were his guides to truth. As his Philadelphia circle and, later, Thomas Jefferson would agree, his God was the wise and benevolent Master Spirit who "made the glorious sun, with his attending worlds . . . and prescribed the wondrous laws by which they move."[23]

Franklin wrote to his father in 1738, "I think vital religion has always suffered when orthodoxy is more regarded than virtue; and the Scriptures assure me that at the last day we shall not be examined what we *thought*, but what we *did;* and our recommendation will be that we did good to our fellow creatures." When the evangelist George Whitefield, grateful for Franklin's offer of lodging for the night, told Franklin that if he made that kind offer for Christ's sake he should not miss a reward, the reply he received was ultramodern: "Don't let me be mistaken; it was not for Christ's sake, but for yours."[24]

From this reasonable man's creed, distrustful of emotionalism and evangelical fervor, theology and dogma were noticeably absent. His rationalism began early. Noticing as a boy the amount of time spent saying grace before meals, he had economically suggested that a single grace for the whole winter's salt meat would be an advantage. Many years later, in his preface to his *Abridgement of the Book of Common Prayer* (1773) he was to suggest a further economy: shorter services would save the time of both ministers and congregations. Though he supported the Presbyterian church—and other churches—in Philadelphia, he preferred to spend Sunday in studying. He used, when he felt he needed it, his own "Articles of Belief and Acts of Religion," compiled in 1728. It began with a quatrain from Cato:

> Here will I hold—If there is a Pow'r above us
> (And that there is, all Nature cries aloud,
> Thro' all her works), He must delight in virtue
> And that which he delights in must be happy.

There followed the characteristic introduction:

I believe there is one Supreme most perfect Being, Author and Father of the Gods themselves.

For I believe that Man is not the most perfect Being but One, rather that as there are many Degrees of Beings his Inferiors, so there are many Degrees of Beings superior to him.

Also, when I stretch my imagination thro' and beyond our System of Planets, beyond the visible fix'd Stars themselves, into that Space that is every Way infinite, and conceive it fill'd with Suns like ours, each with a Chorus of Worlds for ever moving round him, then this little Ball on which we move, seems, even in my narrow imagination, to be almost Nothing, and my self less than nothing, and of no sort of Consequence.

When I think thus, I imagine it great Vanity in me to suppose, that the *Supremely Perfect,* does in the least regard such an inconsiderable Nothing as Man. More especially, since it is impossible for me to have any positive clear Idea of that which is infinite and incomprehensible, I cannot conceive otherwise, than that He, *the Infinite Father,* expects or requires no Worship or Praise from us, but that he is even INFINITELY ABOVE IT.

But since there is in all men something like a natural principle which enclines them to DEVOTION or the Worship of some unseen Power;

And since Men are endued with Reason superior to all other animals that we are in our World acquainted with,

Therefore I think it seems required of me, and my Duty, as a Man, to pay divine regards to SOMETHING.[25]

It was no accident that the climax of Franklin's "Service" was the singing of Milton's "Hymn to the Creator" and the reading of some book or part of a book "discoursing on and exciting to MORAL VIRTUE." His position in the end was a rational but pragmatic deism, in position not far from Gibbon—"the various modes of worship are considered by the believer as equally true, by the philosopher as equally false, by the magistrate as equally useful"—or from Jefferson, in his parallels of the human, the natural, and the divine order of things, or from Addison's hymn to the creation. There was a touch of polytheism, and an acceptance of the Great Chain of Being.[26]

When many years later Tom Paine, who was after all Franklin's protégé, submitted the first draft of *The Age of Reason* to him, Franklin replied, "He who spits against the wind spits in his own face . . . If men are wicked with religion, what would they be if without it?" He took a pew in Episcopalian Christ Church, subscribed in 1737 to the fund to complete the building and in 1751 to the fund to build a steeple, and there he and his wife were in the end to be buried. When his wife missed her prayer book his paper carried a gentle admonition: "Taken out of a Pew in the Church some Months since, a Common-Prayer Book, bound in Red, gilt and letter'd D F on each Corner. The Person who took it, is desir'd to open it and read the Eighth Commandment, and afterwards return it into the same Pew again; upon which no further Notice will be taken." He came to honor virtue far more than orthodoxy; his ethic was social. His friends later ranged from the rationalist Christian Richard Price through the good Anglican Bishop Shipley to the emotional Methodist George Whitefield. Six weeks before his death he summed up his creed in a letter to Ezra Stiles:

I believe in one God, Creator of the Universe. That he governs it by his Providence. That he ought to be worshipped. That the most acceptable Service we render to him is doing good to his other Children. That the soul of Man is immortal, and will be treated with Justice in another Life respecting its Conduct in this. These I take to be the fundamental Principles of all sound Religion, and I regard them as you do in whatever Sect I meet with them.

As to Jesus of Nazareth, . . . I think the System of Morals and his Religion, as he left them to us, the best the World ever saw or is likely to see; but I apprehend it has received various corrupting changes, and I have, with most of the present Dissenters in England, some Doubts as to his Divinity; tho' it is a question I do not dogmatize upon, having never studied it, and think it needless to busy myself with it now, when I expect soon an Opportunity of knowing the Truth with less Trouble . . .

I shall only add, respecting myself, that, having experienced the Goodness of that Being in conducting me prosperously thro' a long life, I have no doubt of its Continuance in the next, though without the smallest Conceit of meriting such Goodness.[27]

Franklin as businessman was thus providentially blessed: everything he touched seemed to turn to print and profit in his hands. Here at least there were few errata, and when there were such, he made them themes for editorials. He opened a stationer's shop and sold or advertised a variety of items: slates and pencils, tea and coffee, cheese and lampblack, lottery tickets and slaves, iron stoves of his own designing and the Crown soap his brothers made in Boston. He began to deal in paper. He imported books; in 1744 his catalog listed 600 volumes for sale. In requesting pamphlets from William Strahan in London, he wrote: "Let me have everything, good or bad that makes a Noise and has a Run: for I have Friends here of Different Tastes to oblige with the Sight of them."[28]

His newspaper was certainly catholic in its journalistic coverage: murders and suicides and the freaks of nature's contriving; a man in Virginia struck dead by lightning with an image of a pine tree imprinted on his body; the birth of triplets; or the story of a young Dutchman who married an old woman and ran off with her money on their wedding night.

(Saturday last) an unhappy man one Sturgis, upon some difference with his wife, determined to drown himself in the river; and she, (kind wife) went with him, it seems, to see it faithfully performed, and accordingly stood by silent and unconcerned during the whole transaction: he jump'd in near Carpenter's Wharff, but was timely taken out again, before what he came about was thoroughly effected, so that they were both obliged to return home as they came, and put up for that time with the disappointment. (February 10, 1730)

The small-pox has now quite left this city. The number of those that died here of that distemper, is exactly 288, and no more. Sixty-four of the number were Negroes; if these may be valued one with another at £30 per head, the loss to the city in that article is near £2,000. (July 8, 1731)

I am about Courting a Girl I have had but little Acquaintance with; how shall I come to a Knowledge of her Fawlts? and whether she has the Virtues I imagine she has?

Answ. Commend her among her Female Acquaintences. (1732)

From New York, we hear that on Saturday se'nnight, in the Afternoon, they had there most terrible Thunder and Lightning, but no great Damage done. The same Day we had some very hard Claps in these Parts; and 'tis said that in Bucks County one Flash came so near a Lad as, without hurting him, to melt the Pewter Button off the Wasteband of his Breeches. 'Tis well nothing else thereabouts was made of Pewter. (June 19, 1732)

[Advertisement] There is to be sold a very likely Negro woman aged about 30 years who has lived in this city, from her childhood, and can wash and iron very well, cook victuals, sew, spin on the linen wheel, milk cows, and do all sorts of house-work very well. She has a boy of about two years old, which is to go with her. The price is reasonable as you can agree.

And also another very likely boy aged about six years, who is son of the above said woman. He will be sold with his mother, or by himself, as the buyer pleases. Enquire of the Printer. (May 3, 1733)

Profiting from his experience in Boston, he was careful as writer and editor to avoid libels and lampoons, and indeed steered clear of political comment. Newspapers did not at that time print editorials or leaders. They influenced opinion by contributions—authentic, anonymous, pseudonymous—usually prepared or edited in the editor's office. At this Franklin was gifted, versatile, and quick. There recur facile and familiar names, Anthony Afterwit and Alice Addertongue, Belinda and Homespun. But the themes are humorous and local, domestic and plebeian. There were no causes here and no crusades, only an easy style and a profitable balance sheet. The battle for freedom of the press in America was fought not by Franklin in Philadelphia but by John Peter Zenger in New York. Franklin carried an account of the Zenger trial, without comment.

He set up former apprentices or journeymen in business in other towns, in varied forms of partnership: James Parker in New York, Thomas Smith and later his own nephew Benjamin Mecom in Antigua, Thomas Whitmarsh and later Louis Timothee in Charleston. He printed the first German hymnbook to appear in America and a short-lived German newspaper, the *Philadelphische Zeitung.* In 1737 Colonel Spotswood of Virginia appointed him postmaster at Philadelphia in place of Bradford; with access to the mails his *Gazette* flourished. "Keep thy shop," said Poor Richard in June 1735, "and thy shop will keep thee." "The Advice of a young Tradesman, written by an old one" in 1748 still reflected the maxims: "Remember that TIME is money . . . Remember that CREDIT is money . . . the Way to Wealth is as plain as the Way to market. It depends chiefly on two words, INDUSTRY and FRUGALITY." He was now no longer a local but a colonial figure: Franklin of Philadelphia. In 1748 at the age of forty-two he had satisfied himself that he was financially secure: his business was worth some £2,000 per year. Accordingly he brought David Hall, his foreman, into partnership with him in Philadelphia—a partnership that lasted harmoniously for eighteen years—and transferred to him executive direction of the printing business at a salary of £1,000 per year. Over the eighteen years the partnership brought Franklin an average of £467 per year. Add his postmastership, his partnerships in New York and Charleston, his real estate—he had by this time a farm near Burlington across the Delaware in New Jersey—and he was, for a Philadelphia tradesman, a man of means. A clerk might earn £25 per year, a tutor £70, the chief justice £200; the governor himself was paid £1,000. Franklin found in trade his own way to wealth.

Early in 1739 a thief stole from his house a "coat lined with silk, four fine homespun shirts, a fine Holland shirt ruffled at the hands and bosom, a pair of black broadcloth stockings, new seated and lined with leather, two pair of good worsted stockings, one of a dark color and the other a lightish blue, a coarse cambric handkerchief marked with an F in red silk, a new pair of calf skin shoes . . . and sundry other things." [29]

With wealth came leisure. "I flatter'd myself that, by the sufficient tho' modest fortune I had acquir'd, I had secured leisure during the rest of my life for philosophical studies and amusements." As always the leisure thus won was not to last long, but the modest competence he had amassed and the great competence he had shown while amassing it formed the foundation on which his public career was built. Not only philanthropy and good works but true freedom, Poor Richard might have said, is the byproduct of economic surplus. And if Franklin himself was not yet a household word, his alter ego was: from 1733 to 1757 "Richard Saunders, Philomath" was the voice of this new and growing society, the voice of the New Man in the New World. He became, in Carl Becker's phrase, "the Sir Roger de Coverley of the masses." [30]

*   *   *

During these years Franklin published *Poor Richard's Almanack*. From 1748, in *Poor Richard Improved,* he added literary and fugitive pieces and doubled its size. In the *Almanack* he printed commonsense observations and wise saws, culled mainly from Rabelais and Swift, Sterne and Lord Halifax. He drew on particular sources for particular years—on James Howell's *Lexicon Tetraglotton* (London, 1660) from 1734 to 1742, and on Thomas Fuller's *Gnomologia* (London, 1732) from 1745 to 1751—"gleanings," he called them, "of all ages and nations." "Why should I give my Readers *bad lines* of my own, when *good ones* of other People's are so plenty?" He made Poor Richard not only the formula for his own financial success but a relished and recognizable figure in any society whether colonial or metropolitan, urban or frontier.

There was nothing new in the idea of an almanac: William Bradford's almanac for Daniel Leeds had been the first thing ever printed in Pennsylvania. When Franklin began planning *Poor Richard,* Andrew Bradford was at one point printing four almanacs, and Keimer had also produced his own. Jacob Taylor, the Quaker poet, produced an almanac each year from 1702 until his death in 1746. No home was complete without one: part calendar, part weather chart, part diary, with alongside and in the margins aphorisms, epigrams, verses, and information for use, for edification, or for amusement. Hoaxes were frequent, especially at the expense of rival almanacs; Franklin drew on Swift here, predicting in his almanac to the hour and the minute when Poor Richard's principal rival, Andrew Bradford's creation Titus Leeds, would die. For Franklin, whose skill lay in exploiting other people's ideas and in chronicling the doings of homespun, humorous characters, the almanac was a natural vehicle. The name of his narrator may have been taken from the actual Richard Saunders who compiled the *Apollo Anglicanus;* the name also occurs in the list of Thomas Denham's Philadelphia customers. Franklin's brother James, now official printer in Rhode Island, was also producing at Newport an almanac of his own entitled *Poor Robin.*

The main source was clearly Swift's *Bickerstaff Papers,* but what Franklin provided, and what was his unique creation, was the fresh and authentic voice, as astrologer and philomath, of an all-too-believable, crotchety, quirkish, and talkative character, the henpecked husband of a shrewish wife, Bridget, "his duchess." Once engaged, one wants to know much more of Richard Saunders, as, earlier, of Silence Dogood. Poor Richard's opening words were:

I might in this place attempt to gain thy favor by declaring that I write almanacs with no other view than that of the public good; but in that I should not be sincere, and men are now-a-days too wise to be deceived by pretences, however specious soever. The plain truth of the matter is, I am excessive poor, and my wife, good woman, is, I tell her, excessive proud; she cannot bear, she says, to sit spinning in her shift of tow while I do nothing but gaze at the stars.

He served up a rich fare: maxims, epigrams, and proverbs, welcome as much for their familiarity as for their terseness; much commonplace moralizing, much worldly shrewdness, not a little bawdiness— for "squeamish stomachs cannot eat without pickles."[31]

If many of the proverbs he used and polished were centuries old, Franklin gave them vigor, clarity and punch, and transformed them in the process. The Scots proverb "A listening damsel and a speaking castle shall never end with honor" became, in Franklin's version, "Neither a fortress nor a maidenhead will hold out long after they begin to parley" (May 1734). The English proverb "God restoreth health and the physician hath the thanks" he changed to "God heals and the doctor takes the fee" (November 1736). He aimed at balance and brevity. "The greatest talkers are the least doers" became "Great talkers, little doers" (April 1733). Some needed little polishing: "None preaches better than the ant, and she says nothing" (July 1736). "A countryman between two lawyers is like a fish between two cats" (February 1737). In other cases Franklin gave the original a new twist, as when he changed the proverb "The King's cheese goes half away in parings" to "The King's cheese is half wasted in parings; but no matter, 'tis made of the people's milk" (June 1735).

Although the items he printed were universal in their range, he never hid his own opinions—that was part of the form. When, in *Poor Richard Improved,* he gave the birthdays or deaths of great and admired men, they were philosophers, scientists, and men of letters: Copernicus and Isaac Newton, William Penn and John Locke, Algernon Sidney and John Calvin. Quite another note was sounded on February 4, 1748, when he recorded the birth of: "Louis the 15th, present King of France, called his most christian majesty. He bids fair to be as great a mischief-maker as his grandfather; or in the language of poets and orators, a Hero. There are three great destroyers of mankind, Plague, Famine, and Hero. Plagues and Famine destroy your persons only, and leave your goods to your Heirs; but Hero when he comes, takes life and goods together; his business and glory it is, to destroy men and the Works of man."

There is a view, held by many, that Poor Richard speaks with the authentic voice of early American capitalism, as well as that of sturdy New World individualism and self-reliance. This view is largely due to the fact that the exhortations to industry and frugality were selected to form the preface to the 1757 *Almanack,* there to be put in the mouth of Father Abraham, and then were separately printed as *The Way to Wealth.* This, as *La Science du Bonhomme Richard,* became fashionable in France, with immeasurable consequences in 1776. It has gone through some 1,300 editions since it was first completed.

Poor Richard had a special flavor and was the foundation of a popular American culture. It was not quite English in its idiom. It had a mixture of Puritan moralizing, yeoman irony, and a dash of cynicism; its humor was rural and small-town rather than urban, as different in style from Fielding as was Mark Twain from Dickens. It sold phenomenally: ten thousand copies a year or one copy for every hundred people in the colonies, the most popular reading matter after the Bible. In the twenty-five years of its existence *Poor Richard* sold more than a quarter of a million copies.[32]

4

WE, THE MIDDLING PEOPLE

ranklin wrote to Cadwallader Colden in September 1748: "I am in a fair way of having no other tasks than such as I shall like to give myself, and of enjoying what I look upon as a great happiness, leisure to read, study, and make experiments, and converse at large with such ingenious and worthy men as are pleased to honor me with their friendship or acquaintance, on such points as may produce something for the common benefit of mankind, uninterrupted by the little cares and fatigues of business." And eighteen months later, in April 1750, he wrote to his mother: "At present I pass my time agreeably enough. I enjoy, through mercy, a tolerable share of health. I read a great deal, ride a little, do a little business for myself, now and then for others, retire when I can, and go into company when I please; so the years roll round, and the last will come, when I would rather have it said, 'He lived usefully,' than 'He died rich.'" [1]

The major leisure activity to which Franklin proposed to devote himself was the study of science, or more properly of what he called—and Scots still call—natural philosophy. "Philosopher" was the word he used of himself and his friends in the Junto. What concerned him was the understanding of the nature of things, in all their variety, and his interests and experiments were, like those of the Junto, immensely wide-ranging. To Franklin, as to Jefferson, it was still possible to take all knowledge to be one's province. It was as a scientist that he first established a reputation that carried his name beyond American shores.

As he anticipated retirement from business he read widely in science, and his authors were English, Dutch, and French: Pemberton's *View of Sir Isaac Newton's Philosophy*, a reminder of his London visit; Hermann Boerhaave's *Elementa Chemiae;* Stephen Hales's *Essays;* Willem Van Gravesande's *Mathematical Elements of Natural Philosophy;* and Jean Desagulier's *Course of Experimental Philosophy,* which he acknowledged had helped him in working on the Pennsylvania fireplace. He was also stimulated by the strongly experimental atmosphere of Philadelphia, with its highly skilled mechanics and artisans, some of whom were members of the Junto—Philip Syng the silversmith, William Maugridge the joiner and mechanic, Nicholas Scull the surveyor, Thomas Godfrey the brilliant self-taught mathematician (one of the few whom Franklin did not find congenial, Godfrey did not remain a member of the Junto for long).

Franklin's eight Atlantic crossings were occasions for recording natural phenomena: ocean temperatures, storms, currents, the partial eclipse of the moon. He was fascinated by all he saw at sea, and especially by the Gulf Stream, of which he was in a sense the discoverer. As early as 1745 he puzzled over why ships should have "much shorter voyages" from America to England than in returning, and regretted that he had not "mathematics enough to satisfy myself" that it was "not in some degree owing to the diurnal motion of the earth." [2]

About the year 1769 or 1770 there was an application made by the Board of Customs at Boston to the Lords of the Treasury in London, complaining that the packets between Falmouth and New York were generally a fortnight longer in their passages than merchant ships from London to Rhode Island, and proposing that for the future they should be ordered to Rhode Island instead of New York. Being then concerned in the management of the American post office, I happened to be consulted on the occasion . . . There happened then to be in London a Nantucket sea captain of my acquaintance, to whom I communicated the affair. He told me he believed the fact might be true; but the difference was owing to this, that the Rhode Island captains were acquainted with the Gulf Stream, which those of the English packets were not. "We were well acquainted with that stream" says he, "because in our pursuit of whales, which keep near the sides of it, but are not to be met with in it, we run down along the sides, and frequently cross it to change our side; and in crossing it have sometimes met and spoke with those packets who were in the middle of it and stemming it. We have informed them that they were stemming a current that was against them to the value of three miles an hour, and advised them to cross it and get out of it; but they were too wise to be counselled by simple American fishermen. When the winds are but light," he added, "they are carried back by the current more than they are forwarded by the wind; and, if the wind be good, the subtraction of seventy miles a day from their course is of some importance." I then observed it was a pity no notice was taken of this current upon the charts, and requested him to mark it out for me, which he readily complied with, adding directions for avoiding it in sailing from Europe to North America. I procured it to be engraved by order from the general post office, on the old chart of the Atlantic, at Mount & Page's, Tower Hill; and copies were sent down to Falmouth for the captains of the packets, who slighted it, however.

On each crossing he made after learning of the current, he kept a careful record of the temperature of the water, and from the resulting data concluded that "a stranger may know when he is in the Gulf Stream, by the warmth of the water, which is much greater than that of the water on each side of it."[3]

London added its own stimulus in 1726; he met Mandeville, author of the *Fable of the Bees*—"A most facetious, entertaining companion"—and Dr. Henry Pemberton, the Secretary of the Royal Society, who had assisted Newton in preparing the third edition of his *Principia;* he always regretted that he had failed to see Newton himself. On his return, his newspaper began to reflect the range of his interests: the weather and waterspouts; why salt dissolves in water; why the sea is sometimes luminous; cures for kidney stones and cancer; mortality rates in Philadelphia; the causes of earthquakes; "On making rivers navigable"; how many people could stand in an area of 100 square yards. George Whitefield's visit to Philadelphia in 1739 raised many issues, including the question of how many could hear him preach from the steps of the Philadelphia Court House: Franklin estimated the number to be 30,000. Everything that crossed his path as apprentice and printer, editor, shopkeeper, and citizen stimulated him to inquire into the Why and How. Even in the midst of political crises after 1765 he would write at length on a scheme for a new alphabet, on his magic squares, on sunspots and whirlwinds, on elephant tusks or the sepulchers of Scythian Kings, or the ways of ants, or of pigeons, or of farmers. He experimented with the qualities of different colors as absorbers of heat. During 1745 he discussed with Cadwallader Colden the nature and functions of pores of the skin and the circulation of the blood. To Jared Eliot in Connecticut he wrote that the strata of seashells in the Appalachians suggested that "It is certainly the wreck of a world we live on."[4]

*   *   *

One incident that came to his notice was especially stimulating. He learned that an eclipse of the moon, which a northeast storm had prevented him from observing in Philadelphia, had been clearly seen in Boston. If northeasters hit Philadelphia before they struck Boston, he concluded, they must move against the wind. His analysis of this— and his description of that analysis—is revealing.

Suppose a great tract of country, land to sea, to wit, Florida and the Bay of Mexico, to have clear weather for several days, and to be heated by the sun, and its air thereby exceedingly rarefied. Suppose the country northeastward, as Pennsylvania, New England, Nova Scotia, and Newfoundland, to be at the same time covered with clouds, and its air chilled and condensed. The rarefied air being lighter, must rise, and the denser air next to it will press into its place; that will be followed by the next denser air, that by the next, and so on. Thus, when I have a fire in my chimney; but the beginning of the motion was at the chimney, where the air being rarefied by the fire rising, its place was supplied by the cooler air that was next to it, and the place of that by the next, and so on to the door. So the water in a long sluce or mill-race, being stopped by a gate, is at rest like the air in a calm, but as soon as you open the gate at one end to let it out, the water next to the gate begins first to move, that which is next to it follows; and so, though the water proceeds forward to the gate, the motion which began there runs backwards, if one may so speak, to the upper end of the race, where the water is last in motion.[5]

Inevitably with Franklin, as with Leonardo da Vinci and with Jefferson, whether to do with ocean currents, windstorms, or stoves for the home, the interest was practical, an interest in useful knowledge: "What signifies philosophy that does not apply to some use?"[6] In 1742 according to his *Autobiography*—but actually, in all likelihood, two years before—he invented "the Pennsylvania fireplace," a cast-iron stove with an open firebox. His curiosity had been engaged even earlier than this. One of the first problems put to his Junto had been "How can smoky chimneys be best cured?" The familiar fireplace might have the comfort of "two warm seats, one in each corner; but they are sometimes too hot to abide in . . . and the cold air so nips the backs and heels of those that sit before the fire that they have no comfort till either screens or settles are provided"; moreover, "a moderate quantity of wood on the fire, in so large a hearth, seems but little; and in so strong and cold a draft, warms but little; so that people are continually laying on more. In short, it is next to impossible to warm a room with such a fireplace." The Dutch or German stove could be placed in the middle of a room, but it gave no sight of the fire, "which in itself is a pleasant thing," and it brought in no fresh air. Franklin's stove was, in a sense, a merger of the open fireplace and the German stove. It retained "the Benefit of Fire" since it was set in the fireplace, but the heat, after rising, was made to descend and circulate before escaping through the chimney, and thus warmed the currents of fresh air as they entered the room. By studying the behavior of hot air, theorizing about its conservation and its transmission by convection as well as by radiation and conduction, and then experimenting, he had made a great, though it might now seem simple and very belated, advance.

The idea was not new: as Franklin pointed out in his account, published in 1774, Nicholas Gauger in France had designed a similar fireplace thirty years before. Franklin's account, however, was significant in itself—and internationally read. He explained the first principles of his fireplace, how and why it worked, listed fourteen advantages of using it, and rebutted criticisms. He turned the stove over for manufacture to Robert Grace, who had helped him to buy out Meredith, and who now owned the Warwick Furnace in Chester County, and, as with all his inventions, he refused to patent it. As a result other ironmongers manufactured and sold the stove. When Franklin moved to London in 1757 he had a stove installed in his Craven Street lodgings and sent one to his Scottish friend Sir Alexander Dick and another to Lord Kames.[7]

When he was again in London, in 1771, he invented a second stove, though he made no public mention of it until ten years later, in a short letter to the Marquis de Turgot. In 1786 he published the details of his second invention in the *Transactions* of the American Philosophical Society under the title "Description of a New Stove for Burning of Pitcoal, and Consuming All Its Smoke." It was built with an inverted funnel that operated as a siphon, causing smoke to descend into the flame instead of rising through the chimney. Smoke was thus eliminated, and soot with it. This stove was never very popular in America, where wood was more available and cheaper than coal—nor was it easy to operate. It should not, its inventor said, be left in the care of ignorant servants "who will with difficulty acquire the knowledge necessary, and will make frequent blunders, that will fill your room with smoke." [8]

Indeed, experience of London's winters reinforced his interest in keeping rooms not only warm but as clean and well ventilated as possible. He was always—to John Adams's later displeasure—a devotee of air baths, open windows, and fresh air. After an illness in 1758, he feared the coming winter and turned his attention to chimneys as well as stoves. He perfected "an easy, simple contrivance . . . for keeping rooms warmer in cold weather than they generally are, and with less fire." He called it a "Sliding Plate"; today it would be referred to as a damper. It consisted of a metal plate that fitted horizontally into the base of the chimney funnel and, when pushed into the funnel, completely closed it off. When drawn out a short distance to create a slight draft, the plate allowed smoke to pass up the chimney while keeping most of the warm air in the room. The heating of rooms was a constant preoccupation; so were cleanliness and the nuisance of smoke. As late as 1785 he wrote a long letter "On the Causes and Cure of Smoky Chimneys." He noted that the nature of smoke and the functioning of chimneys were not generally understood: most people believed that smoke rises because it is lighter than air, but in reality it is heavier. Chimneys function, he held, by allowing atmospheric pressure to push smoke up through them. He was as a result as much architect as scientist, as interested in buildings and their structure as in warming interiors. And, as we have seen, with this went concern with the risk of fire, and with protection from it by insurance and by cooperative organization. [9]

Franklin was as much interested in lighting rooms as in heating them. He devised a new type of candle, made with spermaceti or whale oil. "You will find," he wrote to the Quaker Susanna Wright, whose versatility and longevity matched his own, "that they afford a clear white Light; may be held in the Hand, even in hot Weather, without softening; that their Drops do not make Grease Spots like those from common Candles; that they last much longer, and need little or no Snuffing." He corresponded with Thomas Paine on his claim that he had developed a smokeless candle and later met with him to experiment with methods of making candles burn more brightly. He assisted Peter Kalm with experiments to find a method of preventing candles from dripping. He also devised a four-sided ventilated lamp for use in lighting the streets of Philadelphia, which had the advantage of staying clean much longer and thus giving off more light than the closed globe type of lamp used in London.[10]

*   *   *

From the first, he was captivated by meteorology, in part no doubt with an eye to securing scientific support for Poor Richard's haphazard weather forecasts, the accuracy of which he made a subject of banter with rival almanacs. This led naturally to an interest in electricity. In both Europe and America electricity was something of a rage; itinerant "electricians" traveled around as lecturing showmen selling "shocks" and "magic" to a frightened but fascinated public. For Franklin, this interest came to a head in 1743 when, in Boston, he first met Dr. Archibald Spencer, "a most judicious and experienced physician and man-midwife." Spencer lectured on the discoveries of Newton and Harvey and performed some elementary electrostatic experiments. The following year, at Franklin's suggestion and with Franklin as agent, Spencer visited and demonstrated in Philadelphia. Franklin bought his apparatus and enlisted the aid of the Junto and the Library Company in the experiments. He asked for aid also from the London agent of the Library, the botanist Peter Collinson, who in 1746 sent over an "electric tube." Penn himself provided other equipment. Franklin's experiments completely engrossed his attention, and he sent Collinson detailed reports of his activities. He advanced the study of "the electrical fluid" from a parlor game to science.

Franklin was not the first to establish the identity of lightning with electricity, but he was the first to propose that it could be proved by experiment:

To determine the question, whether the clouds that contain lightning are electrified or not, I would propose an experiment to be tried where it may be done conveniently. On the top of some high tower or steeple, place a kind of sentry-box . . . big enough to contain a man and an electrical stand. From the middle of the stand let an iron rod rise and pass bending out of the door, and then upright twenty feet, pointed very sharp at the end. If the electrical stand be kept clean and dry, a man standing on it, when such clouds are passing low, might be electrified and afford sparks, the rod drawing fire to him from a cloud. If any danger to the man should be apprehended (though I think there would be none), let him stand on the floor of his box, and now and then bring near to the rod the loop of a wire that has one end fastened to the leads, he holding it by a wax handle; so that sparks, if the rod is electrified, will strike from the rod to the wire, and not affect him.[11]

In May 1747 he reported to Collinson "the wonderful effect of pointed bodies, both in *drawing off* and *throwing off* the electrical fire." He observed that a person standing on wax (a nonconductor) was affected differently by an electrical charge from a person standing on the floor. "There have arisen some new terms among us; we say B (and bodies alike circumstanced) are electrised positively; A, negatively. Or rather B is electrised plus; A, minus." He thus reached the idea of electricity as a single fluid, no longer as "vitreous" (produced on glass rubbed with silk) and "resinous" (produced on resin or amber rubbed with wool or fur). He then experimented with "Muschenbrock's wonderful bottle," the Leyden jar. This glass bottle coated on the outside with metal foil and filled with water or shot had become, in Franklin's day, part of the standard equipment of the lay scientist. When charged it could give a considerable shock to many men. It was essentially a primitive condenser, offering a means of "storing" an electrical charge, and opening up the possibility of experiment on a large scale. Franklin, by testing each element in turn, established that the "charge" resided not in the foil or in the water but in the glass itself. And if the charge is contained in the glass because glass is a nonconductor, then the shape of the bottle is irrelevant; the condenser could be made of parallel glass plates with metal sheets affixed to either side—from which comes the parallel plate condenser.[12]

Even as serious scientist he did not lose his sense of humor about his pursuits; he wrote to Collinson in April 1749:

The hot weather coming on when electrical experiments are not so agreeable, it is proposed to put an end to them for this season, somewhat humorously, in a party of pleasure on the banks of Schuylkill. Spirits, at the same time, are to be fired by a spark sent from side to side through the river, without any other conductor than the water; an experiment which we some time since performed, to the amazement of many. A turkey is to be killed for our dinner by the electrical shock, and roasted by the electrical jack, before a fire kindled by the electrified bottle; when the healths of all the famous electricians in England, Holland, France and Germany are to be drank in electrified bumpers, under the discharge of guns from the electrical battery.[13]

His own conclusions he noted as follows: "Electrical fluid agrees with lightning in these particulars: (1) Giving light; (2) Color of light;

(3) Crooked direction; (4) Swift motion; (5) Being conducted by metals; (6) Crack or noise in exploding; (7) Subsisting in water or ice; (8) Rending bodies it passes through; (9) Destroying animals; (10) Melting metals; (11) Firing inflammable substances; (12) Sulphureous smell. The electrical fluid is attracted by points. We do not know whether this property is in lightning. But since they agree in all particulars wherein we can already compare them, is it not probable they agree likewise in this? Let the experiment be made." [14]

Being Franklin, he could not refrain from putting his discoveries to use, even if only to entertain, but he was against exploitation or monopoly. Through all his scientific correspondence he clearly saw himself as a member of an international team of inquirers and experimenters, living by the free interchange of information. His attitude was open and generous, ceaselessly questing, and devoid of vanity. As he put it to Collinson: "since even short hints and imperfect experiments in any branch of science, being communicated, have oftentimes a good effect, in exciting the attention of the ingenious to the subject, and so become the occasion of more exact disquisition and more complete discoveries, you are at liberty to communicate the paper to whom you please; it being of more importance that knowledge should increase than that your friend should be thought an accurate philosopher." [15] Terms he was first to launch into general use became the international language in electricity: armature, battery, brush, charged, condense, electrify, Leyden bottle, minus (negative or negatively), nonconductor, plus (positive or positively), uncharged.

Franklin's accounts of these experiments in his letters to Collinson in London were circulated among the members of the Royal Society and offered to Edward Cave for the *Gentleman's Magazine* in May 1750; they were printed in collected form in 1751, as an eighty-six page pamphlet entitled *Experiments and Observations on Electricity made at Philadelphia in America*. Franklin wrote in language all could understand; in contrast, William Gilbert of Colchester, one of his English predecessors as experimenter, had in 1600 written his *De Magnete* in Latin. Within twenty years no fewer than four English editions of Franklin's tract had appeared, and three in French, one in German, and one in Italian. It was on this that Franklin's European reputation as a scientist was based. "He found," says Carl Van Doren, "electricity a curiosity and left it a science." [16]

He was certainly the first to propose putting the theory to the test by erecting an iron rod on a high tower and drawing off sparks of fire from a storm cloud. He had not done so himself, however, since there was no structure in Philadelphia high enough for the purpose. The experiment was successfully tried in France: first at Marly-la-Ville in May 1752, by Thomas François Dalibard, who had read Franklin's account; and later in Paris. Similar experiments were tried in England, Germany, Russia, and Belgium, and reports of them were circulated. Franklin was known of in Leipzig, Gottingen, and St. Petersburg as one capable of extracting fire from the heavens. Not least was he known of in St. Petersburg, where Professor Georg Wilhelm Richmann was electrocuted during an experiment in 1753. Franklin confirmed his theory without imperiling Christ Church Steeple or himself—and in, as he put it, "a different and more easy manner"—by flying a kite armed with an iron point. This was the charismatic amateur known to every schoolboy, and imitated by many.

Make a small cross of two light strips of cedar, the arm so long as to reach to the four corners of a large thin silk handkerchief when extended; tie the corners of the handkerchief to the extremities of the cross, so you have the body of a kite; which, being properly accommodated with a tail, loop, and string, will rise in the air, like those made of paper; but this being of silk is fitter to bear the wet and wind of a thunder-gust without tearing. To the top of the upright stick of the cross is to be fixed a very sharp-pointed wire, rising a foot or more above the wood. To the end of the twine, next the hand, is to be tied a silk ribbon, and where the silk and twine join, a key may be fastened. This kite is to be raised when a thunder-gust appears to be coming on, and the person who holds the string must stand within a door or window, or under some cover, so that the silk ribbon may not be wet; and care must be taken that the twine does not touch the frame of the door or window. As soon as any of the thunder-clouds come over the kite, the pointed wire will draw the electric fire from them, and the kite, with all the twine, will be electrified, and the loose filaments of the twine will stand out every way, and be attracted by an approaching finger. And when the rain has wetted the kite and twine, so that it can conduct the electric fire freely, you will find it stream out plentifully from the key on the approach of your knuckle. At this key the phial may be charged; and from electric fire thus obtained, spirits may be kindled, and all the other electric experiments be performed, which are usually done by the help of a rubbed glass globe or tube, and thereby the sameness of the electric matter with that of lightning completely demonstrated.[17]

Having confirmed the theory, Franklin was soon concerned with finding a use to which the knowledge could be put:

If these things are so, may not the knowledge of this power of points be of use to mankind, in preserving houses, churches, ships etc. from the stroke of lightning, by directing us to fix, on the highest parts of those edifices, upright rods of iron made sharp as a needle, and gilt to prevent rusting, and from the foot of those rods a wire down the outside of the building into the ground, or down one of the shrouds of a ship, and down her side till it reaches the water? Would not these pointed rods probably draw the electrical fire silently out of a cloud before it came nigh enough to strike, and thereby secure us from that most sudden and terrible mischief?[18]

In Philadelphia, the new Academy and the recently completed State House had lightning rods by 1752. Yet, once again, Franklin refused to patent the lightning rod—or the Franklin rod, as some called it— or to profit by it. "How to Secure Houses etc. from Lightning" appeared in the Preface to *Poor Richard* in 1753. It was for all to read. So too with his tract: it became in the end an international *Vade Mecum* on electrical discourse, in ten editions and four languages; its fifth edition in English constituted a book of 514 pages. He was not just well known but a celebrity, his lightning rods or the absence of them a talking point among the virtuosi, their use or nonuse even an occasion for riots.

It was, however, not for all to accept. There was one loud discordant voice in Europe, that of the Abbé Jean-Antoine Nollet. The Abbé, as a pupil of Charles Du Fay, believed in the two-fluid theory of electricity (as being either vitreous or resinous), and he accepted neither Franklin's unitary theory nor his argument of the efficiency of lightning rods. He considered lightning rods useless and indeed dangerous metal conductors, as likely to attract thunderstorms as to harness their power safely; he cited Richmann's death as evidence. He wrote a critical article in the *Memoirs* of the French Academy, and published in 1753 his *Letters on Electricity,* highly critical of the new ideas. Franklin took note of his criticism in the fourth edition of his own book. He could point with pride to the acceptance of his lightning rod. In July 1773 he could write from London to Professor John Winthrop at Harvard: "Conductors begin to be used here. Many country seats are furnished with them, some churches, the powder magazine at Purfleet, the queen's house in the park . . ." But it was a slow process of persuasion. Franklin was irritated less by Nollet's opposition than by his unscientific tone. The Abbé appealed, he wrote to Cadwallader Colden, "to the superstitious prejudices of the populace, which I think unworthy of a Philosopher."

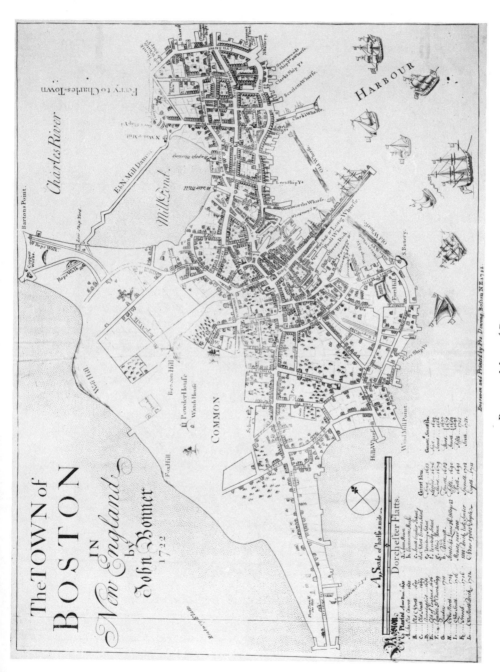

Bonner, Map of Boston, 1722.

Benjamin Franklin, ca. 1746, by Robert Feke.

Deborah Franklin, usually attributed to Matthew Pratt,
but in fact by Benjamin Wilson, 1766.

Mrs. Richard Bache (Sarah Franklin), by John Hoppner.

JOIN, or DIE.

Political cartoon from the *Pennsylvania Gazette*, 1754.

William Temple Franklin, 1790,
by John Trumbull.

A Northwest View of the State House in Philadelphia, 1778,
by Charles Willson Peale.

Benjamin Franklin, 1785, by Charles Willson Peale.

The Library and Surgeon's Hall on Fifth Street, by William Birch. The Library Company moved into the new building in 1790, the year its founder died, and it honored him with a statue in classical garb in the niche above the door.

He speaks as if he thought it Presumption in man to propose guarding himself against the *Thunder of Heaven!* Surely the Thunder of Heaven is no more supernatural than the Rain, Hail or Sunshine of Heaven, against the Inconvenience of which we guard by Roofs and Shades without Scruple.

But I can now ease the Gentleman of his Apprehension; for by some late Experiments I find, that it is not Lightning from the Clouds that strikes the Earth, but Lightning from the Earth that strikes the Clouds.

This was a reference to Franklin's experiment in 1752 and 1753 with a two-part rod, to show that clouds may be sometimes electrified negatively, and to his erection in his home of a number of bells that would be rung, at the approach of a storm, by a clapper suspended by an insulated string, to Franklin's pride and pleasure and to his wife's alarm and distress.[19]

Franklin's lightning rods became a test of enlightenment among men. For centuries in Europe, church bells had been rung at the approach of a storm; indeed, many bells carried inscriptions testifying to their benevolent power to drive away demons, lightning, storm, and tempest. Steeples being high, many bell ringers were killed during lightning storms, and many steeples toppled. Even the good Abbé Nollet had counseled prudence on this, although in doing so he also confessed his ignorance: "I do not know whether sound, considered physically, is capable or not of making a thunder-cloud burst and of causing the discharge of its fire towards terrestrial objects." Peter Van Musschenbroek, the inventor of the Leyden jar, had endorsed Nollet's cautions in a popular physics survey he published in 1751. In an article in Diderot's *Encyclopedia* Musschenbroek scorned the view that thunder and lightning were the work of evil spirits, but he too believed that "thunder can be disrupted and diverted by the sound of several bells or the firing of a cannon; thereby a great agitation is excited in the air which disperses the parts of the thunder."[20]

There was a further mischievous problem: was protection against lightning not a human intervention in God's purpose? Were thunder, lightning, and storm the artillery of heaven, retribution for the sins of mankind? The Junto in January 1760 (while Franklin was absent in London) debated the question: "May we Place Rods on our Houses to guard them from Lightening without being guilty of Presumption?" One who participated was Ebenezer Kinnersley, a Baptist clergyman who had been Franklin's collaborator in his experiments and who lectured widely on electricity; he was prompt to bring forward arguments to prove that in all these experiments and discoveries there

was no presumption against God. John Lining, a correspondent of
Franklin's in South Carolina and himself an experimenter, reported
what Franklin would have found welcome and very much in character: that to quiet the good people of Charleston, who feared that the
erecting of lightning rods might incur divine wrath, the *South Carolina and American General Gazette* "suggested raising lightning rods
to the glory of God."[21]

Controversy only began here. A generation later, it would engage
the attention of two men soon to be not merely enlightenment but
revolutionary leaders in France. When M. de Vissery de Bois-Valé
erected a lightning rod in the 1780s to protect his house in St. Omer,
his neighbors tore it down. They had the law on their side: local laws
prohibited the use of lightning rods. French scientists, however, supported the house-owner and used Franklin's evidence and arguments.
The case went to the Council of Artois. The only major "scientific"
opposition came from Jean-Paul Marat, who believed that the protective power of lightning rods had been exaggerated and that they were
dangerous; he took advantage of the occasion to attack "official"
French science as represented by the Académie Royale des Sciences,
which had refused to admit him to membership. The final plea in the
appeal was made by Maximilien Robespierre, fighting his first case;
his skill in this affair brought him a considerable measure of fame.
Robespierre based his plea on the scientific evidence favoring the use
of rods, but also on the need for progress. He wrote: "The Arts and
Sciences are the richest gifts that God can give to mankind; what
perverse fate has then put so many obstacles in the way of their progress on earth? Do we really believe that the Almighty needs this me-
teor that terrifies us so much?" He sent a copy of his argument to
Franklin, saying that he was happy to salute a man "whose least merit
is to be the most illustrious servant of the world."[22]

The practical success of the lightning rods in securing buildings
against damage by lightning triumphed in the end over scientific jealousy, ecclesiastical dislike, and popular prejudice. Royal displeasure,
however, was more difficult to combat. By 1776 what Franklin called
"knowledge of the power of points" had become entangled with the
politics that led to war. When the British Board of Ordnance asked
the Royal Society to recommend the best method of preserving the
arsenals at Purfleet from danger of explosions caused by lightning,
the Society appointed a committee of five, of which Franklin was one,

to prepare a report. The committee recommended Franklin's system, but one member, Benjamin Wilson, dissented so far as to advocate the use of blunt rather than pointed ends to the rods. Wilson, who had been Franklin's critic in the Royal Society more than twenty years before—critical because jealous—now published two pamphlets, as Franklin said, "reflecting on the Royal Society, the committee, and myself, with some asperity." Franklin made no reply: "I have never entered into any controversy in defence of my philosophical opinions; I leave them to take their chance in the world. If they are right, truth and experience will support them; if wrong, they ought to be refuted and rejected."[23] George III, however, angry at Franklin for his political role and seeking to discredit him, ordered the substitution of blunt for pointed ends on Kew Palace. He asked Sir John Pringle to give an opinion in favor of the change, only to receive the reply that "the laws of Nature were not changeable at royal pleasure." It was then intimated to Pringle "by the King's authority that a president of the Royal Society entertaining such an opinion ought to resign," and he resigned accordingly. He, like Franklin, lost his other posts and exiled himself from London. Whatever the court might do, London gossip made its own comment:

> While you, great George, for safety hunt,
> And sharp conductors change for blunt,
> The nation's out of joint.
> Franklin a wiser course pursues,
> And all your thunder fearless views,
> By keeping to the point.[24]

There was still another controversy, occasioned perhaps by the Boston earthquake of 1755. Did lightning rods actually cause earthquakes? This problem was also made personal in the debate between Professor John Winthrop of Harvard and the Reverend Thomas Prince of Boston. Prince said in his sermon "Earthquakes, the Works of God and Tokens of His Just Displeasure" (printed in Boston in 1755):

The more *Points of Iron* are erected round the *Earth,* to draw the *Electrical Substance* out of the *Air;* the more the *Earth* must needs be charged with it. And therefore it seems worthy of Consideration, Whether *any Part* of the *Earth* being fuller of *this terrible Substance,* may not be more exposed to *more shocking Earthquakes.* In *Boston* are more erected than anywhere else in *New England;* and *Boston* seems to be more dreadfully shaken. O! there is no getting out of the mighty Hand of *God!* If we think to avoid it in the *Air,* we cannot in the *Earth:* Yea it may grow more fatal . . .[25]

In the appendix to this sermon, Prince took note of Franklin's experiments and held that "this Electrical Substance" was "a principal instrument in producing Earthquakes." In *The Pennsylvania Gazette* for December 15, 1737, Franklin had printed an article about earthquakes claiming "that the material cause of thunder, lightning, and earthquakes, is one and the same, viz. the inflammable breath of Pyrites which is a substantial sulphur, and takes fire of itself." This article, however, was taken verbatim from Ephraim Chambers's *Cyclopaedia* and was not a report of Franklin's own views. In a paper to the Royal Society in 1749 the Reverend William Stukeley argued that there was at least a connection between lightning and earthquakes; and the London magazines of the period followed up this view. In the preface he contributed to Franklin's book on electricity, Dr. John Fothergill was driven to emphasize that Franklin's ideas on the causes of lightning were based on hard evidence and experiment and were not part of this general speculation. Winthrop followed the example set by Fothergill: "Philosophy, like everything else, has had its fashions, and the reigning mode of late has been, to explain everything by *Electricity* . . . Now it seems, it is to be the cause of earthquakes . . . The two cases of lightning and earthquakes are no way parallel; . . . the electrical substance, when in the bowels of the earth, is in circumstances essentially different from what it is, when in the clouds of the air." [26]

*   *   *

Franklin as scientist was important not only for the range of his interests and the international stir of opinion he created but also for his attempt, by correspondence and organization, to produce a concerted scientific study of American natural phenomena, and thereby to tighten the cultural bonds of one colony with another and of all with Britain and Europe. There was in his eyes a single and beneficent empire of science and curiosity. In May 1743 he sent a circular letter to various correspondents, proposing the formation of an American Philosophical Society—in form a wider Junto—and an American Philosophical Miscellany, monthly or quarterly. He wanted to establish a system of correspondence on all aspects of the natural world— plants and trees, mines and minerals, maps and surveys, disease and viniculture—and "all philosophical experiments that let light into the nature of things, tend to increase the power of man over matter, and multiply the conveniences or pleasures of life." Where his own mathematics was not strong enough to carry him, as in the study of astronomy, he could at least act as correspondent, and as conveyor of information. Even the 1753 edition of *Poor Richard* noted the imminence of the transit of Mercury, and Franklin printed a four-page pamphlet on how to plot it; unfortunately, thick clouds on May 6, 1753, obscured it. Of this embryonic international society Franklin served as secretary. But the idea was, again, not original to him, and he was not the pioneer. John Bartram, a farmer and botanist, had already been exchanging letters with many correspondents on scientific questions, and had in 1739 suggested to Peter Collinson in England the formation of a society of "ingenious and curious men."

The Philosophical Society made slow progress. But Franklin's correspondents were many, and not only in America: Cadwallader Colden in New York, whom he had first met by chance on the road in Connecticut in 1743; James Bowdoin in Boston; John Winthrop at Harvard, whom Franklin would later nominate for membership of the Royal Society; Ezra Stiles of Newport and Yale; Jan Ingenhousz in Holland (later Vienna); Giambatista Beccaria in Italy; Barbeu-Dubourg, Dalibard, Le Roy, and Condorcet in France; and a host of like-minded spirits, many of them Quakers, in Britain, especially Peter Collinson, Sir John Pringle, and Sir Joseph Banks. The letter of thanks Franklin received from Louis XV after the Marly experiments brought him a pleasure "like the secret pride of the girl in the Tatler who had got a new pair of garters." [27] Even the onset of war in 1776 would not entirely disrupt his contacts with his British scientist-friends. In 1779, at the height of the struggle between colony and mother country, Benjamin Vaughan published in England a selection of Franklin's letters and papers. And with knowledge of his interests came also recognition of his achievements: Master of Arts at Harvard and Yale in 1753 and at William and Mary in 1754; Copley Medalist in 1753; Fellow of the Royal Society in 1756; Doctor of Laws at St. Andrews in 1759; and Doctor of Civil Law at Oxford in 1762. The Philadelphia tradesman was recognized internationally as a man of science: In the end he was a member of twenty-eight learned societies and academies in Britain, France, Germany, the Netherlands, Italy, Spain, Russia, and America.

His strength as a scientist lay in many qualities. He had an endless and persistent curiosity, so that every domestic situation set his mind moving: the ants in his closet and their speed in communicating with each other, or the behavior of pigeons, or the characteristics of a whirlwind he saw in Maryland, about which his host, Colonel Tasker, said "We got this on purpose to treat Mr. Franklin." There was his hunger to question and experiment, using whatever tools lay at hand. And there was his ability to test a hypothesis openly and with total objectivity and then—perhaps the rarest quality of all—to communicate his findings in clear and vivid prose. As he wrote to John Perkins, "If my hypothesis is not the truth itself, it is at least as naked. For I have not with some of our learned moderns disguis'd my nonsense in Greek, cloth'd it in algebra, or adorn'd it with fluxions. You have it *in puris naturalibus*."[28]

Sir Humphry Davy's judgment on Franklin as scientist is hard to better:

A singular felicity of induction guided all his researches and by very small means he established very grand truths. The style and manner of his publication are almost as worthy of admiration as the doctrine it contains. He has endeavoured to remove all mystery and obscurity from the subject; he has written equally for the uninitiated and for the philosopher; and he has rendered his details amusing as well as perspicuous, elegant as well as simple. Science appears in his language in a dress wonderfully decorous, the best adapted to display her native loveliness. He has in no case exhibited that false dignity, by which philosophy kept aloof from common applications, and he has sought rather to make her a useful inmate and servant in the common habitations of men than to preserve her merely as an object of admiration in temples and palaces.[29]

What was striking, however, alongside the genuineness and purity of his spirit of inquiry was his faith that science could and would unlock the mysteries of the universe. This faith was shared by his companions in the Junto, as later by Jefferson and Benjamin Rush, by Rittenhouse and the Bartrams, by Collinson and Priestley.

He did not fail to see the link between politics and science. The general public could be involved not only as beneficiaries but as patrons, backers, insurers, and sources of support. In founding the Pennsylvania Hospital he made this appeal:

the Good particular Men may do separately, in relieving the Sick, is small, compared with what they may do collectively, or by a joint Endeavour and

Interest. Hence the Erecting of Hospitals or Infirmaries by Subscription, for the Reception, Entertainment, and Cure of the Sick Poor, has been found by Experience exceedingly beneficial, as they turn out annually great Numbers of Patients perfectly cured, who might otherwise have been lost to their Families, and to Society.[30]

And when he became a member of the Assembly he could use a new device, the "matching" grant. If individuals would subscribe £2,000, the Assembly would do the same.

This condition carried the Bill through; for the Members who had oppos'd the Grant, and now conceiv'd they might have the Credit of being charitable without the Expence, agreed to its Passage; and then in soliciting Subscriptions among the People, we urg'd the conditional Promise of the Law as an additional Motive to give, since every Man's Donation would be doubled . . . A convenient and handsome Building was soon erected, the Institution has by constant Experience been found useful, and flourishes to this Day. And I do not remember any of my political Manoeuvres, the Success of which gave me at the time more Pleasure. Or that in after-thinking of it, I more easily excus'd myself for having made some Use of Cunning.[31]

If the motives were rooted in the domestic scene—stoves for keeping oneself warm, lightning conductors to protect buildings—and an earlier curiosity, what made them truly scientific was the faith in experiment, the readiness to be governed entirely by it. Experiment remained the core of the discipline:

You require the reason; I do not know it. Perhaps you may discover it, and then you will be so good as to communicate it to me. I find a frank acknowledgment of one's ignorance is not only the easiest way to get rid of a difficulty, but the likeliest way to obtain information, and therefore I practice it: I think it an honest policy. Those who affect to be thought to know every thing, and so undertake to explain every thing, often remain ignorant of many things that others could and would instruct them in, if they appeared less conceited.[32]

*   *   *

By 1751 Franklin was engaged in yet another activity: politics and statecraft. He was elected to the Pennsylvania Assembly and reelected every year for the next decade, including his years of absence in London. This interest came to dominate, though never to swamp, all the others. It was never his first love; science or "philosophy" he would always have put first. And deft though he was at cajolery, for him politics was not cajolery but construction, not the placating of people but the carrying through of plans. He had a remarkable flair for planning practical improvements. To his well-known plans for the civic improvement of Philadelphia, for the defense of Pennsylvania, and for colonial union, he added plans for the abolition of slavery, for an international "United Party for Virtue," for bringing civilization to the natives of New Zealand, and for converting the masses to practicing Christianity—the latter by the simple device of converting a few popular "grandees," for, as he told Whitefield, "men fear less the being in hell than out of fashion."[33] His curiosity in science was always practical, closely linked to his humanitarianism. In one sense, therefore, all his scientific and publishing activities were but prelude to the political; as a politician and statesman he drew heavily on the image he had already made of himself as writer and publisher, folksy philosopher, civic reformer and scientist, with, now, an international reputation.

Franklin in 1751, at the age of forty-five, was no stranger to local or state politics. He had been clerk of the Pennsylvania Assembly since 1736 and a member of the Philadelphia Common Council for the past three years; and in 1749 the Freemasons had elected him Grand Master of Pennsylvania. His life seemed to follow the advice he gave in his *Autobiography:* never ask, never refuse, and never resign. This was no longer a case of *noblesse oblige* but of prosperous *bourgeois oblige* too. He was not likely to be allowed to become conceited; his mother wrote to him on October 14, 1751 (six months before her death): "I am glad to hear that you are so well respected in your town for them to chuse you alderman altho' I don't know what it means nor what the better you will be of it besides the honor of it."[34]

On the political stage he was by no means the unconventional figure he might now seem; the majority of native-born political leaders were inevitably self-made men, though normally their resources came from land, or from shipping and trade. Franklin did not buy his farm in Burlington, New Jersey, until he retired from his printing business, and it never quite became central to his life, for he was first and last an urban product. He was not only self-made; in 1750 he still saw himself as a "Stranger" in Pennsylvania.

The government of Pennsylvania was a proprietary, in which authority lay with the Penn family. The Penns collected quitrents on their grants of land, and they insisted that those lands still ungranted, and which benefited from steadily rising prices, should be exempted from provincial taxation. But William Penn himself had, in his Charter of Liberties in 1701, surrendered the right to make laws for the colony to a single-chamber Assembly, which was to be elected annually. His sons stayed mainly in England, and "reigned" rather than ruled via a deputy-governor on the spot, usually called "the Governor," whom they appointed and instructed. Between these governors and the Assembly, for long Quaker-controlled, arose a steady succession of disputes, usually over finance and almost always over defense. Unwilling to grant very much "for the King's use"—even in the crisis of French invasion in 1754 it voted only £10,000, and that by a vote of seventeen to fifteen—the Assembly yet bridled at any interference by the governor with its power of the purse. There was a mounting sense of grievance that the absentee proprietors, who were also owners and beneficiaries, made no contributions to the cost of government or to the heavy cost of dealing with the Indians. Since, however, no other royal governors did so, why—said the Penns—should they?

In these struggles the Pennsylvania Assembly, like its counterparts in other colonies, came to voice the sentiments of good Whigs, and so to see in the curb it sought to impose on the governor and his prerogatives a check on tyranny reminiscent of that devised in 1688 in Britain: "It is, may it please the Governor, one of the most valuable rights of British subjects, to have their Bills granting money to the Crown, accepted without amendments; a right that cannot be given up, without destroying the Constitution, and incurring greater and more lasting mischiefs than the grant of money can prevent." [35]

One of Franklin's earliest political comments in Philadelphia occurred in the *Gazette* in 1729, when Governor William Burnet of Massachusetts was struggling with that colony's Assembly over his salary. Franklin praised the Massachusetts House for holding to "what *they think* their right, and that of the people they represent." It was the spirit of liberty that "so gloriously distinguished Britons and Englishmen, from the rest of mankind." [36]

With this Whiggish outlook were associated those other notions of 1688: that that government was best which governed least; that government should be "mixed" in character; and that it should represent those who had a stake in society through their ownership of land and property. The formal local and provincial franchise required two years' residence, the acceptance of Jesus as Savior, and the possession of a freehold estate of fifty acres or personal property to the value of £50. A strict enforcement of the freehold qualification would have denied the franchise to some 50 percent to 75 percent of the adult male population. Confusion often arose, however, over the claims of freemen who were not freeholders; and the laws were not always strictly enforced. Colonial society was, in any event, more open to the man of talents than was that of Old England, and property was easier to acquire, but the Whig political code with its concern for property rights was common to both. It was reinforced by the apportionment of seats in the Assembly: Philadelphia, Chester, and Bucks counties were allotted eight seats each in the legislature, and the city of Philadelphia had two. The remaining ten seats were apportioned among the colony's five western counties. Thus two-thirds of the Assembly seats were filled by Philadelphia and its environs, although by the mid-eighteenth century that region contained only half the colony's population. Moreover, those qualified to vote in the east habitually returned their social superiors to the legislature. A small, oligarchic clique of easterners, tied by marriage, religion, and interest, therefore dominated the colony.

Pennsylvania was distinct in being at once a Quaker and a largely German state. If the Penns were by this time Anglican, the Assembly was Quaker-controlled, and its policy of pacifism and friendship for the Indians threw a long shadow over all debates on foreign affairs and defense; more by luck than judgment, pacifism had been a successful policy for over fifty years. There had been no Indian wars, and there were no forts, no army, no militia. The Germans were a disturbing element; they were thrifty and pacific, but in numbers and energy they were seen as a threat to English culture. Few of them had become citizens, and for the most part they supported the Quakers as silent allies in political indifference.

Philadelphia itself was an *entrepôt;* it traded heavily with Britain and the West Indies and was vulnerable to invasion. But it looked west as well as east. The Germans and Scotch-Irish were pushing west and south into Virginia and the Carolinas. The French, based on the St. Lawrence, were pushing south from the great Lakes into the upper reaches of the Ohio valley and onward, via Kaskaskia and Vincennes, to their outlet at New Orleans; thus far they had threatened the uncertain New York frontier and the even less certain Virginia frontier rather than Pennsylvania, but Philadelphia was less than one hundred miles from the frontier.

As printer and publisher of news, as postmaster, as scientist, and now as politician, Franklin was fascinated by the West. In 1751 John Bartram's *Observations . . . in his travels from Pennsylvania to Onondago, Oswego and Lake Ontario in Canada* was published, and in 1755 and 1756 the two parts of Lewis Evans's *Geographical, Historical, Political, Philosophical and Mechanical Essays*. In 1753 and 1754 Captain Swaine's voyages from Philadelphia to seek the North-West Passage were planned—though the *Argo* was to get no farther than Labrador. The West and its infinite extent suggested to Franklin an agrarian expansion that would, he thought, tie a rural hinterland to a metropolitan Britain. Like all men of substance in his day, he was prepared to speculate in land, and it behooved his province to do so, or it would find its western edges formed into a satellite area belonging to Virginia. But all these interests required a western policy, both toward the Indians and for joint intercolonial defense against the French.

By 1747 even Philadelphia found itself involved in King George's War: belatedly, French and Spanish privateers sailed up the Delaware, sacked two plantations, and captured a ship only a few miles below the city. Franklin's first political preoccupation was thus with colonial defense. By 1747 it had become clear that the Quaker-dominated Assembly would not enact the militia bill the governor was urging upon it, and that the colony would take no part, if it could avoid it, in the war. The wealthy merchant class—those Franklin called "the great and the rich"—hesitated to spend money on the defense of Quaker property; it reminded Franklin of the story of "him who refused to pump in a sinking ship because one on board whom he hated would be saved by it as well as himself." One day walking past a Quaker meeting house with William Allen, he "declared that more mischief was hatched in that place than in a meeting of JESUITS at St. Omer."[37]

In a pamphlet entitled *Plain Truth* published in 1747, Franklin argued, in a fashion that was superficially conservative but potentially seditious, that protection and obedience were reciprocal obligations: that it was the duty of the government to protect the people and the duty of the people to obey the government. He never accepted the Quaker view that the state of nature is a state of love; the realist was too strong in him. Since the Quakers were unchangeable in their religious views, "their obstinacy invincible," and the merchant class was selfish, it seemed that "our greatest men, our *Cives nobilissimi* of both parties, had sworn the ruin of the country"; accordingly "the middling people" must set up a voluntary defense association on their own. "All we want is order, discipline and a few cannon." There were, he calculated, sixty thousand former shopkeepers and tradesmen familiar with firearms, "hunters and marksmen, hardy and bold." "The way to secure peace," he said, "is to be prepared for war." His call to arms left nothing to the imagination. In *Plain Truth,* he stressed that the threat came not from disciplined troops but from "licentious privateers": "your persons, fortunes, wives and daughters, shall be subject to the wanton and unbridled rage, rapine, and lust of *Negroes, mulattoes* and others, the vilest and most abandoned of mankind. A dread scene! . . . we, the middling people . . . cannot fly with our families; and if we could how shall we subsist? No, we . . . must bear the brunt." He had learned much from Cotton Mather and from Daniel Defoe. He still honored Defoe's "Great Law of Subordination," but there was evidence now and then in politics of the spirit of a "rising people."[38]

The defense proposals won the approval of the governor, and Franklin was seen fleetingly and inaccurately as an "authority man." They won the approval also of no fewer than ten thousand subscribers, the "Associators," who bought arms and drilled themselves in local regiments and, following New England fashion, elected their own officers. There were ten regiments in Philadelphia, and more than one hundred in the province as a whole. Franklin made suggestions for the training of the volunteers and for the purchase of manuals of arms. He proposed a lottery of 10,000 tickets, selling at £2 each, that raised £3,000 for the Association after providing 2,842 prizes; assisted by £1,500 from the merchants, this made possible the erection of a battery and the purchase of guns from Boston. Franklin even turned over his own lottery winnings of £312 to the Association. Along with Allen, he visited New York to borrow more cannon. They met with Governor George Clinton.

He at first refused us peremptorily; but at dinner with his council, where there was great drinking of Madeira wine as the custom of that place then was, he softened by degrees, and said he would lend us six. After a few more bumpers he advanced to ten; and at length he very good-naturedly conceded eighteen. They were fine cannon, 18-pounders, with their carriages, which we soon [April 1748] transported and mounted on our battery, where the Associators kept a nightly guard while the war lasted, and among the rest I regularly took my turn of duty there as a common soldier.[39]

Franklin himself was chosen colonel of the Philadelphia regiment, but he declined. Both his activities and his sentiments brought him prov-ince-wide popularity; and his forthrightness on this question of de-fense brought a refreshing clarity to the tangled politics of the colony. As he noted of the Quakers: "Indeed I had some cause to believe that the defence of the country was not disagreeable to any of them pro-vided they were not requir'd to assist in it. And I found that a much greater number of them than I could have imagined, tho' against of-fensive war, were clearly for the defensive."[40]

Plain Truth and the voluntary association form an important chap-ter in the Franklin story. Good citizenship and self-defense demanded cooperative action. If it would not come from the Assembly then it would come from outside or, as the Penns would say, "from below." Thomas Penn's reaction was full of proprietary alarm and redolent of privilege, but pregnant too with awareness of things to come. Writing to Lynford Lardner, he held that Franklin's pamphlet had "done much mischief." To Richard Peters, he maintained in 1748: "This As-sociation is founded on a Contempt to Government, and cannot end in anything but Anarchy and Confusion." Of Franklin he wrote: "He is a dangerous Man and I should be very Glad he inhabited any other Country, as I believe him of a very uneasy Spirit. However as he is a Sort of Tribune of the People, he must be treated with regard." Rich-ard Peters himself at first offered verdicts that were favorable to Franklin and the Associators. Their conduct, he reported, "has been remarkably regular and moderate, without any angry Expressions or blustering behavior." Their election of their own officers, he ex-plained, "was look'd upon by the Council only in the nature of a recommendation, the tenor of their Commissions being to receive their Orders from the Governor for the time being according to the rules of War." Peters expressed a belief that the Association might promote the proprietary interest by reconciling the Quakers to de-fense, and so save the British government "the Trouble, and the Quakers the shame, of an Act of Parliament to incapacitate them from sitting in Assembly." Penn's disapproval, however, led Peters to change his view. Writing to Penn in June 1748 he described the Association as an illegal combination that could in due course be used by those hostile to the proprietary interest. James Logan, however, praised Franklin and his achievement and recognized that he was "the principal mover and very soul of the whole."[41]

Franklin's Library Company, the Fire Company, the Hospital, and the militia itself all indicated cooperative rather than individual action, as did his *Proposals relating to the Education of Youth in Pennsylvania* (1749). Again, this proposal was more than a call for the opening of an academy and an outline of a curriculum. In each case a similar method was spelled out. Become aware of what you need: if you really want it, then join others of like mind, as in the volunteer fire company, or pay for it; if funds are short, as they will be, then club together and raise a public subscription where the state's resources are puny; and when the state cannot, or will not, provide public resources, then "the people" must do it for themselves. Almost all Franklin's projects began as self-help, and as insurance. It was a short step then to campaigning for "causes." Because the city watch was poorly recruited, he began a seventeen-year campaign that in the end led to a law taxing property to finance a reliable city watch. A sixpence-per-month levy to have the streets swept led to a law, which Franklin drafted, for paving, lighting, and cleaning them. Franklin reached democratic solutions not from any collectivist or utopian dogma but from a pragmatic, self-help orientation. Always at the root was the conviction that the individual is only truly himself in a gregarious, not in a solitary, setting. The causes were clearly civic, intelligent, and beneficent. It was hard to see where private improvement differed from public welfare, or where the interests of "Us" differed from those of "Them." Franklin arrived at social action from an individualist base. The implications, however, for a community with an absentee governor and a remote government ruling largely by neglect were likely to be profound.

The Peace of 1748 brought an end to the threat of invasion. The Association dwindled away, and neither Franklin nor his colleagues sought to exploit the issue of defense in the October elections of 1748—in contrast to 1764 and later. Yet it is impossible not to notice the democratic implications of the development of the Association, the near-spontaneous action of many public-spirited people, with Franklin in the lead. He was not yet a political animal, and not seeking to use or to dramatize issues. He did not see himself as a solitary or aggressive individual, and he never sought any special glory for himself. The D. H. Lawrence picture of smug vainglory is false to the public actions of the man. For Franklin the line between self-help and social service was elusive. This was not merely because his journal and his role as advertiser bridged the gap between them. It was because for him individual action could never occur in isolation; survival required social solidarity. As Poor Richard said in January 1744, "He that drinks his Cyder alone, let him catch his horse alone."

*   *   *

Defense meant not only arms but the capacity to manufacture them. When in 1750 Parliament enacted the Iron Act, extending its mercantilist veto over colonial manufacturing by forbidding the establishment of new forges and silting mills and insisting on the export to Britain of unprocessed iron, Franklin protested.

His protest, as always, was written, and reflective. His *Observations Concerning the Increase of Mankind, Peopling of Countries etc.*, written in 1751, was one of his first assessments of the relationship between colony and mother country. The pressure of his friends Collinson and Jackson persuaded him to agree to its publication in America in 1754 and in London in 1755. Population, Franklin said, was increasing more rapidly in the Colonies than in the "old settled countries":

I believe People increase faster by Generation in these Colonies, where all can have full Employ, and there is Room and Business for Millions yet unborn. For in old settled Countries, as England for Instance, as soon as the Number of People is as great as can be supported by all the Tillage, Manufactures, Trade and Offices of the Country, the Overplus must quit the Country, or they will perish by Poverty, Diseases, and want of Necessaries. Marriage too, is discouraged, many declining it, till they can see how they shall be able to maintain a Family.

With remarkable accuracy considering his meager statistical base, he predicted a vast increase in the American population by a doubling of numbers every generation. Within a century there would be more British in America than in the motherland. This would open up a matching demand for manufactured goods well beyond the capacity of the home country, "a glorious market wholly in the power of Britain," and the mother country accordingly should not restrain colonial manufacturing: "A wise and good mother will not do it." Franklin did not attack mercantilism as such; he recognized that the system brought obvious advantages to both parties, and he certainly regarded any difference of policy with Britain as minor indeed when compared with the menace presented to both by French expansion in the Ohio Country and to the west of the Alleghenies, as by its threat to the Delaware itself. Expansion unfettered was part of the creed, whether British or American. There was in any case no danger of incompatible interests: "So vast is the territory of North America that it will require many ages to settle it fully; and, till it is fully settled labor will never be cheap here, where no man continues long a laborer for others, but gets a plantation of his own, no man continues long a journeyman to a trade, but goes among those new settlers, and sets up for himself, etc."

Here was the frontier theory, almost fully spelled out. Here too was an awareness of the American potential, of America's uniqueness. It was still for Franklin a British frontier; it was still "the Empire on this side" of the Atlantic. There was no sense of disunity, even if there was a growing awareness of a distinctiveness of character in the New World. And in the first edition of the *Observations,* though tactfully dropped later, was his sturdy, even over-frank, sense of Anglo-American racial identity.[42]

It is a tribute to the *Observations* that it has occasioned a considerable literature. William Appleman Williams has argued that Franklin was so committed to a British imperial view that he wanted to "keep the people busy farming and in that way turn them from domestic manufacturing, while creating a limitless market for British manufactures." This implies a commitment and a deviousness that are not buttressed by a reading of the tract. It is true that Franklin foresaw such space being available, and such lack of density of population, that the American people must for ages be "employed in agriculture chiefly," even more so after Canada was added in 1763. But he did foresee the increase in the need for domestic American manufactures, especially of textiles. He foresaw also the frontier as a safety valve, drawing off the poor of the Middle Colonies and settling them with large families on land not monopolized by great landholders or crowded with surplus workers.

As Alfred Aldridge has shown in his essay "Franklin as Demographer," the *Observations* was part of an interest in demography that had extended over a century and would lead logically to the writings of Malthus fifty years later. Since there were no official censuses, the raw material of prophecy lay in tables of births and deaths. As early as 1731, in the *Pennsylvania Gazette,* Franklin had printed extracts from *The Political State of Great Britain* XL (1731) offering physical and political—and moral—observations on the London rates of mortality. He appended a table of the burials in Boston from 1700 to 1731, from which he concluded: "By comparing the Number of Inhabitants in Boston with the above Account, it appears that not above a 40th Part of the People of that Place die yearly, as a medium."[43]

Franklin's prescience as a demographer may have been hampered by his ethnocentrism. He did not wish to see his America swamped by nonwhites, or even by non-English. He was especially critical of the Germans in western Pennsylvania: "Why should the Palatine boors be suffered to swarm into our settlements and, by herding together, establish their language and manners to the exclusion of ours? Why should Pennsylvania, founded by the English, become a colony of aliens, who will shortly be so numerous as to Germanize us, instead of our Anglifying them?" He went further, and used language that would today be labeled distinctly racist:

The number of purely white people in the world is proportionably very small. All Africa is black or tawny; Asia chiefly tawny; America (exclusive of the newcomers) wholly so. And in Europe the Spaniards, Italians, French, Russians, and Swedes are generally of what we call a swarthy complexion; as are the Germans also, the Saxons only excepted, who with the English make the principal body of white people on the face of the earth. I could wish their numbers were increased . . . Why increase the sons of Africa by planting them in America, where we have so fair an opportunity, by excluding all blacks and tawnys, of increasing the lovely white and red? But perhaps I am partial to the complexion of my country, for such kind of partiality is natural to mankind.[44]

Where the Germans were concerned, he wrote explicitly to Peter Collinson in December 1753, responding to Collinson's suggestions. "Methods of great tenderness should be used," he said, and he went on:

The second Proposal, of an Act of Parliament, disqualifying them to accept of any Post of Trust, Profit or Honour, unless they can speak English intelligibly, will be justifyed by the reason of the thing, and will not seem an hardship; but it does not seem necessary to include the Children. If the Father takes pains to learn English, the same Sense of its usefulness will induce him to teach it to his Children.

The sixth Proposal of Encouraging Intermarriages between the English and Germans, by Donations, &c. I think would either cost too much, or have no Effect. The German Women are generally so disagreeable to an English Eye, that it wou'd require great Portions to induce Englishmen to marry them . . .

The seventh Proposal of discouraging the sending more Germans to Pennsylvania, is a good one; those who are already here would approve of it.[45]

*   *   *

To meet the frontier challenge not only colonial defense and equipment were needed, but joint intercolonial political action. Franklin had long been considering this: he had partners in New York and in Charleston; he had planned in 1740 (but never carried out) a "General Magazine and Historical Chronicler for all the British Plantations in America"; his proposals for the Philosophical Society included a *Proposal for Promoting Useful Knowledge among the British Plantations in North America* (1743). His range was continental. His appointment in 1753, jointly with William Hunter, as deputy postmaster-general for all the colonies brought him to consider colonial union and defense more urgently.

He secured his postmastership by eighteenth-century stratagems. Hearing of the illness of the incumbent controller, Elliot Benger of Virginia, he wrote to Peter Collinson in London, hoping that Collinson might have influence with the authorities: "I am quite a stranger in the manner of managing these applications." He sought the support also of William Allen, chief justice of Pennsylvania, one of the great men of the province, and then—though not later—his friend. Allen authorized his London agent to work for Franklin's cause, just as he had earlier subsidized the medical training of John Redman and, later, of John Morgan, and the artistic training of Benjamin West. Franklin later forgot the part played by his patron. He was prepared, he told Collinson, to spend £300 for any necessary fees or perquisites. "However, the less it costs the better, as 'tis for life only, which is a very uncertain tenure." And "as I have a respect for Mr. Benger I should be glad the application were so managed as not to give him any offence if he should recover." The tradesman had become more than the industrious apprentice; he had moved effortlessly into the world of Lord Chesterfield and the Duke of Newcastle. Franklin was preferred to Cadwallader Colden and John Mitchell, who were also interested in the post, but the application was not totally successful; it was decided that when Benger died the postmastership would be held jointly by Franklin and William Hunter of Virginia, who like Franklin was a printer and a publisher of almanacs. Their joint salary of £600 a year was "to be paid out of the money arising from the postage of letters"—that is, if there was any left over.

This appointment was again at once challenge and opportunity, bringing distinct advantage to the holder. The post carried the prestige accorded to a royal official, and with a territory that stretched the length of the continent, and the ability to travel where he wished on a government expense account. Franklin played down these attractions when asking Collinson to work for his candidacy. In a day when postage was a considerable expense, letters to and from the postmaster-general traveled free. The office would "be suitable to me, particularly as it would enable me to execute a scheme long since formed," he told Collinson, referring to the nationwide or even more ambitious Philosophical Society, "which I hope would soon produce something agreeable to you and all lovers of useful knowledge."[46]

Franklin introduced a uniform method of accounting, careful instructions, and standardized forms for all post offices. He regularized and increased the mail service: in the spring and summer between Philadelphia and New York there were now three services a week, as against only one previously, and two a week from New England to Philadelphia; in the rest of the year there were two a week except in the worst weather. In the year before he sailed for England, the receipts for the colonial post office were greater than for the previous three years together. By 1761 a regular profit from the colonial post office reached London—for the first time. In 1754 Franklin visited all the northern post offices, and in 1755–56 those in Maryland and Virginia. He knew his postal officials, and the roads and ferries that linked them. The colonies for the first time had a profitable, efficient, and unified postal service from Maine to Georgia. On Hunter's death in 1761, Franklin heard of the likelihood of the appointment of John Foxcroft, secretary to Governor Fauquier of Virginia, as his successor. He wrote a courtier-style letter to Lord Bessborough, one of the joint postmasters-general, whose deputies the American officials were:

The Commission I have the Honour so recently to receive from the Goodness of your Lordship and Mr. Hampden, grants the whole Office, Powers and Salary, to the Survivor of the two Persons therein appointed; and therefore, notwithstanding the Decease of Mr. Hunter, there is properly no Vacancy; unless you should think fit to make one by revoking that Commission; which, when my long and faithful Service of 24 Years in the Post Office, is considered, I hope will not be done. During the greatest Part of that time, I had the Burthen of conducting the whole American Office under others, with a very slender Salary; and it has been allow'd that the bringing the Office to what it is, from its former low insignificant State, was greatly owing to my Care and Management. And now that in the Course of Things some additional Advantage seems to be thrown in my Way, I cannot but hope it will not be taken from me in favour of a Stranger to the Office.[47]

Despite this attempt at persuasiveness, Foxcroft was appointed; he served until the British postal service was disrupted by the outbreak of the Revolution.

The postal appointment brought Franklin, besides his £300 in salary, patronage, from which the family promptly benefited. William replaced his father as postmaster of Philadelphia, and when he was upgraded to controller a year later, Joseph Read—a relative of Deborah's—replaced him. Later Peter Franklin came from Boston to fill the post; John Franklin was postmaster in Boston until his death in 1756, when his widow succeeded him. And when Franklin sailed to England in 1757, his partner, James Parker, became controller. Moreover, already well known to "ingenious" men in other provinces, Franklin now came to know the whole area from Boston to Williamsburg at first hand. He carried a responsibility that did not stop at the Pennsylvania line. In 1754 we begin to meet Benjamin Franklin, statesman.

*   *   *

In September 1753 Franklin attended the treaty-making at Carlisle with the Ohio Indians. This was his first experience of Indian consultation, and he found it much less straightforward and infinitely more protracted than consulting with the like minds of Philadelphia. Indeed it never was quite his world: flowery oratory, and all its problems of translation, interrupted by the giving of wampum, and with wild carnival if the demon drink was unleashed too soon. Franklin was one of three white commissioners from Pennsylvania; Richard

Peters of the Council and Isaac Norris, speaker of the Assembly, were the others. The journey by horseback took four days, and they planned to take with them wagonloads of gifts, of blankets and shoes, guns and powder, knives and rum; these were delayed, which was unfortunate, for the tribes put first things first. The commissioners were joined by members of the Assembly from Cumberland county and by local gentlemen and freeholders. There were many Indians; twelve deputies from the Six Nations, three from the Delaware, fifteen from the Shawnee, three from the Miami, and many camp followers. Present as interpreters were Andrew Montour, himself part Seneca Indian, who was later with Braddock, and the able Conrad Weiser; but most of the talking and interpreting were done by Scarouady, an Oneida chief who was the spokesman for the Six Nations. Ceremonial speeches of condolence and exchanges of wampum—as well as interpretation—held things up. So did the insistence on the appearance of the gifts before serious talks began "to wash away the blood" and "to cover the graves of your warriors."

Behind the ritual, all sides were bargaining. The Pennsylvanians wanted peace on the frontier and Indian allies against the French; a month later, Governor Dinwiddie of Virginia, acting independently of the Pennsylvanians, sent the young George Washington with an ultimatum to the French on the Ohio. The Indians at Carlisle were prepared to discuss aligning with the British against the French, but they also wanted fewer Pennsylvanian traders, fewer trading posts, and altogether fewer white men in their hunting grounds. They also wanted—or at any rate, gathered around the council fires, they said they wanted—less of the firewater that spread ruin. At the conclusion of the talks, in fact, rum was distributed freely, and Franklin's observation was that all of them got drunk. When apologizing later, they explained to the white commissioners that the Great Spirit made all things for a purpose, and that rum was made for Indians to get drunk on. For Franklin rum was a beverage that was best for taxes. Perhaps it was no accident that Poor Richard said in 1756, "When you incline to drink rum, fill the glass half with water." Franklin's conclusions were not favorable, least of all to the "vile" Indian traders. Writing to Thomas Pownall in 1756, he expressed distrust of treaty and negotiation: "For my own part, I make no doubt but that the Six Nations have privily encouraged these Indians to fall upon us; they have taken no step to defend us as their Allies, nor to prevent the Mischief done us . . . I do not believe we shall ever have a firm Peace with the Indians till we have well drubb'd them."[48]

He did not see the Indian as any idyllic type of "natural man." Much later, in 1784, he would praise the Indians' hospitality and tolerance, their oratory and pride. The early references, however, are to their simplicity, "happy mediocrity," laziness, and vanity, and the need for blows to keep them honest. He noted that captured whites, raised by the Indians and then freed, were apt to return to a life "of freedom from care and labour." "No European who has tasted Savage Life can afterwards bear to live in our Societies." This is a conclusion the facts would hardly seem to warrant. Nor was his own picture of Indian life suggestive of this freedom from care. He did not see the Indian, as Washington did, as a half-fearsome savage. Equally, he saw no clash of cultures, and no real possibilities of assimilation. The Indian traders were "the most vicious and abandoned Wretches of our Nation." There would always be a frontier, with a forest for forest men. And, given honest trading, a curb on rum, and agreements honored by both sides, red and white men could, he thought, manage to live side by side. Nevertheless, he never quite comprehended the gap between the two worlds. Nor was there any evidence of idealism, any illusions about the brotherhood of man, any pretense of a deeper understanding of the cosmic purpose. The lack of illusion, in his Indian references and in most of his writing, has its own laconic attraction, for its restraint as well as its wisdom.[49]

*   *   *

These varying experiences—as proponent of defense, as student of population growth, as postmaster, as Indian negotiator—all pointed toward a wider role for Franklin. On that role, and on the relationship with Britain, he had already pondered. After reading Alexander Kennedy's *The Importance of Gaining and Preserving the Friendship of the Indians to the British Interest Considered,* which his New York partner James Parker had sent him, he was beginning to work out the strategy and the appropriate tactics for united colonial action. His own suggestion was an intercolonial council, with representatives from all the colonies, meeting by turn in the various capitals, with a governor appointed by the crown. The money needed could be raised by an excise on strong liquors. Again, as with all his projects, it would be a spontaneous colonial movement not imposed from outside, and it would be financially viable. It went beyond Kennedy's proposal of an annual meeting of commissioners, negotiating Indian treaties and fixing provincial quotas of defense contributions, to an intercolonial government. Franklin also meditated on how to get such a plan accepted. He wrote to Parker in 1751:

Now if you were to pick out half a dozen men of good understanding and address, and furnish them with a reasonable scheme and proper instructions, and send them in the nature of ambassadors to the other colonies, where they might apply particularly to all the leading men and by proper management get them to engage in promoting the scheme; where, by being present, they would have the opportunity of pressing the affair both in public and private, obviating difficulties as they arise, answering objections as soon as they are made, before they spread and gather strength in the minds of the people, etc., etc.; I imagine such an union might thereby be made and established. For reasonable, sensible men can always make a reasonable scheme appear such to other reasonable men, if they take pains and have time and opportunity for it; unless from some circumstances their honesty and good intentions are suspected. A voluntary union entered into by the colonies themselves, I think, would be preferable to one imposed by Parliament; for it would be perhaps not much more difficult to procure, and more easy to alter and improve as circumstances should require and direct.[50]

On May 9, 1754 he published in the *Pennsylvania Gazette* an account of the French drive into the Ohio country and of their building Fort Duquesne at the forks of the Ohio. He accompanied it by a cartoon of a snake cut into eight sections (New England, New York, New Jersey, Pennsylvania, Maryland, Virginia, North Carolina, South Carolina), with the caption "Join or Die"—a device that appeared in other colonial newspapers in the same month. The summons had gone out in September 1753 from the Board of Trade for a treaty with the Six Nations, to hear their grievances and to restore goodwill, in order to check French advances. De Lancey, lieutenant-governor of New York, summoned at Albany a meeting of commissioners from a number of colonies to treat with the Iroquois. All the New England colonies sent commissioners, as did Maryland and Pennsylvania; Virginia and New Jersey declined. Twenty-five commissioners were present. Indian grievances were numerous: encroachment of white settlers on their lands; trade between Albany and Canada; the threatened removal of Sir William Johnson from the control of their affairs. But overshadowing these was the need for a plan of defense against the

French, who were moving steadily down the Ohio country, and in 1754 were based on the Allegheny. Governor Shirley of Massachusetts was urging a colonial union; De Lancey himself, skeptical about union, wanted a chain of forts across the northern frontier, to be built and maintained by all the colonies. New York was apt to regard Indian relations as almost its monopoly; Virginia, an absentee, was seeking—somewhat erratically—to establish control over the Ohio Indians, as much for land as for security. The Pennsylvania Assembly sent two commissioners, Franklin and Isaac Norris; the Pennsylvania Council sent John Penn and the secretary of the province, Richard Peters; but the Pennsylvania delegates, unlike those from Massachusetts, were not instructed to take steps to set up any colonial union.

As early as 1751, as we have seen, Franklin had proposed a voluntary union of the colonies. By 1754 he suggested the establishment of a federal council in which each colony would be represented by from two to seven delegates in proportion to its financial contributions, and which would become responsible for defense and Indian policy under a president-general appointed by the crown. On passing through New York he discussed his proposals, now in a memorandum of "Short Hints," with Archibald Kennedy, and sent a copy to James Alexander in New York, asking him to peruse it and then to forward it to Cadwallader Colden. The refusal of the Pennsylvania Assembly to authorize its representatives to consider any plan for colonial union, its refusal to aid Virginia against the French in the upper Ohio valley, and the absence from Albany of any representatives from Virginia or from New Jersey led Franklin now to believe that only an Act of Parliament could manufacture the union he wanted.

The commissioners met in June. They set up a steering committee of one member from each colony—Franklin representing Pennsylvania and Thomas Hutchinson Massachusetts—to prepare a plan for union. The committee reported in four days, recommending substantially Franklin's draft: "one general government" of all the colonies except Georgia and Nova Scotia for defense, expansion, and Indian affairs, with a Grand Council charged to legislate, to make peace and war, and to tax, and a president-general appointed and paid by the crown. Delegates, whose numbers were to be in proportion to each colony's share of taxes, were to be elected by the colonial assemblies every three years; the council, which would meet annually, would discuss Indian affairs and would be responsible for building forts and patrolling the seacoast; it would levy taxes, by a liquor duty or a stamp tax or an excise on "superfluities" such as tea, on the inhabitants of every colony in the union. The president-general—Franklin thought he should be a military man, but the committee disagreed—could veto its acts, but he could not prorogue it or select its speaker. In this plan, therefore, the Council would have more power than the separate colonial assemblies had in relation to their governors, but less power than Parliament enjoyed against the king. Its danger seemed not to be in its democratic character but in the permanence of its institutions, the regularity of its intercolonial meetings, and the federal nature of its authority. Not a single assembly, however, not even that of Pennsylvania, approved the plan. And in Britain, since it had no colonial backing, it was not considered at all. As Franklin put it in his *Autobiography*, "the assemblies did not adopt it, as they all thought there was too much *prerogative* in it, and in England it was judged to have too much of the *democratic*." In fact, Newcastle's Cabinet and the Board of Trade were far more sympathetic to the idea of colonial union than this suggests; but they reasoned that in the emergency now facing the colonies a bill for union would be unwise.[51]

Of Franklin's major part in the Albany conference there can be no question, and there is an almost unanimous view among scholars that his was the major role as author of the Plan of Union. A detailed comparison of the text of the Plan of Union with his "Short Hints" does show some differences as a result of the discussions at the conference, and Franklin said that he "reported the draught in a new form . . . agreeable to the determination of yesterday." It was less specific on sources of revenue than Franklin had been: "such General Duties, Imports and Taxes" as appeared most just should be imposed. Franklin had suggested a possible excise on "superfluities as tea etc."; the Albany Plan recommended that the taxes levied should be aimed at "rather discouraging Luxury, than loading Industry with unnecessary Burthens."

Franklin had envisaged a union of "all the British dominions on the continent"; the final plan excluded Nova Scotia, Georgia, and Delaware (the former two presumably being seen as military outposts supported by annual parliamentary appropriation, the last as having the same governor and council as Pennsylvania). The final version was more specific on representation than the "Short Hints" had been: the numbers ranged from two each for New Hampshire and Rhode

Island to seven each for Massachusetts and Virginia; it was provided, however, that after the first three years the quotas were to be based, as in Franklin's first draft, on the relative amounts of money raised in each colony for the common treasury.

Until July 2 the most hotly debated issue was the one on which Franklin had early yielded; whether an Act of Parliament was the only method for obtaining such a union. The point was carried in the affirmative, though still opposed by some members from Connecticut and Pennsylvania. Connecticut men also continued to hold that too much power was lodged in the president-general, but they went along with the main design. Clause by clause, the report was debated in intervals between Indian conferences and further elaborated, until, on July 9, Franklin was "desired" to reduce it to a finished draft. Next day this draft was accepted, apparently unanimously, for transmission to the assemblies.

The major dissenter from the scholarly consensus that Franklin drafted the Albany Plan has been Lawrence H. Gipson. Gipson contended that Thomas Hutchinson, like Franklin, had drafted a plan before the congress met; that the commissioners considered this draft; and that many of its provisions and even more of its phraseology appeared in the final text that Franklin presented to the congress on the morning of July 10. It is true that in a letter to Governor Bernard in October 1769 Hutchinson said: "At the congress at Albany in 1754 I was in favour of an Union of the governments for certain Purposes and I drew the Plan which was then accepted [but] if I had imagined such absurd notions of government could ever have entered unto the heads of the Americans as are now Publickly avowed I should then have been against any sort of union as I was for it." Thus fifteen years after the event Hutchinson emphatically claimed authorship of the Albany Plan, but some years later he ascribed it to Franklin, equally emphatically, on three occasions. In the third volume of his *History of Massachusetts Bay,* written in England in the 1770s, he declared: "The plan for a general union was projected by Benjamin Franklin, Esq., one of the commissioners from the province of Pennsylvania, the heads whereof he brought with him."[52]

At Albany there was total agreement between the two men. Franklin himself, in the *Autobiography* and in his letters, repeatedly speaks of the plan as his. It was clearly changed only in minor details from his "Short Hints." Although a number of colonial leaders were moving in his direction, the Plan of Union can safely be said to be his in conception, and of it he was the major midwife. It was sad, even tragic, that the infant was stillborn. Franklin reflected on it in the *Autobiography:* "I am still of opinion it would have been happy for both sides of the water if it had been adopted. The colonies, so united, would have been sufficiently strong to have defended themselves; there would then have been no need of troops from England; of course, the subsequent pretence for taxing America, and the bloody contest it occasioned, would have been avoided." And looking backward in 1789 along the road that led from the last war with France through revolution to federal union, he argued that if this or a similar plan had been adopted, "the subsequent separation of the colonies from the mother country might not so soon have happened."[53]

Despite its failure, the meeting in Albany was nevertheless of major importance. From now on Franklin never abandoned the idea of some form of colonial union. From that September until January 1755 he remained in the north. In December 1754, in Massachusetts, he discussed Governor Shirley's variant of the plan: a union not of representatives of the colonial assemblies but of the governors and the colonial councils, with the power to tax reserved to Parliament. Franklin was critical of this on two grounds. First, he believed it wise to associate people with government wherever possible: "they bear better when they have, or think they have, some share in the direction." And second, he objected, then as later, to parliamentary taxation of the colonists; indeed, in 1766 he would reprint the arguments from his letters to Shirley of 1754, to prove that objection to taxes did not begin as a consequence of the Stamp Act proposals.

When Governor Shirley proposed that the colonial assemblies be excluded from any power in the union, Franklin outlined for him the objections that would be made to the exclusion and at the same time set down, on December 4, 1754, attitudes pregnant with meaning for the future:

That the People in the Colonies, who are to feel the immediate Mischiefs of Invasion and Conquest by an Enemy, in the Loss of their Estates, Lives and Liberties, are likely to be better Judges of the Quantity of Forces necessary to be raised and maintain'd, Forts to be built and supported, and of their own Abilities to bear the Expence, than the Parliament of England at so great a Distance . . .

That it is suppos'd an undoubted Right of Englishmen not to be taxed but by their own Consent given thro' their Representatives. That the Colonies have no Representatives in Parliament, and refusing them the Liberty of chusing a Representative Council, to meet in the Colonies, and consider and judge of the Necessity of any General Tax and the Quantum, shews a Suspicion of their Loyalty to the Crown, or Regard for their Country, or of their Common Sense and Understanding, which they have not deserv'd. That compelling the Colonies to pay Money without their Consent would be rather like raising Contributions in an Enemy's Country, than taxing of Englishmen for their own publick Benefit. That it would be treating them as a conquer'd People, and not as true British Subjects . . .

As we are not suffer'd to regulate our Trade and restrain the Importation and Consumption of British Superfluities, (as Britain can the Consumption of Foreign Superfluities) our whole Wealth centers finally among the Merchants and Inhabitants of Britain, and if we make them richer, and enable them better to pay their Taxes, it is nearly the same as being taxed ourselves, and equally beneficial to the Crown. These Kind of Secondary Taxes, however, we do not complain of, tho' we have no Share in the Laying or Disposing of them, but to pay immediate heavy Taxes, in the Laying Appropriation or Disposition of which, we have no Part, and which perhaps we may know to be as unnecessary as grievous, must seem hard Measure to the Englishmen, who cannot conceive, that by hazarding their Lives and Fortunes in subduing and settling new Countries, extending the Dominion and encreasing the Commerce of their Mother Nation, they have forfeited the native Rights of Britons, which they think ought rather to have been given them, as due to such Merit, if they had been before in a State of Slavery.

Here already were spelled out clearly the argument of consent—"it is suppos'd an undoubted right of Englishmen not to be taxed but by their own consent given thro' their representatives"; the argument of distance—Parliament was remote, "and subject to be misinformed"; and the argument that there was, through trade, a "kind of secondary taxes." Franklin was more taken with Shirley's alternative, of colonial representation in Parliament; but he thought that all the acts of trade should then be repealed so that there might truly be created "one community with one interest; which I imagine would contribute to strengthen the whole and greatly lessen the danger of future separations."[54]

However tactically wise it would have been at the time, the strongly imperial note of Franklin's writing in 1754 is worth stressing. The tone was rather of Rudyard Kipling than of Radical Jack, Lord Durham. The empire was Anglo-American and dynamic, deriving its strength from growth, trade, racial character, and enterprise, rather than from restrictive regulation or inhibiting alliances. The energy of Englishmen on both sides of the Atlantic, Franklin believed, would soon extend British influence across all the oceans and to the western limits of America. With the empire thus flourishing, quarrels within it would be submerged; and united, it would easily overcome any combination of enemies. It would be Roman in its sweep, prompt to spare the humble and to crush the proud, *parcere subjectis et debellare superbos;* but it would be also a fifth-century Athens, the "school for all the world."

Franklin had a special dream of establishing British colonies in the Ohio valley. From its natural advantages, he argued, the region "must undoubtedly . . . become a populous and powerful dominion; and a great accession of power, either to England or France." He wrote on July 2, 1756, to the evangelist George Whitefield, proposing that by combining their talents they could render a great service to mankind:

You mention your frequent wish that you were a Chaplain to an American Army. I sometimes wish, that you and I were jointly employ'd by the Crown to settle a Colony on the Ohio. I imagine we could do it effectually, and without putting the Nation to much Expence. But I fear we shall never be call'd upon for such a Service. What a glorious Thing it would be, to settle in that fine Country a large Strong Body of Religious and Industrious People! What a Security to the other Colonies; and Advantage to Britain by increasing her People, Territory, Strength and Commerce . . . In such an Enterprize I could spend the Remainder of Life with Pleasure and I firmly believe God would bless us with Success, if we Undertake it with a sincere regard to his Honour, the Service of our gracious King, and, which is the same thing, the Publick Good.[55]

At this time he did not believe that an enlarged empire would be oppressive to any part of the realm.

*   *   *

The Albany Plan was, however, a by-product. The primary purpose of the Albany meeting in the eyes of London was to draw up a treaty with the Indians. The treaty arrived at was harsh, and it had troublesome consequences. Determined to grasp all the land they could, the Pennsylvania and Connecticut officials tricked the Indians, who did not understand compass courses, into deeding to them a tract stretching from Lake Erie in the north to the southern boundaries of Penn-

sylvania. And, contrary to the custom of the Six Nations, the deed
gave away the land of tribes whose representatives had not signed it.
The commissioners also sought to trick each other; and the area in
Ohio still known as the Western Reserve testifies to Connecticut's
longstanding ambitions for territory in the West.

Shortly after the Albany conference, Franklin drew up a "Plan for
Settling Two Western Colonies in North America." Two were necessary, he held, and they would have to be settled by the older colonies
acting jointly, or else by a charter won in London. One would have a
port on Lake Erie, the other would center on the lower reaches of the
Scioto. His dream of frontier expansion—within a harmonious empire—would persist for twenty years. He was still the Old England
Man. "Britain and her Colonies should be considered as one Whole,"
he wrote to Collinson in May 1754, "and not as different States with
separate Interests." [56]

In the meantime war, not unstimulated by such "legal" trickery
and such dreams, became a serious threat to Pennsylvania and its
neighbors. No central scheme for defense being devised, the initiative
for defense lay with the Board of Trade in England. Accordingly, in
April the Board appointed Sir William Johnson as Northern Superin-
tendent of Indian Affairs, and in the same month Major General Edward Braddock landed at Alexandria, Virginia, at the head of two
understrength regiments of British regulars, some 1,400 men. Braddock, with whatever colonial support might be forthcoming, was, as
military commander-in-chief, to save the seaboard colonies from the
French. He found himself sadly short of horses and wagons. Franklin,
ostensibly present in the role of postmaster, managed to find horses
and wagons for Braddock's baggage train in the campaign to capture
Fort Duquesne. In two weeks he collected 150 wagons and 259
horses by offering fifteen shillings per day for a wagon with four
horses and a driver and two shillings a day for a pack horse with
saddle. To do this, he had to pledge £1,000 of his own resources—
though in the end Shirley, as commander-in-chief, met his claim.

Braddock, rarely effusive, was generous in his praise. He said that
when the governors of Maryland and Virginia failed to provide wagons Franklin undertook to get them, "which he has executed with
great punctuality and integrity, and is almost the only instance of ability and honesty I have known in these provinces. His wagons and
horses . . . are indeed my whole independence." To Franklin person-

ally he wrote that while Virginia and Maryland had promised everything but performed nothing, Pennsylvania had promised nothing but done everything. The Assembly voted Franklin formal thanks.[57]

But all to no effect: Braddock's column was destroyed at the Monongahela eight miles below the fort, Braddock killed, and the frontier ravaged. Indians swept across the foothills of the Blue Mountains, raided to within a few miles of Reading, and laid waste most of Northampton County. Eastern Pennsylvania daily expected invasion.

Franklin's verdict on Braddock's failure has become the standard indictment:

This general was, I think a brave man, and might probably have made a figure as a good officer in some European war. But he had too much self-confidence, too high an opinion of the validity of regular troops, and too mean a one of both Americans and Indians. George Croghan, our Indian interpreter, join'd him on his march with one hundred of those people, who might have been of great use to his army as guides, scouts, etc., if he had treated them kindly; but he slighted and neglected them, and they gradually left him . . . This whole transaction gave us Americans the first suspicion that our exalted ideas of the prowess of British regulars had not been well founded.[58]

It is not quite the whole truth. Braddock made mistakes, and was (until Franklin helped him) left to make them on his own as far as the majority of colonists were concerned. He certainly had an insufficient number of Indian scouts and found them untrustworthy aides. The major cause of the debacle, however, was the falling back of the vanguard when surprised by the enemy, and the confusion that followed among troops who were not well spaced. Officers under Braddock must bear a part of the responsibility for defeat. Although the expedition ended in disaster, it proved that an army could march over the wooded Alleghenies; it taught English troops lessons in wilderness warfare; and the study of its mistakes made possible the successful expedition undertaken by General John Forbes three years later.

The crisis on the frontier, and the attack by a Shawnee war party on the Moravian mission village of Gnadenhutten, seventy-five miles northwest of Philadelphia, led to the dispatch of three commissioners, one of them the portly and by nature sedentary Franklin, to "see and judge" how best to defend Northampton County. Their tasks were to raise troops, dispense arms, and build a line of forts north of the Blue Mountains to defend the Lehigh Gap. Franklin stayed seven weeks, and spent his fiftieth birthday in a rainstorm in the Gap, driven back by the weather in his efforts to reach Gnadenhutten. His account to Debby is customarily easy and affable:

We have enjoyed your roast beef, and this day began on the roast veal; all agree that they are both the best that ever were of the kind. Your citizens, that have their dinners hot and hot, know nothing of good eating; we find it in much greater perfection when the kitchen is four score miles from the dining room.

As to our lodging, 'tis on real feather beds, in warm blankets, and much more comfortable than when we lodged at our inn, the first night after we left home, for the woman being about to put very damp sheets on the bed we desired her to air them first; half an hour afterwards, she told us the bed was ready, and the sheets well aired. I got into bed, but jumped out immediately, finding them as cold as death, and partly frozen. She had *aired* them indeed, but it was out upon the *hedge*. I was forced to wrap myself up in my great coat and woollen trousers, everything else about the bed was shocking dirty.[59]

He found his task in fact daunting—panic on the frontier, a product of rumor as much as of reality, the whole area "evacuated and ruined." Some of his expedients were primitive, almost derisory, such as his suggestion to Conrad Weiser at Reading (by way of James Read) that dogs be used:

They should be large, strong and fierce; and every dog led in a slip string, to prevent their tiring themselves by running out and in, and discovering the party by barking at squirrels, etc. Only when the party come near thick woods and suspicious places, they should turn out a dog or two to search them. In case of meeting a party of the enemy, the dogs are all then to be turn'd loose and set on. They will be fresher and finer for having been previously confin'd, and will confound the enemy a good deal, and be very serviceable. This was the Spanish method of guarding their marches.[60]

The organization of a frontier county at war, devoid of civil authority and of confidence, called on the same skills he had honed in organizing the post office or in marshaling opinion in the Assembly. War, like peace, called for strong native intelligence, speed of decision, an orderly mind, determination to impose order on others, and—always and not least—skill in personal relations. His instructions were specific, as to Captain John Van Etten:

You are to proceed immediately to raise a company of foot, consisting of thirty able men including two sergeants, with which you are to protect the inhabitants of Upper Smithfield, assisting them while they thresh out and secure their corn, and scouting from time to time as you judge necessary on the outside of the settlements, with such of the inhabitants as may join you, to discover the enemy's approaches and repel their attacks ... You are to keep a diary or journal of every day's transactions, and an exact account of the time when each man enters himself with you; and if any man desert or die, you are to note the time in your journal, and the time of engaging a new man in his place, and submit your journal to the inspection of the governor when required ... You are to acquaint the men that if in their ranging they meet with or are at any time attacked by the enemy, and kill any of them, forty dollars will be allowed and paid by the government for each scalp of an Indian enemy so killed, the same being produced with proper attestations ... You are to take care that your stores and provisions are not wasted ... You are to keep good order among your men, and prevent drunkenness and other immoralities, as much as may be, and not suffer them to do any injury to the inhabitants whom they come to protect ... You are to take good care that the men keep their arms clean and in good order, and that their powder be always kept dry and fit for use.[61]

If the qualities were recognizable, the tasks were new: organizing his supply column, felling trees and cutting timber for the stockade, burying the dead, mounting the guns, keeping his five hundred ill-clad men in their thirteen companies informed—and this in persistent rain in the cold of winter in the Blue Mountains. Yet amid it all he found time to note the customs of the Moravians. Hearing that marriages among them were sometimes decided by lot, "I objected, if the matches were not made by the mutual choice of the parties, some of them may chance to be very unhappy. 'And so they may,' answered my informer 'if you let the parties choose for themselves': which, indeed, I could not deny."[62] The reporter and raconteur were always present.

Toward the end he was in charge of an army of 560 men, with his son acting as aide-de-camp; he succeeded in rebuilding the fort at Gnadenhutten and secured the defenses of an area between the Delaware and Lehigh rivers by erecting three stockades. And so he added a new profession to his list: to Bishop Spangenberg and the Moravians he was General Franklin, and on his return he was colonel of the Philadelphia militia regiment. When the regiment marched past his door in review in March, the salute it fired broke some of his electrical equipment; when he went off to Virginia on post office business a week later he was escorted by his officers, mounted, in uniform, and with drawn swords. The proprietors' fears of the "Prime Minister" grew apace. The governor was absent, and the picture of Franklin that reached the Penns in London grew steadily more Satanic.

Franklin's efforts, however, failed to secure the frontier. In April 1756 Governor Morris offered "for the scalp of every male Indian enemy above the age of 12 years, produced as evidence of their being killed, the sum of One Hundred and Thirty pieces of Eight." This measure too had little success. Depredations continued. Within nine months one of Franklin's stockades, Fort Allen, was destroyed. And seven years later William Clapham, left in charge by Franklin, was killed and scalped by Indians twenty-five miles from Fort Pitt. This remained an uneasy frontier, mountainous, restless, and hard to tame.

*   *   *

It is striking how quickly and with what assurance Franklin moved onto a wider stage. Now he was more and more on the move, and very much the politician. In April 1755 he was at Frederick, Maryland, in conference with Braddock, nominally as postmaster, actually as provincial soother of tensions. In the latter part of April and early May he was at Lancaster and York, recruiting wagons—mainly on his own promissory notes—to supply Braddock's army on its ill-fated march. In December, as the Indian assaults devastated the frontier, he was at Bethlehem and Easton organizing the defense of Northampton County; and in January 1756 he was the "general" in charge of this particular front. A month later he was a colonel of the Philadelphia militia. In March 1756 he was in Virginia in his role as deputy post-master-general for North America; in June and July in New York conferring on defense matters with Governor Shirley, who was about to sail for Britain, and then with his successor as commander-in-chief, Lord Loudoun. For one who had retired eight years before to devote himself to "philosophy," Franklin had a public life that was importunate in its claims. Even so it did not prevent letters sent on the line of march, as to Deborah, warm and companionable, and a letter or two to Catharine Ray, his friend of Block Island, Rhode Island, warm and—only just—platonic:

You must practise *Addition* to your Husband's Estate, by Industry and Frugality; *Subtraction* of all unnecessary Expences; *Multiplication* (I would gladly have taught you that myself, but you thought it was time enough, and wou'dn't learn) he will soon make you a Mistress of it . . . that when I have again the Pleasure of seeing you, I may find you like my Grape Vine, surrounded with Clusters, plump, juicy, blushing, pretty little rogues, like their Mama. Adieu. The Bell rings, and I must go among the Grave ones, and talk Politicks.[63]

He had met her in 1755 and traveled in her company. He met her, it seems, only four times in his life. Yet the letters are intimate and close, those of an adopted uncle.

*   *   *

Pennsylvania's capacity to resist attack was marred by the political struggle between largely absentee, and now Anglican and Tory, proprietors and the Quaker-controlled Assembly. The interests of the former were the defense of the colony and the maintenance of the economic status quo, with no invasion by the colony of proprietorial prerogative; the Assembly, though Quaker and, except in a real crisis, pacifist in mood, was far more concerned with reducing the proprietor's power, persuading him to share in the expenses of Indian treaties, taxing his estates, and breaking his power of veto than with fighting Indians on a remote and difficult frontier. The Quaker party, however, was now misnamed. It was no longer Quaker-led; Penn's pacific principles had been eroded by frontier wars and by Indian threats; it was now the party of a minority of the population, and depended less on the Quakers than on the support of the German pietist sects. It was seriously split between the pacifist Quaker followers—"the stiff rumps" Franklin called them—and their more responsible leadership.

Yet, if it had a leader, that leader now was Franklin. He was not a Quaker and not a pacifist, but his program of taxation of proprietary estates and defense of the frontier, and his own business successes and civic concern, made him acceptable to the majority of the members of the Assembly. Liberty and property were for him, as for them, the joint buttresses of their Whiggism. His chief ally was Speaker Isaac Norris, a Quaker who did not share the pacifist scruples of the Quarterly or Yearly Meetings. Franklin came to feel that "Quakerism" was an issue largely kept alive by the proprietorial party to destroy its enemies in the Assembly. For its part, the Quaker party would pass defense bills, but only if allowed to tax the Penn estates. No tax, no defense. There was a strong sense that if government was not formally a matter of contract, it ought to be at least a matter of mutual advantage. Here as elsewhere, however, there were constitutional implications. Note the language the Assembly used in November 1755, much of it drafted by Franklin:

It is, may it please the Governor, one of the most valuable Rights of British Subjects, to have their Bills granting Money to the Crown accepted without Amendments; a Right that cannot be given up, without destroying the Constitution, and incurring greater and more lasting Mischiefs than the Grant of Money can prevent.

   ... In one Thing, indeed, it is our Misfortune, that our Constitution differs from that of England. The King has a natural Connection with His Subjects. The Crown descends to His Posterity; and the more his People prosper and flourish the greater is the Power, Wealth, Strength and Security of his Family and Descendants. But Plantation Governors are frequently transient Persons, of broken Fortunes, greedy of Money, without any Regard to the People, or natural Concern for their Interests, often their Enemies, and endeavouring not only to oppress but defame them, and render them obnoxious to their Sovereign, and odious to their Fellow Subjects. Our present Governor not only denies us the Privileges of an English Constitution, but would, as far as in his Power, introduce a French one, by reducing our Assemblies to the Insignificance of their Parliaments, incapable of making Laws, but by Direction, or of qualifying their own Gifts and Grants, and only allowed to register his Edicts. He would even introduce a worse; he requires us to defend our Country, but will not permit us to raise the Means, unless we will give up some of those Liberties that make the Country worth defending; this is demanding *Brick without Straw,* and is so far *similar* to the Egyptian Constitution. He has got us indeed into *similar* Circumstances with the poor Egyptians, and takes the same Advantage of our Distress; for as they were to perish by famine, so he tells us we must by the Sword, unless we will become Servants to our Pharaoh, and make him an absolute Lord, as he is pleased to stile himself *absolute Proprietary.*[64]

Franklin had no sympathy with the Quakers' passiveness on defense, but he came to share their antiproprietorial views. Only the removal of the proprietary interest would, he thought, allow rational solutions to be found for the basic problems of defense and the imperial relationship. With the advent of war the pacifist Quakers were only a handful in the Assembly; Franklin thus gradually became a leader in a popular party, largely Quaker in its following but now by no means Quaker-led. The fears of the Penns and of the oligarchy men—like his one-time friend William Allen—were now confirmed. Franklin the manipulator was revealed as a "popular" man, an enemy of the Gentlemen's party, a "grand incendiary."

Defense, frontier expansion, and the breaking of the proprietors' power were now emerging as Franklin's three main political preoccupations. The Gentlemen, led by William Allen and by William Smith, the strong-willed and ambitious Anglican provost of the College of Philadelphia, sought to shift the debate from internal to external issues, from taxes to defense, and to indict the Quaker party not only as "democratick" but as cowardly. Smith's efforts to compel the Quakers to take an oath of allegiance and to promise active aid were thwarted by the London Quakers; but the more conscientious Friends withdrew from the Assembly.

The result of the annual election in October 1756 was a vindication of the Quaker party and the policies advocated by Franklin. The newly elected members of the Assembly were in the Franklin group; moreover, four of the twelve remaining Quakers resigned two days after the Assembly convened. Among the new representatives, John Hughes and Joseph Galloway assumed leadership in the legislature during the next decade. Richard Peters reported to Thomas Penn that although "Mr. Allen and his friends have taken a great deal of pains to secure to the Prop[rietor]s and the Governm[en]t the return of one or two reasonable and sensible men, their industry and exertion had been unsuccessful," and a "set is returned of the veriest partisans against the Prop[rietor]s, and moderate measures as cou'd be picked out of this town." This set was led by "ill-disposed persons," his words for Norris and Franklin.[65]

The taxing of all property, including that of the proprietors, now became the central issue. The first struggle over this question, in 1755, had been resolved when, with French and Indian attacks increasing, the proprietors made a free gift of £5,000. This was a gift, not a tax, although it was to be collected in Pennsylvania out of the unpaid money due the Penns as quitrents. Franklin persuaded the Assembly to accept it as offered, stipulating in return that the Assembly alone had the right to grant supplies and to decide as to their "matter, manner, measure and time." The Assembly voted £60,000 on these terms, and the governor assented.

The governor's next line of argument was to request the Assembly to establish a militia, as well as to provide funds for defense. The

Assembly made it lawful for free men to form companies and to elect their officers, subject to the approval of the governor as commander-in-chief; the company of officers would elect regimental officers, and the whole body of officers would draft articles of war. The Assembly appointed a committee of seven, with Franklin at its head, to manage the funds for defense. Increasingly the struggle between the governor and the Assembly was becoming a personal contest between Morris and Franklin.

In August 1756, however, came a new lieutenant-governor, William Denny, a nominee of the Duke of Cumberland. He was forty-seven years of age, small and delicate-looking, but a professional soldier. "A triffler, weak of body, peevish and averse to business," thought Richard Peters, and "extremely near if not a lover of money." Israel Pemberton thought him "weak and corrupt" but preferred a weak to a strong executive. The verdict of historian Nicholas Wainwright seems final: "he was venal, lazy and inept, unsteady and self-pitying, boastful but physically timid and wanting in moral courage—a weathervane sort of person." [66]

Denny began by cultivating Franklin, presenting him with the Royal Society Medal. But he proved during his short tenure to be as unsuccessful as, and more grasping than, his predecessor, and he vetoed the appropriation bill for £100,000 because it once again included a tax on the proprietary estate. The Assembly concluded that the deadlock could be broken only by more direct methods. It adopted a remonstrance against the governor and marched through the streets of Philadelphia to deliver it in January 1757. Again, its constitutional implications were clear:

That the apparent Necessity of so large a Sum for His Majesty's Service, and the Defence of His Province, founded upon the Governor's own Estimate, has obliged us to an Effort beyond our Strength, being assured that Hundreds of Families must be distressed to pay this Tax . . .

That great as the Sum is, and hard for this People to pay, we freely offer it to our Gracious King for His Service, and the Defence of His Colony from His Majesty's Enemies.

That the Proprietaries refusing to permit us to grant Money to the Crown, in this Time of War and imminent Danger to the Province, unless we will consent thus to exempt their Estates from the Tax, we conceive to be injurious to the Interests of the Crown, and tyrannical with Regard to the People.

That we do farther conceive, neither the Proprietaries, nor any other Power on Earth, ought to interfere between us and our Sovereign, either to modify or refuse our Free Gifts and Grants for His Majesty's Service.

That though the Governor may be under Obligations to the Proprietaries, we conceive he is under greater to the Crown, and to the People he is appointed to govern; to promote the Service of the former, preserve the Rights of the latter, and protect them from their cruel Enemies.

We do therefore, in the Name of our most Gracious Sovereign, and on behalf of the distressed People we represent, unanimously DEMAND it of the Governor, as our Right, that he give his Assent to the Bill we now present him, for granting to his Majesty One Hundred Thousand Pounds for the Defence of this Province (and, as it is a Money Bill, without Alteration or Amendment, any Instructions whatsoever from the Proprietaries notwithstanding) as he will answer to the Crown for all the Consequences of his Refusal at Peril.[67]

Largely because of pressure from the new commander-in-chief, Lord Loudoun, who was worried about the defenses of the colony, in the end an appropriation bill was passed that exempted the proprietary estates. The Assembly yielded its claim, however, only because of the emergency. To drive home its firmness, it resolved to send Franklin to London as a special agent to present its case.

Not all were happy with Franklin's new appointment. Dr. John Kearsley, who was later to be mobbed as a Loyalist and to die in consequence, claimed in a letter that Franklin wanted to go to London to support his own interests: "They talk of Sending the Electrician home which is a new delay. He Jumps at going. I am told his office [of postmaster general] shakes. However though he would not go but to Support this falling interest of his own, he is artfully Insinuating that he goes on his Countrys Service. Most Certain am I that he will go at his Countrys Expence for he is wicked enough to Blind the people." Captain Thomas Lloyd also sneered at the proposed mission of Norris and Franklin: "Two of the venerable sages of Pennsylvania are going home with their fingers in their eyes." Richard Peters wrote to the proprietor:

Certain it is that B.F.'s view is to effect a change of Government, and considering the popularity of his character and the reputation gained by his Electrical Discoveries which will introduce him into all sorts of Company he may prove a Dangerous Enemy. Dr. Fothergill and Mr. Collinson can introduce

him to the Men of most influence at Court and he may underhand give impressions to your prejudice. In short Heaven and Earth will be moved against
the Proprietors.

In reply, Penn was full of confidence:

I think I wrote you before that Mr. Franklin's popularity is nothing here, and
that he will be looked very coldly upon by great People, there are very few
of any consequence that have heard of his Electrical experiments, those matters being attended to by a particular Sett of People, many of whom of the
greatest consequence I know well, but it is quite another sort of People, who
are to determine the Dispute between us.[68]

This new assignment posed for Franklin a fundamental political
problem: if "democratick" in Pennsylvania, was he to be so in Britain? He was a "popular" man in Pennsylvania by background and by
tastes; his sympathies lay broadly with the Assembly, not the proprietor: "I conceive a more cordial and thorough contempt for him than
I ever felt for any man living, a contempt that I cannot express in
words."[69] It seemed that only the people could be relied upon to defend themselves. Equally—but contradictorily—he wanted a colonial
union, and in 1757 he was prepared to have it enforced by Act of
Parliament if necessary, whatever might be the consequence of such
an imposition for colonial self-government. Moreover, he held an imperial office, and he had standing as scientist and publisher, statesman
and responsible agent. When he thus for a second time invaded the
London scene, he would find the real dilemma of his life facing him:
the question of to what authority, colonial or imperial, popular or
royal, he gave his true allegiance—if (and his enemies would ask this
from time to time) he was a man capable of holding any true allegiance to any cause outside himself.

His official business took three years: in 1760 the Privy Council
upheld the appropriation bill. But he did not return to Philadelphia
until November 1762. The Assembly voted him a salary of £500 per
year for each of his six years of service, though it was not paid him
until March 1763. His expenses "in the immediate service" of the
province he calculated at £714.10.7.

                    *   *   *

In the spring and summer of 1756 we get glimpses, for the first time,
of the toughening of Franklin's political stance. The militia officers

treated him, said Peters, "as if he had been a member of the Royal Family or Majesty itself." Indeed, he was now in part the prisoner of his own popular image as man of the people, and public praise is heady wine. "The people happen to love me. Perhaps that's my Fault," he wrote to Collinson in November 1756. Cadwallader Colden had written to Collinson of Franklin's "infatuated" persistence in the "Civil confusion." Franklin explained himself to Collinson at length:

The Proprietors, you write me word, are greatly incensed at some Parts of my late Conduct. I am not much concern'd at that, because if I have offended them by *acting right,* I can, whenever I please, remove their Displeasure, by *acting wrong.* Tho' at present I have not the least Inclination to be in their good Graces on those Terms . . . For now I am persuaded that I do not oppose their Views from Pique, Disappointment, or personal Resentment, but, as I think, from a Regard to the Publick Good; but at least I mean well. And whenever they appear to me to have the Publick Good in View, I think I would as readily serve them as if they were my best Friends. I am sometimes asham'd for them, when I see them differing with their People for Trifles, and instead of being ador'd, as they might be, like Demi Gods, become Objects of universal Hatred and Contempt. How must they have managed, when, with all the Power their Charter, the Laws and their Wealth give them, a private person (forgive your Friend a little Vanity, as it's only between ourselves) can do more Good in their Country than they, because he has the Affections and Confidence of their People, and of course some Command of the People's Purses. You are ready now to tell me, that Popular Favour is a most uncertain Thing. You are right. I blush at having valued myself so much upon it.[70]

This querulousness and defensiveness—hitherto rare—would never in future be entirely absent: a partisan note was now part of the man of many parts. He was apt at times to forget that politics was never one-sided. He owed his postmastership to solicitation, and to the support of friends in high places, including William Allen, now his enemy. A year earlier Thomas Penn had written to Peters of a "favor" to Franklin: "I think it no small Act of Friendship that I have recommended him to Sir Everard Falkoner"—Franklin's superior in the Post Office Department. Such patronage assumed that gratitude would follow.[71]

Through the rest of Franklin's life there would be a tension in him not between the scientist and the newsman, which seemed to be the theme of his first forty-two years, nor between the activist and the natural philosopher, but now between the courtier and the political campaigner. This clash would be sharper still after 1757, and in the end the campaigner would triumph. Perhaps it was fitting that the last *Poor Richard* for which he was responsible was compiled in 1757 on the high seas to London. In it there emerged a new persona, in keeping with, and identified with, his creator—"a plain, clean old Man, with White Locks, called Father Abraham." He would enshrine, in *The Way to Wealth,* about one hundred selected earlier sayings, polished and sharpened to make them more telling and to drive home the message that thrift, hard work, enterprise, and sturdy independence were the means to both salvation and success. The virtues preached in *The Way to Wealth* are almost Calvinist as well as capitalist. But, as Franklin ruefully observed, Father Abraham's hearers did not always practice what he preached—any more than did his creator: "The People heard it and approved the Doctrine, and immediately practised the contrary, just as if it had been a common sermon." [72]

Accompanied by his son, William, who acted as his secretary, Franklin left Philadelphia on April 4, 1757. They did not sail from Sandy Hook until June 20, on the packet *General Wall.* For four days they sailed in the convoy of thirty transports conveying Lord Loudoun's troops to Halifax for an attack on Louisbourg. Franklin reached Falmouth after a twenty-seven-day journey, in which he was nearly wrecked on the Scilly Isles. He wrote to Debby: "The bell ringing for church, we went thither immediately, and with hearts full of gratitude, returned sincere thanks to God for the mercies we had received: were I a Roman Catholic, perhaps I should on this occasion vow to build a chapel to some saint; but as I am not, if I were to vow at all, it should be to build a *lighthouse.*" [73]

In striking contrast to his own amused and deflationary style was the pompous tribute paid to him by a commendable anonymous versifier, one of the host of friends and admirers who saw him depart—for now he had courtiers of his own.

> Dear Patriot muse that honest man behold
> Record his Acts in characters of gold.
>
> Who plann'd the Scheme the Associates to unite?
> Who wrote *plain truth* to bring that scheme to light?
> Who bid Yon Academick structure rise?

"Behold the Man!" each lisping babe replies.
Who schemed Yon Hospital for the Helpless poor?
And op'd to charitable use each folding door.
Our Countrys cause, what senator defends?
Void of all partial, or all private ends.
Who to his publick trust has firmly stood?
And built Fort Allen for his Countrys good.
Who form'd a Law our Forces to unite?
And deign'd to execute that Law aright.
Who found out means our Treasury to supply?
Who would not suffer publick faith to die?
Who was the Man brave Braddock did record?
"The only man that with him kept his word."
'Twas he, whose name, the good and just will sound,
While patriot deeds on faithful records stand.

Great thy reward for all thy Labours done,
And at the great Tribunal will be known.
There will thy Genius other worlds survey,
And there adore the glorious God of day.
There Bacon, Newton, will our F—lin greet.
And place him in his Electrisic seat.
O'er Europe, Asia Africk's, science'd Fame,
The Royal Medal will exalt thy name;
Transfer the Palm by thy great genius won
And proudly own America's great son.
If then thy sphere, to Electerise above,
Dart me one ray in pitty and in love
Oh! send thy influence, if permitted, send,
To guide my soul to my beloved Friend.[74]

5

THE OLD ENGLAND MAN

*F*ranklin and his son reached London late on July 26, 1757. They stayed first at the Bear Inn at the Southwark end of the old London Bridge, and were the guests for a short time of Peter Collinson in his sumptuous house at Mill Hill. William Strahan, Franklin's lifelong correspondent, was an early visitor. "For my own part," Strahan wrote to Deborah, "I never saw a man who was, in every respect, so perfectly agreeable to me. Some are amiable in one view, some in another, he in all . . . Your son I really think one of the prettiest young gentlemen I ever knew from America." [1]

Within a few days father and son found handsome lodgings at 36 Craven Street, just off the Strand, near Charing Cross. This was Franklin's home for the rest of his stay in London. His landlady, the widowed Mrs. Margaret Stevenson, found him very congenial and soon adopted him as a sort of foster father and entertaining companion. Soon after his arrival, a series of colds kept him in bed and indoors for some eight weeks. He was cupped. James Fothergill, his friend, became also his doctor. Mrs. Stevenson and her daughter Mary (Polly) nursed him "kindly." [2]

His letters to Polly Stevenson, who quickly became a second daughter to him, are delightful, informative, and teasing. When Polly spent the summer with an aunt in Essex, he wrote to her regularly—on the working of the barometer, the nature and habits of insects, the effect of the heat of the sun on clothing, the movements of the tides in rivers. He added to the last: "After writing six folio pages of philosophy to a young girl, is it necessary to finish such a letter with a compliment? Is not such a letter of itself a compliment?" Polly was intelligent, witty, and affectionate, the daughter he would have liked to have, closer and brighter and more comforting than Sally.

When he died in Philadelphia thirty years later, Polly was at his bedside.[3]

The philosopher did not disregard the London fashions. His personal tastes were always fastidious. In Philadelphia his day began with exercise—a swim in the Delaware, a stint with dumbbells, or, in old age, an "air bath" in the nude. He shaved himself, he said, for the pleasure it gave and to avoid "the dirty fingers or bad breath of a slovenly barber." Each day he dressed carefully in clean linen. His London account books show that the earliest expenses of the new household were for stationery, shoes, wigs, linen to be made into shirts, and cambric for William's handkerchiefs. There was a sword blade to be mended, and such varied purchases as spectacles and a glass, a watch at auction, mourning swords, a sword knot, two pairs of silver shoe and knee buckles, two razors and a case, and copies of the *Gentleman's Magazine*. William, whose wants were greater than his father's—"loans to Billy" is a recurring item in the ledger—was entered in the Middle Temple to study for the Bar. For both Franklins, Craven Street became a convenient, and almost a permanent, London base. There was even space enough in the ample suite of four furnished rooms at the top of the house to install an electrical machine and carry out experiments. "Everything about us pretty genteel," reported the satisfied lodger. A new "court" sprang up around Franklin here, and we see once again in operation his relaxed, inexhaustible capacity for winning friends of both sexes and influencing people of all kinds. And if, despite all his own blandness and benevolence, he found—as all politicians must—critics and even enemies, did not Poor Richard say (March 1756), "Love your Enemies, for they tell you your Faults"?[4]

*   *   *

The London Franklin reached in 1757 was the largest city in Europe, with about 750,000 inhabitants (one-tenth of the population of England), and far larger than either of its two nearest rivals within the Empire, Philadelphia and Bristol. The city's central core extended from Mile End in the east (in the original "City") to Hyde Park in the west and was even more varied in character then than it is today, from the lanes and alleys of Bethnal Green, Wapping, and Rotherhithe on the river to the elegant residences and neighborhoods of the rich, of which the most recent were Portland, Portman, and Manchester squares. Bloomsbury and St. James's had existed for almost a century; Grosvenor, Berkeley, and Cavendish Squares were coming to be the most fashionable addresses. Franklin's own Craven Street, in 1757, was almost at the center of the capital's political and social life.

Much of London was not a healthy place to live. The death rate was far higher than in the countryside, and only constant immigration increased the city's numbers. Though London was better paved and better lit than Paris, and a safer place to walk, much of it stank. Air pollution from domestic coal fires caused smog and black rain. The streets were packed with traffic, and the rattle of wheels on cobbles, together with the cries of hawkers and ballad singers, created a deafening background symphony, destructive of concentration and of sleep. Food was often tainted or stale; the drinking water tasted foul and could, moreover, prove fatal—hence the need for stronger drink. Almost all men of affairs were heavy drinkers. Gout, consequence of the trade treaties with Portugal and of the headier wines that replaced those of France, was the characteristic malady of the century. There were an estimated 759 alehouses in Holborn and 825 in the square mile of the City of London. England drank 8 million gallons of raw gin (called "strip me naked") each year, which represented more than a gallon per man, woman, and child.

Crime, though less prevalent than in other large European cities, was commonplace. The *Whoremongers Guide to London* was sold openly and regularly revised. The widespread prostitution attested to widespread poverty. Unskilled workers poured into the city each year and were lucky if they found jobs paying as much as twelve shillings a week, the price of a pound of tea. Discontent bred in overcrowded, unhealthy conditions; mob violence lay just below the surface of elegant society. Hangings were public occasions, and some dozen criminals were "chopped" at Tyburn every three months.

For those with money in their pockets, London offered an unending round of social gaiety. Franklin must have found it an exhilarating contrast to the gravity encouraged by Philadelphia's Quaker traditions. The French traveler Pierr Jean Grosley, after a visit to London in 1765, wrote of the pleasure grounds at Vauxhall in Lambeth and Ranelagh in Chelsea: "Yet when we compare the splendour to magnificence of these places to the wretched appearance of both houses of parliament, of the courts of justice and even of the King's palace, a foreigner would be tempted to think that the English, supremely fond of pleasure, consecrate the whole grandeur and magnificence of the Kingdom to that favourite idol."[5] Bare-fist fighting and cockfighting were popular. Subscription concerts and balls, the "spectacles" at the Pantheon in Oxford Street, the British Museum, and the Royal Academy were the province of the wealthy. Lord Rockingham did important political business when the races were run at York.

It was an age of distinguished building, as the Adelphi and the Theatre Royal bear witness. In 1762, George III, married and now the father of an heir to the throne, bought a town house of his own, Buckingham House, a red brick mansion built in 1705 by the Duke of Buckingham, and paid £28,000 for it. Renamed the Queen's House, it became the principal royal home in London. The business of the court was carried on in St. James's Palace nearby, where visitors commented on the cramped quarters. In 1760 Westminster Bridge had just been completed. And soon, primarily through the work of the Adam brothers, England, Ireland and Lowland Scotland were to have a constellation of palaces and superb country houses, still among the greatest of their treasures: Woburn and Wentworth Woodhouse, Holkham Hall and Mellerstain, Osterley and Chiswick, Kenwood and Harewood; and they all had parks and lakes, temples and follies and splendid vistas. The eighteenth century was notable for its informal and "natural" parkland gardens, strikingly more romantic than Lenôtre's models of the earlier century. They were carefully proportioned and landscaped, the reverse of the wild and luxuriant flora of the American frontier. To eyes accustomed to the wilderness of the New World, the work of William Kent and Capability Brown, with gazebos and grottoes, Palladian bridges, fountains and pagodas, was as exciting as it was soothing.

For men of fashion it was the fashion to belong to a club. Men of title and substance used Brooks, Boodles, Whites, Crockfords, and Almacks. Charles James Fox or Gentleman Johnny Burgoyne could lose £50,000 a night. Thomas Rowlandson, himself a confirmed gambler, caught the spirit in his sketch "EO or the fashionable vowels"; the EO table stood for Even and Odd. The Sublime Society of Beefsteaks met in Covent Garden; the Literary Club, whose members included Johnson, Reynolds, Burke, and Goldsmith, met at the Turk's Head in Gerrard Street.

To politicians, gossips, and diarists, however, it was the coffeehouse and the newspaper that mattered. The coffeehouses, not the clubs, were Franklin's world. By the mid-eighteenth century there were more than 550 coffeehouses in the metropolis. The coffeehouse served many as a reading room and some as a business address; for all it was a social venue and a political forum. Pro-American radicals like Thomas Hollis, backbench writer-MPs like Soame Jenyns, and colonial agents like Franklin all frequented the coffeehouses to read the latest newspapers or political pamphlets—usually provided gratis by the management—and to discuss the latest news. Samuel Curwen wrote from London in 1775: "America furnishes matter now and then for disputes in Coffee Houses. The disputants talk loud, and sometimes warmly, but without rudeness or ill manners or ill nature, and there it ends. 'Tis unfashionable and even disreputable here to look askew on one another for difference of opinion in political matters; the doctrine of toleration if not better understood, is, thank God, at least better practised than in America."[6]

Coffeehouses became club-like when certain groups favored them. American loyalists adopted various rendezvous as their own small colonial centers in London. Letters headed "from the Massachusetts Coffee house" or "the Carolina Coffee house" were shipped across the Atlantic in steady numbers during the war. As a patron became a regular customer, the landlord of a coffeehouse would offer his establishment as a mailing address, a message center—a true home away from home.

Since 1756 Franklin had been a member of the Royal Society, which met in Crane Court; the Fellows, "the Learned Club," met also at the Grecian coffeehouse in the Strand, within easy strolling distance of Craven Street. Franklin visited the British Museum, recently installed in Montague House. He was a member too of the Premium Society, for the encouragement of arts, manufacturers, and commerce, from which what is now the Royal Society of Arts originated. Six months before his arrival in London he had written to the Society and enclosed twenty guineas "to be applied in premiums for some improvement in Britain, as a grateful though small return for your most kind and generous intentions of encouraging improvements in America. I flatter myself ... that those jealousies of her colonies which were formerly entertained by the mother country begin to subside."[7]

Craven Street, running between the Strand and Hungerford Market on the river bank, was within a few minutes' walk of Whitehall.

For the lawyers are just at the top of the street,
And the barges are just at the bottom.
Fly, honesty, fly to some safer retreat.
For there's craft on the river and craft in the street.[8]

On his first visit Franklin had enjoyed swimming in the river and had been proud of his epic adventure, swimming from Chelsea to Black-friars. Craven Street was also close to Fleet Street, and to the coffee-houses Franklin frequented for their companionship, their news-papers, and their glasses of wine—his own taste was for rum and Madeira—the Dog and Duck, the George and Vulture, the Pennsyl-vania in Birchin Lane, the Crown and Anchor in Shoe Lane, Ye Olde London on Ludgate Hill, and the British (originally St. Paul's) Coffee House in Cockspur Street.

It was at St. Paul's Coffee House that he was a regular caller. The Club of Honest Whigs, as they called themselves, met there on Thurs-days. This was the group to which in retrospect Franklin looked back with warmest memories: Collinson and Pringle, Fothergill, Richard Price and Joseph Priestley, James Burgh, William Rose and John Can-ton, who would, twenty years later, be the friends of America. It was in the world of writers and scientists, Scots and Dissenters, the curi-ous and the questioning, that he felt most at home. Although he met the great, and was the guest of Lord Despencer at Wycombe and of Lord Shelburne to meet the Abbé Morellet, he was never of the Estab-lishment.

In the evening sun, 36 Craven Street also lay in the long shadows cast by Northumberland House, the massive town house of the Dukes of Northumberland. This fashionable political center attracted Wil-liam more than his father, and the son soon became a young man about town. For him the words of Poor Richard (March 1736) had a new significance: "Wealth is not his that has it, but his that enjoys it." His taste for fashion and society, along with his training as a fledgling lawyer in the Temple, would lead him to abandon one girl for an-other, give him different dreams from those of his father, and indeed take him in the end down a Loyalist path.

England's was an aristocratic society, and more stable than the two Jacobite invasions had suggested, especially so once Charles Stuart had retreated into permanent and drunken exile. But it was also, un-like much of Europe, a society that offered ladders to climb. At Eton, sons of lords sat alongside sons of brickmasters—and the aristos paid double fees. If a few hundred titled families were dominant—"the great oaks that shade a country" as Burke called them—many of them were interested in the land, in the revolution taking place on it, and in what came out of it; and so they were closely in touch with the people who worked on it, the vast majority of the population. If it was a nobility with its eccentrics and its rakes, it was a nobility too of service, imagination, and capacity, which pulled toward itself, and sometimes into itself, able men from the middle class, the men of business who as often as not did the day-to-day work: men like Walpole and Burke, the Pitts, John Pownall and William Beckford.

As names like Pitt and Beckford suggest, this was also, in all its contrasts of affluence and poverty, a new and enterprising society. The merchant class mattered increasingly, and commerce was coming to be an avenue to power and acceptance. That power was no longer restricted to London. Bristol had its sugar and tobacco merchants and its own princes of the slave trade. Hull prospered from the Baltic and Dutch trade, Newcastle from coal, and Glasgow from Virginia tobacco. Into this world of enterprise and expansion Americans could move easily, whatever their origins. The first colonial agent, Jeffreys, began as a London grocer but won a knighthood and election to Parliament. It was not only William Byrd who could be as much at home beside the Thames as the James. So could James Crokett of Charleston and William Whiting of Hertford; Jeremiah Dummer and Henry Newman, both Harvard alumni; and Arthur Lee of Virginia, educated at Eton and Edinburgh. Ludwells and Lees of Virginia, Beckmans and Franks of New York, Winthrops and Crugers in Bristol, Huskes and Trecothicks, made up an intimate and personal Anglo-American world into which Franklin—as later Benjamin Thompson and Benjamin West—could move as of right.

*   *   *

The five years from 1757 to 1762 were probably the happiest of Franklin's life. They were so partly because his mission was in some measure successful, and if its success was in other respects a qualified one, Franklin was sufficiently a political animal to appreciate the victory precisely because it demanded some measure of compromise. He was always adept in congratulating himself on being the tactician; his concern was usually with means and rarely with ends. These were happy years also, and more particularly, because of the wide circle of friends in which he moved and the obvious affection in which they held him.

His political undertaking was a slow business. It was "an affair that will take much more time than I expected," he told Galloway; "God knows when we shall see it finish'd, and our constitution settled firmly on the Foundation of Equity and English Liberty." Franklin began by negotiating with the Penns themselves, an unhappy experience in which he got little satisfaction and was shown scant respect. Not normally one to nurse grudges, he never forgot the snubs he received from the Penns and their minions. "When I meet him anywhere", wrote Franklin of Thomas Penn, "there appears in his wretched countenance a strange mixture of hatred, anger, fear and vexation." To Galloway in February 1758 he used unusually venomous language, hoping that the Penns would be "gibbeted up as they deserve, to rot and stink in the nostrils of posterity." He presented the Assembly's complaints to the proprietors in August of 1757. They replied to the Assembly—ignoring him—fifteen months later, and gave no ground at all.[9]

The Quakers were themselves approaching the proprietors through Dr. John Fothergill, not through Franklin. They wanted to make their own treaty with the Indians, and they did not want an open war with the proprietors. Distrustful of the populist in Franklin, they noted the cautions that Fothergill expressed to Pemberton in June 1758:

Benjamin Franklin has not yet been able to make much progress in his affairs. Reason is heard with fear: the fairest representations are considered as the effects of superior art; and his reputation as a man, a philosopher and a statesman, only seem to render his station more difficult and perplexing . . . You must allow him time, and without repining. He is equally able and sollicitous to serve the province, but his obstructions are next to insurmountable: Great pains had been taken, and very successfully to render him odious and his integrity suspected, to those very persons to whom he must first apply. These suspicions can only be worn off by time, and prudence.[10]

Franklin turned to the use of the press in his campaign: he published the views of the Pennsylvania Assembly in the *London Chronicle,* printed by his friend Strahan; in the *Citizen,* until its demise in December 1757; and in the *Gentleman's Magazine.* He aimed, as he wrote to the Assembly in 1758, at "removing the prejudices that art and accident have spread among the people of this country against us, and obtaining for us the good opinion of the bulk of mankind without doors." In June 1759 the tract *An Historical Review of the Constitution and Government of Pennsylvania* appeared, a joint work of Benjamin and William Franklin and Richard Jackson, published by Ralph Griffiths, the editor of the Whig *Monthly Review* (which Strahan also printed): "And who or what are these proprietors? In the province, unsizable subjects and unsufficient lords. At home, gentlemen it is true, but gentlemen so very private that in the herd of gentry they are hardly to be found; not in court, not in office, not in Parliament." Thomas Penn claimed not to be worried by the press campaign: "I suppose you will hear that Mr. W. Franklin has said many imprudent things, but no body will answer him yet tho' he should write again. Appealing to the Publick will always displease the Administration and for that reason I shall not practice it but let them write what they please." [11]

Franklin spent a major part of his time in London in such press campaigning, and some major papers, many of them original and painstaking, emerged. We owe our knowledge of the scale of his press activity to Verner Crane, who traced to Franklin's authorship a number of hitherto anonymous and scattered prints. One of these, in the *London Chronicle* in September 1758, was a formidable indictment of the proprietors, and was no doubt, for the British, surprising reading. Franklin asked twenty-eight questions and concluded with a definitive twenty-ninth: "Whether the frequent clashing of interests between the Proprietors and people of our colonies, which of late have been so prejudicial to his Majesty's Service, and the defence of his dominions, do not at length make it necessary for this nation to enquire into the nature and conduct of these Proprietary Governments, and put them on a better footing?" [12]

By 1759 Lieutenant-Governor Denny had, contrary to instructions, approved an appropriation bill that at last levied taxes on proprietorial lands; he was sharply recalled, but the damage was done. The proprietors then sought to have the Privy Council block his action. After Franklin's counterarguments were heard, and the point noted that the £100,000 approved had already been both printed and spent, a compromise was agreed to. It was essentially a "deal" in chambers, between Franklin and Lord Mansfield. Would Franklin and Robert Charles (the regular agent) sign an engagement that the Penns' estate would not be harmed if the Act were allowed? The agents agreed, and the Act received the royal assent on September 2, 1760. The terms were a victory in principle for Franklin's constituents, but they yielded little revenue. The Penns' surveyed estates were to be taxed only at the same rate as similar estates, and their unsurveyed land was to be exempt. In fact the proprietors paid in tax only one-fiftieth of the sum raised in taxation; but feudalism ceased to hold in Pennsylvania.

In the course of this struggle, Franklin had begun to raise his sights and to campaign overtly for the removal of the proprietary power altogether: for bringing Pennsylvania and its twin, Maryland, directly under the crown. He first sounded out Isaac Norris along these lines in September 1758. He began to write in similar terms to Joseph Galloway. He launched an attack on the Calverts, the Maryland proprietors, in the *London Chronicle.* Later he corresponded with Dr. Thomas Moffat and Martin Howard of Rhode Island, who were similarly at work negotiating for royal government there, and for the replacement of the charter of 1663, which they believed was responsible for Rhode Island's notorious political instability. His friend Richard Jackson counseled caution here: to alter the royal charter and Penn's original charter of privileges could only be done by Act of Parliament, and once such a course were undertaken who knew what might follow? Pennsylvania, like the chartered colonies of Rhode Island and Connecticut, enjoyed remarkable freedom. This was indeed the "secret weapon" of the Penns, and one that Franklin tended to forget. It can be argued that it was imaginative on his part to envision a colonial assembly enjoying a degree of freedom directly under the king, with intermediate and arrogant authorities removed, and that this was a form of high Whiggism—or of Tory democracy. It can also be argued that he thought it possible to be both king's man and Assembly man—and perhaps was as keen to be the former as the latter. Perhaps he likened Parliament to the Assembly, and thought it open to his persuading. He does not seem, in the Albany discussions in 1754 or again in 1760, to have recognized the potential dangers of royal authority when it had become that of a king-in-parliament. When, soon after arriving in London, he met Lord Granville, then presiding over the Privy Council, he was surprised to discover the gap between imperial and colonial standpoints. "The Council," Granville said, and Franklin reported to Isaac Norris in March 1759, "is over all the colonies; your last resort is to the Council to decide your differences, and you must be sensible it is for your good, for otherwise you often would not obtain justice. The king in council is legislator of the colonies; and when His Majesty's instructions come there, they are the law of the land . . . and as such ought to be obeyed." Franklin's letter to Norris continued:

I told his lordship this was new doctrine to me. I had always understood from our charters that our laws were to be made by our assemblies, to be presented indeed to the king for his royal assent, but that being once given the king could not repeal or alter them. And as the assemblies could not make permanent laws without his assent, as neither could he make a law for them without theirs. He assured me I was totally mistaken.[13]

Franklin, who had come to appeal from the proprietors to the king, found that one of the king's ministers thought very much like a proprietor.

He thought Pitt, Charles Pratt (later Lord Camden), and Speaker Onslow "friends to Liberty," but "one may easily conjecture what Reception a Petition concerning Privileges from the Colonies may meet with from those who are known to think that even the People of England have too many." In his letter to Norris of March 1759 he was quite explicit:

From this Sketch of Leading Characters, you will judge, that if the Proprietor does not agree with us, our best Chance in an application is directly to Parliament; and yet that at this Time is something hazardous, for tho' there are many Members in both Houses who are Friends to Liberty and of noble Spirits, yet a good deal of Prejudice still prevails against the Colonies, the Courtiers think us not sufficiently obedient; the illicit Trade from Holland, etc. greatly offends the Trading and Manufacturing Interest; and the Landed Interest begin to be jealous of us as a Corn Country, that may interfere with them in the Markets to which they export that Commodity:—I wish indeed that the illicit Trade could be wholly prevented, for it is not to be justified.[14]

Whatever the ultimate divide, Franklin was moving steadily in these years, if not in a royal, at least in an imperial, direction. This can be seen in his opposition to the proposed Peace of 1761—he thought it would be "unsafe, disadvantageous and dishonourable"— in his satire "On the Meanes of Disposing the Enemie to Peace," which he signed simply "A Briton." It becomes especially clear with his participation in the debate over whether Britain should restore Canada to the French and annex Guadeloupe instead.

He became involved in this issue as early as December 1759, in humorous vein in the *London Chronicle*. The reasons, he said, for returning Canada were:

We should restore it, lest, thro' a greater plenty of beaver, broad-brimmed hats become cheaper to that unmannerly sect the Quakers.

We should restore Canada, that we may *soon* have a new war and another opportunity of spending two or three millions a year in America; there being great danger of our growing too rich, our European expenses not being sufficient to drain our immense treasures . . .

We should restore it, that the French may, by means of these Indians, carry on, (as they have done for these 100 years past even in times of peace between the two crowns) a constant scalping war against our colonies, and thereby stint their growth; otherwise, the children might in time be as tall as their mother.[15]

Having studied the mercantilist case for annexing Guadeloupe rather than Canada—that a rich sugar-providing island was worth far more than an empty wilderness (Voltaire described Canada as "a few acres of snow")—Franklin countered in more sober style with *The Interest of Great Britain Considered, with Regard to her Colonies, and the Acquisition of Canada and Guadeloupe* (1760). The case he made here was at first glance colonial: that only annexing the West would give the British inhabitants in the mainland colonies permanent security against the repeated French and Indian attacks, and only thus would Britain end its drain of blood and cash in defending them:

Now all the kinds of security we have mention'd are obtain'd by subduing and retaining Canada. Our present possessions in America, are secur'd; our planters will no longer be massacred by the Indians, who depending absolutely on us for what are now become the necessaries of life to them, guns, powder, hatchets, knives, and cloathing; and having no other Europeans near, that can either supply them, or instigate them against us; there is no doubt of their being always dispos'd, if we treat them with common justice, to live in perpetual peace with us. And with regard to France, she cannot in case of another war, put us to the immense expence of defending that long extended frontier; we shall then, as it were, have our backs against a wall in America, the sea-coast will be easily protected by our superior naval power; and here "our own watchfulness and our own strength" will be properly, and cannot but be successfully employed. In this situation the force now employ'd in that part of the world, may be spar'd for any other service here or elsewhere; so that both the offensive and defensive strength of the British empire on the whole will be greatly increased.[16]

He moved here to an imperial as distinct from the mercantilist view, and confirmed his arguments by printing as an appendix to this tract a paper he had published five years earlier, *Observations Concerning the Increase of Mankind*. The American population was increasing fast; it would reach one hundred million, but only after many generations. This would not, he contended, lead to a development of manufacturing or to a quest for independence, since the Americans would expand westward as a nation of farmers and would provide ever larger markets for British manufactures:

marriages in *America* are more general, and more generally early, than in *Europe*. And if it is reckoned there, that there is but one marriage per annum among 100 persons, perhaps we may here reckon two; and if in *Europe* they have but 4 births to a marriage (many of their marriages being late), we may here reckon 8, of which one half grow up, and our marriages are made, reckoning one with another at 20 years of age, our people must at least be doubled every 20 years.

. . . But notwithstanding this increase, so vast is the territory of *North America*, that it will require many ages to settle it fully . . .

But in proportion to the increase of the colonies, a vast demand is growing for British manufactures, a glorious market wholly in the power of *Britain*, in which foreigners cannot interfere, which will increase in a short time even beyond her power of supplying, tho' her whole trade should be to her colonies: Therefore *Britain* should not too much restrain manufactures in her colonies. A wise and good mother will not do it. To distress, is to weaken, and weakening the children weakens the whole family.

British exports to North America were increasing, he pointed out, far more rapidly than British exports to the West Indies. Nor was there, in the light of the failure of the Albany Plan, any serious danger of colonial federation. Indeed, on the contrary:

Nothing but the immediate command of the crown has been able to produce even the imperfect union but lately seen there, of the forces of some colonies. If they could not agree to unite for their defence against the French and Indians, who were perpetually harassing their settlements, burning their villages, and murdering their people; can it reasonably be supposed there is any danger of their uniting against their own nation, which protects and encourages them, with which they have so many connections and ties of blood, interest and affection, and which 'tis well known they all love much more than they love one another? . . .

When I say such an union is impossible, I mean without the most grievous tyranny and oppression. People who have property in a country which they may lose, and privileges which they may endanger; are generally dispos'd to be quiet; and even to bear much, rather than hazard all. While the government is mild and just, while important civil and religious rights are secure, such subjects will be dutiful and obedient. The waves do not rise but when the winds blow.[17]

It was impossible to envisage a revolt against Britain "without the most grievous tyranny and oppression"—and in 1760 Franklin did not foresee such oppression. On the contrary, the present war was not a colonial but an imperial struggle: "Our North American colonies are to be considered as the frontier of the British empire on that side. The frontier of any dominion being attack'd, it becomes not merely '*the cause*' of the people immediately affected, (the inhabitants of that frontier) but properly '*the cause*' of the whole body . . . If ever there was a *national war,* this is truly such a one: a war in which the interest of the *whole* nation is directly and fundamentally concerned." [18]

In a letter to Lord Kames in January 1760, he predicted that America would be of great importance to the British Empire:

I have long been of Opinion, that the Foundations of the future Grandeur and Stability of the British Empire, lie in America; and tho', like other Foundations, they are low and little seen, they are nevertheless, broad and Strong enough to support the greatest Political Structure Human Wisdom ever yet erected. I am therefore by no means for restoring Canada. If we keep it, all the Country from St Laurence to Missisipi, will in another Century be fill'd with British People; Britain itself will become vastly more populous by the immense Increase of its Commerce; the Atlantic Sea will be cover'd with your Trading Ships; and your naval Power thence continually increasing, will extend your Influence round the whole Globe, and awe the World![19]

Franklin admired George III, and when the Treaty of Paris was signed he thought it a glorious peace: "the most advantageous for the British nation, in my opinion, of any your annals have recorded." "Happy as we now are, under the best of kings, and in the prospect of a succession promising *every* felicity a nation was ever bless'd with." And in 1763 Shelburne recommended that, while the Appalachians should be regarded as a dividing line between the settlers and the Indians, there should be room left for a projected colonial settlement in the upper Ohio valley. The empire Franklin was proud to serve was, it seemed, to be an expanding one.[20]

*   *   *

During these busy London years Franklin's personal life was also that of an Old England Man. His home was at the heart of things, and his friendships were warm and satisfying. He had, however, a private disappointment. He had hoped that Polly Stevenson would marry his son William, but whatever her feelings might have been, by August 1762 William, whose tastes were expensive, had become engaged to Elizabeth Downes, the daughter of a wealthy sugar planter, so breaking off his earlier engagement to Elizabeth Graeme of Philadelphia.

William had also, early in 1760, fathered an illegitimate son, William Temple Franklin. This did not prevent his being nominated by Lord Halifax, president of the Board of Trade—apparently on the recommendation of Lord Bute, the royal favorite and the king's first minister—as governor of New Jersey, at the age of 31. The young man had sought the deputy secretaryship of South Carolina; he got a richer plum. Presumably his father was seen as a man who must be cultivated by the government. The news was greeted with shock in North America. To John Watts, a New York businessman, it was "a Burlesque on all Government." The Penns were harsher still: John Penn wrote on September 3, 1762, "the whole of this business has been transacted in so private a manner, that not a tittle of it escaped until it was seen in the public papers; so that there was no opportunity of counteracting, or indeed, doing one single thing that might put a stop to this shameful affair." Thomas Bridges, Richard Jackson's brother-in-law, wrote with some amusement to Jared Ingersoll on September 30, 1762: "I hear there was some difficulty in his being Confirmed in his place, for in our Conscientious Age, many Scruples were raised on account of his *being Illegitimate,* which we were Strangers to till very lately."[21] His elevation to the purple makes ironic William Franklin's own remark in June 1760, in a letter to Joseph Galloway about the Canada pamphlet: "I hate Everything that has even the Appearance of Flattery."[22]

The reports in the *London Chronicle* of William's appointment and of his marriage to Elizabeth Downes appeared after his father sailed from Portsmouth in the *Carolina* on August 23, 1762. The elevation to the governorship had been a remarkably well-kept secret. When his father wrote to Lord Kames on August 17, he was laconic about William: "My son presents his Compliments. He stays in England a little longer." [23]

*   *   *

Benjamin Franklin became the close friend of a group, strikingly Scottish in composition, of scholar-scientists and printers. Prominent among them was William Strahan ("Straney"); the two men half-humorously talked of a marriage of Strahan junior to Sally Franklin. Strahan made his mark in the printing business, publishing Johnson's *Dictionary*, Adam Smith's *Wealth of Nations*, and Gibbon's *Decline and Fall*. David Hall, Franklin's partner in Philadelphia, had served as Strahan's apprentice. Strahan became a member of Parliament for Malmesbury in 1774 and for Wootton-Bassett in 1780. He stayed a loyal friend to Franklin through all the trials ahead. Franklin became equally devoted to another Scot, crusty Sir John Pringle, a year younger than himself, who after serving as a professor of moral philosophy in Edinburgh became physician-general to the British forces in Flanders in 1744, settled in London, and was to become president of the Royal Society in 1772 and physician to George III in 1774. His "Observations on the Diseases of the Army" (1752) won him a European reputation. Franklin and Pringle would visit France together in 1767 and in 1769. Another close friend, a Quaker and another Scot, Dr. John Fothergill, attended Franklin when he was ill. Fothergill maintained, at Upton in Essex, one of the finest botanical gardens in Europe. His "Account of the Sore Throat" (1748) was a first recognition of diphtheria. Later, at Ackworth, he founded a Quaker school. As in Philadelphia, so in London: a junto of philosophical spirits grew up around Franklin. Besides the friends already mentioned, they included Richard Price, Joseph Priestley, and James Burgh.

Franklin also traveled to Scotland, where he met William Robertson and David Hume, Lord Kames and Sir William Cullen, Adam Smith and Sir Alexander Dick. He visited St. Andrews, which had made him "Dr. Franklin." He clearly enjoyed and felt at ease in Scotland, as with the Scots in London. Intellectually this was hardly surprising: this was the period when Dr. Aymot boasted that if he stood at the Cross in Edinburgh he could every hour shake fifty men of genius by the hand. Few of Franklin's letters giving any reaction to the sights and sounds and smells of Scotland survive, so that we do not know what he really thought of the tenement lands of Auld Reekie—he stayed in Milne Court, off the Canongate—or of St. Andrews, which at the time had some three thousand people, forty-two ale houses, and only twenty students. But in retrospect he had no doubts. His visit, he wrote to Lord and Lady Kames, constituted the "six weeks of the densest happiness I have met with in any part of my life . . . did not strong connexions draw me elsewhere, I believe Scotland would be the country I should choose to spend the remainder of my days in."[24]

*   *   *

Franklin regularly attended meetings of the Royal Society, and he frequently joined the Scottish fraternity who met at the British Coffee House. In 1760 he was elected a member of the Associates of Dr. Bray, the philanthropic society that advocated schools for blacks in the colonies. In the summer of 1761, with William, he visited Belgium and Holland. In Brussels he was shown the Prince of Lorraine's physics laboratory; in Leyden he met at last his correspondent and fellow-experimenter Peter Van Musschenbroek, just two weeks before the latter's death; at the Hague he and William dined with the British ambassador, Joseph Yorke. For Franklin was not only politician, persuader, and tourist, but philosopher still. His correspondence covers lightning rods and cures for smoky chimneys; the origin of northeast storms; meteors, shooting stars, and new comets; the improvement of typography; the nature of fire; the lunar eclipse of March 1758; the source of the rock salt found in mines; and the melting of powdered amber.

His experiments continued—in electricity and evaporation. In his own room he reduced the opening of his fireplace to three feet by two, and invented an iron frame with a sliding plate that acted as a draft control, with the result that he got more heat from less fuel. "Several of my acquaintance, having seen this simple machine in my room, have imitated it in their own houses, and it seems likely to become pretty common."[25] The effect of chimneys upon ventilation, he thought, had been too little studied. Stimulated in part by a tempting offer of £20,000 from Parliament for any method capable of determining a ship's longitude, and by the encouragement of the Board of Longitude that was set up as a result, he became a correspondent of clock- and watchmakers, and in December 1757 paid the Yorkshireman John Harrison—the eventual winner of the prize—ten shillings and sixpence "to see his Longitude clock." In 1758 he devised a plan for a new kind of clock of his own; it operated with only three wheels and utilized only one hand to show both the hours and minutes, and a separate hand and face to show the seconds. It has had two names: "Franklin's clock" and "Ferguson's clock"; James Ferguson, the English astronomer and mathematician, who wrote the first descriptive account of it, referred to it as "The Franklin Clock." The latter name never came into popular use, however; Franklin took little interest in promoting the invention, in spite of the fact that a number of the clocks were manufactured and distributed in England. On a visit to Birmingham in 1759 Franklin met Matthew Boulton, a foundryman who was experimenting with a steam engine, and they began a correspondence. Some years later Boulton would appeal to Franklin's "fertile genius" for suggestions on improving his model.[26]

When Franklin's four-year-old son had died of smallpox in Philadelphia in 1736, rumors had circulated that he had actually died from inoculation, and Franklin had put an advertisement in the *Pennsylvania Gazette* stating that the child had in fact died "in the common way of infection." Thereafter—perhaps feeling guilty over his youthful criticism of inoculation in Boston when the Mathers had urged it—Franklin became a zealous advocate of the new practice. In 1759 he persuaded the distinguished London physician William Heberden, the first to describe angina pectoris, to write a pamphlet giving simple rules that anyone might follow in inoculating himself and his family—Franklin was always an advocate of "every man his own doctor." *Plain Instructions for Inoculation in the Small-Pox* was originally written anonymously and printed (by Strahan) at the doctor's expense, but believing that its influence would be greater if its eminent author's name were revealed, Franklin sent 1,500 copies of the eight-page pamphlet to David Hall in Philadelphia with instructions that it be given away gratis; he accompanied it with a four-page tract of his own disclosing Heberden's name and providing supporting statistics "because *facts* generally have, as indeed they ought to have, great weight in persuading to the practice they favour." For example, he stated that in the London smallpox hospital, from its opening until 1758, of 3,856 "normal" smallpox cases, 1,002 died, whereas of 1,601 inoculated only 6 died. The facts certainly supported his campaign in favor of inoculation. He had learned a lot in forty years.[27]

He now extended his inventiveness to music. In 1761 he attached a set of graduated glass bowls to a horizontal spindle, which rotated them through a trough of water; when the wet rims were touched, the glasses produced a soft warbling sound. When the poet Nathaniel Evans heard Franklin play this instrument in Philadelphia in 1764, he wrote of its "soft warblings, sounding smooth and clear . . . conveying inward, as they sweetly roll, a tide of melting music to the soul." Gluck performed on the instrument—the armonica—in London; Mozart and Beethoven wrote for it. It was admired at the time, notably by Marie Antoinette, but, perhaps because of its fragility, it never became widely popular; it was also held to cause a nervous tremor in the hands and arms of its players.[28]

Governor Hamilton, who received from Thomas Penn a report of Franklin's spending his time in philosophical matters "and musical performances on glasses," wrote scornfully to Jared Ingersoll:

Your Friend Mr. Franklin, and mine if he pleases, (for it will much depend on himself) is daily expected from England. I cannot find that his five years negotiation at a vast expense to the province hath answered any other purpose with respect to the publick, than to get every point that was in controversy, determined against them. Yet what is this to Mr. Franklin? Hath it not afforded him a life of pleasure, and an opportunity of displaying his talents among the virtuosi of various kingdoms and nations? and lastly hath it not procured for himself the Degree of Doctor of Laws, and for the modest and beautiful Youth, his son, that of Master of Arts, from one of our most famous universities? Let me tell you, those are no small acquisitions to the Publick, and therefore well worth paying for.[29]

*   *   *

There can be little doubt that Franklin liked his London life, on the exciting edge of public affairs and acquainted with the great. He lived well: he had a coach of his own, hired for twelve guineas a month; and he had two black servants, King and Peter, whom he had brought from Philadelphia—though King ran away after a year, making his own comment on the nature of liberty. Franklin sent presents home, two caseloads of them: china and tableware, blankets and tablecloths, a harpsichord costing forty-two guineas for Sally and "I also forgot, among the china, to mention a large fine jug for beer, to stand in the cooler. I fell in love with it at first sight; for I thought it looked like a fat jolly dame, clean and tidy, with a neat blue and white calico gown on, good-natured and lovely, and put me in mind of—somebody." [30]

Certainly Franklin was reluctant to leave Old England, with its "sensible, virtuous and elegant minds." He wrote to Strahan from Portsmouth: "The attraction of reason is at present for the other side of the water, but that of inclination will be for this side. You know which usually prevails. I shall probably make but this one vibration and settle here for ever." And to Lord Kames: "I am going from the old world to the new; and I fancy I feel like those who are leaving this world for the next: grief at the parting; fear of the passage; hope of the future. These different passions all affect their minds at once; and these have *tendered* me down exceedingly." [31]

After nearly ten weeks at sea, Franklin reached Philadelphia, from where he reported to Strahan:

I got home well the first of November, and had the happiness to find my little family perfectly well, and that Dr. Smith's reports of the diminution of my friends were all false. My house has been full of a succession of them from morning to night ever since my arrival, congratulating me on my return with the utmost cordiality and affection. My fellow-citizens, while I was on the sea, had at the annual election chosen me unanimously, as they had done every year while I was in England, to be their representative in Assembly, and would, they say, if I had not disappointed them by coming privately to town, have met me with five hundred horse.

In two years he would, he told Strahan, remove to England, "provided we can persuade the good woman to cross the seas." [32]

6

THE PRIME MOVER

On his return to Philadelphia, Franklin found, as he told Collinson, that his friends were "as cordial and more numerous than ever." In his absence Deborah had moved across Market Street, and in the new sitting room he proudly hung the portrait of Lord Bute, to whom he attributed William's advancement. The high rent of the new house—£80 a year—amazed him. It was not the only aspect of present life in Philadelphia that surprised him. His analysis of the economy in a letter to Richard Jackson in March 1763 was searching and wise:

The Expence of Living is greatly advanc'd in my Absence; it is more than double in most Articles; and in some 'tis treble. This is by some ascrib'd to the scarcity of Labourers and thence the Dearness of Labour; but I think the [Dearness] of Labour, as well as of other Things the Labour of which was long since perform'd or in which Labour is not concern'd; such as Rent of old Houses, and Value of Lands, which are trebled in the last Six Years, is in great measure owing to the enormous Plenty of Money among us. The Crown, I am inform'd, has paid £800,000 Sterling in this Province only, for Provisions Carriages, and other Necessaries in the Service. Beside which, the Province has struck £5 or 600,000 great part of which is still current; and in New Jersey and New York, they have had proportionable Quantities. This is such an over Proportion of Money to the Demand for a Medium of Trade in these Countries, that it seems from Plenty to have lost much of its Value. Our Tradesmen are grown as idle, and as extravagant in their Demands when you would prevail on them to work, as so many Spaniards. But what with burning our Paper yearly, and paying our Debts to England with our Silver, we shall, 'tis to be hop'd, soon reduce the Quantity, and come again to our Senses. And this leads me to an Observation, that your Commerce is now become so profitable, and naturally brings so much Gold and Silver into your Island, that if you had not now and then some expensive foreign War, to draw it off, your Country would, like ours, have a Plethora in its Veins, productive of the same Sloth, and the same feverish Extravagance.

In fact the rise in wholesale commodity prices, while considerable, does not appear to have been nearly so great as Franklin reported. With the monthly averages for the years 1741–1745 taken as a base, the annual arithmetical index of wholesale prices of twenty commodities was 112.5 in 1757 and 140.1 in 1762; the annual geometrical indices for the same years were 110.9 and 134.6 respectively. Falling prices in the latter part of 1763 produced drops in the indices for that year of 2.6 in the arithmetical and 1.6 in the geometrical.[1]

On his return to the Assembly, Franklin was voted £3,000 for his six years of service in England, and he recognized the generosity of his treatment. William, with his bride, arrived in February 1763 to take up residence at Burlington, one of the two capitals of the Jerseys, and only seventeen miles from Philadelphia. In the spring, Franklin set out on a tour of the northern colonies, to inspect the forty-eight post offices now strung out from Falmouth (Portland), Maine, to Norfolk, Virginia, in order to revise and speed up the mail and to establish links with Montreal and Quebec. He covered 1,800 miles and was away from home for seven months, meeting friends and acquaintances all along the way: his son and daughter-in-law in New Jersey; Catharine Ray, now Catharine Greene, in Warwick, Rhode Island, who nursed him when he had a bad fall from his chaise; his old scientist friend Cadwallader Colden, now governor of New York; and his new colleague in the post office, John Foxcroft, in Virginia. His stay in Boston lasted two and a half months, and there was much to savor and enjoy. He sent a recipe for milk punch to James Bowdoin:

Take 6 quarts of brandy, and the rinds of 44 lemons pared very thin, steep the rinds in the brandy 24 hours; then strain it off. Put to it 4 quarts of water, 4 large nutmegs grated, 2 quarts of lemon juice, 2 pound of double refined sugar. When the sugar is dissolved, boil 3 quarts of milk and put to the rest hot as you take it off the fire, and stir it about. Let it stand two hours; then run it thro' a jelly-bag till it is clear; then bottle it off.[2]

*   *   *

Politically, Franklin found the Pennsylvania scene much less appealing than it had been when he left. During his absence he had been reelected each year to represent the city of Philadelphia in the Assembly. He was soon active on no fewer than eleven committees, many concerned with the drafting of bills. The initiative in the colony was now passing from Quakers to frontier Scotch-Irish, and, the peace with France notwithstanding, the frontier was unsettled. In 1763, within three months of Shelburne's approval of a plan for settlement on the upper Ohio, a new minister at the Board of Trade, Hillsborough, countermanded it. The line of civil settlement was fixed; colonists west of it were ordered out, and the area became a responsibility of the military. But this move, disturbing to potential settlers, came too late to placate the Indians. In May 1763, Pontiac rose in open rebellion. Within six weeks every western post except Detroit and Fort Pitt (Duquesne renamed) had fallen. Although Colonel Henry Bouquet routed the Indians at Bushy Run in August, he suffered heavy losses of his British regulars, and not until 1766 did Pontiac submit. The Pennsylvania frontier felt neglected and vulnerable, and its inhabitants dreamed up deadly weapons: smallpox-infected blankets should be sent to the Indians as presents; dogs should be sent to hunt them down (a tactic Franklin himself had earlier suggested).

Franklin, in his letter to Jackson in March 1763, when the terms of the peace settlement were known, returned to his plan for new colonies, a plan he had strikingly neglected during his years in London: "Since all the Country is now ceded to us on this Side the Missisipi, is not this a good time to think of new Colonies on that river to secure our Territory and extend our Commerce; and to separate the Indians on this side from those on the other, by intervening Settlements of English, and by that means keep them more easily in order? What think you now of asking for a Slice of Territory to be settled in some manner like that I once propos'd?" When in London, he had talked much to Jackson about advancing a plan for a western colony, and had made contact with Sir Matthew Fetherstonehaugh, an M.P. and a protégé of the Duke of Newcastle, with John Pringle and with John Sargent. Fetherstonehaugh brought contact with the Duke of Newcastle, and Pringle with Lord Bute; and the last contact had already brought the governorship for William. There were here the beginnings of what became known as the Vandalia project, the name chosen in tribute to the queen's German origins. It was at this time called Pittsylvania. It would check the resurgence of French power, Franklin maintained; it would attract ten thousand families as settlers, and there would be room for ten times that number.

As for keeping the Indians in order, Franklin believed tact and discretion were called for. He was critical of Lord Amherst's parsimony toward the Indians, as were the old Indian hands Johnson and Croghan:

We should let the Indians feel as little as possible, the Superiority we have acquir'd, and should treat them with as much Consideration, for some time at least, as we did while the French Power in America subsisted: And as they never negotiate among themselves, or call any Meeting of another Nation or Tribe, without Presents, they ought not to have been omitted on this Occasion by us. The Indians think us so wealthy, and that we have such Plenty of everything valuable to them, that if we omit so essential and so establish'd a Ceremony, it cannot be through Want, it must proceed from Contempt. I hope, however, that this Mistake of ours, if it was one, will soon be rectified.[3]

In June 1763, after news broke of the Pontiac conspiracy, he wrote again to Jackson, who by that time was Pennsylvania's official agent. His letter showed an anthropologist's understanding but also called for the use of force:

The Indians are disgusted that so little Notice has lately been taken of them, and are particularly offended that Rum is prohibited, and Powder dealt among them so sparingly. They have received no Presents: And the Plan of preventing War among them and bringing them to live by Agriculture, they resent as an Attempt to make Women of them, as they phrase it: It being the Business of Women only to cultivate the Ground: their Men are all Warriors.

Perhaps these Causes have jointly contributed to produce the Effect. I think too, that we stoop'd too much in begging the last Peace of them; which has made them vain and insolent; and that we should never mention Peace to them again, till we have given them some severe Blows, and made them feel some ill Consequences of breaking with us.

Modern historians, notably Howard Peckham, have corroborated Franklin's interpretation. Peckham places the blame for the Pontiac uprising chiefly on Amherst's shortsighted policy of refusing to supply the Indians with presents, ammunition, and rum, although he does not discount French intrigue and the encroachment of settlers on Indian lands. As Jackson was to tell Franklin in December, however, the news of the Indian uprising and of frontier wars did imperil Vandalia. "Affairs here never were so mutable," he wrote. And as for Dr. Pringle, he "altogether declines any Concern in our Schemes only because he says he makes it a Rule to prevent Views of profit from intruding on the Quiet necessary a Life of Literary Pursuit and Speculation."[4]

The frontier saw itself as powerless because underrepresented in the Assembly. In December 1763 a band of exasperated frontiersmen, largely Scotch-Irish, from Donegal and Paxton townships raided a small village of peaceful Christian Indians at Conestoga in Lancaster County, and killed six of them. A fortnight later they stormed the workhouse at Lancaster and massacred the remaining fourteen, who had been put there for protection. Other friendly Indians on the upper Susquehanna asked the governor for protection. When the Assembly ordered the Paxton Boys arrested and sent east for trial, however, the Boys took the law into their own hands; they set off on a march east to secure a redress of grievances by force and to wreak vengeance on those Christian Indians converted by the Moravians, about 140 in number, who had been brought east for safety and were under guard on Province Island in the Schuylkill River. The rioters declared that they would kill not only the Indians but Joseph Fox, a prominent member of the Quaker party, and Israel Pemberton, the main target, who they believed had incited the Indians to resist white settlers. This prospect was alarming to the good and pious folk of the city of brotherly love; even Quakers looked for weapons of defense. The governor called a public meeting at the State House, which more than three thousand attended in a driving cold rain. One of Franklin's tasks in 1764 was to organize yet another Association—six companies of footsoldiers, one of artillery, and two troops of horse—to defend the city against this invading army; another was to go out, and with six other emissaries, exercise his blarney on them. The band of 250 toughs was stopped and turned back at Germantown, in part by his persuasions. "And within four-and-twenty hours," he wrote to Fothergill, "your old friend was a common soldier, a councillor, a kind of dictator, an ambassador to a country mob, and, on his returning home, nobody again." His *Narrative of the Late Massacres in Lancaster County* is an eloquent and savage account and, for once, the writing lacks urbanity:

They would have been safer among the *Moors* in *Spain,* though they had been *Murderers of Sons;* if Faith had once been pledged to them, and a Promise of Protection given. But those have had the Faith of the *English* given to them many Times by the Government, and, in Reliance on that Faith, they lived among us, and gave us the Opportunity of murdering them. However, what was honourable in *Moors,* may not be a Rule to us; for we are *Christians!* They would have been safer it seems among *Popish Spaniards,* even if

Enemies, and delivered into their hands by a Tempest. These were not Enemies; they were born among us, and yet we have killed them all. But shall we imitate *idolatrous Papists,* we that are *enlightened Protestants?* They would even have been safer among the *Negroes of Africa,* where at least one manly Soul would have been found, with Sense, Spirit and Humanity enough, to stand in their defence. But shall *Whitemen* and *Christians* act like a *Pagan Negroe?* In short it appears, that they would have been safe in any part of the known world, except in the neighbourhood of the CHRISTIAN WHITE SAVAGES of *Peckstang* and *Donegall!*[5]

The leaders of the Paxton Boys, Matthew Smith and James Gibson, presented to the governor a declaration of remonstrance that raised issues other than frontier defense and representation. It charged that a "certain Society of People" were too friendly to the Indians, and that one in particular had kept up relations with them "as if he had been our Governor." The reference was to Israel Pemberton, "King of the Quakers," the founder of the Friendly Association for Regaining and Preserving Peace with the Indians by Pacific Measures. Pemberton knew how much the frontiersmen hated him because of his activities on behalf of the Indians, and when the Paxton Boys were approaching Philadelphia he prudently left town.[6]

The Paxton Boys dispersed, and once they had gone no action was taken, by Franklin or by anyone else, on the issue of representation. And when in March 1765 the Indians who had been at the center of the original storm were escorted back to the upper Susquehanna and to the village their Moravian friends called Friedenshutten (Tents of Peace), their number had fallen from 140 to 83—not from the guns of white raiders but from their more serious and persistent enemies, dysentery and smallpox. The Indians were in fact no permanent threat to the douce burgers of Philadelphia.

*   *   *

The crisis did have other and more serious consequences. It threw the established pattern of proprietary government versus Assembly once again into sharp, but now suddenly twisted, focus. Thus far the Quakers, though less and less prominent and active in the Assembly, had supported the dominant party; it was indeed spoken of as the Quaker party. The Quakers were somewhat suspicious of Franklin but were still more critical of the Penns. Franklin was not slow in his own writings to emphasize the Penn family's abandonment of its

Quaker faith for Establishment Anglicanism. But because the Friends were very divided on defense, the Quaker Meeting for Sufferings of September 13, 1764, "decided not to take a stand on the issue." Similarly, the German pietistic sects had hitherto been on the Assembly side. Now, as reputed "friends of the Indians," they too were unpopular, and many residents of the eastern counties had less sympathy than ever for them.

The Scotch-Irish Presbyterians on the frontier had even less respect for the Assembly. For them as ever the faith was militant. Of those he called the Irish Presbyterians, Franklin wrote to Jackson that they "piqu'd at the Reflections thrown on them by the Quakers for the late Riots and Murders, have join'd the Proprietary Party, by which they hope to acquire the Predominancy in the Assembly, and subdue the Quakers."[7] Two of the three assemblymen who voted against the petition for a royal takeover came from the frontier counties; the third, John Dickinson, until now associated with the Quaker party, thought the takeover inexpedient—he was, throughout his career, frequently to be found on the hesitant side. So the crisis gave the majority in the democratic West (though not all in Lancaster County or in the predominantly German county of Berks) a platform for their criticism of the Assembly and its leaders, and allowed them dramatically to expose the Assembly's apparent indifference to the needs of the frontier. Murderers of Indians could not, it seemed, be brought to trial; law and order were at risk. From the crisis the proprietary party thus derived a certain support in 1764, even if to support them was to uphold what otherwise seemed an anachronistic and fading cause. As Franklin was aware, the proprietary cause did best in military crises on the frontier. Quakers for their part moved in each crisis rapidly away from pacifism.

The rioters had carried with them to Philadelphia a petition from York, Cumberland, and Lancaster counties that not only expressed the views of the Scotch-Irish but ascribed the misfortunes that had befallen the frontier to the fact that the West was underrepresented in the provincial Assembly. A representation of only ten from the five western counties (Lancaster, York, Cumberland, Berks, and Northampton) against the twenty-six representatives of the three older counties and two from the city of Philadelphia was considered "oppressive, unequal and unjust, the cause of many of our Grievances."

William Penn's Charter of Privileges had provided that, in case the three Lower Counties on the Delaware should split off and form a

separate Assembly (as they did in 1705), the three counties of Philadelphia, Chester, and Bucks should elect eight representatives each
and the city of Philadelphia two. The charter said that no county
should have fewer than four representatives, but said nothing about
representation of new counties that might be formed later. When the
five newer counties were created, they had relatively small popula-
tions and were understandably allowed fewer assemblymen: Lancaster had four, Cumberland and York two each, and Northampton and
Berks one each. No significant complaints of underrepresentation
arose until the Indian incursions of 1763–1764 led to a belief in the
frontier counties that the Assembly was indifferent to their interests.
By that time, the combined population of the newer counties had
grown to the point where it almost equaled that of the three original
counties, including the city of Philadelphia. On the basis of population, then, the two sections should have had about equal representation—although the older region paid taxes in 1760 amounting to approximately half again as much as did the "back counties." [8]

Representation in Pennsylvania was not proportional, any more
than elsewhere. Its unevenness, however, was not a premeditated design on the part of the Quaker party to keep the opposition from
gaining power, easy though it was to see it that way. At the time of
their establishment the new counties had adequate representation in
the legislature in terms both of numbers and property. The people of
York and Cumberland counties, created in 1749 and 1750 respectively, were concerned about the issue of representation only on the
outbreak of war, when they wanted aid. Because of the expense involved, they had at times neglected to elect members to the Assembly,
or had chosen Philadelphians to represent them; William Allen of
Philadelphia was regularly elected to the legislature by Cumberland
County. Again, the charge that eastern conservatives deliberately put
the suffrage qualification beyond the reach of many people is hard to
sustain. The majority of adult males easily met the property-owning
requirement for the suffrage, but for those living in Philadelphia the
requirement of £50 in property in the city did exclude most of the
working population. If the system was inegalitarian, however, equality of representation was far from being a generally accepted principle anywhere in the English-speaking world. Indeed, Pennsylvania
had a more equitable system than the pre–1832 British House of
Commons.

Yet, all this said, after the affair was over there was a curious indif-

ference to the issue of representation, on the part of the Assembly and
of Franklin. He had visited the frontier and become a "general" there
a decade earlier. If the Paxton Boys were murderers, Franklin himself
had earlier urged vigorous action against Indians. For one with a
dream of the West, he showed little interest in the acute and worrying
questions of representation, taxation of its land, and administrative
methods of handling Indian affairs. For him these were now lesser
questions, lost in the larger crusade against the proprietors, who
seemed all too likely to profit from frontier clashes.

The tensions on the frontier also threw into sharper focus the continuing dispute over the taxation of the proprietary estates. Reinforced in their determination that the proprietors should pay taxes on
their lands on the same terms as ordinary citizens, the Assembly
drafted a bill accordingly, and there ensued months of bitter altercation with the new governor, John Penn. "Is it consistent with Justice
to the good People of this Province, to insist on taxing the best and
most valuable of the Proprietaries' Lands no higher than the worst
and least valuable of People's Lands in a common Tax, to be levied
for the defenses of the whole?" While this dispute over one bill was
in progress, disagreement also arose over a militia bill: the Quakers
were still unwilling to bear arms, but the province needed a defense
force. Franklin and the Assembly demanded a law similar to one that
had been enacted in 1755, permitting voluntary enlistment, allowing
the choice of company officers by the common soldiers and barring
the use of courts-martial. The governor insisted on the right of appointment of officers; the Assembly disagreed. This disagreement
would become an issue in the election of the following year.[9]

*   *   *

The Paxton Boys affair destroyed for once Franklin's image as a
smooth and crafty operator. In these months his writing reveals a new
degree of venom. His letters to Richard Jackson about the Penns in
particular carry an unusual bitterness. He had now been campaigning
against the proprietary connection for at least six years. His arguments are no longer either seriously marshaled or jocularly put; the
persiflage has gone. He scorned the argument that the proprietary
interest served as a protective buffer between vulnerable colony and
reformist ministry. He saw the proprietors as selfish, mean, and mer-

cenary; they had abandoned not only their Quaker faith but common humanity. He held that by amending or vetoing militia and money bills, and by refusing to contribute a fair share to the public treasury, they had weakened the efforts of the Assembly to defend the province. Governor John Penn, after the Paxton affair, resumed a policy of offering bounties for Indian scalps, male and female alike. His conduct—"his dropping all inquiries after the murderers and his answering the disputes of the rioters privately" and his insults to the Assembly—had brought "him and his government into sudden contempt. All regard for him in the Assembly is lost. All hopes of happiness under a proprietary government are at an end." [10]

The "Resolves upon the Present Circumstances," which Franklin helped draft for the Assembly in March 1764, and which were unanimously adopted, put a compelling case and raised new as well as old issues. They defined the issue squarely as one of province versus proprietors: "1. That it is the Opinion of this House, that the Proprietaries of this Province, after having delegated their Powers of Government, can be justly or legally considered in no other Light than as private Owners of Property, without the least Share or constitutional Power of Legislation whatever." This view had been given support by the Board of Trade report of June 1760, which criticized the Penns expressly because "they seem to have Consider'd themselves only in the narrow and Contracted view of Landholders in the Province, and to have been regardless of their Prerogatives as long as their Property remained secure." The "Resolves" went on to list twenty-six items, among them:

4. That it is high Presumption in any Subject to interfere between the Crown and the People; and by his private Instructions to a Deputy Governor, enforced by penal Bonds, prevent the Crown's receiving, and the People's granting, the Supplies required, and necessary for the Defence of His Majesty's Province . . .

13. That the present Proprietary Demand, of having the *best and most valuable* of their located uncultivated Lands, rated and assessed no *higher* than the *worst and least valuable* of the located uncultivated Lands belonging to the Inhabitants, is equally unreasonable and unjust with any of their former Claims . . .

14. That the Proprietaries taking Advantage of Times of public Calamity to extort Privileges from the People, or enforce Claims against them, with the Knife of Savages at their Throat, not permitting them to raise Money for

their defence, unless the Proprietary arbitrary Will and Pleasure is complied with, is a Practice dishonourable, unjust, tyrannical and inhuman . . .

19. That the Power insisted on by the Governor, of marching any Number of the Militia to any Part of the Province, and keeping them there during any Time, at Pleasure, without the Advice and Consent of the Commissioners, who are to pay them, is a Power that may be used so as greatly and unnecessarily to harrass the Freemen of the Province, and cannot safely be trusted in the Hands of a Proprietary Governor . . .

26. That this House will adjourn, in order to consult their Constituents, whether an humble Address should be drawn up, and transmitted to His Majesty, praying that he would be graciously pleased to take the People of this Province under His immediate Protection and Government, by compleating the Agreement heretofore made with the first Proprietor for the Sale of the Government to the Crown, or otherwise, as to his Wisdom and Goodness shall seem meet.[11]

Franklin buttressed this appeal in a long Preface to Joseph Galloway's speech of May 24, 1764, supporting a change to royal government; he always thought this Preface one of the best of his pieces of writing. It was witty, pungent, sarcastic, and humorous, an impressive reply to William Smith's Preface to the defensive speech of John Dickinson opposing change:

Pleasant, surely it is, to hear the Proprietary Partizans, of all Men, bawling for the Constitution, and affecting a terrible concern for our Liberties and Privileges. They who have been, these twenty Years, cursing our Constitution, declaring that it was no Constitution, or worse than none, and that Things could never be well with us, 'till it was new-modell'd, and made exactly conformable to the British Constitution. They who have treated our distinguishing Privileges as so many Illegalities and Absurdities; who have solemnly declared in Print, that though such Privileges might be proper in the Infancy of a Colony, to encourage its Settlement, they became *unfit for it* in its grown State, and *ought to be taken away:* They, who by numberless Falshoods, propagated with infinite Industry, in the Mother Country, attempted to procure an Act of Parliament for the actual depriving a very great Part of the People of their Privileges: They too who have already depriv'd the whole People, of some of their most important Rights, and are daily endeavouring to deprive them of the rest! Are these become Patriots, and Advocates for our Constitution? Wonderful Change! Astonishing Conversion! Will the Wolves then protect the Sheep, if they can but persuade 'em to give up their Dogs? Yes; The Assembly would destroy all their own Rights, and those of the People; and the Proprietary Partizans are become the Champions for Liberty!¹²

There was much truth as well as propaganda here. Smith had advocated an Act of Parliament that would have had the effect of barring Quakers from the Assembly, depriving Germans of the right to vote until they had acquired "a sufficient Knowledge of our Language and Constitution," and requiring that all newspapers, almanacs, and legal documents in the province be written in English.¹³ Others in the proprietary faction, such as William Allen and Gilbert Tennant, had been talking in similar fashion.

After passing the "Resolves," the Assembly had adjourned for seven weeks, in order to carry on consultations over the issue of a change of government. In May it seemed clear that the Assembly had the support of the majority of the people, with petitions, Franklin boasted, signed "by a very great number of the most substantial inhabitants." There were mass meetings, broadsides, and a petition to the king, which in one form was written in German and in another suitably reworded form was written for Quakers. After the seven-week campaign, the petitions for a royal takeover had 3,500 signatures, and only four members of the Assembly voted against it. The signatures came, however, largely from Philadelphia, where only one in ten of Pennsylvanians lived. The back country was still to be heard from. By September there were 15,000 against.

In the pamphlet war that this crisis occasioned, which ran on into the propaganda campaign for the October election, Franklin's writing showed a high quality. Not only with the "Resolves" and the Preface to Galloway's speech, but with a broadside entitled *Explanatory Remarks* and then his *Cool Thoughts on the Present Situation of Our Public Affairs*, Franklin reinforced his case. Perhaps without fully realizing the implications, however, he touched in *Cool Thoughts* on issues that would bedevil Anglo-American relations in the decade ahead. He sought to minimize the possible threat royal government might bring to liberty of conscience and liberty of worship, rights that had been solemnly and perpetually guaranteed by William Penn in the Charter of Privileges of 1701. He was at pains to point out that when similar changes had been made in other colonies, like South Carolina and the Jerseys, there had been no threat to religious liberty. He discounted the danger that royal government might lead to Episcopacy. And he boldly raised the issue of a contribution to defense; Jackson had been warning him that a parliamentary tax levied on the colonies would be required to support the cost of British troops there.

That *we shall have a standing Army to maintain,* is another Bugbear rais'd to terrify us from endeavouring to obtain a King's Government. It is very possible that the Crown may think it necessary to keep Troops in America henceforward, to maintain its Conquests, and defend the Colonies; and that the Parliament may establish some Revenue arising out of the American Trade to be apply'd towards supporting those Troops. It is possible too, that we may, after a few Years Experience, be generally very well satisfy'd with that Measure, from the steady Protection it will afford us against Foreign Enemies, and the Security of internal Peace among ourselves without the Expence or Trouble of a Militia. But assure yourself, my Friend, that whether we like it or not, our continuing under a Proprietary Government will not prevent it, nor our coming under a Royal Government promote or forward it, any more than they would prevent or procure Rain or Sunshine.[14]

This was a long way from the Franklin of 1775, or even of 1766. While he was seeking royal government, the Penns, William Allen, and Richard Jackson in London were busy thwarting the plans for a proposed stamp duty. They thought it unconstitutional, and got it delayed. Franklin merely thought it, at that point, impractical. If there were to be taxes, there would be a new game to play. "If you choose to tax us, give us members in your legislature, and let us be one people." Perhaps the British government should have offered bigger inducements than a governorship to an illegitimate son.[15]

Yet, however justified the case for change, and however clear the evidence of governmental weakness in Pennsylvania revealed by the march of the Paxton Boys, the contrary case made in rebuttal, especially in the series of anonymous *Plain Dealer* pamphlets, was also formidable. "If our Government should now be changed, we must lose a great many valuable privileges." William Allen warned that the king's little finger would weigh more heavily on the colony than all the Proprietor's loins. The Assembly approved the petition for a change to royal government only after expanding and explaining Franklin's draft. Franklin had proposed very briefly to ask the king to preserve merely "the Privileges that have been granted" to his subjects in Pennsylvania by his royal predecessors. The final text specified more definitely "those Civil and Religious Privileges" that had been instrumental in encouraging the first settlement "of this Wilderness

Country, to the Extension of the British Dominions and Commerce," and had been and still continued to be important in drawing "many Thousands of Foreigners" to settle in Pennsylvania and become his majesty's subjects.[16]

Governor Penn had no doubt where the center of trouble lay: not in Paxton and Donegal but closer to home, in Philadelphia. He wrote to his uncle Thomas, the major proprietor, on May 5, 1764:

Mr. Franklin may be consider'd as the chief Cause of this faction being carried to its present height, for it is observ'd by everybody that while he was in England there was at least an appearance of Peace and Quietness, but Since his return, the old Sparks are again blown up and at present the flame rages with more violence than ever. I really believe there never will be any prospect of ease or happiness here, while that Villain has the liberty of Spreading about the poison of that inveterate Malice and ill Nature, which is so deeply implanted in his own black heart. He certainly looks upon Mischief, in the light other people do upon Virtue, as carrying with it its own reward. This is the best way I can account for his present Politicks.[17]

The Assembly saw things differently: it elected Franklin as Speaker. The opportunity arose when Isaac Norris, unwilling to sign the petition, pleaded ill health and resigned after fourteen years as Speaker. He had long opposed proprietary government, but as a Quaker he foresaw a threat to the Quakers' religious privileges—they had more freedom in Pennsylvania than in England—and he was unhappy and embarrassed by the prospect ahead. Franklin was elected to replace him, and thus when the petition was approved by the Assembly it bore his name as Speaker.

The petition, "that Your Majesty would be graciously pleased to resume the Government of this Province making . . . Compensation to the Proprietaries for the same," contended that government by proprietaries had been found from experience to be "inconvenient, attended with many Difficulties and Obstructions to your Majesty's Service, arising from the Intervention of Proprietary private Interests in publick Affairs, and Disputes concerning those Interests." Such government, it was held, was "weak, unable to support its own Authority, and maintain the common internal Peace of the Province."[18]

*   *   *

The call for a constitutional change led to a shift in party alignment. A number of influential Quakers joined with the proprietary leaders

in launching a "New Ticket," under which banner they hoped to
unite all opposition to the proposal for a change in government. Most
of them were strict Friends, led by Israel Pemberton, who held, val-
iantly but against the tide, to a rigid interpretation of their pacific and
other religious principles. They shared the Presbyterian fear that if
Pennsylvania became a royal province there would be not only king
but also bishop, or at least that the Church of England might endeavor to restrict religious liberty. The vote in October 1764 in Philadelphia (city and county) turned out to be very close, so the stand
taken by these Quakers may have been the deciding factor in throwing five seats to the proprietary party. They had also some influence
on the Moravians of Northampton County, where a proprietary man
was returned. Ironically, the proprietaries were also supported by
William Smith and other Anglican leaders, who counted on the votes
of about half of the churchmen in the city, welcome though the
thought of a bishopric might be to some of them. The College of
Philadelphia, which had fifteen Presbyterian teachers, lent its weight
to the proprietary cause. Presbyterian ministers, prompt to express
their views on state as well as church, sent circular letters throughout
the province exhorting church members to vote the New Ticket. This
curious coalition of Anglicans, Presbyterians, Germans, and some
Quakers was a novel and formidable phenomenon.

*   *   *

The election of October 1764 followed months of pamphleteering on
a host of issues: defense of the frontier, policy toward Indians, taxation of proprietorial lands, Assembly versus proprietors, New Ticket
versus Old—and on the personal character of the antagonists. Franklin was the target of many printed attacks: "I bore the personal abuse
of five scurrilous Pamphlets, and three Copperplate Prints, from the
Proprietary Party, before I made the smallest Return; and they began
to think they might continue to affront me with Impunity." Some of
the writing on both sides was elevated; some of it on both sides was
vicious. William Allen paid a schoolmaster named Dove £25 for a
print with derogatory verses that would hurt Franklin's reputation.
"Tit for Tats"—verses and epitaphs in a "lapidary style"—were especially popular:

To the much esteem'd Memory of
B_____ F _____ Esq; L.L.D;
The only man of his day
In Pennsylvania,
Or perhaps of any age or in any country,
Whose *ingrate Disposition* and *Badness of Heart*
(These enormous Vices) Ever introduced to
POPULARITY.

. . . . .

By assuming the merit
Of other mens *discoveries*,
He obtain'd the name of
A PHILOSOPHER.
By meanly *begging* and some Times *buying*
HONORARY DEGREES,
From several *Colleges* and *Universities*,
He obtain'd the Character of
A Man of LEARNING.

. . . . .

And by an Address, peculiar to himself,
He found the Way to climb to Promotion
Upon the shoulders of FRIENDS
Whom a few Years before
He *proposed* to, and even *boasted* that he would *Ruin*.
Thus, rising by degrees
From the meanest Circumstances
To a Politician of the first Magnitude,
He became perfectly acquainted
With every Zig Zag Machination
And triming Contrivance,
Peculiar to that Science.
Quick as the Flashes of Lightning,
Darted from a Cloud,
He would sometimes *level*
ALL DISTINCTIONS,
Pull down the very Walls
Of Power,
And fatally destroy the *Safeguards*
of JUSTICE

. . . . .

He lived, as to the Appearance of Wealth,
In Moderate Circumstances.

His principal Estate, *seeming* to consist,
Till very lately,
In his Hand Maid BARBARA
A most valuable *Slave,* The *Foster-Mother*
Of his last Offspring Who did his dirty Work—
. . . . .
Providence for wise tho' secret Ends,
Lately depriv'd him of the Mother
OF EXCELLENCY.
His Fortune was not however impair'd,
For he piously witheld from her
MANES
The *pitiful* Stipend of *Ten Pounds per Annum,*
On which he had cruelly suffered her
To STARVE: Then stole her to the Grave in Silence
Without a Pall, the covering due to her dignity
Without a Groan, a Sigh or a Tear
Without a *Tomb,* or even
A *Monumental Inscription*
. . . . .
Devoid of Principles and
Ineffably mean;
Whose Ambition is POWER:
And whose intention is
TYRANY
. . . . .[19]

The voters were reminded not only that Franklin's son was illegitimate but that Franklin had said harsh things about "Palatine boors" and "Christian White Savages" and "Piss-brute-tarians." He had, allegedly, passed off Ebenezer Kinnersley's experiments as his own; he had lived well in London at public expense; contrary to the Assembly's instructions, he had invested in British stocks the parliamentary grant for Pennsylvania's wartime expenses, and had thus lost money for the province. He had been bribed: his consorting with virtuosi and his honorary degrees—former governor James Hamilton had said—were "no small acquisitions to the public, therefore well worth paying for." He had come from "the meanest Circumstances," he was skilled at "every Zig Zag Machination." He was Dr. Double-face.[20]

Franklin's friend John Hughes offered to give to the Pennsylvania Hospital £10 for any proof of the charges made. Galloway accused

Dickinson—whose pen and oratory had become rhetorical instruments of the proprietaries—of looking to political rewards. Dickinson replied that at least he had scrupulously avoided remunerative public offices. He also repeated the charge that Franklin had mishandled provincial funds while in England; in fact, even William Allen had agreed that Franklin had carried out that part of his assignment competently.

Amid the mutual savagery and scurrility—and Dickinson even challenged Galloway to a duel—it is significant that in the 1760s, unlike what happened in the 1790s, deism was not singled out for attack; that the gospel of success, as distinct from the success itself, was not held up to scorn; and that no one accused Franklin of campaigning against the Penn's lands in order to compel them to sell large stocks of it to interested parties. There was much that was still common ground. But it was nevertheless a contest that was polemical, wounding, and personal.

*   *   *

The result was clear enough. The Old Ticket won. Of the thirty-six members elected to the Assembly in 1764, only eleven were proprietary partisans. In Philadelphia County, however, three of the eight members were proprietary men; and the city of Philadelphia filled its two seats with proprietary supporters. The two leaders of the Quaker party, Franklin and Galloway, were defeated—though very narrowly—Franklin in the city and Galloway in the county. The margin was of 25 votes out of 4,000 polled. Galloway "agonized in death like a mortal deist who has no hopes of a future existence," wrote Charles Pettit to Joseph Reed in London; "Mr. Franklin died like a philosopher." In fact, Pettit said, the result was due to an error of tactical judgment on how long to keep the polls open rather than to any matter of high principle:

About three in the morning, the advocates for the new ticket moved for a close, but (O! fatal mistake!) the old hands kept it open, as they had a reserve of the aged and lame, which could not come in the crowd, and were called up and brought out in chairs and litters, &c., and some who needed no help, between three and six o'clock, about two hundred voters. As both sides took care to have spies all night, the alarm was given to the new ticket men; horsemen and footmen were immediately dispatched to Germantown &c., and by nine or ten o'clock they began to pour in, so that after the move for a close, seven or eight hundred votes were procured, about five hundred or near it of which were for the ticket . . .[21]

Franklin blamed his defeat quite simply on the loss of the German vote. The New Ticket in the event was strong in the city, with Isaac Norris, Joseph Richardson, and John Dickinson at the top of the list. In the West, the proprietary party also carried the counties of Cumberland, York, and Northampton, and elected one of the four members from Lancaster County. The result, disappointing as it was to the proprietary party in that the popular cause triumphed, nevertheless represented great gains for the proprietors over previous years. There was, as ugly portent, a greater degree of political division in the province along racial and sectional lines than ever before.

*   *   *

There is a further paradox in the confused story of the 1764 crisis. By the time the election was held, the proprietors had in fact decided to yield on the disputed point of the taxation of their uncultivated lands—though as a matter of equity, and not, they said, because of the petition. They made their decision in May, on the advice of their London solicitor, Henry Wilmot. Governor Penn received news of the decision in August, but he chose, not wishing to add fuel to the flames or to concede Franklin's and the Assembly's case in advance, to hold back the announcement of this retreat. Both Allen and Smith, who had been in London in 1764, also knew of the concession. Since this had been the original cause of contention, the proprietors supposed that "the dispute on the mode of taxation must now be entirely settled." In subsequent letters to the governor and other supporters in Pennsylvania during the summer and autumn, Thomas Penn emphasized that he and his brother had given in, not through fear of an application to the crown for a change in government, but because "there does appear some equity" in the Assembly's argument. He admitted to Smith in October that "at this distance of time, no Person here that considers [the stipulation] looks upon it in any other light than that the Assembly contended for."[22]

Governor Penn preserved official silence until January 17, 1765, when he addressed a circular letter to the commissioners of appeal informing them of the proprietors' decision, and asking them and the county commissioners and local assessors to interpret the Supply Act in the way the Assembly had wanted from the start. The Assembly passed the proposed bill on February 7. Penn then returned it, however, with an amendment relating in an unspecified way to the taxation of the proprietors' town lots. On this neither side would yield to the other, and the bill failed to pass. Twice thereafter—in September 1766 and January 1774—the Supply Act of 1764 was successfully amended in other particulars, but never in the controversial matter of the assessment and taxation of proprietary lands.

Had the governor been more candid, the history of the colony—and of Franklin—might have been very different. Richard Jackson may have written to Franklin of the proprietors' concession in a lost letter of June 14, but Franklin had not heard of it in September. He had borne, he said, "the personal abuse of five scurrilous pamphlets . . . The breach is now become irreparable, and the difference between the Proprietaries and the Province irreconcilable."[23] In any event, there was no reconciliation because of the unresolved controversy over the taxation of the proprietors' town lots. The struggle now was continuous and increasingly one of fundamentals.

*   *   *

The new Assembly, still firmly Old Ticket in character, voted down an attempt to have the petition to the king rescinded. Although he had been defeated in the election, Franklin was reappointed as provincial agent to Britain. It was not a unanimous appointment: the vote was nineteen to eleven, and among the eleven were John Dickinson of Philadelphia County and William Allen of Cumberland.

William Allen, once Franklin's patron, now used unusually violent language. Franklin was, he said, "fully freighted with rancour and malice"; he was "a turbulent plotter." William Smith became a savage critic. Franklin was ambitious and time-serving: "Here in America his delight is in contention, anarchy and opposition to government. And then, when he has created an embassy for himself, and gets on the other side of the Atlantic, he shifts with the scene; puts off the noisy demagogue, forgets the cause of his employers, truckles for preferment for himself and his family, and boasts services he never performed." Smith also called him an Anti-Penn: "the prostitute writer, the whispering incendiary, the avowed desperado surround him." Franklin now had dangerous and rapier-sharp enemies. A formal remonstrance against his appointment was entered in the Assembly's

"Votes and Proceedings" and then printed in the *Pennsylvania Journal*. It was Dickinson's handiwork:

Because it is well known that Mr. Franklin has had a principal Hand in proposing and promoting the Petitions for a Change of Government, which now appear contrary to the Sentiments of more than three Fourths of the Province, and he may be justly supposed to have a fond partiality for his own Schemes: Because it appears highly necessary to engage the Influence of our honourable Proprietaries to assist in preventing, if possible, any unnecessary Burthens being laid upon the Province, against whom Mr. Franklin entertains such a rooted Enmity, that they cannot take joint Council for the public good: Because, especially as both Mr. Franklin and his Son hold Offices of considerable Profit and Honour under the Crown, the Remonstrants cannot expect that a Gentleman of his moderate Fortune will sacrifice his Interest for the Sake of the Province, which he must necessarily do, if he but seems to oppose the Measures of the Ministry, and which our present Circumstances require an Agent to do, with unshaken Resolution and Fidelity.[24]

In November 1764 Franklin published his "Remarks on a Late Protest," signed and written in the first person, as a rebuttal of Dickinson's "Protest" against his appointment. Here for the first time he sounds genuinely on the defensive, disappointed by defeat, hurt and vulnerable. He prepared for his departure under a cloud, a man in retreat. He instructed Sally to be circumspect, and to go to church. He left behind a new brick house rising on the south side of Market Street, three storeys high, with three rooms to a floor, and with the kitchen in the cellar; it was insured in 1766 for £500. He concluded the "Remarks" by taking leave "(perhaps a last leave) of the Country I love, and in which I have spent the greatest part of my Life. Esto Perpetua. I wish every Kind of Prosperity to my Friends, and I forgive my enemies."[25] It sounded very final. Less than two weeks after being appointed, he had gone. He was to be away more than ten years, and may well have expected never to return. He was never to see his wife again.

*   *   *

It is impossible to study this two-year spell of Franklin's life in Philadelphia without concluding that he was now personally much happier in London than in Pennsylvania, that he had more open and bitter enemies in America than in Britain, and that he now saw this experience as but an interlude in his life on the eastern side of the Atlantic.

He was out of place now in Philadelphia, at odds with frontiersmen, with Germans, with the friends of the proprietors, and with Quakers. And he had been defeated at the polls, however narrowly. Although his cause had triumphed in the election, he himself had not.

In 1764, for the first time in his life, Franklin misread the signs, both in Pennsylvania politics and in London. Why? He lost his seat in the Assembly after thirteen years as a member. He hurt himself by the bitterness of his own journalism, and by the evidence of his lack of real sympathy with Quakers and Germans. The savage criticisms of him got under his skin. Some personal difficulties were now apparent. He was never really accepted into "Society" either in Philadelphia or in London. Yet in Philadelphia William Smith was, although even more a "foreigner," equally devoid of a base, equally opportunistic. If Franklin got on well with Logan, what went wrong with his relations with William Allen? There was a similar failure in London, and it was not due solely to the snobbery of the British Establishment. Perhaps the core of his misjudgment was his attitude toward the Penn family. Was his vendetta against them necessary? By 1764 he was savagely antiproprietarial, even as he was intensely royalist and imperialist. The vendetta and its bitterness, and the role of popular and "democratic" leadership into which it cast Franklin, lost him the chance of playing the other role in which he had shown such talent: that of conciliator. He was never permitted to play that part in London. Yet if the Penns were to surrender their province, it was persuasion, not enmity, that was needed. The fault was in the man as much as in the stiff imperial system.

In his isolation he was increasingly becoming, through events as much as by personal inclination, the London man. He had, almost alone, aided Braddock in 1755. He had, in 1764, established close relations with Bouquet; and that Swiss-born professional soldier saw the Pennsylvania situation as clearly as did Franklin, and saw it objectively. He also saw the need for a conciliation between London and Philadelphia. Writing to Franklin from Fort Loudoun in August 1764, he made the point that what the colony lacked was "the weight of a third power . . . to act as mediator . . . But that will be impracticable in America till Time has produced Nobility and Wealth." Without this, Bouquet saw no prospect of true stability in the government of the province. Had Franklin played the role of mediator that Bouquet recognized—the role for which in Philadelphia he had had a long apprenticeship—his own fortunes, and his country's might have been very different.

By campaigning conspicuously against the proprietors, Franklin aligned himself with royal government. By 1764 there was no longer approval in Britain for colonies of a feudal kind; in that year the Privy Council rejected the plea of the Earl of Egmont for the island of St. John (now Prince Edward Island) for himself and his heirs. Franklin here was on the government's side. It is true that the same logic weakened his own plea for the establishment of a new colony or colonies in the Ohio country or on the banks of the Scioto, but the colonies Franklin favored need not have taken the proprietorial form of Pennsylvania or Maryland. A "royal" colony might be established in the Ohio country, but with generous land grants to individuals. Egmont after all did not get his colony, but he did obtain smaller tracts of land on the island. In the spring of 1764 Jackson had expressed a hope of interesting Franklin in a grant of land in Nova Scotia, and Franklin had been receptive to the idea; Jackson was one of twenty-three men in Great Britain who received large grants of land in June and July, 1764. Of these, nineteen, including Jackson, were awarded 20,000 acres each; the others lesser amounts. In his ambitions (not merely personal) for the West in 1764, Franklin was much closer to the thinking of the men of business in London and Philadelphia and of the Board of Trade than were most members of the Quaker party. He had heard that his name was one of the fifteen (William Allen's was another) recommended to the Privy Council as commissioners to settle the disputed boundary between New York and New Jersey. He took this as an indication of ministerial recognition of his standing, though the commission was not in fact set up until 1767.

Moreover, Franklin was by nature accommodating rather than rebellious, with the talents of the conciliator. His way of life in London, and now for some years in Philadelphia, had been very easy and comfortable. He was familiar with colonial leaders, advocates of colonial union like Francis Bernard and Thomas Hutchinson in Massachusetts, who were decidedly not "democratick" in their leanings. In working for the dissolution of the proprietary charter he would perforce become—was it entirely unwillingly?—an ally of men who, with very different motives and backgrounds from his, wanted the republican charters of Connecticut and Rhode Island repealed. To win over the Ministry he must stand well with them, and yet by every link of society and of connection they were close to the proprietors. Being many-sided—affable by nature and democratic by instinct, loyal to his Assembly but with his strong and loyal view of empire— he was himself highly vulnerable. He had interests in western land; as postmaster he held a crown appointment worth £300 a year, which for years the Penns had been trying to have taken from him; and his son had been since 1762 a royal governor. For one who had come up the hard way, Franklin now had clearly a lot to lose. And he had put it in some peril. According to Thomas Penn, Lord Halifax had said that the "Resolves" of May 1764 were "a kind of Rebellion against his Majesty's Government, and that Mr. Franklin must be turned out, if he does not alter his conduct." The scale of his vendetta against the Penns, and the virulence of his writing, weakened the part he might have played in London. He went thus not as a conciliator but as a prickly and argumentative advocate of change.[26]

But he still had his friends and supporters. When he departed from Philadelphia on November 7, three hundred wellwishers accompanied him on horseback on the sixteen-mile ride to Chester, where he boarded his ship, giving him a rousing demonstration of their loyalty and esteem. A letter written by one of the participants gives a stirring description of the scene. Franklin, according to this anonymous witness,

was attended by a very great Number of the reputable inhabitants of this City and County; and on his embarking, was saluted by a number of Cannon, and the Huzza's of the People; and an Anthem was sung, (composed here) suitable to the Occasion. He was rowed on board the Ship *King of Prussia* . . . by Ten Freeholders of the White-Oak Company, in their Barge, they attending on Purpose; in short, the Respect that was paid to this great and truly deserving Patriot, can hardly be set forth, nor the Joys shewn on the Occasion, be express'd.

This witness also recorded the text of "The Anthem Sung at Chester," the best literary expression of honor and respect for Franklin produced in the 1764 campaign, which indicates the near-royal adulation he inspired:

> O LORD our GOD arise,
> Scatter our Enemies
>   And make them fall.
> Confound their Politicks,

Frustrate such Hypocrites,
Franklin, on Thee we fix,
    GOD Save us all.

God save great George our King
Prosper agent Franklin
Grant him success.
Hark how our rallies ring
God save our gracious King
From whom all Blessings spring
Our wrongs redress.[27]

Franklin's ship made speedy progress—thirty days from land to land—and he covered the seventy-two miles from Portsmouth to London in one short winter's day. The eager speed availed him little: Mrs. Stevenson was out when he arrived, and he caught a violent cold in the chill December weather. Yet now, it seemed, it was in Craven Street, not Market Street, that the fifty-eight-year-old Dr. Franklin felt most at home.

7

TWO VIEWS OF EMPIRE

*T*he crossing in 1764 took thirty days. It allowed the usual plumbing of ocean depths and the plotting of ocean currents. It allowed reflection too. Franklin came from what he called the empire "on this side," for in 1764 his view of empire was already transatlantic; the Whitehall-and-Westminster view was never his. What—before the storms began—was the difference between the two views?

In 1763, after the conquest of Canada from the French, and with the prestige enjoyed by William Pitt, wartime secretary of state and planner of victories, there was in London a newfound national pride. For the first time since the defeat of the Spanish Armada in 1588, an element that can be described as "Imperial" can be detected running through the thinking of the policymakers.

This is not to be confused with the jingoist and populist imperialism of the late nineteenth century; there was no trace in it of Disraeli's pride in the East, or of the pomp and pageantry of the Victorian and Edwardian heyday. It had no cheap popular press to blow hot air upon its coals. It had, rather, a Roman note, an awareness of the need for armed protection of trade routes and of the need for security on the frontiers—and indeed of the grandeur and ambitions of family oligarchs using the wealth of their estates, but also drawing on the profits that overseas investment and commerce brought them. Even Pitt, a popular hero to whom statues were erected in North America as well as in England, owed his beginnings to family profits made in the East India trade. This sense of empire had four distinguishing characteristics: mercantile, administrative, parliamentary, and strategic.[1]

*   *   *

Britain, like all other European powers, expected her colonies to supply raw materials and articles that could otherwise be obtained only from foreign rivals, and in return to purchase manufactured goods from the mother country. The colonies had been founded expressly for profit: profit for those who settled the land, for the proprietor to whom a charter was granted, for the country under whose direction the whole venture was risked. The objective of the state was that of any other merchant—profit and a favorable balance of trade. The laws that systematized these developments, insofar as they ever were systematized, were built around the Navigation Acts of 1651 and 1660 and given a comprehensive form in 1696: they confined the carrying trade within the Empire to British or colonial ships; they listed or "enumerated" the commodities that could not be shipped to foreign countries (sugar, cotton, indigo, tobacco, and later naval stores, rice, furs, copper); the Staple Act of 1663 required that all exports from Europe to the colonies be shipped via England; and to prevent competition with Britain certain colonial manufactures —woolen cloth (1699), beaver hats (1732), and iron goods (1750) —were prohibited from being exported outside their locality of production.

Contemporaries believed as an article of faith that the economic subordination of the colonies brought immense advantages to Britain. As the *London Magazine* of 1766 put it, "The American is apparelled from head to foot in our manufactures . . . he scarcely drinks, sits, moves, labours or recreates himself, without contributing to the emolument of the mother country." By 1770 exports to the colonies equaled Britain's entire exports in 1704. The colonies were now important as markets, as well as the suppliers of raw materials. The British merchant marine flourished. The adverse balance of trade in many colonies led to dependence on British merchants or factors for credit; and shippers, shipbuilders, and ship factors, ship and foreign insurance firms, and British merchants and manufacturers—often, as the colonists believed, the manufacturers of the shoddier articles— benefited from the system.[2]

There can be no denial that the colonies were seriously affected by the system; indeed, their economies were permanently shaped by it, and in some measure their expansion hindered. Most of them were debtor communities. They could not mint coins. Paper money was, at least in theory, banned as legal tender lest they pay their debts with depreciated paper; yet a sound currency was unobtainable. (A parliamentary statute forbade the use of paper money first in New England and then, in 1764, in all the colonies, but paper money remained in circulation in all of them.) The diversity of colonial currencies in itself handicapped local economic development. The iron industry of the Middle Colonies was curbed, and the South's concentration on tobacco led to periodic overproduction and slumps in prices. The New England colonies, having no commodities to send to Britain in exchange for manufactures, tried to encourage local industry and to develop their own trade with the West Indies, exchanging timber, fish, horses, beans, and shoes for sugar and molasses; and Pennsylvania exported grain. Since the British West Indies were not large enough to absorb the products of New England and the Middle Colonies, the surplus timber and fish were sold to the French West Indies. The British West India interest, however, demanded the cessation of a trade that might be ruinous to their already perilous sugar economy. The result was the Molasses Act of 1733, an attempt to put a prohibitive duty on colonial imports of sugar and molasses from the French and Spanish West Indies. Its enforcement would have ruined the New England traders for the sake of the British West Indies. Failure to enforce it, however, brought the law and its officials into contempt. This trade between the French islands and Boston, Newport, and Providence flourished even more during the Seven Years' War than in the years of peace, owing as much to the collusion of customs officers as to the cupidity of colonial importers. By 1763 it was thought of in Britain not merely as illicit but as treasonable.

Nevertheless, the Navigation Acts were neither mischievous nor wicked. Indeed, the system was much less oppressive than that of France or Spain, and it brought some important advantages to the colonies. Tobacco had a monopoly of the home market. There were bounties for the production of indigo, lumber, and naval stores that totaled some £65,000 a year for the thirteen colonies by 1776. New England's shipbuilding industry flourished; in 1775 approximately one-third of all the ships employed in the total British carrying trade had been built in New England yards. And in Chesapeake Bay clipper-schooners were being built and used. Despite the Iron Act of 1750, the expansion of the iron industry continued; by the outbreak of the Revolution there were more furnaces and forges in production in the colonies than in England and Wales, producing pig iron and bar iron of excellent quality. If this was in part due to the availability of supplies of iron ore and charcoal, it was due also to the availability of capital. The colonies were growing fast, and were being encouraged in their growth by credit from Britain. Moreover, the plantation colonies fitted into the mercantile system admirably; the economies of the South and the Caribbean and of Britain were in large measure naturally complementary. Where there was discord, the casualness of administration, the charter privileges of the colonies, and even the shoals and sandbars of their coasts combined to make enforcement of unpopular laws obligingly difficult. And until 1763 Britain carried the burden of colonial defense and gave colonial goods and ships protection abroad. Indeed, the colonists fully realized this. Sustained smuggling was confined mainly to two articles, tea and molasses. For the rest, the system brought prosperity, assured markets, and easy credits. Where it hurt, it was tacitly evaded.

As a result, historians have now some hesitation in accepting the indictment of mercantilism that was fashionable in the free-trading nineteenth century, which paid as much respect to Adam Smith as to Edmund Burke and which condemned the running of great nations "by the maxims of the counter." While there was clearly much that was irksome in the trade and navigation laws, in the heavy drain on colonial specie that drove the colonies to do business in foreign territories, and in heavy indebtedness, the colonies had come into existence not for political but for economic reasons, "for England's profit, not her glory." Colonial prosperity had been largely the consequence of the laws of trade. "The Act of Navigation," said Burke, "attended the colonies from their infancy, grew with their growth and strengthened with their strength. They were confirmed in obedience to it even more by usage than by law."[3]

There is now abundant evidence that it was not primarily from a distaste for mercantilism that the Americans rebelled. Much can be made of Virginian indebtedness to Britain, but Washington expressly countered the proposal, made in 1774, to withhold remittances due from Virginia to British merchants: "whilst we are accusing others of injustice, we should be just ourselves, and how this can be, whilst we owe a considerable debt, and refuse payment of it to Great Britain, is to me inconceivable. Nothing but the last extremity can justify it."

The debts did not weigh with him or his planter friends as a reason for separation; even in crises planters lived by a code. As late as 1775 Franklin, whose code of conduct was always more adaptable, was willing to have the Navigation Acts reenacted in each and every colony if Britain would only drop her claim to the right to tax. The first Continental Congress accepted the Acts of Trade.[4]

The Acts presented no great impediment to colonial trade, but the tightening of regulations after 1764 induced real bitterness toward British customs and revenue collectors, stamp officials, and enforcement agents. The clashes of 1765 and thereafter arose out of distaste not for the old mercantilism but for the new imperialism, its overzealous officers and what seemed to be their "racketeering," and the many seizures that followed the new and irksome bonding regulations. The correspondence of George Washington with the merchants Hanbury and with Robert Cary, his London agent, and of John Hancock with the house of Harrison and Barnard in London, suggests that it was the sharp practice of the factors in Britain that angered the colonists; shoddy goods and the querying of bills—not the system itself but the ways in which it was abused—brought hostility.

For in 1763 the failures of the mercantile system seemed to the British government far more striking than its merits. Ever since the emasculation of the 1733 Molasses Act, Yankee traders had ignored the law. Colonial governors had long complained; as early as 1743 Governor Shirley of Massachusetts thought the whole system in danger of collapse and wanted offenders against the Acts of Trade to be tried in the courts of Vice-Admiralty. By 1750 the smuggling trade was averaging £500,000 per year in American exports. During the Seven Years' War trade with the enemy flourished even more, and Pitt instructed governors and naval officers to stamp it out. This prompted an inquiry into the colonial customs service, an inquiry that revealed that it cost far more to maintain than it collected, and confirmed that it was both inefficient and corrupt. As a result, customs officers were ordered to their posts in America and forbidden to carry out their duties by deputy; they were promised half of the proceeds of all ships and cargo condemned after seizure; they were freed from civil suits for damages in colonial courts; colonial governors and military and naval officers were ordered to help them in enforcing the law; and a new Vice-Admiralty court was established at Halifax, Nova Scotia. A new apparatus of officialdom and, it was hoped, of efficiency was set up. Franklin was aware of the dangers in such revived and, as it seemed, hungry vigilance. He reported to Boston:

The course and natural progress seems to be, first, the appointment of needy men as officers, for others do not care to leave England; then, their necessities make them rapacious, their office makes them proud and insolent, their insolence and rapacity make them odious, and being conscious that they are hated, they become malicious; their malice urges them to a continual abuse of the inhabitants in their letters to administration, representing them as disaffected and rebellious, and (to encourage the use of severity) as weak, divided, timid, and cowardly. Government believes all; thinks it necessary to support and countenance its officers; their quarrelling with the people is deemed a mark and consequence of their fidelity . . . I think one may clearly see, in the system of customs to be exacted in America by act of Parliament, the seeds sown of a total disunion of the two countries.[5]

In keeping with this policy of customs enforcement came the Revenue (Sugar) Act of 1764, a reinvigoration of the Molasses Act of 1733. It had been discussed in the Board of Trade since 1750, but the colonial agents had managed, by concerted action for thirteen years, to block it. The new vigor swept away their protestations. The duty on foreign molasses was lowered from sixpence to threepence a gallon, but that on sugar was increased; heavy duties on French West Indian products were imposed and were to be enforced; importation of rum or spirits from foreign colonies and trade with the French islands of St. Pierre and Miquelon were forbidden. Smugglers were hit by it; Yankee distillers were given a monopoly at home, for which they showed no gratitude; there were some concessions to South Carolina's rice exports, which compensated New England not at all. And it was ominously stated in the preamble to the Act that these duties were designed to raise a revenue to meet the costs of colonial defense, and that such a policy was just. The Act was accompanied by a Currency Act prohibiting the use of paper money as legal tender in all the colonies.

The Sugar Act could be opposed on economic grounds. Franklin put this colonial case forcibly in a letter to Peter Collinson from Philadelphia in April 1764:

I think there is scarce anything you can do that may be hurtful to us, but what will be as much or more to you. This must be our chief security, for interest with you we have but little: the West Indies vastly outweigh us of the Northern Colonies. What we get above a Subsistence, we lay out with you for your Manufactures. Therefore what you get from us in Taxes you must lose in Trade. The Cat can yield but her skin. As you must have the whole Hide, if you first cut Thongs out of it, 'tis at your own Expence. The same in regard to our Trade with the Foreign West Indian Islands. If you restrain it in any degree, you restrain in the same Proportion our Power of making Remittances to you.[6]

New England and the Middle Colonies no longer fitted the British system but were now part of an American system that had grown up around shipbuilders and smugglers, traders to Africa and the Caribbean, iron manufacturers, and sugar importers. If Britain proposed to enforce mercantilism, there was a competing mercantilism arising now in America itself. Nevertheless the mercantilistic policy of the mother country was not, at mid-century, a major American grievance; and at a later time many Americans, including Franklin, would, at least as a tactical argument, urge a return to the good old ways as practiced before 1763.

*   *   *

The second imperial strand was administrative. The administration of the colonies was the responsibility of the Privy Council and primarily of the secretary of state for the Southern Department, acting on the advice of the Board of Trade and Plantations. The Board examined all laws passed by the colonial assemblies and occasionally imposed a royal veto on them. It drafted instructions to colonial governors, recommended appointments, and gave advice. None of its members had had colonial experience, and they invariably and exclusively reflected mercantile opinion.

In the early part of the eighteenth century the Board had declined in influence. There was no consistency of opinion as to its powers. The Earl of Halifax, on becoming its president in 1748, sought to extend its authority, and began a campaign for the creation of an American department. From 1752 to 1761 the Board had the right to appoint colonial governors and to control all ordinary correspondence with them. In 1757, with Pitt's support, Halifax was admitted to the Cabinet. He was a clear-headed imperialist and wanted the colonies taxed for their own defense. This new efficiency, again antedating 1760, along with Pitt's zeal and success as secretary of state, brought Parliament into the day-by-day matters of administration; increasingly the Commons took an interest and at times an initiative—rarely unselfish or high-minded—in colonial patronage, in the workings of the laws of trade, or in curbing American manufacturers. And this parliamentary curiosity, which at home appeared a guarantee of liberty against royal or bureaucratic power, appeared in colonial eyes at best as meddling interference, and in the end as a new species of tyranny.

The power of the Board of Trade declined after Halifax retired in 1761. The Board was never an effective and not always a sympathetic colonial office, close though its contacts were with merchants and colonial agents. Whenever it proposed major expenditure, particularly for colonial defense, it met opposition from Parliament and the Treasury; it could in the last resort only advise and recommend, not enforce.

Nor did the creation, in 1768, of a third secretaryship of state, for American affairs, improve matters. The Earl of Hillsborough, despite his experience at the Board of Trade, was quite unsuited to the post, and his powers were never precisely defined. When the office had been first proposed, the Duke of Newcastle had spoken of a "Secretary for the Indies." Although by 1768 the office was concerned with the American colonies, it was not until Lord George Germain became its holder in 1775 that it would come to rank as equal to the two earlier secretaryships. What vigor there was under Hillsborough (1768–1772) and Lord Dartmouth (1772–1775) came from the office of its permanent secretary. This post was held by John Pownall as secretary of the Board of Trade (1748–1768) and then as undersecretary for the colonies (1768–1770); although his brother had been a governor of Massachusetts, Pownall knew of the colonies only at second hand, and he favored a policy of coercion. He was succeeded by William Knox, who served until the department was abolished in 1782. Knox had estates in Georgia as a rice planter; he had been an agent for Georgia in London (1762–1765), but he had lost his post because of his advocacy of the Stamp Act. He favored the creation of a colonial aristocracy and the inclusion in Parliament of representatives from the colonies. It was from Pownall and from Knox that the first drafts of bills came. The frequent changes of ministry and their fluctuating membership gave these permanent officials considerable influence.

Even after 1768, however, no one single agency in London held exclusive responsibility for the colonies. The Commission of Customs, the Secretary-at-War, the Admiralty and the Admiralty Courts, the Surveyor-General of the King's Woods, the Postmaster-General, the Bishop of London—all were involved. Much time was spent in consultation and discussion among them; still more was wasted in the physical effort of reaching the appropriate authority. The Admiralty alone had fifteen branches scattered in all parts of the town. Any rapid dispatch of business was almost impossible in London; it took a further five weeks at best to pass the results on to the colonies; a similar period followed in waiting for a reply. "Seas roll and months pass between the order and the execution," said Burke.[7]

The result of this was that the British government was parliamentary and—as it saw itself—free at home, but inefficient, bureaucratic and "royal" abroad. Indeed, at a time when separatist feeling in the colonies was very strong and the political structures and societies of the colonies varied, centralization was increasing, not decreasing, in London. More and more colonies were coming under the control of the crown—the fate Franklin sought for Pennsylvania. In 1752 colonial governors were reminded that they must abide by their instructions and that all colonial laws should be brought into conformity with royal instructions. It was all too possible for Americans, for whom the pattern of imperial government had not changed since 1660, to see themselves by the 1770s as protesting against a tyranny like that of Charles I. When, after 1763, Parliament increasingly associated itself with the king in colonial matters, it appeared in American eyes as remote and unrepresentative: not as the guardian, but as the enemy, of liberty. The Declaration of Independence was America's Grand Remonstrance. For by 1776 the enemy was seen less as bureaucratic inefficiency and indifference—under which the colonies had flourished—than as parliamentary interference. The imperialism was now parliamentary too.[8]

*   *   *

Before 1763 Parliament had played little part in colonial rule, either in theory or practice. There is hardly an Act of Parliament for the colonies before 1763 that is not a trade bill. At various times, however, the Board of Trade, in its efforts to establish a homogeneous system of administration, tried to extend the royal prerogative in the colonies, and itself brought forward measures to make the private proprietary colonies royal. Parliament was slow, and reluctant, to interfere with colonial charters or to tighten the system, but in 1729 it did authorize the transfer to the crown of the rights of the Carolina proprietors, and in the 1730s it appropriated considerable sums to help establish Georgia. For the rest, it confined itself mainly to trade regulation, and left the administration of the colonies to the executive. Parliament was of course more powerful in theory than in fact; the years from 1733 to 1763 were marked by debilitating factional politics, but there was no serious questioning of its ultimate legislative authority. The year of the Stamp Act, 1765, saw the publication of the first volume of Blackstone's *Commentaries on the Laws of England:* "There is and must be in every state a supreme, irresistible, absolute and uncontrolled authority, in which the *jura summa imperii,* or rights of sovereignty, reside; this supreme power is by the constitution of Great Britain vested in the King, Lords and Commons." [9]

Parliament's sensitiveness to its own rights was very evident in the attitude toward America of George Grenville, First Minister from 1763 to 1765. After the repeal of his own Stamp Act, Grenville consistently opposed all suggestions for a return to the old system of requisitions or for a revenue derived from quitrents, on the grounds that all such funds would be crown revenues, beyond the control of Parliament. British parliamentary imperialism was born in 1763. It took the form of legislative enactments—Grenville had "a rage for regulation and restriction," said Burke. Power over remote territories and increasingly alien peoples was now to be political as well as economic; trade could flourish by means of war; Oceania would now give law to the sea. [10]

A number of Members of Parliament had colonial experience as serving officers, especially naval commanders on the North Atlantic station, soldiers, or governors. The seven ex-governors of mainland or West Indian colonies and the two dozen with military or naval experience were almost all hard-liners, scornful of the colonists as soldiers. Ex-governor William Shirley of Massachusetts, Franklin's correspondent and commander-in-chief back in 1754, had favored Franklin's Albany Plan but even then thought it too permissive of colonial variety; he wanted a clear British imperium over all the colonies. Ex-governor Thomas Pownall, elected to the House of Commons in 1767 and becoming a supporter of Lord North, outlined in his *Administration of the Colonies* a plan for a grand marine dominion. And Francis Bernard, governor of Massachusetts from 1760 to

1769, reinforced the theme by urging on Barrington, the secretary-at-war, a general uniform system of government established by "the Supreme Imperial Legislature to which all members of the Empire, whether represented or not, are subject in all matters and things." And even in the worst crisis of all, in 1773–1774, the liberal Burke was still skeptical of colonial representation in the British House of Commons because "Opposuit natura—I cannot remove the eternal barriers of the creation." This parliamentary imperialism especially irritated Franklin. Not only were there no colonial M.P.'s, but his own role as an agent representing, by 1770, four colonies was unclear and his legitimacy repeatedly challenged. "My opinion has long been," he wrote to Cushing in 1771, "that Parliament had originally no right to bind us by any kind of law whatever, without our consent." [11]

This Parliament, however unrepresentative geographically of American—and of British—opinion, was by no means unrepresentative of the emerging economic forces in Britain. Lady Sarah Osborne wrote in 1768: "The landed interest is beat out, and merchants, nabobs, and those who have gathered riches from the East and West Indies stand the best chance of governing this country." John Gay, the author of *The Beggar's Opera,* could write:

> Now Commerce, wealthy goddess rears her head,
> And bids Britannia's fleets their canvas spread;
> Unnumbered ships the peopled ocean hide,
> And wealth returns with each revolving tide. [12]

Financing the defense of the extended Empire was not its most difficult, although it became in Parliament its most controversial, aspect. In 1763 Britain had emerged from the most expensive war in its history; despite unprecedented wartime taxation, the national debt stood at £133,000,000, an increase of £60,000,000 since 1755. What is often forgotten, however, is that the method of financing the colonial wars had long been a subject of debate: Robert Dinwiddie as lieutenant-governor of Virginia and Halifax as president of the Board of Trade had both urged a tax on the colonies. In the years 1754–1756 the Board had discussed this and other schemes. By 1763 the issue was urgent. The public debt, Lord North estimated, fell on the Englishman to the extent of eighteen pounds per person per year, but on the colonist only to the extent of eighteen shillings. The American paid an average sixpence per year in taxes; his counterpart in Britain paid twenty-five shillings. And the size of the national debt was in some degree Pitt's responsibility. In 1757 he had destroyed the extensive civilian powers conferred on Braddock and Loudoun, the commanders-in-chief from 1755 to 1757, and had substituted the old requisition system. He asked for men from the colonial governors; the colonial assemblies voted them and were then granted a reimbursement of part of, often most of, the cost by Parliament. That there were few difficulties in this system was not due to Pitt's planning or choice of commanders but to Britain's generosity: the five campaigns after 1757 cost Britain £866,666. The colonies offered high rates of pay and high bounties to recruits, and the specie on credit they received helped them in the process to wipe out their own debts. As Stanley Pargellis has shown, this reckless expenditure was unnecessary; the bulk of the fighting was done by regulars sent from Britain.

Parliamentary opinion was reinforced by the colonial dispatches, whether from governors or soldiers. There was in 1763 no respect for American fighting qualities. Amherst and Forbes, Loudoun and Gage, all with experience of the French and Indian Wars, were unanimous in their scorn for colonial troops. Frank sentiments were also being voiced against assemblies and freedom of debate. General Guy Carleton, serving as governor of Quebec, wrote in 1768: "A popular Assembly, which preserves it's full Vigor and in a Country where all Men appear nearly upon a Level, must give a strong bias to Republican Principles." By 1769 Parliament regarded Boston as a city where contention too rapidly became treason. What the colonists saw as a clash of sovereignties was not viewed sympathetically in London. Lord North condemned the Massachusetts constitution because of its dependence on "the democratic part." Germain went further: "I would not have men in mercantile cast every day collecting themselves together and debating on political matters." [13]

In his private opinions, Gage, who knew the local situation well, was clearly unsympathetic. He wrote to Barrington as early as January 1767: "The colonists are taking great strides towards Independency; it concerns Great Britain by a speedy and spirited Conduct to shew them that these provinces are British Colonies dependent on her, and that they are not independent states." Such sentiments abound in the dispatches of colonial governors. As early as 1768 Governor Bernard thought all government in Massachusetts "at an end" and the mob dominant. Demagogues in America were "determined to bring all real power into the hands of the people." The only hope was to increase the powers of the governor—and to institute a colonial nobility, "appointed by the King, for Life, and made independent." Recalled home and made a baronet, by 1773 Bernard was a close adviser of North. He had long pressed for the removal of the executive power in Massachusetts "from the democratic part of government." [14]

But even the more sympathetic ministers could be quoted to the same purpose. When the New York Assembly refused to enforce the Quartering Act of 1765—empowering the billeting of troops in inns and uninhabited houses—it was the liberal Earl of Shelburne, a supporter of Pitt, who pressed for the removal of the governor of New York, Sir Henry Moore, and his replacement by a man "of a Military Character" with authority "to act with Force or Gentleness as circumstances might make necessary." In the party negotiations of 1767–68, even the Old Whigs were ready to consider taking office on a policy of asserting or maintaining—they argued over the terminology—"the rights of Great Britain over her colonies." Both sides began to use words of similar high-sounding principle, words on which it was impossible to compromise. As late as 1770 Pitt, who had been translated to the upper house as the Earl of Chatham, declared that the Americans "must be subordinate. In all laws relating to trade and navigation, this is the mother country, they are children; they must obey and we prescribe." [15]

And the Boston Tea Party produced an almost unanimous chorus: "The popular current," wrote Burke, "both within doors and without, at present sets sharply against America." Dartmouth, in the summer of 1774, spoke for an almost united opinion when he wrote privately to Joseph Reed in Pennsylvania that "the supreme legislature of the whole British Empire has laid a duty (no matter for the present whether it has or has not the right to do so, it is sufficient that we conceive that it has) . . . The question then is whether the laws are to be submitted to? If the people of America say 'No,' they say in effect they will no longer be a part of the British Empire." [16]

If any doubts remained in London, they were dispelled by the election of 1774, in which North had an ample majority, giving him less need for caution in government, and in which the American question had played little part. Gage reported wearily that mobs were now hunting and harrying his councillors as earlier they had bedeviled stamp agents and customs officials. He wanted reinforcements, preferably mercenaries from Germany: "These provinces must be first totally subdued before they will obey." When the trusted lieutenant on the spot held such opinions, the time seemed to have come for firmness. It was in Britain, not America, that the die was cast; it was there that vacillation had in the end to give way to obstinacy.[17]

This third element in the pattern, the emergence of parliamentary imperialism, was the most dangerous of all. By 1763 a doctrine of explicit sovereignty was emerging; it was to feed hungrily on the events of the next decade. Stimulated by the recent war and by the evidence of colonial half-heartedness and dealings with the enemy, and reinforced by the views of the commanders on the spot, there now ran through the writings and reports of a number of officials a recurring emphasis: let the law be enforced.

*   *   *

There was also a belief, implicit in mercantilism, that the colonists should, as in the past, bear the main weight of their own defense. But that defense now involved the protection of a vastly extended Empire and could no longer be left to colonial militia or volunteers, supplemented by expeditions from Britain in every crisis. The new and little-known territories in Canada and Florida, moreover, had few white inhabitants, and those of doubtful loyalty. They could be controlled, or for that matter surveyed, only by garrisons of regular troops. There was a need for a permanent British army in the colonies.

The problem of strategy and defense in 1763 was composed of many strands: the protection of the Indians and the honoring of treaties with them; the importance of the fur trade; the disposal of land if and when it was bought from the Indians; the claims of colony against colony and of one land company against another; the siting of forts and garrisons; the relationship of the new territory to the older settlements, some of which had claims from sea to sea; and not least the character of the colonies' government. These issues continued to baffle Americans after 1783 as much as they baffled British officials in 1763. The defense of the frontier was the most intractable problem of all, and one concerning which Americans, then and later, were as hesitant, selfish, and culpable as British officials.

The great debate had been proceeding since Halifax took over the Board of Trade in 1748, and it went beyond both administration and finance, and beyond the question of sugar islands versus Canada. The acquisition of Canada and the trans-Allegheny country by Britain in 1763 posed for the first time the issue of native versus settler, a problem later British imperial administrators would meet repeatedly in southern and central Africa. The fur trade and frontier peace together demanded the protection of the Indians in their hunting grounds, extensive though they were. Inevitably this ran counter to the frontier expansion and land hunger of the settlers thrusting north, west, and south, with speculators not far behind them. The frontier represented America's own imperialism, an imperialism that did not cease in 1776. It was rough and ready in its methods, antinative in its essence, and scornful of the remote control of London. The liberty it sought in the West was liberty to take Indian lands.

In 1754, on the failure of the Albany Plan, the British government had put relations with the Indians under the direction of its American commander-in-chief, Braddock. It created two superintendencies divided by the Ohio, and appointed to the northern Sir William Johnson and to the southern first Edmund Atkin and, on his death in 1761, John Stuart. Johnson and Stuart were outstandingly able, but they could not maintain peace indefinitely: treaties were hard to enforce; frontiersmen were aggressive for land; each colony competed with its neighbors; traders were greedy for furs and generous with firewater and firearms; all parties were quick to anger—and to brutality. There was an ugly war with the Cherokees from 1759 to 1761.

Three months after the signing of the Treaty of 1763, and after the decision was taken to retain Canada and the Floridas, came the uprising of the northwestern Indians under Pontiac, the Ottawa chief. Although Henry Bouquet defeated the rebels, every western station except Detroit and Fort Pitt had been captured by them, and some two hundred settlers and traders had been killed. Only four colonies— New York, New Jersey, Connecticut, and Virginia—gave any aid against them. It was three years before there was real peace in the new territory between the Ohio and the Great Lakes, and it was achieved almost entirely by British regulars.

Before the Pontiac uprising, in October 1763, the Grenville ministry had issued a proclamation forbidding colonial governors to authorize surveys or to grant patents for any land beyond the "source of any of the rivers which fall into the Atlantic Ocean from the West or Northwest." The new West was closed to settlers and to speculators. It was to be an Indian reserve under military control, with free access for traders under careful regulations. And separate governments were established for Grenada, Quebec, and East and West Florida.

There was much to be said for this policy, revolutionary though it was. Until the Seven Years' War, land settlement had been encouraged. But bulwarks against the French were needed no longer, even if French incursions could not be entirely ignored. The fur trade was now safely in British hands, and land settlement would destroy its profits. The farther west the settlers moved, the harder they would be to control. The settlement of the West would draw labor from the East, and could only be done at the expense of the Tidewater. And unless defense was to be still more burdensome, the Indians must clearly be pacified. They had been promised security in their land titles by wartime treaties; they supplied furs; they were a potential market for manufactures. The line protecting them would divert white settlement, it was hoped, to Canada, Georgia, and Florida, and thus continue the development of the Tidewater areas. The line of demarcation was not immutably fixed. Limited settlement was to be permitted at the discretion of colonial governors, particularly in the bitterly contested reaches of the Upper Ohio, but the land was to be fairly bought. It was a worthy blueprint devised by worthy men, placid and passionless.

Yet it is easy to see how unpopular the Proclamation Line was in the colonies, especially to frontiersmen eager for land and security, to land speculators, and to colonial governments with western claims. It was never, of course, fully honored; no civil government was provided before 1776; the line was steadily pushed back by settlers and companies using methods more dubious than fair. Governors as well as planters and merchants combined to flout the law. What is not always fully appreciated is that while successive administrations did in the end accept the changing line of advance as a result of the pressures brought on them in London by agents and merchants, they were now being advised also by a new element, the military and the Indian superintendents, who came to form a new imperial bureaucracy on the frontier. It was well informed, simple-minded, practical; these were men on the spot, facing problems about which they could be neither placid nor passionless.

They were British regulars, or like Johnson, British-Indians, drawing their pay and their status from Britain; they were remote from the

Tidewater and not very amenable or sympathetic to it; some were Swiss *condottieri* like Bouquet and Haldimand, doing a job for pay and doing it well; they were suspicious of the land companies and their rascally agents—even if they themselves owned vast tracts of land. From sad experience they dismissed colonial fighting ability. They had only a little less contempt for many of the instructions they received from Whitehall. They were a military caste whose first and major task, as with all responsible soldiers, was to prevent war from breaking out. They represented a new pressure group, remote from London but directly in touch with the frontier.

The British government listened to men of experience now living in London, like Bernard, Pownall, and William Bollan, but after 1763 it listened more carefully to the soldiers on the spot. The colonists of course distrusted a peacetime standing army, fearing that it might be used whenever there was local trouble. The picture of the colonies furnished to London after 1763 by men like Bouquet and Johnson would have given the colonies still more reason for alarm. For to these men the peace of the frontier was too important to be left to civilians. Part of the responsibility for the British determination after 1774 to impose its will on the colonies rests with the dispatches received from Gage, who was commander-in-chief from 1763 to 1774 and whose pleas, like those of all commanders-in-chief, were for still more troops. If London grew quite adamant by 1774, this was not just the obstinacy of weakness but also the reflection of the judgment of Britain's own frontiersmen, its soldier-governors and Indian administrators.[18]

To these problems of the frontier was added the mounting British view that the colonies must make some contribution to the costs of their own defense. The benefits and cost of defense are hard to quantify. Before 1762, Britain had maintained a standing army in America of 3,000 men. After 1763 it was increased to 7,500, primarily to protect an unmapped frontier, from New Orleans via Kaskaskia and Vincennes to the Great Lakes, against Indian incursions. Its largest bases were in Jamaica, Mobile, and Halifax, Nova Scotia. At a minimum, the annual cost must have totaled around £200,000. The colonists minimized or ignored this sum; to them the underpaid "lobsterbacks" were a rival labor force, rowdy and unwelcome and, at least in rhetoric, an instrument of a tyrannical government.

While the Grenville ministry asked the colonial agents to suggest how a contribution to defense costs might be levied, and, none forth-coming, proposed in the end a stamp tax, all ministries could agree on other measures. Smuggling must be curbed, and in the years of Britain's wars with France, illicit trade with the French West Indies was also treason.

It was views such as these, far more than any wish of George III "to be a King" or the corruption of the British electoral system, so much deplored by Franklin, that was the "cause" of British intransi-gence. It was this monopolist, home-centered, class-oriented, and re-stricted Empire to which, as early as 1757, Franklin had begun to feel alien. And behind it now was pride, success in arms, and a realization of power. By 1770, references to John Bull recur in Franklin's writing. So too does the statement "Every lady of Genoa is not a Queen of Corsica," a reference to Genoa's declining control of the island over which it had exercised suzerainty for four hundred years, and to Cor-sica's war of resistance against Genoa and France. There was a par-allel here: in 1763 a foreign conqueror had similarly been excised from part of North America. "Every Englishman," Franklin said, "considers himself a King of America, and peculiarly interested in our subjection; it gratifies his pride . . . We have no other resources but in our own virtue and resolution . . ." There was, he told Lord Kames, too much talk of "the sovereignty of Parliament and the sovereignty of this nation over the colonies, a kind of sovereignty the idea of which is not so clear, nor does it clearly appear on what foundation it is established." [19]

And there was in North America after 1763 an unmistakable sense of freedom, release, and bravado. Free now from the French threat on their frontiers, the Americans could be proud and boastful too. The demographic explosion continued, unworried by frontier wars; the Great Awakening further stimulated a democratic challenge in state as well as church. The policies of London would have to be more sympathetic and ingratiating if they were to hold colonial allegiance.

This was a far larger and more daunting problem than any Frank-lin had faced in Philadelphia. But he brought to it not only his in-telligence, his experience, and his faith in "the empire on this side" but also his belief that problems were for solving—given mutual goodwill.

Every Abridgement of the Power of the Mother Country, where that Power was not prejudicial to the Liberties of the Colonists, and every Diminution of the Privileges of the Colonists, where they were not prejudicial to the Welfare of the Mother Country, I, in my own Mind, condemned as improper, partial, unjust and mischievous; tending to create Dissensions, and weaken that Union, on which the Strength, Solidity, and Duration of the Empire greatly depended . . . Hence it has often happened to me, that while I have been thought here [in England] too much of an American, I have in America been deem'd too much of an Englishman.[20]

Franklin was increasingly the man in the middle. For there was now emerging in the colonies a matching firmness and pride in their own constitutional system, in their own promise, and in their own abnormal growth. William Knox saw it as early as 1768. He recounted that when the colonial agents "were sent for lately by Lord Hillsborough, and acquainted that if they would waive the point of right, and petition for a repeal of the duties as burdensome and grievous, Administration were disposed to come into it. The agents, however, declared they could not leave out the point of right, consistent with their present instructions, but should inform their respective colonies, and so it rests." In 1769 Dennys De Berdt remarked that "when ever these Acts are repealed, the question of right must be kept out of sight . . . . and the repeal must be on the foot of inexpediency."[21]

The solution, if it was to be found, lay with the men of expedients, not those of high principle—with Burke, with De Berdt, and with the Franklin of an earlier day. But by 1774 Franklin too would be driven to beliefs in "rights" and in "justice," and to the language of "self-evident truth." That way lay conflict.

*   *   *

Was there already emerging from Franklin an alternative view of empire? His political philosophy, evolving steadily since 1751, similarly had a number of component threads: demographic, agrarian, economic, constitutional, and even racial. But at its core was Franklin's incapacity, as a Bostonian Philadelphian living in London, with close friendships with Scots, Welsh, and Irish, to make the Londoner's distinction between England and America. He insisted that America was a part of England, or at least as much part of it as Scotland was; and at least until 1768 he was as ready to settle permanently in London as he had been to move to and settle in Philadelphia.

He maintained, as in the Canada pamphlet, that the blood spent in the West during the war was not spent for the colonies alone but for the whole nation. The Indian trade, he held, was a British interest; the French and Indian War was fought to defend territories of the crown, and to defend a trade that was purely British; it was therefore really a British war. He could make no distinction; he was an Anglo-American. Britain's military and diplomatic strength lay, he believed, in its connection with America, and on it depended the European balance of power. The kingdom, similarly declared Richard Henry Lee at the first Continental Congress, could not exist without the commercial connection with America. The belief that America was the key factor in Europe's prosperity would lie at the heart of Franklin's later role in France.

Franklin's major writing of 1767, which he signed "Benevolus," was the article "On the Propriety of Taxing America." In it he rebutted at length eight major propositions, and in rebutting them made the converse clear.

1. *That the colonies were settled at the expense of parliament.* If we examine our records, the journals of parliament, we shall not find that a farthing was ever granted for the settling of any colonies before the last reign, and then only for Georgia and Nova Scotia . . .

2. *That they received their constitutions from parliament, which could not be supposed to give away its own power of taxing them.* The charters themselves show that they were granted by the King . . . parliament had no participation in these grants, and was not so much as consulted upon them . . .

3. *That they have been constantly protected from the Indians at the expense of Parliament.* No grants for that purpose appear on our records, and the fact is, that they protected themselves, at their own expense, for near 150 years after the first settlement, and never thought of applying to parliament for any aid against the Indians . . .

4. *That the two last wars were entered into for their protection.* The truth is, that the war with Spain, 1739, was occasioned by the Spaniards interrupting with their guarda costas the British trade, carried on indeed in the American seas, but in British ships chiefly, and wholly with British manufactures . . .

5. *That the colonies refused to contribute their share towards the expense of those wars.* The fact is, that in the first war, upon requisitions from the crown, the colonies sent between 3 and 4000 men to join our army in the siege of Carthagena; and in the last war they raised and paid 25,000 men, a number equal to those sent from Britain; which was far beyond their proportion . . .

6. *That the colonies are great gainers by the event of the last war.* There is

to be sure a great extent of country conquered. It was however ceded not to the colonies, but to the crown, which is now granting it away in large tracts to British gentlemen . . .

7. *That the colonies pay no taxes.* There cannot be a greater mistake than this. They have their own civil and military establishments to support, and the public debt . . . to discharge, for which heavy taxes are and must be levied among themselves . . .

8. *That the colonies contend the parliament of Britain has no authority over them.* The truth is, that all acts of the British legislature, expressly extending to the colonies, have ever been received there as laws, and executed in their courts, the right of parliament to make them being never yet contested, acts to raise money upon the colonies by internal taxes only and alone excepted. In granting their money to the crown, they think their assent is constitutionally necessary . . . and they think it hard that a parliament in which they have no representative, should make a merit to itself by granting *their money* to the crown without asking their consent, and deprive them of the privilege of granting it themselves, which they have always enjoyed, never abused, and are always ready and willing to exercise on behalf of the crown when occasion shall require, and the usual requisitions are made to their assemblies. This is the *sole point* that has been in dispute.[22]

Inevitably, Franklin spent much of his time in London—as agent, in the end, for four colonies, as correspondent, and always as journalist—in penning such pieces of rebuttal. These protests had begun as early as 1750; but even then he moved to a positive and colonial counter-assertion, which was the basis for a contrary statecraft. A careful reading of his letters, of Benevolus, and of the evidence he gave before the House of Commons in 1766, suggests that what became explicit by 1774 was implicit as early as 1766, and that it had four component strands.

The first strand of his counterimperialism was demographic. His attitude was rooted in the view he had first voiced in the *Observations* of 1751: that the rapid increase of the American population would not lead to a development of manufacturing or to a quest for independence; instead, the Americans would remain a nation of farmers and would provide even larger markets for British manufactures. He drew a picture of a transatlantic empire living in happy relationship to the mother country. "The foundations of the future grandeur and stability of the British Empire lie in America," he wrote to Lord Kames in January 1760. "I am, therefore, by no means for restoring Canada. If we keep it, all the country from the St. Lawrence to the Mississippi will in another century be filled with British people. Britain itself will become vastly more populous, by the immense increase of its commerce; the Atlantic sea will be covered with your trading ships; and your naval power, thence continually increasing, will extend your influence round the whole globe, and awe the world!"[23]

He admired George III, and in 1763 he thought the Treaty of Paris a glorious peace. In the same year Shelburne recommended setting aside land for a projected colonial settlement in the upper Ohio valley; the empire Franklin was proud to serve was to be an expanding one. And at this point it was still in essence mercantilist. It would, he hoped, plant new colonies in the West, and they would need officials; it would help with bounties and tariffs against foreign competition. But, although accepting such trade restrictions as a fact of the economic world, he did not like them, any more than he liked trade monopolies, or the regulation of prices, wages, or the quality of goods.[24]

In 1751, when Franklin composed the *Observations*, he was as ardent an expansionist and as intense an imperialist as Pitt himself. His imagination was fired, as was Pitt's, by the limitless prospect of power and grandeur that opened before the British Empire in those years. In the next decade he threw most of his energy into the work of consolidating what he called the Empire "on this side." In Pennsylvania he stirred the provincials to measures of defense; in Albany he took the lead in devising a scheme of intercolonial federation; in London he argued vigorously for westward expansion. He put it thus to Lord Kames in 1767:

I have lived so great a part of my life in Britain, and have formed so many friendships in it, that I love it, and sincerely wish it prosperity; and therefore wish to see that Union, on which alone I think it can be secured and established. As to America, the advantages of such a union to her are not so apparent. She may suffer for a while in a separation from it; but these are temporary evils that she will outgrow ... America, an immense territory, favoured by Nature with all advantages of climate, soil, great navigable rivers, and lakes etc., must become a great country, populous and mighty; and will, in a less time than is generally conceived, be able to shake off any shackles that may be imposed on her, and perhaps place them on the imposers. In the mean time, every act of oppression will sour their tempers, lessen greatly, if not annihilate, the profits of your commerce with them, and hasten their final revolt; for the seeds of liberty are universally found there, and nothing can eradicate them. And yet, there remains among that people so much respect, veneration and affection for Britain, that if cultivated prudently, with kind usage, and tenderness for their privileges, they might be easily governed still for ages, without force, or any considerable expense. But I do not see here a sufficient quantity of the wisdom that is necessary to produce such a conduct, and I lament the want of it.[25]

He had immense confidence in the future of an America looking to the West. He believed that it would grow and flourish, inside or outside the connection with Britain—just as Washington, much less reflective but with some knowledge too of the West, believed that America could never be conquered by a British army supplied from the ocean and dependent on its fragile grip on the coast. He had given his allegiance to an Empire of Anglo-American culture. His London years, too, had confirmed his strong bent toward territorial imperialism. They were the years when Pitt's leadership offered prospects of continuing expansion and optimism. He was, however, already drawing strikingly different conclusions from those of Pitt.

Franklin was a westerner, and in a minority indeed. His first emergence on the wider stage in the late 1740s had coincided with the tensions in the West. And yet however stormy the western prospect became in the 1750s, Franklin always saw it as golden. He was interested in it as an inquiring natural philosopher; he published the maps of Lewis Evans. He joined forces with the group of British officials and farsighted provincials who began to agitate for a more vigorous and unified western policy. Like the Virginia planters and his Philadelphia business acquaintances, he realized that the West held rich possibilities of profit through land speculation. Soon after the Albany Congress of 1754 he elaborated the commissioners' proposals for western settlements in his *Plan for Settling Two Western Colonies,* a plan he never abandoned through the next two tortured decades.

The same logic led him to stress the need for the retention of Canada and the West. Population in the continental colonies doubled at least every twenty-five years; with a rising standard of living, colonial consumption of British goods increased at an even faster pace. By contrast, imports to the West Indies, where population was static, had "long been at a stand." To say this was to ignore the major merit of the sugar colonies in mercantilist eyes: that their exports to Britain greatly exceeded those of the continental colonies. His stress upon colonies as markets for British manufacturers, while never totally ignored by the mercantilists, was not for them central; as far as they were concerned the colonies were still chiefly valuable as sources of raw materials. Franklin's roots, however, were American, not British, and his eyes were on the future, not the past.

A second strand in Franklin's thinking was his faith in agriculture. He always thought it not only the most independent employment but in some respects the noblest: land gave security and freedom. He had planned in 1748, on selling his printing house, to retire to Burlington, where he bought three hundred acres. He hoped, when the break with Britain came, that his son would give up his governorship and "settle in your farm. 'Tis an honester and more honourable, because a more independent, Employment." Only such personal independence allowed a man to be truly free, or, as his century put it, to be "virtuous." To Mrs. Catharine Greene in Rhode Island he wrote in the last year of his life, now in a philosophic rather than an avuncular vein: "I think agriculture the most honourable of all employments, being the most independent. The farmer has no need of popular favour, nor the favour of the great; the success of his crops depending only on the blessing of God upon his honest industry."[26]

These Jeffersonian sentiments expressed by such a citydweller ought not to be surprising. Agriculture was the major occupation of the American colonies, and Franklin identified himself from the beginning of his political career with the group in Pennsylvania who were clearly the agrarians. His views were reinforced when he visited France in 1767 and met the Physiocrats. He shared their theory that agriculture was the major source of wealth, and their opposition to trade regulation. As early as 1747 he argued for free trade among the colonies; as early as 1754 he was questioning the Acts of Trade. In his eyes the conditions in the colonies were a striking confirmation of the truth of the Physiocrats' doctrines, and he believed that the American opposition to English commercial restrictions and tax policy was based upon their own economic principles. He considered the soil the only true source of national wealth, and the encouragement of agricultural production the key to prosperity.

There seem to be but three ways for a nation to acquire wealth. The first is by *war,* as the Romans did, in plundering their conquered neighbors. This is *robbery.* The second by *commerce,* which is generally *cheating.* The third by *agriculture,* the only *honest way,* wherein man receives a real increase of the seed thrown into the ground, in a kind of continual miracle, wrought by the hand of God in his favour, as a reward for his innocent life and his virtuous industry.

In all his urbanism, he was also—as were all Americans—a believer in an agrarian system and an agrarian social order.[27]

This agrarianism was at the center, thirdly, of his economics—and also put him in the paper-money camp from the beginning. Schemes for supplying a more abundant currency by provincial issues of paper had long had the support of debtor farmers, small tradesmen, and the lesser merchants engaged in local commerce. In 1729 he had written and printed *A Modest Enquiry into the Nature and Necessity of a Paper-Currency.* His argument in favor of a sufficient currency, based on land security, to stimulate trade, immigration, and agricultural expansion, ran counter to British mercantilist doctrine and to the plans not only of the British government but of colonial merchant capitalists. As he later recounted, his *Enquiry* "was well received by the common people in general; but the rich men dislik'd it, for it increas'd and strengthen'd the clamour for more money, and they happening to have no writers among them that were able to answer it, their opposition slacken'd, and the point was carried."[28] Franklin profited personally; he received the contract to print the money, and he was launched upon his political career. As he prospered, he modified his views. His worries over inflation in Pennsylvania, in 1762 and again during the Revolution, led him to a more businesslike caution in securing the state and continental notes; he always retained, however, his original agrarian bias on the money question.

His agrarianism was linked with his demographic analysis. He saw it as folly born of ignorance for London to seek to convert the rapidly multiplying community of husbandmen and consumers of British manufactures into manufacturers of their own necessities. Despite his encouragement after 1765 of the colonial tactic of nonimportation, and of American manufacturing as an economic tactic in the struggle with Britain, he remained unconvinced of the social desirability of industrialization. In 1773 his study of the mortality tables for industrial towns in the north of England gave him grim proof of the "Unwholesomeness of Manufacturing Life" as countries became industrialized. "Farmers who manufacture in their own Families what they have occasion for and no more," he wrote, "are perhaps the happiest people and the healthiest." Despite his later image as the voice of incipient capitalism, Franklin was as loyal as was Jefferson to the dream of an agrarian utopia in America. And he saw that, in crises, the American farmers had great resources in their own industry.[29]

He had thus something of the agrarian's distaste for what it is now fashionable to call "the control of the money supply." Neither in Philadelphia nor, thirty years later, in Passy did he like the mother country's grim and largely unsuccessful efforts to check colonial paper currency passing as legal tender. To Samuel Cooper he wrote from France in 1779:

The Effect of Paper Currency is not understood on this Side the Water. And indeed the whole is a Mystery even to the Politicians, how we have been able to continue a War four years without Money, and how we could pay with Paper that had no previously fix'd Fund appropriated specifically to redeem it. This Currency, as we manage it, is a wonderful Machine. It performs its Office when we issue it; it pays and clothes Troops, and provides Victuals and Ammunition; and when we are obliged to issue a Quantity excessive, it pays itself off by Depreciation.[30]

The third strand in Franklin's imperial vision was his advocacy of colonial union. In all his career—as in his work for the post office, and in the Albany Plan—this is a recurring faith. Not that he had any illusions about the ease of accomplishing it: the colonies were jealous of each other, and if entirely independent they would soon be at war with one another. Only the authority of the king, Franklin believed, would prevent open outbreaks. He thought at first that such union could be achieved by reason, by men of goodwill talking together. By 1754, however, after the failure at Albany, he doubted whether union could be achieved without an Act of Parliament. And clearly it was easier for the Board of Trade to deal directly with each colony than with a colonial union.

The fourth strand in his view of the North Atlantic empire was Franklin's mounting distaste for mercantilism and state control, and his turning toward free trade. He moved steadily from criticism of British restraints on American industry to his proposals in 1754 for the total revision of the Navigation System. By 1760 Hume's "Jealousy of Commerce" had reinforced him in the view that trade between nations was mutually advantageous, rather than a form of economic warfare in which one nation always profited at another's expense. He hoped, he told Hume, that the Essay would "abate the jealousy . . . of the commerce of the colonies" and promote "the interest of humanity or common good of mankind." By 1774 he contributed to the second edition of George Whatley's *Laws and Policy of England relating to Trade* notes that anticipated the views of Adam Smith, whose friend he was. He expanded what he had written a decade earlier: "Perhaps, in general, it would be better if Government medled no farther with Trade, than to protect it, and let it take its Cours . . . No nation was ever ruin'd by Trade, even seemingly the most disadvantageous."[31]

None of these assumptions could easily be reconciled with British mercantilism, with its view of the world as having limited resources for which all mercantilist empires must compete. Franklin knew from his own experience and from his study of population statistics that resources were not limited or static and that in the New World there was vast undeveloped country in the West. He recognized that in a new country there was a place for some stimulus to and protection for home industry, and in any case he disliked what he called "foreign Gegaws," so he did not entirely oppose import restrictions. But with growth of population, direct taxes would replace the dependence for revenue on imports at the ports. The growth and the expansion would absorb both home and foreign products, so that a beneficial and modest government stimulus could march easily with free trade at the ports. His dream was of a developing international system of almost-free trade, each country fostering its own specialties and flourishing by their exchange.[32]

Given these elements of his thought—demographic growth, agrarian foundations, colonial union, and a preference for free trade—it was inevitable that Franklin should in the end evolve an attitude to government different from that prevailing in Whitehall. His doctrine was clear. His Empire was closer to a commonwealth of equal members than to a mother country with subservient dependencies. The Americans wished, he believed, "for nothing more than a permanent union with Britain, upon the condition of equal liberty." He sought for each part of the Empire an equal dispensation of protection, rights, and privileges. In the discussions at and after the Albany Conference, he had been greatly taken with the proposal of Governor

Shirley of Massachusetts of some form of colonial representation in Parliament. He wrote to Shirley that such a union would be very acceptable to the colonies, provided that they had a

reasonable number of representatives allowed them; and that all the old acts of Parliament restraining the trade or cramping the manufactures of the colonies be at the same time repealed, and the British subjects *on this side the water* put, in those respects, on the same footing with those in Great Britain, till the new Parliament, representing the whole, shall think it for the interest of the whole to reenact some or all of them . . . A Parliament, in which they are fairly represented, would be vastly more agreeable to the people, than the method lately attempted to be introduced by royal instructions, as well as more agreeable to the nature of an English constitution, and to English liberty.[33]

Franklin hoped at this point for a "consolidating Union" or imperial federation, with "a fair and equal representation of all parts of this empire." This was more than reform of Parliament or limitation of its powers; he was already envisaging a true imperial legislature. He spoke of it at times as "A Bill of Rights," at other times as "A great Constitutional Charter." The claim was for civil, not natural, rights—he was no revolutionary.[34]

The Stamp Act Congress swept his plea aside, however, and Franklin, always the realist, abandoned it. The repeal of the Stamp Act gave, in any event, a false optimism, the belief for a time that a strong enough protest would persuade Parliament. But he never accepted the idea of parliamentary supremacy that, for instance, Dickinson expressed in his *Farmer's Letters*. In any case colonial representation in Parliament was then impracticable; a voyage usually took four to six weeks and was fraught with risks. Franklin was moving steadily toward the advocacy of what a century later would be called "dominion status." "The sovereignty of the Crown I understand. The sovereignty of the British Legislature out of Britain I do not understand." "Parliament has power only within the realm." In assessing his own evolution, after the confrontation in the Cockpit in 1774, he said that at the time of the Stamp Act he became convinced that "the bond of union was not in Parliament but the King." The colonies, he told William in 1768, were "so many separate states, only subject to the same King, as England and Scotland were before the Union." And he wrote in his "Causes of the American Discontents":

But a new kind of loyalty seems to be required of us, a loyalty to P[arliamen]t; a loyalty that is to extend, it is said, to a surrender of all our properties, whenever a H[ouse] of C[ommons], (in which there is not a single member of our choosing) shall think fit to grant them away without our consent; and to a patient suffering the loss of our privileges as Englishmen, if we cannot submit to make such surrender. We were separated too far from Britain by the ocean, but we were united to it by respect and love, so that we could at any time freely have spent our lives and little fortunes in its cause: But this unhappy new system of politics tends to dissolve those bands of union and to sever us for ever.[35]

There was here an imperialism of its own, land-based and expansionist, even if not yet looking to expand across salt water. It was agrarian and utopian, liberal and nongovernmental, but English, not polyglot, in character. The faith was in people, not bureaucrats, and in the free farmer. Although always himself an urban figure, he shared the physiocratic assumptions of Jefferson. He was still an Old England man and rising remarkably through an open Atlantic society. But the faith was transatlantic, and nonelitist, and had a viability of its own if the winds came to blow.

8

ONE COMMUNITY
WITH ONE INTEREST

*F*ranklin's congenial surroundings in London, in a familiar street near his friends in the coffeehouses and in the Royal Society, were equally convenient for visits, even strolls, to Whitehall and Westminster. There he had to persuade those who were members of the Privy Council or had access to it to support his plans for a royal takeover of the colony whose Assembly he represented. By 1764 the king's First Minister was George Grenville, Pitt's brother-in-law but totally different in character and style, the least pliable of men. First and last the accountant, Grenville had been busy for a year exploring devices for raising a colonial revenue to defray the cost of the defense of the territories won from France in 1763.

The major imperial problem, revenue raising, promptly overshadowed the lesser, the petition against the proprietors. The latter was delicate indeed: not only was Franklin personally vulnerable, his fellow agent Richard Jackson, himself an M.P., counseled caution; Jackson thought that the days of proprietary colonies were numbered anyway, and that patience would be the wiser course. There was a ten-month delay until, in November 1765, the Privy Council ruled that the king had no power to interfere between proprietor and people. The petition was formally "postponed for the present," but all concerned knew that this meant "for ever and ever."[1]

In 1763 the Treaty of Paris gave Britain a vast new dominion, not only of Quebec and the Maritimes, but across the Alleghenies, the "land of the western waters." It would need to be explored, mapped, and eventually settled. It would need defending against France, should that power return, and against the Indians. A permanent establishment of some ten thousand men was contemplated. Defense on such a scale would have to be paid for. Jackson warned Franklin that Parliament would "infallibly" seek to raise £200,000 annually in the colonies. The device being mooted was a Stamp Act—unless the colonies could produce an alternative proposal within the year. A contribution toward their own defense was, it was held, eminently justified, and even a stamp tax would bring in less than a quarter of the cost. To the colonists, however, the stricter enforcement of customs regulations now being planned, and the policy of currency deflation, already hurting, were part of the cost and could threaten the colonial economy.

Despite the warnings of the troubles ahead—proposals of this sort had been discussed and speculated upon for over a year—Franklin was curiously blind to their character and their extent. In January 1764 he had written to Richard Jackson, "I am not much alarm'd about your Schemes of raising Money on us. You will take care for your own sakes not to lay greater Burthens on us than we can bear; for you cannot hurt us without hurting your selves." It was, as we have seen, the proprietary party leaders and William Allen who spoke out in Pennsylvania in opposition to parliamentary policy. Franklin found himself with curious allies, governors or ex-governors like Bernard and Thomas Pownall. His claim that by being pliant he had secured the abandonment of the proposal in the Mutiny Act to quarter troops on private houses won little attention and less praise. Franklin's initial comments were the shrewd and rather cynical views of the adroit politico. "The cat can yield but her skin," he had put it to Collinson in April 1764.[2]

In June 1764, when Franklin read the terms of the Stamp Act, he still stood by his view. He wrote to Jackson: "Experience only will inform us clearly, how short it will fall of procuring on one hand the Good, and producing on the other hand the Evil, that People engag'd in different Interests expect from it. If it is not finally found to hurt us, we shall grow contented with it; and as it will, if it hurts us, hurt you also, you will feel the hurt and remedy it." He abandoned the simplicity of his earlier position of 1754—that there could be no taxation without consent—and took to equivocation. Although he never accepted Jackson's view that Parliament had a right to impose any kind of law it chose but should as an act of discretion refrain from imposing internal taxes, he did accept Jackson's distinction between

taxes for trade regulation (external) and taxes designed to raise revenue (internal). This distinction, drawn also by Daniel Dulany of
Maryland in his *Considerations on the Propriety of Imposing Taxes
in the British Colonies . . . by Act of Parliament* (1765), then and
subsequently has thrown an obscuring veil over the debate on the
Stamp Act and other Grenville measures. As Edmund and Helen
Morgan have shown, this distinction was not in fact generally drawn
in the colonies. But by accepting it, and by using it to help obtain the
repeal of the Stamp Act in 1766, Franklin gave British parliamentar-
ians a false view of the character of American opposition to British
legislation. His own views were clear as early as June 1764 in his
letter to Jackson:

I note what you say of the Colonies applying for a Stamp Act. In my opinion
there is not only no Likelihood that they will generally agree in such an
Application, but even that any one Colony will propose it to the others. Tho'
if a gross Sum were generally requir'd of all the Colonies, and they were left
to settle the Mode of raising it at some general Congress, I think it not unlikely that instead of settling Quotas, they would fall on some such general
Tax, as a Stamp Act, or an Excise on Rum, &c. or both; because Quota's
would be difficult to settle at first with Equality, and would, if they could be
made equal at first, soon become unequal, and never would be satisfactory;
whereas these kind of Taxes would nearly find their own Proportions.[3]

Franklin himself, like Hutchinson, opposed the Stamp Act, and had
alternative proposals to offer in his preliminary discussions with
Grenville and with Thomas Whately of the Treasury. He would, like
Hutchinson's rival James Otis, have preferred colonial representation
in Parliament, as he told Cadwalader Evans in May 1766: "My private Opinion concerning a union in Parliament between the two
Countries is, that it would be best, for the Whole. But I think it will
never be done . . . The Parliament here do at present think too highly
of themselves to admit Representatives from us, if we should ask it;
and, when they will be desirous of granting it, we shall think too
highly of ourselves to accept of it." He came gradually to modify this
farsighted view. In 1754 he had favored representation on condition
that the colonies were allowed "a reasonable number" of members
and "that all the old Acts of Parliament restraining the trade or
cramping the manufacturers of the Colonies were at the same time
repealed." The second condition was politically quite unrealistic, as
he must have known. Gradually he discarded the idea of colonial rep-

resentation, though he never completely rejected it prior to the final break with the mother country. Some of his statements that seem on the surface to favor representation may be construed, not as advocacy of it, but rather as arguments against legislation for the colonies by a body in which they were unrepresented. In any event the Stamp Act Congress of 1765 rejected this proposition: "The people of these colonies are not, and from their local circumstances cannot be, represented in the House of Commons in Great Britain."[4]

As an alternative to the stamp tax Franklin preferred a return to the "usual constitutional way" of requisitions from the king and responsive votes from the Assembly. Grenville—or Whately for him— retorted that this had not worked in the past, since assemblies had not agreed on, or been prompt to raise, the required sums. Franklin suggested, again, that the power to tax might be conferred on some form of colonial union. In particular, he put up to Grenville the proposal that Parliament should establish a general loan office in America and devote the interest from it to the purpose of defense. Both minister and Parliament, however, were firmly against allowing paper money to circulate as legal tender. Assured that Parliament had a right to tax the colonists, and equally assured that the stamp duties would be acceptable, Grenville was probably determined upon the Stamp Act scheme from the first, although he offered to consider all alternatives.

On February 27, 1765, the Stamp Act was approved by the Commons with little dissent—"nothing of note in Parliament, but one slight day on the American taxes," wrote Horace Walpole—and by the Lords on March 8, without a division; it became law on March 22 and went into force on November 1.[5] Legal documents and commercial papers, almanacs and newspapers, dice and cards, had to bear the imprint of a stamp, and the paper or parchment was to be sold by officially appointed distributors. The stamp for a college degree was to cost two pounds; for a bill of lading, fourpence; for an appointment to an office worth twenty pounds a year, ten shillings; for an office worth more than twenty pounds a year, four pounds; for a liquor license, four pounds; for a pack of cards, one shilling; for a pair of dice, ten shillings; for a newspaper on a half sheet of paper, one halfpenny; on a whole sheet, one penny; for a pamphlet, one shilling; for an advertisement, two shillings; for an almanac, twopence; for a grant from a governor, six pounds. And so on, through fifty-five articles. Even so, it would not meet more than one-fifth of the estimated burden of the force: it would provide some £60,000 toward the military budget of £300,000 for the twelve regiments projected.

An internal tax it was, and now the law of the land. For Franklin reason was always superior to principle; he had opposed the plan and lost; if you cannot beat them, join them, as Poor Richard might well have said. Between February and June there are very few references to the Stamp Act in Franklin's correspondence, and no awareness of the gathering storms on the other side of the Atlantic. Realizing that to counter the British assertion of the right to tax—on which even the Rockinghams insisted—with assertions of an American right to be taxed only with consent would only increase tension, he advised his friends to make the best of it. He wrote to Charles Thomson in July 1765: "We might as well have hinder'd the Sun's setting . . . But since 'tis down . . . let us make as good a Night of it as we can. We may still light candles. Frugallity and Industry will go a great way toward indemnifying us. Idleness and Pride tax with a heavier Hand than Kings and Parliaments; if we can get rid of the former, we can easily bear the Latter." And from Thomson came the rejoinder:

I much fear instead of the candles you mention being lighted, you will hear of the works of darkness . . . Our Liberties and most essential privileges are struck at: Arbitrary courts are set over us, and trials by juries taken away: The Press is so restricted that we cannot complain: An army of mercenaries threatened to be billeted on us: The sources of our trade stopped; and, to compleat our ruin, the little property we had acquired, taken from us, without even allowing us the merit of giving it; I really dread the consequence. The parliament insist on a power over all the liberties and privileges claimed by the colonies, and hence require a blind obedience and acqiescence in whatever they do: Should the behaviour of the colonies happen not to square with these sovereign notions, (as I much fear it will not) what remains but by violence to compel them to obedience. Violence will beget resentment, and provoke to acts never dreamt of: But I will not anticipate evil; I pray God avert it.[6]

Despite this vehemence from the shrewd Irish-American, when Franklin was asked by Whately to recommend "discreet and repu-table" Americans for the post of stamp distributor, he suggested his friends John Hughes for Pennsylvania, William Coxe for New Jersey, and Zachariah Hood for Maryland, all of whom were offered the posts; he advised Jared Ingersoll, agent for Connecticut, to accept the Connecticut post himself. He even sent over some extra supplies of paper (pointlessly, since newspaper would require special prestamped paper) and some stamped legal blanks to David Hall to be sold in his shop. In 1765 he seemed to see no clear line between profit, patronage, and patriotism. In any case, why quarrel with a fait accompli? Even when the storm broke, he urged Hughes (in August 1765) to stay loyal to the government: "A firm loyalty to the Crown and faithful adherence to the Government of this nation, which is the safety as well as the honour of the Colonies to be connected with, will always be the wisest course for you and I to take, whatever may be the madness of the populace or their blind leaders, who can only bring themselves and country into trouble, and draw on greater burdens by acts of rebellious tendency."[7]

*   *   *

On this occasion, as earlier in Philadelphia in 1763, Franklin misread the political horoscope, and he misread it on a number of fronts. He opposed but did not fight the Stamp Act; his zeal against the Penns brought him strange bedfellows and, however falsely, a "royal" reputation; he missed the deeper implications of Parliamentary taxation. It is impossible not to conclude that the astigmatism was in large measure due, like the gout, to good living and self-indulgence; it was due also to the blinkers he wore after his fight in Philadelphia. He was still the political operator, not yet aware that there was a role of patriot to play.

It is difficult to see in the pliable and patient *apparatchik* of 1764–65 the outline of the future patriot. Franklin was no ideologue, no campaigner for causes, no revolutionary; he lived for the political game, the game of adjustment and mediation. His friends were conservatives, several of them officials soon beset by Stamp Act mobs. His temper was pacific and compromising; he hated disorder and mob violence, by Paxton Boys, by followers of the stormy John Wilkes in London, or later by Sons of Liberty. And he distrusted legalisms. In 1762 he had returned from England an enthusiast for empire and still, uncritically, an Anglophile. Like most Americans, he admired the young king, George III; more vividly than most he had conceived the ideal of an expanding Anglo-American empire of power and culture. He also believed that if the new measures injured

America they would be seen to injure Englishmen also and would be repealed. He was slow to grasp the historic significance of the Grenville program, despite the warning shots fired by Richard Jackson and by Thomson. He did not want to be diverted from his goal of a royal colony. He did not detect yet the rumblings of the earthquake.

The consequences were soon to become clear. A spontaneous movement of opposition to the Stamp Act sprang up in colony after colony. As Thomas Hutchinson—whom Franklin's sister, Jane Mecom, thought "the Gratest ornement of our Country, and the most Indefateguable Patrioat"—wrote to Franklin, it was not safe "to advance anything contrary to any popular opinions whatsoever." Too many influential groups—lawyers, merchants, printers—were hurt by the Stamp Act, too many interests were threatened (by, for instance, the power of Vice-Admiralty courts), and too much fear existed of further taxation for the measure to be acceptable. In the Virginia House of Burgesses Patrick Henry brought in resolutions condemning the Stamp Act and claiming that Virginians could be taxed only by their own Assembly. Franklin had expected that the circulation of the *Gazette* would drop by a tenth, but that it would "gradually recover again." David Hall told him that, on the contrary, the number of newspapers "decreases prodigiously." Hall warned him of the scale and savagery of the protests: "There seems to be a general Discontent all over the Continent, with that Law, and many thinking their Liberties and Privileges, as English Men lost, or at least in great Danger, seem Desperate. What the Consequences may be, god only knows; but, from the Temper of the People, at Present, there is the greatest Reason to fear, that the Passing of that Law will be the Occasion of a great Deal of Mischief." Sons of Liberty appeared, well led and well organized. Hutchinson's stately home in Boston, with its books and thick carpets, was looted. When stamp distributors like Andrew Oliver in Boston, Augustus John in Rhode Island, and John Hughes in Philadelphia were hanged in effigy, they and their colleagues resigned their posts. "A sort of frenzy or Madness" gripped the people, wrote Hughes.[8]

It was inevitable in this tension that the colonists should see Franklin, the agent sent to London to redress their grievances, not as agent but as enemy. Nothing that the Penns had ever done was quite as serious as the Stamp Act. In Philadelphia it was rumored that Franklin had framed the Act himself, encouraged its passage, and profited by it, that he had been paid money for recommending stamp officers, and that he had been promised a high post by the crown. Some of the anger the Philadelphia rioters showed toward John Hughes was clearly aimed at Franklin. A cartoon showed a Devil whispering in Franklin's ear, "Thee shall be agent, Ben, for all my dominions," with below it, the lines:

> All his designs concenter in himself,
> For building castles and amassing pelf.
> The public 'tis his wit to sell for gain.
> Whom private property did n'er maintain

There was talk of setting fire to Franklin's new house on Market Street. William Franklin hurried from Burlington and urged his mother and sister to take refuge with him in New Jersey. Deborah Franklin let Sally go, but she herself would not move. One of her brothers came to stay with her, and one of her husband's nephews. She wrote to her husband on September 22, 1765:

I sente to aske my Brother to Cume and bring his gun all so we maid one room into a Magazin. I ordored sum sorte of defens up Stairs such as I Cold manaig my self. I sed when I was advised to remove that I was verey shuer you had dun nothing to hurte aney body nor that I had not given aney ofense to aney person att all nor wold I be maid unesey by aney body nor wold I stir or show the leste uneseynis but if aney one Came to disturbe me I wold show a proper resentment and I shold be very much afrunted with aney bodey.

A fortnight later, on October 9, she sent a vivid account of the plight of John Hughes:

I have bin to see Mr. Hughes who I found a littel better and a bel to stir himself which I know will give you pleshuer and the more so as you will hear no doubte hough he has bin yoused and by men that better things mought be expeckted from firste to have the bells mufled and send two Drumes a bought the town to raise the mobe and send them under Mr Hughes window then send meisegers to tell him that they was a Coming and wold be thair in a minit and all moste terreyfi his wife and Children to deth and after this the man who was at the head of thier afair to Compleymente him self with the merrit of preventeing the mobe from falling on and distroying Mr Hughes and his whole family[.][9]

The Stamp Act Congress met in New York in October. Delegates from nine colonies petitioned for repeal of the Act and, in all their expressions of loyalty, stood firmly by the principle of no taxation without representation. "The Times are Dreadful, Dismal, Doleful, Dolorous and Dollar-less," moaned the *Pennsylvania Journal* on its masthead on October 31. On November 1, church bells rang in sorrow. At Portsmouth, New Hampshire, a copy of the Act was buried with due pomp; on the coffin lid was inscribed "*Liberty* aetas 145, *Stamp'd.*" By that date every stamp agent had resigned; Hughes had been forced to do so—despite Franklin's pious exhortation otherwise—by simple fear for his skin:

> He who for a Post or base sordid Pelf
> His Country Betrays, Makes a Rope for himself.
> Of this an Example, Before you we Bring
> In these Infamous Rogues, Who in Effigy Swing.

At the Stamp Act Congress it was John Dickinson of Pennsylvania, leader now of the proprietary party, who drew up the Declaration of Rights and Grievances denying the right of Parliament to tax the colonies. Petitions for repeal of the Act were sent to London. Merchants organized to stop importing British goods. And, with the fall of Grenville in July 1765 on the Regency Bill question and the accession of the Rockingham ministry, there came a turn of the tide.

*   *   *

The campaign in London for what began as the suspension and became the repeal of the Stamp Act was brilliantly organized: petitions, audiences with important ministers, complaints from British merchants and manufacturers at the loss of trade, the use of the press. Strahan, writing to David Hall in February 1766, testified to Franklin's efforts:

The Assiduity of our Friend Dr. Franklin is really astonishing. He is forever with one Member of Parliament or other (most of whom by the bye seem to have been deplorably ignorant with regard to the Nature and Consequence of the Colonies) endeavouring to impress them; first, with the Importance of the present Dispute; then to state the Case clearly and fully, stripping it of every thing foreign to the main Point; and lastly, to answer Objections arising from either a total Ignorance, a partial Knowledge, or a wrong conception of the Matter . . . By this means, however, when the Parlt. reassembles, many Members will go into the House properly instructed, and be able to speak in the Debates with Precision and Propriety, which the Well-wishers of the Colonies have hitherto been unable to do . . . All this while, too, he hath been throwing out Hints in the Public Papers, and giving Answers to such Letters as have appeared in them, that required or deserved an Answer.—In this Manner is he now employed, with very little Interruption Night and Day.

Franklin did not hesitate. If he had erred in judgment before, and hesitated just too long, the only way to salvage his own good name and to win ministerial approval for his charter plans was to work for repeal.[10]

On November 6 he was with Lord Dartmouth, the new president of the Board of Trade, who was popular with Americans because of his reputation for piety, and on November 10 with the new First Minister, Lord Rockingham. Rockingham's group had replaced Grenville's after much uncertainty and intrigue; the new First Lord of the Treasury, the official title of the man in whom the king invested authority, was only known to the public, said Horace Walpole, "by his passion for horse-races." Franklin's arguments were again essentially tactical: the Act could not be enforced without serious economic consequences to Britain and the risk of "a future total separation"; it could be suspended for a term of years and then quietly dropped without raising questions of the constitutional right to tax; a parliamentary enquiry should be set up; more would be given voluntarily than would ever be got by parliamentary taxation; one way to raise the money without taxes would be to set up a loan office.[11]

For his part, William Franklin handled his own situation in New Jersey with considerable finesse, resting his case on the fact that neither he nor the stamp distributor there, William Coxe, had received any orders from home about carrying the Act into execution. "Indeed, for any Man to set himself up as an Advocate for the S[tamp] Act in the Colonies is a meer Piece of Quixotism, and can answer no good Purpose whatever. And if he is an Officer of Government he not only becomes obnoxious, but is sure to lose all the Authority belonging to his Office."[12]

For a wider public Franklin turned to the press. He was, first and last, the penman of persuasion, "the engineer of the American propaganda machine in London," as Verner Crane has described him. Anonymity in political controversy was the fashion of the day. In any case Franklin, as a crown appointee, had a job at risk, and as colonial agent, too obviously a cause to plead. His arguments would appear stronger if they seemed to come from a less interested source. We know now that, signing himself Homespun, Pacificus, Traveller, and probably Americus, Justice, and O, Franklin sought to educate the British public on the issues. The war of 1756–1763 had been in Britain's interest, and for British trade; Americans had played their full part; if they were raising matters of constitutional principle, had they not learned these from "your *Seldens,* your *Lockes* and your *Sidneys.*" "If they are mistaken 'tis their misfortune not their fault." Nor could he refrain from satirizing British ignorance of America, with his tale of the grand leap of the whale up the falls of Niagara. At one time, explaining that the colonists were not entirely dependent on British woolen goods, he declared: "The very tails of the American sheep are so laden with wool that each has a little car or wagon to keep it from trailing on the ground." If the chuckle was never far below the surface, sarcasm was touched with acid; the appeal was basically to reason and good sense. He now published, in Strahan's *London Chronicle* on February 6–8, 1766, his letters to Shirley of a decade earlier. They were written with an introduction by "A Lover of Britain." [13]

A side-effect of the anonymity was the concealment not only of Franklin's personal contribution but of the steady development of his political views. The recently appointed agent of the Massachusetts Assembly, Dennys de Berdt, a London merchant of Dutch descent, charged Franklin with indifference to those who campaigned for repeal, and claimed that only when it was clear that a majority in the Commons was likely did he speak out. "Why," he asked, "does not the Pennsylvania agent write? He has leisure and a masterly pen." These charges were welcomed and broadcast by the Penns and their party in Pennsylvania, glad to have ammunition with which to puncture the reputation of the bland and rotund agent. They were voiced with gusto by William Bradford in his *Pennsylvania Journal,* carrying on the half-friendly, half-envious rivalry with Franklin of his uncle and grandfather. Bradford had been in the crowd threatening Hughes, and the proprietary group had been prompt to attack the Stamp Act. Yet in the October 1765 elections they did badly—although when the new Assembly voted to keep Jackson and Franklin as joint agents, the vote for the former (27 to 3) was stronger than that for the latter (22 to 8).

In the last analysis, the day was won not by the appeal to reason or even by constitutionally buttressed arguments about taxation or sovereignty or the status of colonial assemblies, but by the economic pressures and petitions of twenty-five commercial centers in Britain, and especially by the arguments of the merchants of London, Bristol, and Glasgow. This pressure group was set up at a meeting of merchants at the King's Arms tavern on December 4, under the chairmanship of the Boston-educated merchant Barlow Trecothick. They it was, as well as Franklin, who appeared before the Committee of the Whole House set up to investigate the matter. They had been marshaled and rehearsed by Trecothick, who perhaps more than anyone deserves credit for securing repeal. And behind him were the London hosier Robert Grafton, Obadiah Dawson of Leeds, the goldsmith George Masterman, the Hanburys, who bought for Washington and were in the Ohio Company, and the Glasgow tobacco merchant John Glassford. The movement for repeal was the work of a lobby of British and West Indian merchants worried about their lost profits. They estimated that orders worth £700,000 had been countermanded, and that in all, in future hopes and past debts, some £4 million worth was at issue. Rockingham was driven by this pressure to move from the policy of "amendment and curtailment" of the Act to its outright repeal.

The hearings lasted a fortnight; thirty witnesses were heard. Trecothick's evidence was more substantial than Franklin's, but it was Franklin's that, rightly, got the attention. For his was a genuine American voice, and he gave his evidence—and gave answers, many of them rehearsed, to the 174 questions put to him—with an aplomb, lucidity, brevity, infinite grasp of information, and sweet reasonableness of manner that revealed a rare quality of balance and judgment, of statistics and sentiment:

Q. What was the temper of America towards Great Britain before the year 1763?
A. The best in the world. They submitted willingly to the government of the Crown, and paid, in all their courts, obedience to acts of parliament. Numerous as the people are in the several old provinces, they cost you nothing in forts, citadels, garrisons or armies, to keep them in subjection. They were governed by this country at the expense only of a little pen, ink and paper. They were led by a thread. They had not only a respect, but an affection, for Great Britain, for its laws, its customs and manners, and even a fondness for its fashions, that greatly increased the commerce. Natives of Britain were always treated with particular re-

gard; to be an Old England-man was, of itself, a character of some respect, and gave a kind of rank among us.

Q. Don't you think they would submit to the stamp-act, if it was modified, the obnoxious parts taken out, and the duty reduced to some particulars, of small moment?

A. No; they will never submit to it.

Q. Was it an opinion in America before 1763, that the parliament had no right to lay taxes and duties there?

A. I never heard any objection to the right of laying duties to regulate commerce; but a right to lay internal taxes was never supposed to be in parliament, as we are not represented there.

Q. Then no regulation with a tax would be submitted to?

A. Their opinion is, that when aids to the Crown are wanted, they are to be asked of the several assemblies, according to the old established usage, who will, as they have always done, grant them freely. And that money ought not to be given away without their consent, by persons at a distance, unacquainted with their circumstances and abilities. The granting aids to the Crown is the only means they have of recommending themselves to their sovereign, and they think it extremely hard and unjust, that a body of men, in which they have no representatives, should make a merit to itself of giving and granting what is not its own, but theirs, and deprive them of a right they esteem of the utmost value and importance, as it is the security of all their other rights.[14]

The case was strong because it was not specific. It was grounded in constitutional claims, but they were not yet made explicit or primary. The tax was impracticable, it was inexpedient, and it would lose the mother country the respect and affection of the colonists. The Act was repealed in February 1766 by 275 votes to 167. Franklin wrote to Charles Thomson in September 1766 that there were enough claimers "of Merit in obtaining the Repeal. But, if I live to see you, I will let you know what an Escape we had in the Beginning of the Affair, and how much we were obliged to what the Profane would call *Luck,* and the Pious, *Providence.*"[15]

As a performance Franklin's interview was remarkable. He was no orator, and he was never again to attempt such a role. But the *Examination*—of which by the following year there were editions in French and German—is still a model of how to be interviewed. He was again the hero of the hour. He had upheld the cause of America before Parliament and won a great victory for his countrymen. In Pennsylvania even the proprietary party had to admit some good in him. In Philadelphia the coffeehouses gave presents to every man on the ship that brought the news of repeal. Punch and beer were free to anybody who would drink the health of the king. Three hundred gentlemen in the State House, guests of the governor and the mayor, toasted Franklin and resolved that on the king's birthday in June they would all wear suits of British manufacture and give their homespun to the poor. On the king's birthday the salutes were fired from a barge named the *Franklin*.

Franklin celebrated the repeal appropriately. To Debby, he wrote in April 1766:

As the Stamp Act is at length repeal'd, I am willing you should have a new Gown, which you may suppose I did not send sooner, as I knew you would not like to be finer than your Neighbours, unless in a Gown of your own Spinning. Had the Trade between the two Countries totally ceas'd, it was a Comfort to me to recollect, that I had once been cloth'd from head to foot in Woollen and linnen of my Wife's Manufacture, that I never was prouder of any Dress in my Life, and that she and her Daughter might do it again if it was necessary . . . I have sent you a fine Piece of Pompador Sattin, 14 yards, cost 11 shillings per yard; a Silk *Negligee* and Petticoat of brocaded Lutestring for my dear Sally, with two dozen Gloves, 4 Bottles of Lavender Water, and two little Reels.[16]

After February 1766 his reputation, if it had ever been really imperiled, was now restored. The criticisms almost totally disappeared. When he requested permission to return in 1766 the Pennsylvania Assembly refused and reappointed him agent. He became also agent for Georgia (1768), New Jersey (1769), and Massachusetts (1770)— which together would have brought him a more than ample £1,100 a year had he been paid regularly. In fact he did not receive payment from Massachusetts until after the Revolution broke out and he was still awaiting that from Georgia in 1785. He was eventually granted three thousand acres of land in Georgia in settlement. He counseled the colonists to behave prudently; Parliament must appear to be convinced of the need for surrender, not to have it thrust upon it. To make the point clear, the Rockingham government asserted in the Declaratory Act that Parliament had, if it chose to use it, the power to bind the colonies in all cases whatsoever. The continuing argument based on "supreme authority" on the one hand and "rights" on the other, on abstractions and universals, worried Franklin—as later it worried Burke. For that course, he knew, could lead only to mutual declarations of fervent and increasingly rigid high principle, noble, conflicting, and disastrous.

*   *   *

In the nine years that followed repeal, Franklin emerged as the voice of colonial America, agent for four colonies, counselor for all. He took upon himself the congenial role of flatterer and cajoler, smoother of quarrels, compromiser of differences, archconciliator.

Charged as agent to represent colonial views, he came more and more to be a delegate, a pleader at the bar of British opinion. He did so by petitions and interviews, by articles and pamphlets—he wrote at least 126 newspaper articles in the decade 1765–1775—by organizing the London end of the various nonimportation campaigns. He got little public credit, for middlemen rarely do. His impartiality itself became suspect. He was held "in England, of being too much of an American, and in America of being too much of an Englishman." Trying to see both sides, however, made his own views on the vexed question of constitutional rights become steadily clearer, and steadily more "American" than "British." By 1770 he was contending that colonies and mother country were united only "as England and Scotland were before the Union, by having one common Sovereign, the King." Gradually even this happy view was to weaken, for the more he saw of British politics at close range the more disillusioned he became. He moved in a circle largely composed of critics and Dissenters, and if his own way of life was indeed snug and highly respected, he nevertheless came to be less and less enamored of the British scene: "A people," he thought in 1768, "who are ungratefully abusing the best Constitution and the best King . . . any nation was ever blest with." [17]

A letter to Lord Kames of February 1767 indicated the weakening of Franklin's faith in the idea of American representation in Parliament:

I am fully persuaded with you, that a consolidating Union, by a fair and equal Representation of all the Parts of this Empire in Parliament, is the only firm Basis on which its political Grandeur and Stability can be founded. Ireland once wish'd it, but now rejects it. The Time has been when the Colonies might have been pleas'd with it; they are now indifferent about it; and, if 'tis much longer delay'd, they too will refuse it. But the *Pride* of this *People* cannot bear the Thoughts of it. Every Man in England seems to consider himself as a Piece of Sovereign over America; seems to jostle himself into the Throne with the King, and talks of OUR *Subjects in the Colonies.* The Parliament cannot well and wisely make Laws suited to the Colonies, without being properly and truly informed of their Circumstances, Abilities, Temper, &c. This it cannot be without Representatives from thence. And yet it is fond of this Power, and averse to the only Means of duly acquiring the necessary Knowledge for exercising it, which is desiring to be *omnipotent* without being *omniscient* . . .

He reverted to his other plans: a return to the requisition system, or his old favorite, a general loan office to be established by Parliament, "appropriating the interest to the American Service." This, he told Galloway in October 1766, "Would be a lighter and more bearable Tax than the Stamps, because those that pay it have an Equivalent in the Use of the Money; and that it would at the same time furnish us with a currency which we much wanted, and could not obtain under the Restrictions lately laid upon us."[18]

In 1765 Franklin's position had been close to that of Burke; he did not question the right of Parliament to enact the Stamp Act, but the expediency of doing so. It seems clear now that one reason for his evasions and cautions in 1765 was his concern with these constructive alternatives to parliamentary taxation. He was seeking a program of financial reform that would not depart from his position of 1754. In his correspondence in that year with William Shirley he had rehearsed all the arguments of 1765–66; direct taxes laid by Parliament ran counter to the "undoubted Right of Englishmen not to be taxed but by their own Consent given thro' their Representatives." Then, he had admitted that "secondary taxes, incidental to the Regulation of Trade" they did not object to. His letters of 1754 were reprinted in Strahan's *London Chronicle* in February 1766 as ammunition for the debates on the repeal of the Stamp Act.[19]

By 1768 Franklin had abandoned the distinction between external and internal taxes. The right to regulate trade, however tenable under the logic of the mercantile system or by resting the argument on Parliament's absolute right to do anything (as the Declaratory Act asserted), was vulnerable because it forbade Americans to buy manufactures from foreign countries. His economic liberalism and his awareness of the rapid expansion of the American community compelled him forward to a radical view of the empire as a commonwealth of free peoples joined in allegiance to the King. The radicalism lay not in the tactics nor in the constitutional theory but in the faith, evident as early as the *Observations on the Increase of Mankind* in 1751, in the natural fecundity and growth of the New World. In any case, the Americans had never been precise about the distinction between internal and external taxation. What they were clear about was that there must be no taxation for revenue except by their own consent.

By 1767 tensions were rising again. The Chatham administration replaced that of Rockingham in 1766 but, with the prime minister ailing and remote, crotchety and querulous, the responsibility for policy lay with his loyal but embarrassed deputy, the Duke of Grafton. Issues were piling up. New York merchants were petitioning once more against the Revenue Act of 1764; they were requesting the establishment of a vast number of free ports; the New York Assembly steadily refused to comply with the Quartering Act or to provision British troops. Massachusetts was quarreling with Governor Bernard, and the General Court had passed a bill compensating those who had lost property during the Stamp Act riots, but had added a provision granting general pardon, indemnity, and oblivion to the rioters. There was almost universal agreement in Great Britain that this addition was a grave usurpation of the king's sole power of pardon. In Great Britain, when such an Act of Parliament seemed to be required, agent Charles Garth reminded the South Carolina Committee of Correspondence, the king sent the completed text to the House of Lords and it received its first reading in the Lords and then in the Commons while the members stood with bared heads.[20]

Opinions in Britain too were hardening: even the Rockingham Whigs and William Beckford, West India merchant and Lord Mayor, were losing patience; even Chatham, it was thought, was all for stern measures. And in Chatham's absence, it was the brilliant but erratic Charles Townshend, the Chancellor of the Exchequer, who actually determined American policy. Grafton was compelled in 1767, by a proposal carried against his wishes, to reduce the land tax in Britain in order to relieve the burden on the country gentlemen, the major economic interest in the country and in the House of Commons. To cover the loss of revenue involved, Townshend undertook to obtain American revenue by the introduction of new duties on colonial imports of glass, lead, paints, paper, and tea. As external duties at the ports, these were not open to the charges brought against the Stamp Act; but as duties on British-produced goods, they were quite impossible to reconcile with mercantilism. From their proceeds Townshend proposed to meet not only the cost of defense but also the salaries of royal officials, and thus to reduce the control exercised over these officials by colonial assemblies. Franklin reported that he heard Townshend declare this in the House of Commons and go on to say that after that, "he did not expect to have his Statue erected in America . . . Mr. Grenville joined him fully—what they will do with us in the End, I cannot say."[21]

Moreover, the machinery for enforcing trade regulation was improved: colonial justices were authorized to issue writs of assistance, permitting a right of search of homes and stores by customs officers; Vice-Admiralty courts were established at Halifax, Boston, Philadelphia, and Charleston; and an American Board of Customs Commissioners, directly responsible to Britain, was established in Boston and armed with a galaxy of revenue cutters and sloops, searchers and spies. The governor of New York, which had refused to comply with the Quartering Act, was instructed not to approve of any measure of the Assembly until the Assembly showed itself more obedient to the will of Parliament.

The major American reply to the Townshend legislation came from Franklin's Pennsylvania rival John Dickinson, in his *Letters from a Farmer in Pennsylvania,* a British edition of which Franklin printed and for which he wrote a preface. Dickinson admitted the parliamentary right to regulate trade, but denied the right to tax, whether the tax was internal or external. And the difficult line between duties for regulation and those for revenue was, he said, to be discovered by examining the intent of a parliamentary measure. Franklin did not accept this logic, which he thought oversubtle. "The more I have thought and read on the subject," he wrote to his son in March 1768, "the more I find myself confirmed in opinion that no middle doctrine can well be maintained." Something, he wrote, "might be made of either of the extremes: that Parliament has a power to make *all laws* for us, or that she has a power to make *no laws* for us; and I think the arguments for the latter more numerous and weighty than those for the former." He began now to see useful case studies in the Channel Islands, Scotland, and Ireland; the bond of union, he continued to argue, "is not the Parliament but the King." Parliament had no power to bind the colonies without their consent, and what she claimed to possess was no less than usurpation.[22]

He realized that this was dangerous country to explore. Perhaps, as the editors of the Franklin *Papers* argue, he was busy convincing himself:

he was not yet fully convinced by his own logic, or at least not yet ready to deny in practice, as distinct from theory, Parliament's right to impose regulatory duties. Two years earlier, in his examination before the House of Commons, he had mentioned the argument that the authority of Parliament was indivisible, and that to deny its right to levy internal taxes was to deny its right to make any laws for the colonists. "At present they do not reason so," he had concluded, "but in time they may possibly be convinced by these arguments." He himself was now in the process of being convinced.[23]

He was careful to keep this dominion-theory view to himself, aware that even his liberal friends like Jackson or Thomas Pownall, and liberal imperialists like Chatham, did not, indeed could not, question the "supreme authority" of Parliament. And to question it among the Tories would have brought the heavens down. "In sovereignty there are no gradations," thundered Dr. Johnson. But sovereignty now meant something different on different sides of the ocean.

The clearest exposition of Franklin's position in 1768 is expressed in his "Causes of the American Discontents before 1768" printed in the *London Chronicle* in January of that year. Verner Crane has called it "perhaps the most famous contribution by Franklin, after the *Examination,* to the propaganda of the American Revolution." It grew out of a speech to a group that included members of Parliament. It appeared anonymously, signed F-S, in the *London Chronicle* and after much editing—"it seemed only to paw and mumble," said Franklin, who had meant it "to scratch and bite." He was still tactful, but there was now a threatening note. And along with familiar arguments there were, very tentatively, now new ones:

It was well known, that the Colonies universally were of opinion that no money could be levied from English subjects, but by their own consent given by themselves or their chosen Representatives: That therefore whatever money was to be raised from the people in the Colonies, must first be granted by their Assemblies, as the money raised in Britain is first to be granted by the House of Commons: that this right of granting their own money, was essential to English liberty: And that if any man, or body of men, in which they had no Representative of their chusing, could tax them at pleasure, they could not be said to have any property, any thing they could call their own . . .

We are truly a loyal people. Scotland has had its rebellions, and England its plots against the present Royal Family: but America is untainted with those crimes; there is in it scarce a man, there is not a single native of our country who is not firmly attached to his King by principle and affection. But a new kind of loyalty seems to be required of us, a loyalty to P[arliamen]t; a loyalty, that is to extend, it is said, to a surrender of all our properties, whenever a H[ouse] of C[ommons], in which there is not a single member of our chusing, shall think fit to grant them away without our consent; and to a patient suffering the loss of our privileges as Englishmen, if we cannot submit to make such surrender. We were separated too far from Britain, by the Ocean, but we were united to it by respect and love, so that we could at any time freely have spent our lives and little fortunes in its cause: But this unhappy new system of politics tends to dissolve those bands of union, and to sever us for ever.

Thus indirectly, but now publicly, Franklin reached the core of the problem. Loyalty to the king, yes. But not blind loyalty to a Parliament in which the colonists were unrepresented. The Parliament that—since 1688—saw itself in Britain as a check on tyranny and a protector of liberties was seen by an increasing number of Americans as something very different, a distant, corrupt, and arrogant oligarchy. For the mother country and for the king there was continuing affection, but not for Parliament. As one of Franklin's marginal comments of 1769 puts it, the Americans used to speak of the mother country, but "her late conduct entitles rather to the name of Step-Mother." [24]

*   *   *

Equally stimulated by absence and by that distance that lends enchantment, Franklin came to express more and more often his love for America, his "dear Country." A new note was now emerging: of pride in America as a distinct entity. But there was no change as yet in tactics. Franklin was aware that, after the Cabinet changes of January 1768 and the new prominence of Lord Hillsborough as minister of the newly created American Department, he was personally vulnerable. So he walked softly. Avoid dogma and trim your sails; "stoop as you go . . . you will miss many hard bumps." It was the voice not only of Poor Richard but of Cotton Mather; it was still the discreet man's gait. To surrender on form, but retain the substance, was as ever the Franklin method. If continuing the claim to tax "please you, continue it as long as you please, provided you never attempt to execute it. We shall consider it in the same light with the claim of the Spanish monarch to the title of King of Jerusalem."[25]

In 1768, however, the position had not yet hardened. In the summer came a general election, bringing no more clarification, least of all on the American question. And Franklin's own personal position was still open. Indeed, during that year, when his critics were asking how he could reconcile serving the crown as absentee postmaster with criticizing its policies in the press, he had some hopes of an undersecretaryship in the Grafton ministry, which succeeded Chatham's. The Duke—whom he never met face to face—intended, he was assured, "to do something handsome for me." This was one of the reasons, though not the only one, why he stayed on in London at the age of sixty-two. From the tone of a letter to his son that July, there can be little doubt that he would have accepted such a post had it been offered. But the ministry did not make the offer. It hesitated between promotion and dismissal, for this was a dangerous man. It half hoped to persuade him to resign from his postmastership in expectation of something else—which it might then find was not available. He himself knew, he told William in the same letter, that from the Grenville group there could be no expectations—for his country or himself: "If Mr Grenville comes into power again, in any department respecting America, I must refuse to accept of any thing that may seem to put me in his power, because I apprehend a breach between the two countries; and that refusal might give offence. So that you see a turn of a die may make a great difference in our affairs. We may be either promoted, or discarded; one or the other seems likely soon to be the case, but it is hard to divine which."[26]

Franklin's ultimate failure to avert independence—and he had a lot to lose by it—in part lay in his overreliance on his own skills as lobbyist and operator. To use these skills he had to be nearer to those he sought to influence. After January 1768 his persuasions fell on deaf and increasingly distant ears. He showed little interest in that year's elections. His focus was too narrow, too provincial. His chief concern was still with Pennsylvania, for which he was carrying on the old struggle to have proprietary replaced by royal government. He was also acting ostensibly for Pennsylvania, though in fact for the other colonies as well, in attempting to have restrictive legislation—not only the Townshend Acts but the Sugar Act, the Currency Act, the Quartering Act—repealed or at least substantially modified. In this many-sided effort he was completely unsuccessful. Moreover, none of the "friends of America" were in office. Henry Conway, who had been in charge of American affairs as Secretary of State for the Southern Department, was forced from office in January; Lord Shelburne held on only until autumn; Grenville, the arch protagonist of the strong line with America, threatened to return to power; Hillsborough, now in essence "Minister for America," became more and more Grenvillean; Chatham was a cipher, Grafton evasive.

There were thus many reasons why the public Franklin—and even the Franklin of many private letters—was ultra cautious. Indeed in these years western lands, the affairs of the new house being built for him in Philadelphia, his scientific interests, and his own travels dominate his attention far more than do the American issues. He did not protest strongly when troops were sent to Boston in the summer of 1768. The elections of 1768 went unmentioned in his correspondence. For the first few months he had hopes of Hillsborough. He was still the Establishment man—even if he felt now a deep unease on the basic question: What was the authority of Parliament over the American colonies?

The Townshend measures proved effective: between 1768 and 1774, £30,000 were collected annually, at a cost of £13,000 per year. They were consequently vehemently opposed. The Massachusetts General Court issued a "Circular Letter" (the work of Samuel Adams, James Otis, and Joseph Hawley) appealing to other assemblies and claiming that only the colonial assemblies could tax the colonists. Governor Bernard branded this as seditious—as did Hillsborough—and ordered it withdrawn; the General Court refused to withdraw it by a vote of ninety-two to seventeen. The "Circular Letter" was endorsed by seven other colonies.

Rioting, endemic in eighteenth-century society, now became recurrent. Liberty Poles were torn down as soon as erected, rarely without bloodshed. Customs agents were attacked in Boston, New York, and Providence. When, in June 1768, customs officers attempted to seize John Hancock's sloop *Liberty* with a load of Madeira aboard, they were driven to take refuge in Castle William, on an island in Boston Harbor, to escape mob violence. They put out appeals for help to Gage and to Admiral Hood. When the Boston garrison was increased by two regiments of infantry—an act Franklin likened to "setting up a smith's forge in a magazine of gunpowder"—the officers found themselves socially boycotted, the privates, physically assaulted.[27] The Boston town meeting declared that the regiments could remain in the colony only by authority of the Assembly. When Hancock deeded his new concert hall to the town, he stipulated that no British revenue, army, or navy officer should be admitted to it. According to Hutchinson, who had replaced Bernard as Acting Governor in August 1769, the situation when the troops landed was very close to revolution.

It was so because on these questions in these years the British merchants had not rallied to the American cause as they had in 1765, partly because their trade with other areas, especially Europe, was now more prosperous and they could ride out the storm. But the main reason was that the boycott of British goods had not been as effective in the colonies as it had been earlier—it had been notably less effective in the South and, to Franklin's embarrassment, in Pennsylvania. Colonial merchants became alarmed at the violent features of the nonimportation movement, frightened of the power of the mob and its radical leadership; others were quite ready to continue to trade and to prosper at the expense of their more dedicated countrymen. The boycott was now a political instead of an economic weapon, the work of the town meeting rather than the counting house. New York merchants, who tried hardest to honor the boycott, protested that other towns were more active in resolving what they ought to do than in doing what they had resolved. Thus the motion for the repeal of the Townshend Acts, introduced in Parliament by Thomas Pownall in April 1769, was easily defeated. And Franklin's newspaper campaign for repeal—the *Colonist's Advocate* series—seemed to be fruitless.

Yet, precisely because the tensions in Britain were less acute, even Hillsborough could promise in May 1769 that no further taxes would be laid on America, and that in the next session of Parliament the Townshend duties would be looked at afresh. It was clearly unwise for Britain to tax her own goods when they were sold abroad. And when Lord North took office in 1770, the government concluded that the Townshend policy was unprofitable and—on the day of the Boston Massacre, as it happened—withdrew all the duties except that on tea. North promised that there would be no new taxes. The Quartering Act was quietly allowed to expire. Again, face had to be saved, and the tea duty was retained (by a margin of a single vote in the Cabinet) "As a mark of the supremacy of Parliament, and an efficient declaration of their right to govern the colonies." It accorded, Franklin thought, "with the idle notion of the dignity and sovereignty of Parliament." New York City abandoned nonimportation after a house-to-house inquiry, and other ports gradually followed. Indeed, once partial repeal was enacted, the merchants' agreements were abandoned—against Franklin's urging, for he now believed not only that they had been effective in 1765–66 but that an embargo on British goods would stimulate colonial manufactures and thus strengthen the domestic colonial economy. Virginia was the last to give way, in July 1771.[28]

*   *   *

The anonymity of much of his writing in these years has had the effect of concealing the development of Franklin's own views. He appears primarily as reporter, a conveyor of other people's moods. Verner Crane has demonstrated the value here of Franklin's marginalia in the tracts and pamphlets he was reading. It is clear from these that now central in his thinking was the principle of colonial legislative autonomy. Representation in the House of Commons was not in prospect. The House elected in 1768 was no more sympathetic or better informed than its predecessor. Parliamentary taxation was a danger, and an issue on which it was now clear there would be colonial resistance. In the margin of the *Protest against the Bill to Repeal the American Stamp Act of Last Session* drafted in 1766 by members of the House of Lords, he wrote: "The Sovereignty of the Crown I understand, the sovereignty of the British Legislature out of Britain, I do not understand." In January 1766, in a newspaper letter signed N.N., he had already argued that the extent of parliamentary power in the dominions was a contentious and complex issue. He was sure that resolutions of Parliament's right to legislate for the colonies, incorporated in the Declaratory Act, would be seen as "unconstitutional and unjust." "It is to be wish'd it had not asserted it," he wrote in his copy of the first of the Lords' *Protests*, "or asserted it with some Limitation as when qualified etc."; and in his copy of the second *Protest* he entered an emphatic counterprotest against the Declaratory Act. In his own examination in the House he held: "The Colonies are not supposed to be within the realm; they have assemblies of their own, which are their parliaments, and they are, in that respect, in the same situation with Ireland." When William Knox—the former rice planter and industrious pamphleteer, who was agent for Georgia until 1765 and three years later became undersecretary in the new American Department—contended that the constitution of Great Britain "acknowledges no authority superior to the legislature, consisting of Kings, lords, and commoners," Franklin queried, "Does this Writer imagine that wherever an Englishman settles, he is Subject to the Power of Parliament?" Knox's description of the colonists as subjects of Great Britain he rejected totally, in what represented a denial of the sovereignty of a British Parliament over the colonies. "The people of G. Britain are Subjects of the King. G.B. is not a Sovereign. The Parliament has Power only within the Realm."[29]

There was, of course, the central difficulty that Parliament had repeatedly exercised a right of restraining colonial commerce; it had prohibited manufactures, and it had taxed the products of one colony when they were moved to another. When Knox in his pamphlet, *The Claim of the Colonies to an Exemption from Internal Taxes Imposed by Authority of Parliament, Examined* (1765) asserted that he found "almost as many instances of the parliament's exercising supreme legislative jurisdiction over the colonies, as there have been sessions of parliament since the first settlement of America by British subjects," Franklin's scribbled comment was a laconic "wicked."

By 1770–71 Franklin's private view of the power of Parliament was thus coming to rest on two assumptions: that Parliament had acted wickedly in the past, and that the line should now be drawn: "My opinion has long been that Parliament has originally no Right to bind us by any kind of Law whatever without our Consent. We have indeed in a manner consented to some of them, at least tacitly. But for the future methinks we should be cautious how we add to those Instances, and never adopt or acknowledge an Act of Parliament but by a formal Law of our own . . ." When English writers brought forward the precedents of the Hat Act, or the Navigation Acts, Franklin was ready to acknowledge a tacit consent, which gave those statutes separately a validity in America but which manifested no general consent and hence conferred no general legislative powers. In some fashion or other, laws binding upon the Americans must receive their assent: in their own assemblies, in a common council representing the assemblies, in a properly representative Parliament, or, as in the past, in the crude fashion of colonial submission to reasonable legislation. With respect to taxation, at least, Franklin made this very clear. "The Trust of Taxing America," he said in 1766, "was never reposed by the People of America in the Legislature of Great Britain."[30]

But he still hoped for what in a letter to Lord Kames he had called a "consolidating union": "On the other hand, it seems necessary for the common good of the empire, that a power be lodged somewhere, to regulate its general commerce: this can be placed nowhere so properly as in the Parliament of Great Britain." In a letter of May 9, 1766, to Cadwalader Evans, he was somewhat more explicit: "It would certainly contribute to the strength of the whole, if Ireland and all the dominions were united and consolidated under one common council for general purposes, each retaining its particular council or parliament for its domestic concerns." The creation of such a "consolidating union" must be the result of some formal act of union such as had earlier united England and Scotland: an act that by "ascertaining the relative Rights and Duties of each" would put an end to disruptive disputes. And he still believed that issues, even issues of principle, could be compromised.[31]

When now he questioned the parliamentary right to tax, however, he had taken—albeit unconsciously—a step nearer separation. He made it plain in a letter to Samuel Cooper (June 8, 1770), which he must have known would be widely circulated. In this he attacked the whole concept of parliamentary sovereignty in the Empire, and urged his American friends to stop implying that they accepted it. The Empire, he now held openly, was composed of states with coequal legislatures and a common sovereign, the "dominion parliaments" view that anticipated later British imperial history. This was a view welcome in Boston, where the Massachusetts House of Representatives was worried about the rumors of the governor's secret correspondence with London and afraid that their charter was at risk. Franklin's step to the left, politically, coincided with his election as agent for the Massachusetts House, an election that was far from unanimous; in Massachusetts he had been seen up to now as complaisant and compromising. He could now speak for four colonies out of thirteen, and one of the four was the seedbed of dissent.

For this very reason, he was vulnerable to attack in London as an unfaithful officer of the crown: he was still a postmaster-general. When news of his efforts to maintain the nonimportation agreements reached London, he found himself savaged in the press. He was, however, true to Poor Richard's homilies and "deficient in that Christian virtue of resignation." Again, as at the time of the Stamp Act, he said what he thought, "refused to change my political opinions every time his Majesty thought fit to change his ministers," and retained his office.[32]

The three-year interlude of Anglo-American concord from 1770 to 1773 is deceptive in the Franklin story. By 1770 Franklin's intellectual position had hardened: *suaviter in modo,* yes, or as long as possible, but intellectually now *fortiter in re.* In his own mind, he had reached the view that "we are free subjects of the King, and that fellow subjects of one part of his dominions are not Sovereigns over fellow subjects in any other part." The sovereign was, he held,

the sole legislator of his American subjects, and in that capacity is, and ought to be, free to exercise his own judgment, unrestrained and unlimited by his Parliament here. And our Parliaments have right to grant him aids without the consent of this Parliament . . . Let us, therefore, hold fast our loyalty to our King, who has the best disposition towards us, and has a family interest in our prosperity; as that steady loyalty is the most probable means of securing us from the arbitrary power of a corrupt Parliament, that does not like us, and conceives itself to have an interest in keeping us down and fleecing us.[33]

The fable he inserted in the *Public Advertiser* in January 1770, was apposite:

A Lion's Whelp was put on board a Guinea Ship bound to America as a present to a Friend in that Country: It was tame and harmless as a Kitten, and therefore not confined, but suffered to walk about the Ship at Pleasure. A stately, full-grown English Mastiff, belonging to the Captain, despising the Weakness of the young Lion, frequently took it's *Food* by Force, and often turned it out of it's Lodging Box, when he had a Mind to repose therein himself. The young Lion nevertheless grew daily in Size and Strength, and the Voyage being long, he became at last a more equal Match for the Mastiff; who continuing his Insults, received a stunning Blow from the Lion's Paw that fetched his Skin over his Ears, and deterred him from any future Contest with such growing Strength; regretting that he had not rather secured it's Friendship than provoked it's Enmity.[34]

Ever since the glorious Revolution of 1688 and the Acts of Union of 1707, the course of British constitutional development had increasingly emphasized the sovereignty of the crown in Parliament. Any sphere of royal influence outside the purview and control of Parliament was suspect—as appeared soon afterward in the controversies over the reform of the government of India. Kings, Lords, and Commons, all alike, would then have considered proposals of divided sovereignty unconstitutional, even heretical. Franklin never seems to have realized this: what he saw as liberalism could not be seen as such in London. At least, not yet. He was born at least seventy years too soon to win the title of Imperial Statesman.

* * *

Franklin was still dreaming another dream, and it too demanded caution: the Grand or Ohio or Vandalia Project. It had been planned in 1766 by the Philadelphia Indian-trading firm of Baynton, Wharton, and Morgan, in conjunction with William Franklin, Sir William Johnson, George Croghan, Galloway, and Hughes. They petitioned the crown for a tract of land in the area bounded by the Ohio, Mississippi, Wisconsin, and Wabash rivers; their request began by asking for two million acres and ended by claiming twenty million. In September 1766 Franklin had not held out very high hopes. He wrote to William:

I have mentioned the Illinois affair to Lord Shelburne. His Lordship had read your plan for establishing a colony there, recommended by Sir William Johnson, and said it appeared to him a reasonable scheme, but he found it did not quadrate with the sentiments of people here; that their objections to it were, the distance, which would make it of little use to this country, as the expense on the carriage of goods would oblige the people to manufacture for themselves; that it would for the same reason be difficult both to defend it and to govern it; that it might lay the foundation of a power in the heart of America, which in time might be troublesome to the other colonies, and prejudicial to our government over them; and that people were wanted both here and in the already settled colonies, so that none could be spared for a new colony.[35]

A month later it was the cost that seemed the major obstacle. What seemed to be turning the tide, however, was Sir William Johnson's trade and friendship with the Indians, and Franklin's own evidence that the Indians themselves sought a settlement of the boundary question. Croghan had acted on his own; he and a group of thirty-nine Pennsylvania "associates" (probably merely convenient straw men) had negotiated a purchase from the Indians of forty thousand acres west and southwest of Lake Oswego in New York, and had then procured from Governor Moore of New York formal permission to make the purchase.

By October 1767 Franklin was more hopeful. Shelburne presented his proposed western policy to the Cabinet on September 11, 1767, and the Cabinet voted at once to refer it to the Board of Trade for report. The plan warmly supported the proposal for several new governments in the interior of British North America. "I returned last night from Paris, and just now hear that the Illinois settlement is approved of in the Cabinet Council, so far as to be referred to the Board of Trade for their opinion, who are to consider it next week."[36]

The hope now was that the trade and the cost of administration would be transferred from the crown to the colonial governments, and thus the high cost of the Indian superintendencies and of Indian agents would be saved; with a reward for Sir William Johnson in one of the new colonial governorships. Franklin and John Hughes and friends in Philadelphia were to be awarded a grant of twenty thousand acres in Nova Scotia, a claim which, in the end, was passed on to William and proved worthless. Hopes rose still higher with the news that in the treaty of Fort Stanwix in 1768 Johnson had persuaded the Iroquois to cede part of the area in compensation for the damage done to "these suffering Traders" by Pontiac, even if this treaty was not valid until approved by the crown.

The group used every device open to them. From 1769 Samuel Wharton and William Trent were in London soliciting support, and winning over Thomas Walpole, the London banker and nephew of Sir Robert, Thomas Pownall and Lord Temple, Todd of the post office, Strahan and Jackson, Lords Camden and Hertford, and not least Lord Gower, head of the Bedford group and no friend of Hillsborough. The Bedford group's objective was simple, and political: to bring down North by bringing down Hillsborough, his strongest henchman in the Cabinet. Through Strahan, who was his publisher, David Hume was appealed to, and Hume in turn sounded out Lord Hertford, who may have talked to George III. The colony's changing name (Illinois to some, Indiana to others) had once been changed to Pittsylvania to win that great man's goodwill. Now it became Vandalia, because the queen was said to be descended from the royal line of the Vandals. In 1769, renamed again, the Grand Ohio Company was formed, to obtain and to exploit a vast grant in the trans-Allegheny West. It offered to pay just over £10,000, and, after twenty years, a quitrent of two shillings for every hundred acres of cultivated land.

Benjamin Franklin, 1767, by David Martin.

Twyford, where Franklin began his *Autobiography*, today.

Franklin's London home, 36 Craven Street, today.

Benjamin Franklin and Lady Friend, Craven Street, 1767, by Charles Willson Peale.

Franklin Before the Privy Council in the Cockpit, 1774, by Christian Schuessle.

Congress Voting Independence, with Franklin "fast asleep in his chair,"
by Robert Edge Pine and Edward Savage.

Hillsborough's appointment to the new Colonial Office transformed matters. Hillsborough, as an Irish landowner, foresaw and
feared—with accuracy—a massive migration from Ireland. He may
well have deliberately urged the group to bid for high stakes in the
belief that it would be beyond their capacity, and that of the Treasury,
to carry through. Whether or not Franklin was correct to suspect him
of this duplicity—he argued later that Hillsborough had pressed him
to step up the demand from two and one-half million to twenty million acres—the relationship between the two was bitter and personally tense. Franklin wrote of him as early as 1771:

His Character is Conceit, Wrongheadedness, Obstinacy, and Passion . . . I
hope, however, that our Affairs will not much longer be perplex'd and embarrass'd by his perverse and senseless Management. I have since heard, that
his Lordship took great Offence at some of my last words, which he calls
extreamly rude and abusive. He assured a friend of mine, that they were
equivalent to telling him to his Face, that the Colonies could expect neither
Favour nor Justice during his Administration.[37]

Hillsborough believed, with most of the members of the Board of
Trade, that remoter colonies were dangerous to British interests. It
had been a settled policy, as he later said, to confine

the western extent of settlement to such a distance from the sea coast as that
those settlements should lie within the reach of the trade and commerce of
this kingdom, upon which the strength and riches of it depend, and also of
the exercise of that authority and jurisdiction which was conceived to be
necessary for the preservation of the colonies in a due subordination to, and
dependence upon, the mother country.

It would be better to leave the country west of the Alleghenies wholly
to the Indians and the fur trade, forbidding white emigration there
until the eastern colonies were solidly populated. Hillsborough
seemed not to understand, as Shelburne understood, that emigration
was all but irresistible. He had none of Franklin's faith in population
increase and in western opportunity. His doubts were reinforced by
the consistent opposition of rival bidders for land in Virginia, especially its successive governors, to these plans for a land-grab in the
Ohio country. Governor Dunmore certainly had plans of his own. So
had New York and New Jersey. When finally the Vandalia proposal
reached the Privy Council in 1772, Hillsborough reported against it.
Wharton's and Franklin's masterly rebuttal—and the self-interest and
hopes of profit from speculation of a number of councillors—won

the day. Hillsborough had threatened to resign if the grant was made. It was with this hope, more perhaps than anything else, that Gower and his colleagues approved the proposal. Hillsborough resigned in August. Prime Minister North, ever unwilling to resign but ever protesting at the burden of office, soldiered on.[38] Franklin had no illusions, however, that he had destroyed a political career.

Franklin of course hoped to profit financially from this scheme, far more than from any of his other activities; but the hope was set in the larger context of his faith in endless expansion. Just as he was coming to believe that the colonies were subject only to the king, and hence politically coequal with Great Britain, so he was coming to believe that they were economically freestanding and capable, if left alone, of populating the wilderness. His interest in canals, machinery, the culture of silk in the colonies, like his emphasis on the rapid rise in the population, was part of his sense of a burgeoning economy. Despite this victory, the crisis of 1773 finally put paid to the western plans.

Whatever the tensions, there was still a code among gentlemen in the eighteenth century. When Franklin visited Ireland in 1771, not long before Hillsborough's resignation, he was a guest at Hillsborough's home. His host was "attentive to everything that might make my stay in his house agreeable, and put his eldest son Lord Kilwarling into his phaeton with me, to drive me a round of forty miles that I might see the country, the seats, manufacture, etc., covering me with his own greatcoat lest I should take cold." But Franklin went on to comment suspiciously to Thomas Cushing: "I shall think all the plausible Behaviour I have described . . . as meant only, by patting and stroaking the Horse, to make him more patient while the Reins are drawn tighter and the Spurs set deeper into his Sides."[39]

*   *   *

The years from 1770 to 1773 were, Vandalia apart, relatively quiet, and Franklin enjoyed his grand climacteric. His enemies were defeated or lying low; the mood was benevolent. In August 1772 he was lyrical in writing to William:

As to my situation here, nothing can be more agreeable, especially as I hope for less embarrassment from the new minister; a general respect paid me by the learned, a number of friends and acquaintance among them, with whom I have a pleasing intercourse; a character of so much weight, that it has protected me when some in power would have done me injury, and continued me in an office they would have deprived me of; my company so much desired that I seldom dine at home in winter, and could spend the whole summer in the country-houses of inviting friends, if I chose it. Learned and ingenious foreigners, that come to England, almost all make a point of visiting me; for my reputation is still higher abroad than here. Several of the foreign ambassadors have assiduously cultivated my acquaintance, treating me as one of their *corps,* partly I believe from the desire they have, from time to time, of hearing something of American affairs, an object become of importance in foreign courts, who begin to hope Britain's alarming power will be diminished by the defection of her colonies; and partly that they may have an opportunity of introducing me to the gentlemen of their country who desire it. The King, too, has lately been heard to speak of me with great regard.[40]

He was happy in his domestic London circle. It included not only Mrs. Stevenson and Polly but his grandson Temple, and Sarah Franklin, daughter of one of his Northamptonshire cousins, living in Craven Street as yet another second daughter to him. The "Craven Street Gazette," his genial parody of royal gazettes, testifies to his contentment. Here he recounts with due pomp the doings of Her Majesty's Court when Her Majesty (Mrs. Stevenson) is absent and where clearly he reigns as uncrowned king, disguised as Big Man, Great Person, or Dr. Fatsides:

This morning Queen Margaret, accompanied by her first maid of honour, Miss Franklin, set out for Rochester . . . It is whispered that the new family administration, which took place on Her Majesty's departure, promises, like all other new administrations, to govern much better than the old one.

We hear that a certain Great Person (so called from his enormous size) of a certain family in a certain street is grievously affected at the late changes, and could hardly be comforted this morning, though the new ministry promised him a roasted shoulder of mutton and potatoes for his dinner.

It is said that the same Great Person intended to pay his respects to another great personage this day, at St. James's, it being coronation day; hoping thereby a little to amuse his grief, but was prevented by an accident, Queen Margaret, or her maid of honour, having carried off the key of the drawers so that the lady of the bedchamber could not come at a laced shirt for His Highness. Great Clamours were made on this occasion against Her Majesty.

Other accounts say that the shirts were afterwards found, though too late, in another place. And some suspect that the wanting a shirt from those drawers was only a ministerial pretence to excuse picking the locks, that the new administration might have everything at command.[41]

In 1770 Polly Stevenson married the surgeon, anatomist, and Copley medalist William Hewson. Hewson died in 1774 of a wound incurred during dissection. Franklin's attitude to Polly's children, his godchildren, was that of a grandfather. Both Polly and his friend Joseph Priestley were in the end to settle in Pennsylvania. In the late summer of 1772, when the house became too crowded, Franklin and his housekeeper moved across the street—to his confusion, and to the discovery that he had many more books than he realized. Young Temple was at school in Kensington; American visitors and callers were innumerable.

He took a special pleasure in his friendship with Jonathan Shipley, the bishop of St. Asaph, and his wife and five young daughters. It was at Twyford, the bishop's country house near Winchester, in 1771, that he began the *Autobiography,* in the form of a letter of advice and reminiscence to his son. He conveyed the warmth of that household in a letter to Debby in August 1772:

The bishop's lady knows what children and grandchildren I have, their ages, etc. So when I was to come away on Monday the 12th in the morning, she insisted on my staying that one day longer, that we might keep my grandson's birthday. At dinner, among other nice things, we had a floating island, which they always particularly have on the birthdays of any of their own six children; who were all but one at table, where there was also a clergyman's widow now above a hundred years old. The chief toast of the day was Master Benjamin Bache, which the venerable old lady began in a bumper of mountain, a variety of Malaga wine. The bishop's lady politely added: "And that he may be as good a man as his grandfather." I said I hoped he would be much better. The bishop still more complaisant than his lady, said: "We will compound the matter and be contented if he should not prove quite so good." [42]

He was now an habitué of the Society of Arts and of the Royal Society, the center of a wide circle of scientists, dissenters, and friends of America. Sir John Pringle was a particularly close friend. When Boswell saw Pringle and Franklin together, he commented: "Sir John, though a most worthy man, has a peculiar sour manner. Franklin again is all jollity and pleasantry. I said to myself 'Here is a prime contrast: acid and alkali.'" [43]

Always the most clubbable of men, and still with a preference for rum and Madeira, in London he followed a busy social round: erratically at the Dog Tavern or the Star and Garter in Pall Mall, at the New England Coffee House in Threadneedle Street or the Pennsylvania Coffee House in Birchin Lane, where young American law students gathered, or among the Scots in the British Coffee House in Cockspur Street. He loved a chat and a laugh, a glass and a song, as much as ever. On Mondays he was usually at the George and Vulture off Cornhill, and on alternate Thursdays regularly at St. Paul's (later the London) Coffee House, to meet his companions of the Club of Honest Whigs, and to savor the house's special dishes—Welsh rarebits and apple puffs—and its porter and beer, at a fixed charge of eighteen pence a head.[44]

Wherever he went, Franklin attracted the questioning, dissenting, and scientifically curious. It was to plain folk with stimulating minds that he responded. The theater attracted him not at all—it is strikingly absent from his correspondence. He met only a few of the great: he made three visits to Lord Despencer's house in West Wycombe in Buckinghamshire, another to Lord Shelburne's to meet the Abbé Morellet, and a five-day stay with Lord Hillsborough; but he was never of the Establishment. Despencer's name was no automatic passport to social acceptance; he was the Sir Francis Dashwood of the Hellfire Club. And Shelburne was always something of an outsider. Apart from Shelburne (for whom for eight years Priestley was librarian), the Earl of Bessborough (for a time postmaster general), Despencer, and the Earl of Molton of the Royal Society, a fellow scientist interested in lightning rods for his Brook Street house, Franklin made hardly any close or friendly contact with any peers. He was rarely entertained at the great houses, and, it seems, never inside the clubs. Neither by rank nor wealth was he of the elect in an England where the oligarchs ruled.

Franklin's experiments continued, but with longer and longer interruptions: experiments with his "musical glasses," the heating of rooms, the design of clocks, the effect of oil on water, phonetic spelling, lightning rods for St. Paul's, the causes of lead poisoning, whirlwinds and waterspouts, the raising of grapes, the cultivation of the silkworm in Pennsylvania, countering colds. He came close indeed to the understanding of infection and contagion:

I hope, that after having discovered the Benefit of fresh and cool Air applied to the Sick, People will begin to suspect that possibly it may do no Harm to the Well . . . I have long been satisfied from Observation that besides the general Colds now termed Influenzas (which may possibly spread by Contagion as well as by a particular Quality of the Air) people often catch Cold from one another when shut up together in close Rooms, Coaches, etc., and when sitting near and conversing so as to breathe in each other's Transpiration; the Disorder being in a certain State . . . Travelling in our severe Winters, I have suffered Cold sometimes to an Extremity only short of Freezing, but this did not make me *catch Cold.* And for Moisture, I have been in the River every Evening two or three hours for a Fortnight together, when one would suppose I might imbibe enough of it to *take cold* if Humidity could give it; but no such Effect followed.[45]

The way to avoid colds was to eat and drink temperately, take enough exercise, and breathe as much fresh air as possible. He was always a believer in cold air baths.

He was seeing through the press the fourth edition of his *Experiments and Observations,* and assisted preparations to observe the transit of Venus in 1769. His curiosity prowled as always down unexplored paths: the speed of canal boats, the making of glass, the effects of the Gulf Stream upon transatlantic navigation; the problems of mining coal. On his travels he was, as always, uninterested in the aesthetic, little impressed by the beauty of nature, averse to social analyses as such. In 1767 he met James Watt, and through his correspondence with Matthew Boulton he was interested in the progress of the steam engine. By coincidence he visited the Carron Iron Works in Scotland in 1771 when parts of the first steam engine were being cast. He was utterly unromantic: "Many people are fond of accounts of old Buildings and Monuments, but for me I confess that if I could find in my travels a receipt for making Parmesan cheese, it would give me more satisfaction than a transcript from any inscription from any old Stone whatever." But some social observations were now creeping in, and he drew proudly nationalist conclusions. A tour of Ireland in 1771, when he was lionized in Dublin and admitted to the floor of the Irish House of Commons as a member of an "English Parliament," nevertheless made him nostalgic for America:

I have lately made a tour through Ireland and Scotland. In these Countries a small part of Society are Landlords, great Noblemen, and gentlemen, extremely opulent, living in the highest affluence and Magnificence; the Bulk of the People Tenants, extremely poor, living in the most sordid Wretchedness in dirty Hovels of Mud and Straw and cloathed only in Rags.

I thought often of the Happiness of New England, where every man is a Freeholder, has a Vote in public Affairs, lives in a tidy, warm House, has plenty of good Food and Fewel, with whole Cloaths from Head to Foot, the manufactury perhaps of his own Family. Long may they continue in this Situation![46]

Frugality he no longer practiced and only occasionally preached. It was a doctrine for the young—or the newly wed. He knew that for himself it did not come easily: "Frugality is an enriching Virtue, a Virtue I could never acquire in myself but I was lucky enough to find it in a Wife who thereby became a Fortune to me." Affluent living, however, did not hold for Sally or her husband, Richard Bache, when they married in 1767. He had urged delay when Debby reported their wish to marry. When he met his son-in-law for the first time in 1771, when visiting the Bache family in Preston, he still urged caution on him. Bache hoped for a political appointment in England and had brought £1000 with him to help secure it. His father-in-law was firmly against it, and recommended a course mindful of his own career. Bache should open a store in Philadelphia, like Franklin before him. Franklin wrote to his daughter:

I am of Opinion that almost any Profession a Man has been educated in is preferable to an Office held at Pleasure, as rendering him more independent, more a Freeman, and less subject to the caprices of Superiors. And I think that in keeping a Store, if it be where you dwell, you can be serviceable to him as your Mother was to me; for you are not deficient in Capacity, and I hope are not too proud . . . For your Encouragement I can assure you that there is scarce a Merchant of Opulence in your town whom I do not remember a young beginner with as little to go on and no better Prospects than Mr. Bache. That his Voyage hither might not be quite fruitless I have given him £200 sterling, with which I wish you good Luck.[47]

This austerity was not visited on William when he was young, or on young Temple, both of whom were spoiled. For himself, conviviality did not march with abstinence. He had a special preference for old Madeira, and in his Paris years his cellars were to be well stocked.

There was time in 1766 for a two-month visit to Germany (the spa at Bad Pyrmont, then Hannover, Göttingen—where he and his traveling companion, Sir John Pringle, were elected to the Royal Academy—Cassel, and Frankfurt), and in 1767 and 1769 to France, where he was presented to the king and queen at Versailles (but "No Frenchman shall go beyond me in thinking my own King and Queen the very best in the world and the most amiable"). His French visit, indeed, stirred his pride in Britain. Writing to Samuel Cooper, he hoped that "nothing that has happened or may happen will diminish in the least our loyalty to our Sovereign, or Affection for this nation in general. I can scarcely conceive a King of better dispositions, of more exemplary virtues, or more truly desirous of promoting the welfare of his subjects." He was aware, he told Cooper, of French interest in the British colonies. "But Europe has its reasons. It fancies itself in some danger from the growth of British power, and would be glad to see it divided against itself. Our prudence will, I hope, long postpone the satisfaction our enemies expect from our dissensions." There was still an Old England man here—or one nostalgic for Craven Street? Had it not been for the unresolved and now all but irreconcilable political divisions in the Anglo-American world, Franklin's would have been an idyllic existence. It would not stay so much longer.[48]

*   *   *

Politically Franklin remained a tactician of the "ca'canny" style, a counselor of nonviolence. But when the next crisis broke he had to speak for the most radical colony of them all. In his letters to Samuel Cooper, Thomas Cushing, James Bowdoin, and the Massachusetts Committee of Correspondence a more strident note is heard. Discretion was now as hard to preach as to practice. He wrote in May 1771 to the Committee of Correspondence (Otis, Cushing, and Samuel Adams):

I think one may clearly see, in the system of customs to be exacted in America by act of Parliament, the seeds sown of a total disunion of the two countries, though, as yet, that event may be at a considerable distance. The course and natural progress seems to be, first, the appointment of needy men as officers, for others do not care to leave England; then, their necessities make them rapacious, their office makes them proud and insolent, their insolence and rapacity make them odious, and, being conscious that they are hated, they become malicious; their malice urges them to a continual abuse of the inhabitants in their letters to administration, representing them as disaffected and rebellious, and (to encourage the use of severity) as weak, divided, timid and cowardly.[49]

In 1772 violence began to reappear. When Rhode Islanders boarded the revenue cutter *Gaspee*, aground off Pawtucket, overpowered her crew, wounded her commander, and burned the ship, the law officers could not agree on appropriate action. The commission of investigation was given immense—and to the colonists frightening—powers but proved unable to discover any conspirators. Yet there had been eight boatloads of them; they had been led by men of social distinction in the colony, including its most eminent merchant, John Brown; and they had acted quite openly. Civil disobedience could hardly go further. To counter it, the culprits—if they had been found—would have been taken to England for trial. Also to counter it, Governor Hutchinson of Massachusetts announced that henceforward he and the judges of the Superior Court would receive their salary directly from the crown. It was to meet this threat that Sam Adams put out a call at a Boston town meeting for the creation of a standing committee of correspondence. For it he prepared a list of infringements and violations of rights, an impressive summary of the colonial viewpoint. Other committees were promptly organized, ready to concert action if there should be need. "It is natural to suppose," wrote Franklin to Thomas Cushing, "that if the oppressions continue, a congress may grow out of that correspondence."[50]

Franklin still pleaded for peaceful protest, for cool tempers. To Cushing he wrote in January 1773:

Our great security lies, I think, in our growing strength both in Numbers and Wealth; that creates an increasing Ability of Assisting this Nation in its Wars, which will make us more respectable, our Friendship more valued and Enmity feared; thence it will soon be thought proper to treat us not with Justice only but with Kindness, and thence we may expect in a few Years a total Change of Measures with regard to us; unless, by a Neglect of military Discipline, we should lose all martial Spirit, and our western People become as tame as those in the eastern Dominions of Britain, when we may expect the same Oppressions; For there is much Truth in the Italian Saying: "Make yourselves Sheep, and the Wolves will eat you." In confidence of this coming change in our favour, I think our Prudence is meanwhile to be quiet, only holding up our Rights and Claims on all Occasions in Resolutions, Memorials, and Remonstrances; but bearing patiently the little present Notice that is taken of them. They will all have their Weight in Time, and that Time is at no great Distance.

And again in March: "In the meantime I must hope that great Care will be taken to keep our People quiet; since nothing is more wished for by our Enemies than that by Insurrections we should give a good Pretence for increasing the Military among us and putting us under more severe Restraints."[51]

When the Massachusetts Assembly declared its legislative independence of Parliament, Franklin pleaded with Lord Dartmouth not to lay the news before Parliament. As he reported in a letter to Cushing in May 1773, he told Dartmouth, "In my Opinion, it would be better and more prudent to take no Notice of it. It is *Words* only. Acts of

Parliament are still submitted to there. No Force is used to obstruct their Execution. And while that is the Case, Parliament would do well to turn a deaf Ear and seem not to know that such Declarations had ever been made. Violent Measures against the Province will not change the Opinions of the People. Force can do no good." Dartmouth replied, "I do not know that Force would be thought of; but perhaps an Act may pass to lay them under some inconveniences till they rescind that Declaration." Franklin thought such an Act unwise: "It is likely *that* it will only put them as heretofore upon inventing some Method of injuring this country till the Act is repealed; and so we shall go on injuring and provoking each other instead of cultivating that Good Will and Harmony so necessary to the general Welfare." [52]

To this tense situation, in which until now he had been the archconciliator, Franklin now made four decisive contributions. The clash with Hillsborough had made him enemies. He proceeded to anger them still more by publishing in the *Gentleman's Magazine* in September 1773 an anonymous and unusually savage satire, "Rules by Which a Great Empire May Be Reduced to a Small One." Purporting to be a ministerial brief presented to Hillsborough when he assumed office, it listed the steps by which America had been estranged as if they had been deliberate acts of policy: "Suppose them always inclined to revolt, and treat them accordingly . . . By this means, like the husband who uses his wife ill from suspicion, you may in time convert your suspicions into realities." Choose inferior, rapacious, and pettifogging men for governors and judges in the provinces. Support them against all complaints from the governed. Reward them for having governed badly, when at last they have to resign or be recalled. When you want money from the colonies, "despise . . . their voluntary grants, and resolve to harass them with novel taxes." If they petition for redress, scorn their petitions. Use the revenues to pay salaries or pensions "to every governor who has distinguished himself by his enmity to the people and by calumniating them to their sovereign." If the provincial parliaments claim any rights, dissolve them or adjourn their meetings to some inconvenient place.

XV. Convert the brave, honest Officers of your Navy into pimping Tidewaiters and Colony Officers of the Customs. Let those who in Time of War fought gallantly in Defence of the Commerce of their Countrymen, in Peace be taught to prey upon it. Let them learn to be corrupted by great and real Smugglers; but (to show their Diligence) scour with armed Boats every Bay,

Harbour, River, Creek, Cove, or Nook throughout the Coast of your Colonies; stop and detain every Coaster, every Woodboat, every Fisherman, tumble their Cargoes and even their Ballast inside out and upside down; and, if a Penn'orth of Pins is found unentered, let the Whole be seized and confiscated. Thus shall the Trade of your Colonists suffer more from their Friends in Time of Peace than it did from their Enemies in War . . .

XX. Lastly, invest the General of your Army in the Provinces with great and unconstitutional Powers, and free him from the Controul of even your own Civil Governors. Let him have Troops enow under his Command, with all the Fortresses in his Possession; and who knows but (like some provincial Generals in the Roman Empire, and encouraged by the universal Discontent you have produced) he may take it into his Head to set up for himself? If he should, and you have carefully practised these few *excellent Rules* of mine, take my Word for it, all the Provinces will immediately join him; and you will that Day (if you have not done it sooner) get rid of the Trouble of governing them and all the Plagues attending their Commerce and Connection from thenceforth and for ever. Q.E.D.[53]

He drove the harsh lesson home with a second hoax, "An Edict by the King of Prussia," which proclaimed that Britain had been settled by colonists from Germany, had never been emancipated, and had hitherto yielded little revenue to "our august house." "And whereas it is just and expedient that a Revenue should be raised from the said Colonies in Britain, towards our Indemnification; and that those who are Descendants of our ancient Subjects, and thence still owe us Obedience, should contribute to the replenishing of our Royal Coffers as they must have done had their Ancestors remained in the Territories now to us appertaining. We do hereby ordain and command"—that duties be laid on all goods exported from Britain or imported into it, and that all ships to and from Britain

touch at our port of Koningsberg, there to be unladen, searched, and charged with the said duties . . .

And lastly, Being willing further to favour Our said Colonies in Britain, We do hereby also ordain and command that all the Thieves, Highway and Street-Robbers, Housebreakers, Forgerers, Murderers, So[domi]tes and Villains of every Denomination, who have forfeited their Lives to the Law in Prussia, but whom We in Our great Clemency do not think fit here to hang, shall be emptied out of our Gaols into the said Island of Great Britain, *for the better peopling of that country.*[54]

Franklin and other guests derived great amusement from it when it was read during his visit to Lord Despencer's. He told his son with glee that Paul Whitehead, the author of *Manners,* a popular satirical poem just published,

came running in to us, out of breath, with the paper in his hand. "Here," says he, "here's news for ye. *Here's the king of Prussia* claiming a right to this kingdom." All stared, and I as much as anybody; and he went on to read it. When he had read two or three paragraphs a gentleman present said: "Damn his impudence, I dare say we shall hear by next post that he is upon his march with one hundred thousand men to back this." Whitehead, who is very shrewd, soon after began to smoke it, and, looking in my face, said: "I'll be hanged if this is not some of your American jokes upon us." The reading went on and ended with abundance of laughing, and a general verdict that it was a fair hit; and the piece was cut out of the paper and preserved in my lord's collection.[55]

The hoax brought no amusement, however, in Whitehall.

*   *   *

Franklin's third contribution to the controversy was an attack on Hutchinson, written under the nom de plume "A New England-Man" and published in the *Public Advertiser* of March 1773. The governor had, in an address to the Massachusetts Assembly, made the issue squarely one of sovereignty. "As a friend of both Countries being concerned with both, I wish Governor Hutchinson had thought of some other Subject for his speech, and not revived needlessly a dispute that can end in nothing but mischief."[56]

The fourth contribution was his role in the affair of the Hutchinson letters. Between 1767 and 1769 Hutchinson, then lieutenant-governor of Massachusetts, and Andrew Oliver, then secretary of the province, had written a number of letters to Thomas Whately, Grenville's former secretary, urging drastic measures against the colonies. "There must be an abridgement of what are called English liberties," wrote Hutchinson. Officers of the crown should be made independent of the colonial assemblies, thought Oliver. In 1772, after the deaths of Grenville and Whately, these letters were shown to Franklin by an unknown member of Parliament—John Temple's name was mentioned later, as was Thomas Pownall's, but Franklin never revealed his source. Franklin, with the source's permission, sent the letters to Thomas Cushing in Boston, with strict instructions that they could be shown privately to the colonial leaders but neither copied nor printed, and that they must be returned. They might work their effect better if seen by a few and talked about by many, he thought, "As distant objects seen only through a mist appear larger." And the effect he claimed to expect was a conciliating one: "I cannot but acknowledge that my resentment against this country for its arbitrary measures in governing us, conducted by the late minister, has, since my conviction by these papers that those measures were projected, advised, and called for by men of character among ourselves, and whose advice must therefore be attended . . . my own resentment, I say, has by this means been exceedingly abated. I think they must have the same effect with you; but I am not, as I have said, at liberty to make the letters public." [57]

Despite the veto on publication, the letters were printed in Boston. The London news sheets speculated on their source. A duel was fought in Hyde Park between William Whately, his brother's executor, and John Temple, who was accused of stealing the letters. Neither was satisfied, though Whately was wounded. A second duel was planned, and in order to exonerate Temple, Franklin revealed that he had been responsible for sending the letters to Boston. His admission came on Christmas Day, 1773; nine days earlier, the Boston patriots had celebrated the Boston Tea Party.

In retrospect, the affair of the Hutchinson letters appears a trivial incident. The opinions expressed by Hutchinson and Oliver were neither especially inflammatory nor more outspoken than those which many of their circle were regularly expressing; these letters were private, sent to a member of Parliament no longer in government; they had already been seen by several members of Parliament, and were known about by many more. Nor were they the first opinions pro or con to be thus privately and publicly canvassed and discussed. In Hillsborough's days as secretary, Franklin's own correspondence appears to have been regularly read in transit—a fact of which he was aware, and of which he warned Galloway as early as 1766 and Cushing in 1771.

And yet a storm of indignation broke over Franklin after he admitted sending the letters. In 1774 he was seen as "the most mischievous man in England," at least a thief and at worst a traitor; as the ringleader and puppet-master of rebellion, saying smooth things publicly in London but treacherously pulling the strings of rebellion in Boston; as the Brer Fox of the story, laying low but grinning high. It was, of course, like all legends, far removed from the truth. But it ended Franklin's long and expert labors for preserving what he now called that "fine and noble China vase," the British Empire.[58]

The political tensions now became personalized as Franklin versus Hutchinson. The Massachusetts petition for Hutchinson's removal as governor came up before the Privy Council in January 1774. There were present not only thirty-six privy councillors but a noble company of the politically interested. Among the spectators were Burke and Priestley, the young Jeremy Bentham, the American Edward Bancroft, Dartmouth, and Hillsborough. Only Despencer could be counted on as a friend of Franklin. Hutchinson was represented by counsel, in the person of Alexander Wedderburn, the formidable Scottish advocate, one-time follower of Bute and then of Wilkes, and now North's solicitor-general. He was already known to Franklin as an opponent of the Vandalia project. Franklin asked for a postponement to prepare his own case; he could not use witnesses without betraying secrets; and while he was at work, news broke in London of the Boston Tea Party. The government claimed to be convinced that a great conspiracy was being planned. And thus the case, in form that of Massachusetts versus Hutchinson, became in fact that of the British government versus Franklin.

Franklin, in a coat of Manchester velvet, stood silent throughout the hearing on the advice of his friends. Wedderburn's attack on him lasted an hour and was a brilliant piece of invective—"a furious philippic against poor Dr Franklin" was Burke's phrase. Franklin was a thief, a man without honor, "the true incendiary . . . and abettor," "the first mover and prime conductor," "the actor and secret spring" of the Committee of Correspondence in Boston; his object was to remove Hutchinson—who had discerned his intentions—and he was "possessed with the idea of a Great American Republic"; Franklin was indeed already behaving as though he were the minister of "a foreign independent state." Wedderburn fed on accumulated resentments that had been building up for twenty years: of the Pennsylvania boss, of the critic of proprietary government, of the colonel in whose honor a suspect militia fired salutes, of the writer of anonymous articles, of the officeholder revealed as conspirator, of the all-too-knowledgeable expert witness of 1766, of the know-it-all agent of colonial assemblies claiming rights to which they had no title. And he voiced a general theme, though he hid it in Latin, quoting Juvenal:

Nunquam ... amavi hunc hominem, "I never liked the man." The solicitor-general's virtuoso effort was a political and personal triumph. The petition for Hutchinson's removal was pronounced "groundless, vexatious, and scandalous"; Franklin was dismissed from his position as deputy postmaster-general; and in Parliament the Coercive Acts were passed to close the port of Boston, to move the capital to Salem, to curb town meetings and fetter political freedom in Massachusetts; Hutchinson did lose his post as governor, but only to be replaced by a soldier, Commander-in-Chief Gage. Boston, obstinate and ungovernable as it now seemed, must be brought to heel. The reaction in the colonies was equally extreme: the call went out to summon a Continental Congress. Franklin's years of devious politics had reaped a whirlwind.[59]

There can be no question that Wedderburn's attack was a turning point in Franklin's career. He had certainly not willed it thus; he was the least "incendiary" of political animals. Now he had to be even more circumspect: William Whately threatened him with a libel suit; there were rumors that the government would reveal a treasonable correspondence between Franklin and Boston. He published little that was new, though he did reprint in Strahan's *London Chronicle* in August and September "The Causes of the American Discontents." His letters, he now felt sure, were opened; if it came to blows in Boston, he would almost certainly be arrested. Now more than ever he needed all his wiliness, or his fate would be worse than Brer Fox's. He kept a cool and sullen silence. His optimism did not entirely desert him; after the call for a Continental Congress and the debate—so reminiscent of 1754 and this time so nearly successful—on Galloway's Plan of Union, he still hoped for a firm economic boycott of British goods and then the intervention of British merchants, following the pattern of nine years before. A boycott of British manufacturers, he pleaded in October,

would in a peaceable and justifiable way do everything for us that we can wish. I am grieved to hear of Mobs and Violence and the pulling down of Houses, which our Friends cannot justify and which give great Advantage against us to our Enemies . . . I am in perpetual Anxiety lest the mad measure of mixing Soldiers among a People whose Minds are in such a state of Irritation, may be attended with some sudden Mischief; for an accidental Quarrel, a personal Insult, an imprudent Order, an insolent Execution of even a prudent one, or twenty other things may produce a Tumult, unforeseen and therefore impossible to be prevented, in which such a Carnage may ensue as to make a Breach that can never afterwards be healed.[60]

A decade, however, had passed: what had been effective deterrence in 1765 was not so in 1774. The election of November 1774 in Britain was held quickly, before the boycott could take effect in the trading towns, and in a mood of high patriotism; this time there was no retreat, no redress. Burke had said little on America in the election campaign in Bristol; after it, Trecothick was no longer a member of Parliament. Neither in Westminster nor outside it, in the commercial or the political nation, was there sustained opposition to the firm line etched in the Boston Port Bill. "The die is cast," said the best of kings. "The Colonies must triumph or submit."

*   *   *

In one sense, of course, it is an oversimplification of the causes of the Revolution to trace many of them to Franklin's ordeal in the Cockpit. The hardening of British mercantile opinion thanks to prosperity, the snap election of 1774, the pressures for firmness: these owed nothing to Franklin and were formidable in themselves. Even less was he responsible for the Tea Party, which he condemned and in compensation for which he pledged his entire fortune, if only the offensive acts of Parliament were repealed; or for the movement for the summoning of a Continental Congress, which he greatly welcomed. These were events too remote for him to be seen as their engineer.

Yet in another sense Franklin's ordeal of January 29 is a microcosm of the causes of the Revolution, the moment of truth. To him the gulf then became obvious and unbridgeable. A moderate who had worked for peace was made a victim by ugly and irrational forces, rooted in the certainty of their prejudices. The language in which he was attacked was vindictive and savage; he was presented as an organizer of rebellion, which—until then—he certainly was not. The attack on him was foolish, for many of his ties and interests strengthened his natural caution: his crown office, his son's governorship, his wish to replace the Proprietors by a royal government, his hope for a vast land grant in the West, all made him, and might have kept him, loyal. The arrogance of Wedderburn in 1774 was in some respects an index of a national arrogance. Though distinguished by talent and important by office, Franklin met few of the men of power; far fewer in

England than in France. More and more he lamented the indifference of Englishmen "to what passes in such remote Countries as America." As late as February 1775, he professed to hope with Galloway that a constitution might be settled, "But if 'tis to be settled, it must settle itself, nobody here caring for the Trouble of thinking on't."[61]

By 1775 the dream of a consolidating union was totally abandoned. To Galloway's Plan of Union, Franklin was disposed to add preliminary conditions that he must have known were quite unobtainable, in view of the failure of his underground negotiations for a reconciliation: "Before establishing the Union, it would be necessary to agree on the following preliminary Articles": repeal of the Declaratory Act and of all Acts altering colony charters and laws; repeal of all Acts laying duties and restraining manufactures in the colonies; reenactment in "both Parliaments" as projected by Galloway, or otherwise by Parliament and the colonial assemblies, of only such portions of the Acts of Trade as were beneficial to the whole Empire; and control of the residuum of the colonial customs by the colonies.[62]

The fluctuations of Franklin's imperial planning between colonial home rule and imperial federation, between a somewhat romantic idealization of the good old ways and projects for a new constitution, reflect no real instability of purpose. His was a flexible mind grappling with the problem of *libertas et imperium* amid confusions of politics and mounting passions of controversy, which in the end would defeat all programs. By 1775 his imperialism and his sense of colonial evolution were in conflict. No longer did he hope for a continuing union under a benevolent ruler; he no longer had confidence even in the sovereign. Many of the objectionable measures, he wrote to William as early as July 1773, "have been, I suspect, very much the King's own, and he has in some cases a great share of what his friends call firmness."[63]

Franklin's last formal attempt at reconciliation was made through Chatham. Chatham had been greatly impressed by the statesmanlike actions of the Continental Congress. It denied the right of Parliamentary taxation without colonial consent and demanded the repeal of the irritating measures passed since 1763, but for the rest its language was moderate: "We ask only for peace, liberty and security. We wish no diminution of royal prerogatives, and we demand no new rights." The rights it wanted guaranteed were in fact the familiar trinity of "life, liberty and property." To all this Chatham responded. By late

1774 the two men were closely in touch, the hero's carriage conspicuous in Craven Street, "which flattered not a little my vanity." In January 1775, with Franklin a spectator, Chatham moved in the Lords
for the recall of troops from Boston; in February he asked for parliamentary recognition of the Congress, a pledge by Parliament not to
levy revenue measures on the colonies without the consent of the provincial assemblies, and in turn, for American recognition of "the supreme legislative authority and superintending power of Parliament."
But it was all to no effect. Chatham in fact remained preoccupied with
"authority," haunted by the fear of rebellion. For Franklin personally
he had gracious words: a scientist who compared with Boyle and
Newton, one who was "an honour, not to the English nation only,
but to human nature." For his part, Franklin might be flattered, but
in the end he was disenchanted. Chatham always spoke at great
length, never listened to replies, and left without concluding anything.
One day Franklin visited him at his country estate, carrying with him
documents incorporating a plan of reconciliation. Franklin arrived at
nine in the morning, listened for six hours to Chatham's wit and elo-
quence, and left at three in the afternoon with his papers untouched
and the subject of the conference not even broached. Chatham's proposals in the Lords were rejected. Indeed, as Franklin wrote four days
later to Charles Thomson, "though on so important a Subject, and
offered by so great a Character, and supported by such able and
learned speakers . . . [the proposals were] treated with as much Contempt as they could have shown to a Ballad offered by a drunken
Porter." These lords who claimed "Sovereignty over three millions of
virtuous, sensible people in America . . . appeared to have scarce Discretion enough to govern a Herd of Swine. *Hereditary legislators!*
thought I. There would be more Propriety, because less Hazard of
Mischief, in having (as in some University of Germany) *Hereditary
Professors of Mathematics.* But this was a hasty Reflection; for the
elected House of Commons is no better, nor ever will be while the
Electors receive Money for their Votes and pay Money wherewith
Ministers may bribe their representatives when chosen." [64]

In retrospect the scale of parliamentary corruption left its mark.
Later he would often tell his French friends that if the people of the
United States had given him one-quarter of the cost of the war to be
used in bribery, he could have bought independence for them. By the
time the details reached him of Galloway's Plan of Union, which the

Continental Congress rejected, he had no illusions left. He no longer believed in an imperial legislature. There was no longer a place for reason and persuasion when irrational and corrupt men were in control.

> When I consider the extream Corruption prevalent among all Orders of Men in this old rotten State, and the glorious public Virtue so predominant in our rising Country, I cannot but apprehend more Mischief than Benefit from a closer Union . . . Here Numberless and needless Places, enormous Salaries, Pensions, Prerequisites, Bribes, groundless Quarrels, foolish Expeditions, false Accounts or no Accounts, Contracts and Jobs devour all Revenue and produce continual Necessity in the Midst of natural Plenty. I apprehend, therefore, that to unite us intimately will only be to corrupt and poison us also . . . However, I would try anything, and bear anything that can be borne with Safety to our just Liberties, rather than engage in a War with such near relations, unless compelled to it by dire Necessity in our own Defence.[65]

A little more, and Franklin, in disgust and desperation, would be ready to embrace the idea of independence.

In this sense Franklin did personify and dramatize the divide. He was in his London years always on the fringe of British policymaking, never—except perhaps in February 1766 at the bar of the House of Commons—at the center, never accepted by the oligarchy of land-owners who made the major decisions. Indeed he was seen in 1774 as their enemy. He was an American, spokesman of a cause now seen in London as stubborn and unyielding, perverse and recalcitrant. He was an agent, less an ambassador in the twentieth-century sense than a man of business in the eighteenth-century sense, and regarded as the organizing executive behind the scenes. He was an Opposition man, who hobnobbed with the dissenters and with the men who inflamed the public through the press. He was close to men of learning, his very role as Philosopher and "Dr." Franklin striking an alien note. By origins he was a tradesman and that special novelty, a townsman, familiar with commerce and manufacture, his arguments disturbing as much because of their content of statistics as their content of satire. "Able and artful" was Lord Mansfield's comment on the *Edict by the King of Prussia,* but the artfulness now seemed that of the Artful Dodger, with more of craft than courtesy. He was assiduous as writer, and known to be active, witty, and near-libelous under too many other names than his own. He was bland and smooth, or, in a hostile thesaurus, devious and double-faced. He was now all too often using the language of American rights. He was irritating just because of his obvious merits, his incapacity to hide his talent under a suitable show of deference, and his skill in easy argument and socratic questioning. Most of all, and where he differed from Wedderburn and Burke, and from his friends Sandwich and Despencer, he was in the end uncomplaisant. They would all of them work their passage into social acceptance. Reluctantly he would not. There was behind the imperturbability a touch of Puritan iron. No more at sixty-nine than at seventeen would he sell his pride, or that of his newfound country, to keep his comfort.

*   *   *

"It seems," Franklin said, "that I am too much of an American." He had many talks with Admiral Lord Howe, who hoped to lead a peace mission and sought his support. His friends Fothergill and Barclay, who were busy with a petition from the London merchants, hinted at Dartmouth's interest in still more attempts at mediation. But Franklin could do no more in London; his place was at home, now that it was made crystal clear to him that in London he had become an alien. To be both British and American was now impossible; a man must choose. As he told Lord Hyde, "if any supposed I could prevail with my countrymen to take black for white, and wrong for right, it was not knowing either them or me; they were not capable of being so imposed on, nor was I capable of attempting it." When asked what would satisfy the Americans, he replied with a piece of paper on which he wrote:

	call your Forces,
	store Castle William,
	pair the Damage done to Boston,
	peal your unconstitutional Acts,
	nounce your pretensions to Tax us,
Re	fund the duties you have extorted; after this
	quire, and
	ceive payment for the destroyed Tea, with the voluntary
	grant of the Colonies, and then
	joice in a happy
	conciliation.[66]

Barclay and Fothergill could do no more in the end than encourage him to urge America to stand firm. "The salvation of English liberty depended now on the perseverance and virtue of America." On February 20, he was saddened by the news from Philadelphia that Deborah had died in December after a stroke. On March 20, he embarked at Portsmouth in the Pennsylvania packet, bound for Philadelphia.[67]

While at sea he wrote at length for his son's eyes a secret history of his recent negotiations. He recognized that it was a chronicle of failure: already defeated at the polls in Philadelphia in 1764, he had now been savaged in the Privy Council rooms in the Cockpit and deprived of his postmastership, so that now he had failed as an Imperialist. It was hard to see why: he had the respect of the learned, of the Royal Society and of the Society of Arts; his writings brought him acclaim and Poor Richard's *mots* were familiar currency; he had as propagandist, political agent, and postmaster served the cause not of American independence but of federal union; he was the most rational and unrevolutionary of men, who had even offered to pay the costs of the tea damaged in Boston Harbor. A form of federalism not unlike his own had been urged on the Continental Congress by his friend Joseph Galloway, to fail by only one vote; his view of Empire was all but identical with that of Edmund Burke, reelected M.P. for Bristol in 1774, to whom the Empire was "an aggregate of many states under a common head," and to whom also the line between the central and the local was always "extremely nice." His politics, like Burke's, were Whig: the primacy of the local assembly, the freedom of the individual in trade, religion, thought, and advancement inside a system resting on property and deference. No one in Britain, he found, wanted an independent America.[68]

Yet the failures were real: to overturn proprietary government, to obtain a new colony in the West, to restore harmony. Even his reputation as smoother and fixer had gone. Neither the Stamp Act nor independence was of his doing. But the "fine and noble China vase, the British Empire" was breaking in his hands.[69]

There had been bad luck. Of the five native North Americans who in his London years were in the House of Commons, Brice Fisher of South Carolina, M.P. for Boroughbridge, died in 1767; John Huske, Boston merchant and M.P. for Maldon, called by Horace Walpole a "wild absurd man, very conversant with America," died in 1773; and Barlow Trecothick, his ally in securing the repeal of the Stamp Act, was ailing after 1770 (he died three weeks after Franklin reached Philadelphia). He had too few friends in either house; and the West Indian, military, and landed blocs of members had heavily outnumbered the meager North American lobby. He had made hardly any contact even with Burke until the last few months of his mission.[70]

Moreover, to both houses his journalism—his forte in Philadelphia—had been unwelcome, even an irritant. He had always been happier in the coffeehouses of the Strand and among the Scots and dissenters than in the corridors of power. When he sought Burke's aid in December 1774 to present a petition to the Commons from the Congress, he invited him not to a meeting in Parliament, but to Waghorn's Coffeehouse outside—and Burke, who was agent for New York as well as M.P., declined. The arrogance of those dressed in a little authority always made him bitter: the Penns, Grenville, Hillsborough, Wedderburn. Again, product of a different world, he overstated the case against the status quo and the static view of Westminster by labeling it, simply, corruption. It was no more so than any other contemporary political system, colonial America's included. The House of Commons was of course unrepresentative: property in land was represented, people and movements of opinion were not. Voting—in both Britain and America—was oral, noisy, and much influenced by Bacchus. But a Parliament that only sixty years before had managed to curb royal power, and which a century before had had to execute one it saw as tyrant, could not easily accept a view of monarchy that would give the monarch independent authority and territory overseas. Dominion status would become acceptable only when kings and queens accepted that they reigned over all their dominions, but did not rule in any. But the distinction between ruling and reigning was as hard to grasp—by Franklin and by his contemporaries—as, in twenty years time, would be the idea of the separation of powers inside an extensive republic.[71]

It was a tired and disappointed man who went ashore at the Market Street Wharf on a mild night, May 5, 1775.

9

THE UNGRATEFUL INCENDIARY

By the time Franklin reached Philadelphia on May 5, 1775, the shots fired at Lexington Green and Concord Bridge on April 19 had echoed through the colonies. Franklin was appointed a Pennsylvania delegate to the Second Continental Congress, which convened in Philadelphia five days after his arrival. He reported to a friend that summer:

I found at my arrival all America from one End of the 12 united Provinces to the other, busily employed in learning the use of Arms. The Attack upon the Country People near Boston by the Army had rous'd every body and exasperated the whole Continent; The Tradesmen of this City were in the Field twice a day, at 5 in the Morning, and Six in the Afternoon, disciplining with the utmost Diligence, all being Volunteers. We have now three Battalions, a Troop of Light Horse, and a Company of Artillery who have made surprising Progress. The same Spirit appears everywhere and the Unanimity is amazing.[1]

The Congress was attended by sixty-five delegates, and Georgia sent five in September. They met in a room where for many years Franklin had sat, first as a clerk, then as a deputy. But most of the faces he saw were those of strangers. He knew George Washington, whom he had met as Braddock's aide twenty years before. A majority of those present had been youngsters when Franklin retired from business. His only contemporary was Stephen Hopkins of Rhode Island, with whom he had attended the Albany Congress in 1754. The dominant voice in the Pennsylvania delegation was that of his old enemy John Dickinson, who still refused to put a lightning rod on his house.

The delegates to the Second Congress faced a formidable task.

"When fifty or sixty men have a constitution to form for a great empire," said John Adams, "at the same time they have a country of fifteen hundred miles extent to fortify, millions to arm and train, a naval power to begin, an extensive commerce to regulate, numerous tribes of Indians to negotiate with, a standing army of twenty-seven thousand men to raise, pay, victual, and officer, I shall really pity those fifty or sixty men." They could request but not order, advise but not demand, recommend but not legislate. The thirteen colonies resembled "a large fleet sailing under convoy," said Adams. "The fleetest sailers must wait for the dullest and slowest." "The Management of so complicated and mighty a Machine, as the United Colonies, requires the Meekness of Moses, the Patience of Job, and the Wisdom of Solomon, added to the Valour of Daniel."[2]

The fundamental issue was the relationship of this illegal assembly to the mother country. The majority of the delegates were against independence, and a final appeal to the king was drafted: John Dickinson's Olive Branch Petition. To Adams it was the product of "a certain great fortune and piddling genius," giving "a silly cast to our whole doings." On this, however, Franklin had clearly moved forward from his position of the year before. In his conversations with Chatham in August 1774, he had still held to his dream of an ever-growing western Empire "as far as the South Sea." In his "Rules by Which a Great Empire May Be Reduced to a Small One" he argued that empires begin to crumble at their extreme outposts; the British system had been so far preserved only because the provinces had been in great measure allowed their own government. In talking with fellow Americans, however, Franklin showed another face. Josiah Quincy, Jr., who had been sent over to London from Boston to check on Franklin as well as on the political situation in general, wrote back reassuringly to Massachusetts in November 1774: "Dr Franklin is an American in heart and soul. You may trust him;—his ideas are not contracted within the narrow limits of exemption from taxes, but are extended upon the broad scale of total emancipation. He is explicit and bold upon the subject, and his hopes are as sanguine as my own, of the triumph of liberty in America."[3]

A few weeks earlier Franklin had expressed to Jonathan Williams his pleasure in the zeal with which the other colonies had supported New England. Even if they were to desert her and all Europe were to join Britain in attempting to enslave her, he was sure that "she would finally succeed." He seemed now to see no other way. As he wrote to Priestley in July 1775, Franklin was very skeptical about the results of giving Britain "one more chance, one opportunity more, of recovering the friendship of the Colonies; which however I think she has not sense enough to embrace, and so I conclude she has lost them forever." John Adams was more outspoken: "Power and artillery are the most efficacious, sure and infallible conciliatory measures we can adopt."[4]

There was now a clear recognition of the need for defense—although it was still defense against a "parliamentary army." When Patrick Henry arrived in Philadelphia, he brought the tale of Governor Dunmore's seizure of powder from the Horn in Williamsburg on April 27. Two weeks later Ticonderoga and Crown Point were captured by a mixed band of volunteers under the colorful and quarrelsome leaders Ethan Allen and Benedict Arnold. With curious facility for a nonmilitary people unfamiliar with the organization of war, the delegates in the Congress agreed to aid Massachusetts by raising an army and choosing a commander. "A powerful Army on the side of America," said Joseph Warren of Massachusetts, was "the only means left to stem the rapid progress of a tyrannical ministry."[5]

On June 16, 1775, George Washington accepted with his customary protestations the commission of commander-in-chief. He wrote to his wife, Martha, at Mount Vernon assuring her that he would be home by Christmas. There is no evidence that he felt himself the leader of a revolution. Yet such he was, for on the next day came the first battle of the war, Bunker Hill. The British casualties were 1,150 out of 2,500 men engaged—the price paid for what a participant called an "absurd and destructive confidence." The Americans lost 400 out of some 1,500 engaged.

Accompanying these steps the Congress issued, on July 6, its Declaration of the Causes and Necessity for Taking Up Arms. Although it rejected independence, it asserted that Americans would rather die than be enslaved. The war thus began at least a year before the Declaration of Independence, with the shots fired at Concord Bridge and Bunker Hill, with Washington's appointment, and with this Declaration. It began as a defense of the colonies against "the tyranny of irritated ministers," in order to bring them to terms; it was to be short, only a demonstration of force. But here again events were now not so easily controllable. What might have been intended as a further pressure on London was taken in London as confirmation of revolution. "Government can never recover itself but by using determined measures," wrote Gage to Dartmouth. "I have no hopes at present of any accommodation, the Congress appear to have too much power, and too little inclination . . . and it appeared very plainly that taxation was not the point, but a total independency." The king was convinced of it. He proclaimed the colonies to be in a state of rebellion.[6]

*   *   *

From the moment of his return Franklin had been under no illusions about this. Indeed, he had fewer illusions than many who had been thus far the radicals. A few were suspicious of him—was he a spy or friend? He had no doubts now: Americans would fight and fight well, and it would be a long war. From the start he was in favor of opening the ports to trade with the world and importing foreign military supplies. He became now the organizer of revolution: a member of committees for the defense of Philadelphia, for the printing of a continental currency, for the manufacture of saltpeter, and for the organization of the post office, of which he became first postmaster-general. The royal post office was discontinued; Philadelphia became the center of the new system, with a chain of posts from Falmouth (now Portland, Maine) to Savannah. As a member of the Pennsylvania Committee of Safety he worked on a model musket for home defense, and on a boom of logs and iron with which to block the passage of British warships should they threaten the Delaware. He organized the militia, selected officers, hunted out lead and medical supplies.

What interested him most was the government of the emergent nation. He went back to his Albany project and read to the Congress in July a paper, "Articles of Confederation and Perpetual Union," which became in emasculated and limited form the basis of the Constitution of 1781. It was an ambitious project: the United Colonies could include Canada, the Floridas, the West Indies, and Ireland if they so wished. At the center there should be a unicameral Congress, with delegates elected according to the male population of each colony. If it was in some respects a strongly centralized government that he proposed, the Congress controlling war and peace, land policy, and new colonies, it was in other respects strikingly less so, with no power to tax. Less a student of constitutions than John Adams, Franklin was more daring; here, as in the Pennsylvania Constitution of 1776, were those "democratick" dangers which the Founding Fathers later so much feared, unicameralism and centralization. But Franklin had seen so much of "mixed" government in London that he was skeptical about it; it seemed to him synonymous with corruption and incompetence. He was certainly less sympathetic toward states' rights than the Founders were to be. In his 1775 draft the office of presidency-general, as outlined in the 1754 plan, disappeared; the door was left open for this Congress to be a third house of a British Parliament, or for total independence. This last was still for the majority of delegates a fearsome prospect. It was less so for Franklin, since it seemed to him now all but inevitable. He had a confidence in the American future that was consistent with his optimism of twenty-five years before, when he had written the *Observations Concerning the Increase of Mankind*. On October 3, 1775, the day before he left for Cambridge to confer with Washington on how best to supply and provision the army, he wrote cheerfully to Priestley: "Britain, at the expence of three millions, has killed one hundred and fifty Yankies this campaign, which is twenty thousand pounds a head . . . During the same time sixty thousand children have been born in America."[7]

Two weeks later the Congressional Committee (Franklin, Lynch of South Carolina, and Benjamin Harrison of Virginia) and their three servants were in Washington's camp. Gage had been replaced by Sir William Howe, but the British forces were still shut up in Boston. The New England companies that the Congress had adopted as the Continental Army were made up of volunteers who would soon be free to go home, as many of them meant to do, and Washington asked that a new army be formed, of twenty thousand men enlisted for at least a year, with better discipline and more abundant supplies. The committee sat for four days, planning the reorganization of the army, revising the articles of war, making rules for the exchange of prisoners and for the disposal of prizes taken at sea by the armed schooners (one of them named the *Franklin*) that were now harassing British supply ships. At the end of the conference, Washington still had hopes and promises rather than an army, but New England had some reason to believe that the other colonies would continue their support, and the Congress had shown itself willing to assume, so far as it could, a general responsibility.

Franklin was now commissioner as well as committee member. In the spring of 1776, he went north in the company of Samuel Chase and Charles Carroll of Carrolton to seek to persuade the Canadians to join their brothers of the south. For arms had already failed. In the summer of 1775 the Congress had planned its first major offensive, the liberation of Canada. Two columns had advanced on Canada that autumn, one under Richard Montgomery going by way of Ticonderoga, the other under Benedict Arnold and Daniel Morgan of Virginia proceeding along a little-known route, through the forests of Maine, up the Kennebec River, over the Dead River portages, and down the Chaudière, and emerging on the St. Lawrence opposite Quebec. The battle, on New Year's Eve, was a disaster. Montgomery was killed; Arnold was carried off the field with a ball through his leg; Morgan and 370 others were taken prisoner. The wrecked army was ravaged by a smallpox epidemic, but it continued the siege through the long Canadian winter.

The weather that defeated the army also defeated Franklin, who was now over seventy. The party left New York on April 2, 1776, and traveled up the Hudson by way of Albany and the Schuyler home at Saratoga to Fort George. They embarked on Lake George on clumsy open flatboats, and had to sail through snow and ice, landing from time to time on the rough shore to build a fire, to warm themselves and drink tea. The journey from New York took twenty-seven grim days. At night some of them slept in the woods, the others (including Franklin) under awnings on the boats, in beds they had brought with them. They set out each day at four or five in the morning, landed when they were hungry or cold, steered with the current, and came to St. John's on the afternoon of April 27. In calèches ordered from Montreal they drove, over bad roads, to the St. Lawrence, again took to water, and at Montreal on April 29 were met by Arnold, now a general, with a salute from the cannon of the citadel to the "Committee of the Honourable Continental Congress . . . with the celebrated Dr. Franklin at their head." He was near exhaustion and his legs swollen with dropsy.

From the first, Franklin realized that the task was beyond his, or anyone else's, skill. The army had only four thousand men and was in appalling condition—without tents, bread, shoes, stockings, shirts. One in ten was sick, some of them from smallpox; those who did not have it lived in fear of it. The men had not been paid, they had no adequate equipment, and the food was atrocious. As Franklin reported, General Wooster was "unfit, totally unfit" for command and should be replaced. The American appeal was weakened by the tone of the Congress's Address to the People of Great Britain, adopted on October 21, 1774, which complained that the Quebec Act extended the dominion of Canada at American expense. It used dangerous and inflammatory language:

by their numbers daily swelling with Catholic Emigrants from Europe and by their devotion to Administration so friendly to their religion, they may become formidable to us and on occasion be fit instruments in the hands of power to reduce the ancient free Protestant Colonists to the same state of slavery with themselves ... Nor can we suppress our astonishment that a British Parliament should ever consent to establish in that country a Religion that has deluged your Island in blood and dispensed impiety, bigotry, persecution, murder and rebellion through every part of the world.[8]

The attitude revealed here was disturbing, and proved to be decisive: only a handful of the eighty thousand French Canadians could be won over, even though they did not wish to act aggressively and there were few troops available to protect them. There were not more than four hundred British Protestants in Canada, at least half of whom were loyalist in sentiment. The facts were as disturbing as the language. Before 1776 Catholics were allowed freedom of worship in only two colonies, Maryland and Pennsylvania, and even in these they were denied the franchise. By contrast, the Quebec Act not only had guaranteed religious freedom to Catholics but had also provided civil government for those in the West who for a decade had been without it.

The army was desperately short of supplies, money, and credit. It had debts of £14,000 and was short of another £6,000 in hard cash; Franklin gave £353 of his own, in gold. Lacking pay, the army behaved badly: priests were treated with little respect, and troops returning to the United Colonies on grounds of sickness left their baggage behind because they were weighed down with their booty. Word reached Montreal on May 6 that British reinforcements had reached Quebec by sea. There was no hope here. Franklin returned in May, sick in body and even more in mind: "The army must starve, plunder or surrender." Canadians stayed firmly loyal to Britain: they were angered by the fact of invasion; they were skillfully held in line by Sir Guy Carleton; and, overwhelmingly Catholic, they were grateful to

London for the liberalism shown in the Quebec Act. Not all Franklin's persuasion could offset the damage done by the earlier American expressions of detestation of this Act as at once Popery and tyranny. It was one of his least successful missions and one of his least happy experiences, and he paid it little subsequent attention. He was never one to ruminate long on his defeats.[9]

*   *   *

The news of the British proclamation that the colonies were in rebellion had reached Philadelphia in November 1775. On December 6 the Congress renounced all allegiance to Parliament—though not yet to the king. Franklin wrote to his friend Charles Dumas at the Hague and to Jacques Barbeu-Dubourg, the Paris translator of his works, to begin inquiries whether in the event of independence any state in Europe would become an ally "for the benefit of our commerce." From November 29 he was a member of perhaps the most important group of all, the Committee of Correspondence, charged with "corresponding with our friends in Great Britain, Ireland and other parts of the world." His fellow members were John Dickinson, John Jay, Thomas Johnson, and Benjamin Harrison; Robert Morris joined them later. This was in essence a committee on foreign affairs. From the start it was important, and in its operations it was melodramatic: secret codes and invisible ink were *de rigueur,* and by 1782 no one could be sure who was spying on whom. In December Arthur Lee, who had replaced Franklin as Massachusetts agent in London, was instructed by the Congress to seek with great discretion—a quality with which he was not richly endowed—to discover the attitudes of the European powers toward the colonies. Lee met Beaumarchais, courtier and dramatist, and each took to political intrigue with enthusiasm. Lee outlined the needs of America and its capacity to exchange tobacco for military supplies; Beaumarchais talked to all he met in French society, and wrote *La Paix ou la Guerre.* And on March 3, 1776, Silas Deane of Connecticut, thinly disguised as Timothy Jones, merchant— a disguise that deceived no one, least of all the British—was sent to France formally to seek aid. His instructions were drafted by Franklin. He was to go to Dubourg, "a man prudent, faithful, secret, intelligent in affairs," who would introduce him to American sympathizers and, it was hoped, to the French foreign minister, Vergennes. He should stress less diplomacy than economics; American trade "was rapidly increasing with our increase of people"; he should discover whether France would be willing "to enter into any treaty or alliance . . . for commerce or defense, or both." Franklin had also made contacts with Penet and Pliarne, the Nantes merchants, offering a barter trade of tobacco for military supplies. They were to trust Dubourg and no one else. In 1776 they handled a shipment of arms from the royal arsenal, with Vergennes's approval. And Lord Stormont, the British ambassador in Paris, was fully aware of the correspondence between Dubourg and Franklin, and reported it to Lord Weymouth in London.[10]

Until the formal proclamation of independence, however, Franklin opposed suggestions of formal requests for aid from foreign governments. The idea of a political alliance with France, the old and absolutist and Catholic enemy, was far from welcome; it was aid, military and economic, that was needed, if possible without strings. He had spelled it out before leaving London in his "Dialogue between Britain, France, Spain, Holland, Saxony and America." John Adams, always the Puritan, thought a link with France might "embarrass us in after times and involve us in future European wars. Franklin, although he was commonly as silent on committees as in Congress, ventured so far as to intimate his concurrence with me in these sentiments." Adams did see in Dr. Franklin, he told Abigail, "a great and good man. I wish his colleagues from this city were all like him."[11]

For France the American situation of 1775 posed acutely difficult problems. The French ministers Choiseul and Vergennes sought to undermine British power. Franklin had been accorded extravagant welcomes on his visits in 1767 and 1769. "I fancy that intriguing nation would like very well to meddle on occasion, and blow up the coals between Britain and her Colonies," he had written in 1767, "but I hope we shall give them no opportunity." Now the opportunity was being offered—but not universally welcomed. To weaken Britain and ruin her prestige, certainly; although France had renounced any intention of regaining Canada, she had an empire to protect, and if possible increase, in the Caribbean, and two inadequate islands in the St. Lawrence as fishing bases. Expansion here or elsewhere would be possible only at Britain's expense. To call into existence a new nation friendly to France would weaken Britain still more. But to weaken Britain was one thing; to aid rebellion, and a rebellion of vehement Protestants, quite another. This viewpoint was strongly endorsed by

France's ally, Spain; and should there be outright war, Spain's naval support was believed to be essential to balance British sea power. There were also voices, like that of Turgot, the French finance minister, still raised to query not only the wisdom of aid but whether the funds allowed it. And if, out of the crisis, the North government fell in Britain, to be replaced by a new coalition led by francophobic Chatham, would aid to rebels not be rashness indeed? To these considerations diplomacy had to be added. In December 1775 the suitably named Achard de Bonvouloir reached Philadelphia to assure the committee that France had abandoned all thoughts of reannexation of Canada; and would welcome American independence, but could not abet it fully or openly until it was avowed.[12]

For its part, the not-yet-independent country could not make war without arms or money, and to obtain these it needed to open its ports to other countries than Britain—which was to become in fact, if not in form, independent. Moreover, in September 1775 scattered attacks on the king had begun to appear in the colonial press. The enemy was now less Parliament and a parliamentary army than royalty and all its legions. In January 1776, with the publication of Tom Paine's brilliant pamphlet *Common Sense,* of which a hundred thousand copies were circulating by the spring, came the theory that was implicit in all these developments. The king, who sixteen months before had been described as the "loving father" of his people, was now "the royal brute." "The blood of the slain, the weeping voice of nature cries, 'Tis time to Part.'" The ties of a century and a half were dissolving in a tidal wave of antimonarchical feeling. Washington read the pamphlet and was convinced. Every day and by every post, said John Adams, demands for independence rolled in on the Congress like a torrent. In February, however, the Congress defeated Franklin's proposal to open the ports. In March John Adams admitted that they had moved from fighting half a war to fighting three-quarters of a war, but even this was not independence: "Independence is a hobgoblin of so frightful mien that it would throw a delicate person into fits to look it in the face."[13] In April Carter Braxton thought that if independence were asserted, "the Continent would be torn in pieces by intestine wars and convulsions"; Dickinson thought that in thirty years' time a separate commonwealth would split off to the north of the Hudson River. And even if independence was the outcome, how dependable and even desirable were these new Bourbon allies that had, so little time before, been old enemies? The prospect of French support was one thing, alliance quite another. There had been little commercial or cultural contact between the thirteen colonies and the Bourbon states; they had fought over fisheries and the fur trade and the lands of the interior; the French and their courts were seen as synonymous with immorality, poverty, and cruelty. And if American counsels were so divided, how sure could France be of the result?

Britain had declared the colonists to be in rebellion and proclaimed a blockade. She was now seeking to destroy coastal towns: Norfolk, Charleston, Falmouth. She was avowedly seeking foreign troops— German, as the colonists knew, and Russian, as they heard it rumored. Dunmore's recklessness in threatening a Negro insurrection in the South led to a curfew for slaves, patrolling of towns, and panic on Tidewater estates. In May, the Congress instructed the colonies to suppress British authority and to establish governments elected by the people. By that time, North Carolina, Massachusetts, and Virginia had instructed their delegates to the Congress to vote for separation from Britain. On June 24 the Congress passed the Allegiance and Treason Resolves, branding the king an enemy. On June 7, under instruction from the Virginia Assembly, Richard Henry Lee introduced his resolution that "these United Colonies are, and of right ought to be, free and independent States." John Adams seconded. The Congress ordered that Governor William Franklin of New Jersey, already arrested, should be held prisoner in a Connecticut jail.

There was still no unanimity; delegates from the Middle Colonies and from South Carolina were under instruction to oppose a motion for separation, and John Dickinson and James Wilson of Pennsylvania were loud in their opposition. Their case was not of ends but of means. They accepted by June that there could no longer be any form of unity with Britain, but they doubted, as conservatives always are apt to do, whether the time was ripe. The speech made in opposition to independence by Dickinson is as moving a statement, and as severe an indictment of Britain, as the ultimate Declaration itself.

Because of the opposition to independence of Pennsylvania, New Jersey, South Carolina, and New York, a final vote was postponed for three weeks. On June 11 a committee was set up—Jefferson, Franklin, Adams, Roger Sherman, and Robert Livingston—to draft a Declaration of Independence "in case the Congress agree thereto." The draft was Jefferson's (though voices still are heard saying that this too was Paine's handiwork) and altered but slightly. Franklin was never an addict of grandiloquence in style, and the language of "natural rights" was unusual to him. He was responsible for Jefferson's ringing truths being described as "self-evident" rather than as "sacred and undeniable." Where Jefferson had said "reduce them to arbitrary power," Franklin made it read "reduce them under absolute despotism." Jefferson said that the king had made American judges dependent on his will "for the tenure of their offices, and amount of their salaries." Franklin made it more precise by changing the last four words to "the amount and payment of their salaries." To Jefferson's charge that the king had given his assent to acts "for taking away our charters, and altering fundamentally the forms of our governments," Franklin added a third clause, inserted between the other two— "abolishing our most valuable laws"—in recollection of the many acts passed by the Pennsylvania Assembly and invalidated by Parliament. American petitions, Jefferson said, had been "answered by repeated injury." Franklin strengthened, if not exaggerated, it to "answered only by repeated injury." Jefferson's accusation that foreign mercenaries were being sent to "deluge us in blood" was modified by Franklin to the less rhetorical "destroy us." In the end, the Congress dropped the whole accusation as brought against the British people.

When Jefferson fumed over the changes, he recalled later, Franklin counseled him:

I have made it a rule whenever in my power, to avoid becoming the draftsman of papers to be reviewed by a public body. I took my lesson from an incident which I will relate to you. When I was a journeyman printer one of my companions, an apprentice hatter, having served out his time was about to open a shop for himself. His first concern was to have a handsome signboard with a proper inscription. He composed it in these words: "John Thompson, hatter, makes and sells hats for ready money," with a figure of a hat subjoined. But he thought he would submit it to his friends for their amendments. The first he showed it to thought the word "hatter" tautologous, because followed by the words "makes hats" which show he was a hatter. It was struck out. The next observed the customers would not care who made the hats. If good and to their mind, they would buy, by whomever made. He struck it out. A third said he thought the words "for ready money" were useless, as it was not the custom of the place to sell on credit. Everyone who purchased expected to pay. They were parted with, and the inscription now stood: "John Thompson sells hats". "Sells hats?" says his next friend.

"Why nobody will expect you to give them away. What then is the use of that word?" It was stricken out: and "hats" followed it, the rather as there was one painted on the board. So his inscription was reduced ultimately to "John Thompson" with the figure of a hat subjoined.[14]

The draft was presented to the Congress on July 1. After nine hours of debate, four colonies still were not in favor: Pennsylvania and South Carolina opposed it; Delaware was divided; the New York delegation was unable to vote because they awaited instructions from home. It was decided to postpone the final vote for a day. By the evening of July 2—Caesar Rodney having ridden eighty miles on horseback and in pain from Dover to break the deadlock in his delegation—Delaware had voted in support. South Carolina had come in, and Pennsylvania also, but by a very narrow margin. New York alone, of all the colonies, failed to vote. The resolution was thus approved on July 2, and on the fourth the Declaration was formally adopted. On July 8, it was read in public in the State House yard, the Liberty Bell clanged lustily, and the royal coat of arms was torn down from the State House wall and burned in a great bonfire. The Declaration was not signed until August 2, when a fair copy had been engrossed on parchment; and when Franklin said—or is said, by no less an authority this time than John Hancock, to have said—"Gentlemen, we must now all hang together, or we shall most assuredly hang separately." The story may well be apocryphal, but Jared Sparks accepts it as part of the canon.[15]

The war that was declared was not the war prepared for: the enemy now was monarchy, the goal no longer merely independence but republicanism, the rights claimed no longer "the rights of Englishmen" but "natural rights." When Lord Howe, now with his brother the general commanding in New York, wrote Franklin a letter suggesting offers of pardon, the reply was rough: "It is impossible we should think of submission to a government that has with the most wanton barbarity and cruelty burnt our defenceless towns in the midst of winter, excited the savages to massacre our peaceful farmers and our slaves to murder their masters, and is even now bringing foreign mercenaries to deluge our settlements with blood."[16]

To many colonial families, like the Fairfaxes and Coffins, the Randolphs and Bulls, the Moultries and Curwens, the final separation from the mother country brought personal tragedy and heartache; it wrenched son from father, brother from brother. For Franklin the

split came late. William had been his companion on many journeys:
to the Pennsylvania frontier in 1755; through England and Scotland
in the halcyon years of 1757–1762; in the Netherlands in 1761. William had been popular, good-looking, and easy-mannered, and his
father had taken pride in his success as governor of New Jersey.
Throughout Franklin's second spell in London, 1764–1775, the correspondence between father and son had been extensive and cordial,
and especially close on Indian affairs; William was his associate in the
Vandalia project. William had in fact handled his colony with skill.
He improved roads and alleviated conditions for debtors in prisons.
He stayed on—and stayed in touch with his Assembly—long after
other governors had fled. He was helped by the absence of firebrands
and radicals in his province, and by the lack of local newspapers. He
built a three-story brick house for himself in Burlington, developed a
farm of some six hundred acres at Rancocas Creek, and ran a stable
of horses. In explaining his success to his father in 1771 he had given
some hint of a difference in temperament: "I think that all Laws until
they are repealed ought to be obeyed and that it is the Duty of those
who are entrusted with the Executive Part of Government to see that
they are so." Even after Franklin's own dismissal in 1774, his caution
led him to discourage any idea of resignation in his son. He wrote to
William in February 1774:

Some tell me that it is determined to displace you likewise, but I do not know
it as certain . . . Perhaps they may expect that your Resentment of their Treatment of me may induce you to resign and save them the shame of depriving
you when they ought to promote. But this I wou'd not advise you to do. Let
them take your place if they want it, tho in truth I think it is scarce worth
your keeping it since it has not afforded you sufficient to prevent your running every year behindhand with me. But one may make something of an
Injury, nothing of a Resignation.

William Franklin did not resign, nor did he share his father's political
sentiments. "You," Franklin wrote to him on September 7, "who are
a thorough Courtier, see everything with Government Eyes." [17]

When it came, the breach was sudden, total, and unforgiving. Almost a decade later, in August 1784, he would write to William:
"Your situation was such that few would have censured your remaining Neuter, *tho there are Natural duties which precede political ones
and cannot be extinguish'd by them.* This is a disagreeable Subject. I
drop it." [18]

In his father's will, William received the worthless claims to the Nova Scotia lands, whatever books and papers he had in his possession, and the cancellation of his debts to Franklin's estate. In other words he received nothing, with the final comment "The part he acted against me in the late war, which is of public notoriety, will account for my leaving him no more of an estate he endeavoured to deprive me of." The father carried his hurt to the grave. The mask of blandness of countenance cracked where William was concerned. William died in exile and in poverty in 1813, two years after the death of his second wife. (His first wife, Elizabeth, had died in July 1776, while William was in prison in Connecticut; Washington had not granted permission for him to see her as she lay dying.)

*   *   *

There was iron now in Franklin's soul. This was a man who, with all his amiability and persuasiveness, could be bitter and could nurse a grievance. He had enemies. In turn, he could be an enemy. He had never forgiven the Penns. He would never forgive Wedderburn, and part of the bitterness of these months in 1775 and 1776 was a legacy of the Cockpit. He would never forgive his son, or his son's wife, Elizabeth, whom in large part he blamed for William's Loyalism. Bland, cool, calm, yes. But charity and forgiveness were coming to be rare features in his character. It did not do to cross him now. The asperities were sharper, the hesitations fewer. In July 1775 he wrote a singular and unhappy letter to William Strahan, a letter that might have been designed for public effect, since it was never sent: "You are a Member of Parliament, and one of that Majority which has doomed my Country to Destruction—You have begun to burn our Towns, and murder our People.—Look upon your Hands! They are stained with the Blood of your Relations!—You and I were long Friends:—You are now my Enemy,—and I am, Yours, B. Franklin." Or perhaps he merely felt that it went too far. For he and Strahan kept up their friendly correspondence as long as they could—until the last regular packet from England to America.[19]

Franklin's response to the final letters from Strahan showed that the moderate in him was still alive. He wrote from Philadelphia in October 1775:

You wish me to come over with Proposals of Accommodation. Your Ministers have made that impracticable for me, by prosecuting me with a frivolous

Chancery Suit in the name of Whately, by which, as my Sollicitor writes me, I shall certainly be imprisoned if I appear again in England. Nevertheless, send us over hither fair Proposals of Peace, if you choose it, and nobody shall be more ready than myself to promote their Acceptation. For I make it a Rule not to mix personal Resentments with Public Business.[20]

If this was not a revolutionary, and certainly no grand incendiary, this was clearly a man nursing a deep hurt. Britain's "fondness for conquest as a warlike nation," her "lust of dominion" as an ambitious one, "atrocious injuries," "wanton barbarity," "tyranny and obstinacy"—these phrases, used in his exchanges with Lord Howe, are for him novel, and signal the end of a phase. He had turned full circle, however reluctantly, from monarchist to republican.

There is clear evidence of the extent of his transition in the Pennsylvania constitution of 1776. It was drawn up by a constitutional convention, to which he was elected at the head of the Philadelphia delegation of eight, and over which, as Pennsylvania's best-known figure, he presided. The convention met on July 15—the date originally set had been July 8, but that had become instead the public, and very boisterous, celebration of the proclamation of the Declaration of Independence. Certainly at the time the new constitution was seen in Pennsylvania as at least as significant as the now-more-famous document of a week before.

The constitution provided for a General Assembly, elected by all freemen over twenty-one who paid taxes and all nontaxpaying sons of freeholders, regardless of their religious allegiance (although all the delegates to the Constitutional Convention were required to affirm belief in the divinity of Christ and the divine inspiration of the Bible). It omitted all propertyholding requirements in the holders of public office; and it provided for an executive council of twelve, one from each county, elected for three-year terms, which would choose a president of Pennsylvania, to serve as a formal figurehead on state occasions; for annual elections, legislative debates open to the public, and the rotation of office-holders; for the doubling of western representation (until a census could be taken, each county and Philadelphia would have six representatives) and for a Council of Censors, to prevent any violation of the constitution itself.

The ultra-democratic features of the document—especially its plural and vetoless executive and its single-chamber assembly—and the fact that it was the first of the new constitutions gave its contents dramatic value in America and in Europe. From the beginning it was seen in France as Franklin's special handiwork. "The doctor, when he went to France in 1776, carried with him the printed copy of that Constitution, and it was immediately propagated through France that this was the plan of government of Mr. Franklin . . . Mr. Turgot, the Duke de la Rochefoucault, Mr. Condorcet and many others became enamoured with the Constitution of Mr. Franklin." The acerbity indicates the source of this quotation: John Adams. "He (Franklin) did not even make the constitution of Pennsylvania, bad as it is. The bill of rights is taken almost verbatim from that of Virginia. That of Pennsylvania was written by Timothy Matlack, James Cannon, Thomas Young and Thomas Paine."[21] In fact, Paine was not present in person, although James Cannon, who was, often echoed Paine's views, and the new constitutional structure did bear close resemblance to that outlined in *Common Sense*. It certainly represented a sharp break with the past: no governor, a council clearly subordinate to a single-chamber Assembly, and many few faces. Not a single member of the new executive council had held office in the last colonial government. Utopianism lay just below the surface: candidates for office were instructed to be conspicuous for a "firm adherence to justice, moderation, temperance, industry and frugality," and "laws for the prevention of vice and immorality shall be made and constantly kept in force." One of the first acts of the new state government in fact was to send into exile twenty of the most prominent Quakers in Philadelphia—the so-called Virginia exiles—including Elijah Brown, Henry Drinker, Thomas Wharton, and Israel and James Pemberton. It seemed that the days of Allens and Chews, Cadwaladers and Logans, Penns and Shippens had passed for good.

Before long, around this constitution the old party lines would regroup: many Presbyterians and Scotch-Irish and the majority of back-country farmers supported the constitution of 1776, the so-called Constitutionalists; the majority of Quakers and Anglicans, and many Philadelphians (including Robert Morris, Thomas Willing, and James Wilson), the so-called Republicans, were highly critical. Half or more of the people were, it seems, opposed to it, and its short reign was stormy. As early as October 1776 eastern political leaders met and passed thirty-two resolutions against the constitution, and they campaigned against it throughout the war. A totally new constitution was enacted in 1790. And by 1788 each side claimed Franklin as being not only the document's author, which he was not, but as being one of them—which, given his flexibility, he probably was.

It was, nevertheless, with this constitution that Franklin became publicly associated, and indeed, in 1788 when it was under bitter attack, he defended it. Clearly, whatever his sympathies, he could not have been a very active participant; in June, on returning from Canada, he had been ill with what he described as gout, but which seems to have been a distressing mixture of boils and psoriasis; he was physically exhausted by the Canadian experience. Yet, five days after the opening of the state convention he was also elected a delegate to the Federal Congress; he said later that in 1776 he had been busy twelve hours a day on public business. Nor did his chairmanship permit active work in committee; he was involved in the committee on style, and when the convention adjourned, it thanked him for his chairmanship, and for his "able and disinterested advice," without indicating what expressly he had advised. Of the convention's sixty-three meetings, he presided in fact only at nineteen, and missed nine (four of them while on his journey to meet with the peace commissioner, Lord Howe); there is no way of discovering how many of the other thirty-five sessions he attended. We know that he spoke once—but then oratory was not his forte, and his taste was always less for theorizing than for problem-solving.

There were at the convention younger, and even keener, republican voices than his. They had emerged in his ten-year absence, during which he had become remote from his province. He had always had enemies—in the proprietary party, and among Germans and westerners. One of the new voices was that of James Cannon, Franklin's fellow delegate from Philadelphia, who was responsible for the drafting of the document. George Bryan, who led the majority in the convention, was a Scotch-Irish Presbyterian who had arrived only in 1752 and had defeated Franklin in the bitter contest of 1764. Franklin had made his mark not one but two generations earlier, climbing a more difficult ladder; to many now he was too old and distant. But now that the king's men had gone, and, after the Cockpit affair, he was clearly something of a hero, and even a martyr. There might be here a name to conjure with.

We know that with one of the constitutional provisions Franklin did not agree: the clause requiring the members of the legislature to take an oath affirming belief in God, in future rewards and punishments, and in the divine inspiration of the scriptures. He insisted that "no further or more extended Profession of Faith should ever be exacted." Nor did he endorse the provision by which slavery was recognized as a legal institution in Pennsylvania. One section of the document did have his total endorsement: "If any man is called into public service to the prejudice of his private affairs, he has a right to a reasonable compensation; and whenever an office, through increase of fees or otherwise becomes so profitable as to occasion many to apply for it, the profits ought to be lessened." He had always held to this view: public service was an honorable activity, not to be monopolized by men merely of ambition or of avarice. He attributed the ills of Britain less to the king than to "the enormous salaries, emoluments, and patronage of great offices," of which cabals and factions and "violent divisions" were, he held, the result. It would not happen in Pennsylvania.[22]

To the unicameralism that he supported in 1776 Franklin held firm until the end. He always saw a second chamber in terms of the Upper House in Britain; with a few exceptions, he had no taste for *aristos* or for men wielding power and patronage, as did the British peers. Or, at best, a second chamber would be just another Governor's Council of the local great and the local good, able to bribe when they failed to persuade. Such division could, he believed, spell the exploitation of the people. He had, as always, a fable to suit the occasion. It was the story of "the snake with two heads and one body . . . She was going to a brook to drink, and in her way was to pass through a hedge, a twig of which opposed her direct course. One head chose to go on the right side of the twig, the other on the left, so that time was spent in the contest; and before the decision was completed the poor snake died of thirst."[23]

*   *   *

By 1775, and despite his age, activity itself became satisfaction enough: membership of the committee of safety, of the state constitutional convention, of the Congress, and of the newly constituted post office, all of them activities in or around Market Street; winning friends, influencing and smoothing people. Add the diplomatic journeys to Canada and to Lord Howe. It is not surprising that when he sat in a chair he was often noticed to be asleep. But then he had never been sought for his skill as an orator, or as a crusader for causes. A natural politician with his unique diversity of experience was, as always, immensely useful: though now presented as leader and as hero, he was in fact in Pennsylvania now a figurehead, an *apparatchik* in a new elite now going for republicanism and independence.

In August, after Washington's defeat on Long Island, Congress was approached by Lord Howe in his role as peace commissioner, and a committee of three—Franklin, John Adams, and Edward Rutledge—waited upon him on Staten Island. The discussions came to nothing, because Howe, though empowered to grant pardons to the "rebels" who submitted, could not treat with the Congress or the state governments as independent bodies. Tempers worsened and attitudes polarized still more.

Franklin was already at work on a plan for a series of commercial treaties with sympathetic states in Europe, if they could be found. Deane's reports from Paris were encouraging. So, on September 26, 1776, the Congress decided to send a commission of three to negotiate a treaty with France. Franklin, Deane, and Jefferson were first chosen; when Jefferson declined, Arthur Lee replaced him. Franklin helped to draft his own instructions. He thought it unlikely that France would allow the United States to "sink in the present contest," but she might think that "we are able to support the war on our own strength and resources longer than in fact we can do." The need was clear: an "immediate and explicit declaration of France in our favour, upon a suggestion that a reunion with Great Britain may be the consequence of a delay." The risk was equally clear: of alliance and entanglement. This he did not welcome: "A virgin state should preserve the virgin character, and not go about suitering for alliances . . . I was over-ruled; perhaps for the best." To go abroad to contrive not a marriage of true minds but a mere liaison of convenience called for uncanny deftness of touch; he had to bargain not just from weakness but from nakedness; and to bargain with a power that was in American eyes the old enemy, Catholic, despotic, and immoral.[24]

As for himself, he was over seventy, and a widower. New men with radical views were in office, if not in full control, in Pennsylvania. His son was now a Loyalist, and irrevocably estranged. "Don't go, pray don't go," urged his favorite sister, Jane Mecom. He saw himself, however, as expendable; "I am old and good for nothing," he told Benjamin Rush, "but as the store-keepers say of their remnants of cloth . . . I am but a fag end, and you may have me for what you please." [25] Before leaving Philadelphia he lent to Congress some three or four thousand pounds, and left his papers in the safe keeping of his old ally of the Pennsylvania struggles, Joseph Galloway, now, it seemed, safely retired to the country. He sailed on October 26 in the three-masted sloop *Reprisal,* with its eighteen six-pounder guns; it had already served as a raider of British merchant ships for the Philadelphia firm of Willing and Morris. It was, however, so frail that it foundered on its return voyage. "A miserable vessel," he called it, "improper for those northern seas"; the accommodation was so "miserable" that he was almost "demolished"; they were chased by British men-of-war, though they captured two small prizes just off the French coast; when they reached Quiberon Bay storm-force winds prevented them from moving up the Loire to Nantes. On landing, he had "scarce strength to stand." He took with him for company his two grandsons: William's son Temple, aged sixteen, who would act as his secretary, and Benjamin Franklin Bache, aged seven. Once again, the journey was put to good use: his seventh crossing gave him yet one more opportunity to study the characteristics of the Gulf Stream.

10

BONHOMME RICHARD

The Paris Franklin reached in December 1776 was not strange to him; he had visited it twice already, in Sir John Pringle's acerbic company, in 1767 and 1769. He left little trace of these visits in his correspondence, except of his meetings with the Physiocrats, with the economist François Quesnay and Thomas-François Dalibard, his translator and correspondent through the years, his contacts with Barbeu-Dubourg over the publication of his scientific papers, and his presentation at court. He appreciated the honor of being presented but was aware of the reasons: the French foreign minister, the Duke of Choiseul, was seeking, he thought, "to blow up the coals between Britain and her colonies." Franklin, after all, then thought his own "King and Queen the very best in the world, and the most admirable." His main contacts on these visits had been with boatmen and porters: "I know not which are the most rapacious, English or French; but the latter have, with their knavery, the most politeness."[1]

His Paris was of course prerevolutionary, not yet the handsome, well-planned Paris of the Haussmann era. The city was cradled in its hills, its streets cobbled and crooked, narrow and congested, with few sidewalks, and usually wet from the open sewers that ran in the gutters. It lay on a very old waterway to the sea, at the center of a fertile and forested basin. At a time when London had 750,000 people, and New York fewer than 100,000, Paris had some 650,000. In the eighteenth century, as Franklin had discovered by living two hundred yards from it, Londoners enjoyed their Thames; it flowed through their lives and past their gardens, and it was still a pleasant if increasingly crowded and polluted waterway. The Seine was more exclusive and cleaner than the Thames, and even more at the center of its city's life. After being "clarified," the Seine water was sold from door to

door. Most of the bridges were owned and operated by private con-
cessionaires, who levied tolls; two rows of shops lined the sidewalks
of the Pont Neuf.

The Île de la Cité, then as now, lay on the river like a great stone
barge moored at its historic heart, with Notre Dame at its eastern
end; it was then dominated by the Palais de Justice—ravaged by fire
just before Franklin's arrival—and the Conciergerie. Although the
Jesuits had recently been expelled, the Paris Franklin knew was still
ecclesiastical, dotted with churches and monasteries and peopled by
clerics. Churches would not have surprised him, nor the cattle yards
and slaughter houses, moneychangers and jewelers—sights as familiar in London as in Paris. He would have noticed the *quais* at which
goods were loaded and unloaded: Bercy for wines, La Rapée for timber, Macas for wood, La Grève for fruit, La Gare for oil. Because of
the expense and difficulty of land transport, goods and passengers
were still conveyed as far as possible by water. Any print of the Seine
at Paris in the eighteenth century shows it lined with rows of boats
discharging supplies from the great hinterland tapped by its tribu-
taries.

Franklin's Paris was rich in history. The Rue St. Honoré was the
"main street" from east to west, from the Bastille to the just-
completed Place Louis XV. Ange-Jacques Gabriel's handiwork was
the largest square Franklin would see in all the world; within fifteen
years it was to be renamed the Place de la Révolution. It was, said
Arthur Young, who toured France before the Revolution, "not properly a square, but a very noble entrance to a great city." The Rue
Royale had been built forty years before, and Louis XIV had been
honored by triumphal arches at the Porte St. Denis and the Porte St.
Martin. If the city did not have the royal parks of London, the
Champs de Mars had been laid out six years before, and the gardens
of the Palais Royal, the Tuileries, and the Luxembourg were now over
a century old.[2]

The reason for these peaceful developments was clear. After the age
of Louis XIV, the threat of invasion or of civil war no longer hung
over France, and the ramparts around Paris and other cities, which
had already often spread beyond them, were converted into public
spaces and promenades. Formal gardens were laid out, enclosed with
balustrades, peopled with statues, and shaded by trees. Boulevards
replaced the old walls, triumphal arches replaced the fortified gates.

Building enjoyed an unprecedented expansion. Contemporary maps are dotted with the word *chantiers,* buildings under construction. So much building and rebuilding augured great prosperity. A new Théâtre Italien, a new Théâtre Français, a new Mint on the quai de Conti, a splendid grain market, the domed Halle aux Blés were erected. The last was completed in 1782, in time to be the scene for a public festival to celebrate the Peace Treaty of 1783; in July 1790, its walls draped in black, it would be the scene for a commemorative tribute to Franklin before three thousand people. Paris was expanding—the new areas of the Chaussée D'Antin and the Faubourg du Roule were fashionable, and expensive.

To the south of the city, on Sainte Geneviève's mount, was rising Jacques-Germain Soufflot's domed church, relic of Louis XV's vow after his recovery from illness at Metz in 1744; by the time it was completed in 1790 it would so vividly recall the Roman Pantheon that it would become a sepulchre for *les grands hommes;* Voltaire and Mirabeau were the first to be entombed there. It was already beginning to cast its shadow over the Latin quarter, which since Abelard's day had been the haunt of scholars and controversialists, and of the mendicant orders of the Sorbonne, the great marketplace of western ideas. Around the cobbles of Notre Dame and in its side streets the power of the church was visible, with its attendant monasteries, convents, and schools. On the right bank along the Rue St. Honoré the wealth of merchants was conspicuous, but on the left bank it was ideas that mattered.

The roads of France showed the influence, as did so much else, of a centralizing ruler. In 1767 Franklin had noted how good the roads were and noted too the complaints of the "peasants" over the *corvée:* "obliged to work upon the roads full two months in the year without being paid for their labors. Whether this is truth, or whether like Englishmen, they grumble, cause or no cause, I have not yet been able fully to inform myself." Radiating out from Paris, wide and straight, the roads were determined by the political predominance of the capital and by military rather than by economic considerations. Arthur Young repeatedly mentions the quality of the French roads and the lack of traffic on them, even in the neighborhood of great cities. His comments on the streets of Paris itself, however, are not favorable: "The streets are very narrow, and many of them crowded, nine-tenths dirty and all without foot-pavements. Walking, which in London is so pleasant and so clean that ladies do it every day, is here a toil and a fatigue to a man and an impossibility to a well-dressed woman."[3]

Outside Franklin's cloistered existence this was a world of a few very rich and many poor. The rich were privileged and largely exempt from taxes, as was the church. Some four thousand *aristos* owned great estates and held bishoprics and commissions in the military. Perhaps one in four peasants owned land outright—some as relatively prosperous *laboureurs,* others (as Arthur Young found) "poor and miserable, much arising from the minute division of their little farms among all the children." Half or more were poor sharecroppers, or *métayers,* who owned no capital and shared their produce on a fifty-fifty basis with their landlords; a quarter perhaps were landless laborers or rented tiny plots. If his legal disabilities were less oppressive than in many other states, the French peasant carried a heavy burden of taxation: tithes to the church; *taille, vingtième, capitation,* and *gabelle* (salt tax) to the state; and to the seigneur of his parish a varying series of tolls, services, and indirect payments. These varied greatly in the different regions of the country, but, in years of bad harvests and depression, they all proved to be oppressive and resented burdens.[4]

Industrial change was just beginning in France. In 1789 there were 20,000 spinning jennies in England and only 900 in France. There was already, however, a public alertness, and a popular press was about to develop. There was no daily paper before the *Journal de Paris* began to appear in 1777. But in the last decade before the Revolution the growth of the periodical press was striking: there were 35 papers and periodicals of all kinds in France in 1779, and 169 in 1789. Meanwhile, the writings of the Enlightenment—the tracts and treatises of Montesquieu and Rousseau, the *Encyclopedia* of d'Alembert and Diderot, Raynal's *History,* Voltaire's political satires and letters—had begun, in numerous guises and translations, to circulate outward from Paris and the Netherlands. The American Revolution and its aftermath, like the news of Franklin's electrical experiments in an earlier decade, produced a fresh crop of tracts and commentaries that extended still further the boundaries of enlightened and educated public opinion. In this fermenting and cosmopolitan world, as fifty years earlier in Philadelphia and twenty years earlier in London, Franklin quickly felt at home.

Of Versailles, we have what from Franklin is a rarity, a physical description. In 1767 he wrote to Polly Stevenson: "the range of build-

ing is immense, the Garden Front most magnificent all of hewn stone
. . . but the Waterworks are out of repair, so is a great part of the
Front next the Town, looking with its shabby half Brick Walls and
broken Windows not much better than the houses in Durham Yard.
There is in short both at Versailles and Paris a Prodigious Mixture of
Magnificence and Negligence, with every kind of Elegance except that
of Cleanliness, and what we call Tidyness." [5]

Across the river from Paris and on the road to Versailles lay Franklin's Passy. In 1776 it was already a bourgeois suburb, but it was then
almost a mountain village; the land dropped down to the Seine more
sharply than today. Passy is now, like its neighbor Auteuil, swallowed
up in the sixteenth *arrondissement,* in the long shadow of the Palais
de Chaillot. In Franklin's day it ranked as one of the loveliest of the
small villages ringing the city. Surrounded by forests and vineyards, it
was less a single village than a cluster of villes, with four royal châ-
teaux, a parish church, and a scatter of houses and shops. It owed its
reputation to its sulphurous springs, well known for their alleged me-
dicinal and therapeutic qualities; Franklin drank much of its good but
malodorous *eau rouge.* Passy was a small-scale French edition of
Bath, with assembly rooms, a small theater, and flower gardens
within sight of the leafy park on the Chaillot hill. Franklin put up a
lightning rod on the house at what is now 66 rue Raynouard.

*   *   *

Franklin landed on December 3, 1776, at Auray. After waiting three
days in Quiberon Bay with the ship at anchor, because winter storms
held up its approach, he finally was perilously put ashore in a fishing
boat. Auray he found to be "a wretched place," and he stayed no
longer than necessary before traveling the seventy miles to Nantes.
This was a major port for the American and the slave trade, much
less exposed than Le Havre, and it would flourish during the American war. In Nantes were the offices of the Pliarne brothers and their
Alsatian associate Pierre Penet, who had visited America a year before, had contacts with the Browns of Rhode Island, and made plans
with the Committee of Secret Correspondence to send supplies. With
credits from the Swiss banking house of Schweighauser, they supplied
15,000 weapons—to the embarrassment of Vergennes, the French
foreign minister, who thereupon charged Beaumarchais, the play-
wright turned adventurer, to do the same, but more discreetly. Beau-

marchais set up a fictitious company, Roderigue Hortalez et Cie, as an instrument for French government assistance under disguise—a disguise that deceived no one. The American Congress also had an agent at Nantes in Thomas Morris, half-brother of Robert; he proved to be irresponsible and a drunkard, and within a month Franklin would reprimand him for not transferring to the commissioners' account the money he obtained from the sale of prizes and cargoes. Nantes was to become also John Paul Jones's headquarters, and here Franklin was to place as his own agent his grandnephew Jonathan Williams (whom he was apt to call "cousin Jonathan"): conscientious and always worried, always obliging and always much obliged. By 1783 the banking house, then of Dobrée and Schweighauser, had lent more than 10,000 livres for the cause.

Franklin spent twelve days at La Barberie, the country home of Barthelemy-Jacques Gruel, a substantial merchant whose wealth came from Santo Domingo. He was looked after there by the Jogues family, one of whom, Thérèse, had married Jacques-Donatien Le Ray de Chaumont, a wealthy shipper, slave trader, and army supplier who had made a fortune out of the East Indies trade. From the first, Franklin was in the welcoming grip of the Chaumonts—welcoming and watchful.

His 250-mile journey from Nantes to Paris was a slow but triumphal procession. He wrote to his sister on December 8, "You can have no conception of the respect with which I am received and treated here by the first people, in my private character; for as yet I have assumed no public one." He was wined and dined by the literary and scientific notables en route. He was entertained by the Duke de Choiseul, the Duke de la Rochefoucauld, and the Prince de Broglie—welcomed by the great as he had never been in England. He reached Paris on December 20, 1776, cocooned in adulation. And his correspondence from now on reflects his contentment. The French, he told Josiah Quincy, were "a most amiable nation to live with. The Spaniards are by common opinion suppos'd to be cruel, the English proud, the Scotch insolent, the Dutch avaricious etc, but I think the French have no national vice ascrib'd to them." In the salons of Paris, and among intellectuals, America and travelers' tales of it were already fashionable. In the New World, they dreamed, simplicity would be rewarded, virtue triumphant, and Nature enthroned. Republican and classical Rome, it would seem, would be reborn in Boston. Franklin fitted easily into this setting. When he was sounded out on his religious views, the critical spirits of the *philosophes* relaxed: "they discovered that he is a believer in their own religion—that is to say, that he has none at all."[6]

In France Franklin was already a familiar name: the versatile author of *Poor Richard* and of scientific works, the defender of the rights of the colonies in 1766, elected in 1772 one of the eight foreign associates of the Academy of Sciences. Rousseau's friend Joseph Bertier had written to him in 1769 that France "is your country as much as England is. You would be here in the midst of Franklinists, a father in his own country."[7] His scientific paper *Observations and Experiments on Electricity* had been translated, on Buffon's urging, by Dalibard and appeared in French in 1752 and again in 1756; it had appeared also in two elegant quartos edited by Barbeu-Dubourg as one of the *Oeuvres de M. Franklin* in 1773, which included also his *Observations Concerning the Increase of Mankind, The Way to Wealth,* and the reflections of *Le Pauvre Henri,* and some of his earlier contributions to the Physiocrats' journal, the *Ephémérides du Citoyen.* The verses beneath the handsome portrait that served as frontispiece to the *Oeuvres* expressed the universal admiration:

> Il a ravi le feu des Cieux,
> Il a fait fleurir les Arts en des Climats sauvages,
> L'Amérique le place a la tête des Sages,
> La Grèce l'aurait mis au nombre de ses Dieux.

The lines were translated for the English press in 1774—perhaps by Franklin himself?—

> To steal from Heaven its sacred fire he taught;
> The arts to thrive in savage climes he brought;
> In the New World the first of Men esteem'd;
> Among the Greeks a God he has been deem'd.

The government, however, unwilling as yet to recognize the rebellious colonies lest the rebellion peter out too quickly, could not openly receive him. Stormont, the British ambassador, reported his arrival to Lord Weymouth: "I look upon him as a dangerous engine, and am very sorry that some English frigate did not meet with him by the way."

I shall endeavour to discover what Franklin *does,* but shall seldom trouble your Lordship with account of what he *says;* my reason, my Lord, is this. I have already traced him so far as to know that to different people he holds different and indeed quite contradictory language; for instance to some he says that the Americans will never submit, to others that General Howe will soon bring about an accommodation. This weak conduct, which will soon be known in such a prating town as this, will confirm the general suspicion of his duplicity."

The ambassador indeed threatened to leave his post if "the chief of American rebels" ever set foot in Paris. But Stormont stayed on; Franklin arrived, and high society and the populace took him to their hearts.[8]

To Vergennes Franklin was a likely instrument of French imperial revenge on Britain; to the Encyclopedists and Physiocrats he was a "natural man" from an idyllic republican wilderness; to bluestockings he was a rustic philosopher with a plain dress, unpowdered gray hair, unpretentious manners, and civilized tastes, with an approving eye for the ladies and a neat democratic wit. The Comte de Ségur wrote of him:

The most surprising thing was the contrast between the luxury of our capital, the elegance of our fashions, the magnificence of Versailles, the surviving evidence of Louis XIV's mode of life, the polite haughtiness of our nobility— and Benjamin Franklin. His clothing was rustic, his bearing simple but dignified, his language direct, his hair unpowdered. It was as though classic simplicity, the figure of a thinker of the time of Plato, or a republican of the age of Cato or Fabius had suddenly been brought by magic into our effeminate and slavish age, the eighteenth century. This unexpected visitor charmed us all the more as he was not only a novelty but appeared when literature and philosophy were astir with demands for reform, for change, and for a universal love of liberty.[9]

Franklin lived first in the Hôtel d'Entragues in the rue de l'Université, then in the Hôtel d'Hambourg in the rue Jacob; and from March 1777 in Passy, first in a garden pavilion five minutes away from the main house, and after 1779 in a wing of the Hôtel Valentinois, put at his service by Chaumont. In 1780 Chaumont rented another part of the house to an admirer of Franklin's, the beautiful Yvonne de Polignac, whom the mob during the Terror would tear limb from limb. The estate was spacious and attractive, and the *hôtel* stood on the crest of a bluff with terraces and formal gardens, a lake and avenues of clipped lindens, leading down to the Seine. Paris lay half an hour's drive to the east, Versailles ten miles away to the west.

Franklin was fortunate in his friend and landlord, though it seems unlikely that chance led Chaumont to become his patron and benefactor. Chaumont was wealthy, enterprising, and ambitious. He was a Grand Master of Water and Forests, Director and Intendant of the Invalides, and a Mason (as were Dobrée and Schweighauser). His ceramics factory on the Loire produced many Franklin medallions. He was a government contractor, a supplier of army uniforms and outfitter of ships, one of the privileged Farmers-General, a kinsman of Maurepas, the first minister, and a friend of Vergennes and Sartine, the Navy Secretary. He shared their anglophobia, and hoped to exploit the war situation to his own advantage to become "le grand munitionaire des Americains," the financial counterpart to Lafayette. This was a man of power and influence. He had a great château at Chaumont sur Loire, between Blois and Tours, to which he owed his prefix "de," and the purchase of which had been been financed by his success as a merchant prince in the East Indies. He had bought the house at Passy, its furnishings and the estate, for 140,000 livres six months before, just in time to allow it to be a base for an important visitor. For Franklin life here was a splendid edition of Craven Street. Mme de Chaumont arranged, and at times acted as hostess at, his dinner parties; and the domestics were his to command.

Chaumont had his own agent in America, John (Jean) Holker, who after 1778 became France's first consul-general in Philadelphia. He was, in all his enterprises, liberal toward the great new cause, ready to invest in it lavishly. Chaumont was to spend two million francs, almost his entire fortune, aiding the Americans; he said that he would take no rent from Franklin until the American cause was triumphant. The deal they made was carefully itemized: Franklin would pay six francs a meal (about 4400 per year) plus six for every guest; when he dined separately he would pay his own wine bill, and when he entertained guests separately and was supplied by his hostess he would meet the total bill. This was a strict commercial transaction.[10]

The Duc de Croy was impressed by the residence, and by the relatively frugal meal "without soup," but he praised the fish, the excellent American pudding, and the pastry. "Everything there breathed," he said, "simplicity and economy well befitting a philosopher." John Adams, by contrast, denounced the luxury: "at what rent I never could discover, but from the Magnificence of the Place, it was universally expected to be enormously high." Chaumont explained to Adams in 1778, "When I consecrated my house to the use of Dr. Franklin and his associates who might share it with him, I made it fully understood that I should receive no compensation . . . I pray you, Sir, to permit this arrangement to remain which I made when the fate of your country was doubtful."[11]

In December 1782, after the preliminary peace treaty with Britain was signed, Chaumont, then on the eve of bankruptcy, did send Franklin a bill. Franklin replied that he had not occupied the main residence for the whole of the period; in 1784 they settled on 15,000 livres in back rent, plus a bonus. The rent for Franklin's final year at Passy was 6,000 livres. The house had to be sold in the Chaumont bankruptcy proceedings; it no longer exists, but Leray, Chaumont's son, later an American citizen, was to build a replica at Leraysville in upstate New York. At the end of the war Congress at last recognized the elder Chaumont's services by the only gift available to it: a grant of land in the New World. By that time, however, he—like Penet of Nantes also—was ruined.

Franklin's life at Passy was one of public modesty but private affluence. He had no fewer than nine servants, and his account of the food and drink indicates a regal style for so staunch a republican. Breakfast, at eight on weekdays and at nine or ten on Sundays, was bread and butter, honey, and coffee or chocolate or their fair equivalents, such as Franklin's tea. For dinner at two there was a joint of beef or veal or mutton, followed by fowl or game, with two sweets, two vegetables, pastry, hors d'oeuvres, butter, pickles, radishes, two kinds of fruit in winter, four in summer, two compôtes, cheese, biscuits, bonbons, and ices twice a week in summer and once in winter. The cellar was as generous as the table. In February 1779 Franklin had access to 1,041 bottles of wine: more red and white Bordeaux, less Burgundy, a little champagne, a great deal of sparkling white wine, a good deal of vin rouge ordinaire (probably for the servants), and 48 bottles of rum. In September 1782 his stock was 1,203 bottles. To feed his household of four, plus the nine servants, he paid Jacques Fink, his majordomo, 1,300 francs a month. Not much of this, it seemed, actually reached butcher and baker; after Franklin left, the police were chasing Fink. "He was continually saying of himself, 'Je suis honnête homme'," said Franklin, "But I always suspected he was mistaken: and so it proves." [12] The hire of his carriage and horses, and the wages and clothes of his coachman, cost 5,018 livres a year. Franklin's annual salary from Congress was 11,428 livres, with "reasonable expenses." Arthur Lee found that in fifteen months Franklin drew 12,214 livres from the bank for his private account. He must have spent that much or more on average each year in France. Some of his compatriots thought him lavish, and he himself said in June 1782, that frugality was "a virtue I never could acquire in myself." Moreover—or so he told Mrs. Stevenson in London—he "dined abroad, six days in seven." If Franklin could justly claim that he lived more plainly than any other ambassador in Paris, his gout is nevertheless self-explanatory. The austerity of the Puritan and Quaker influences of his past was forgotten.

Not that he was really worried over the charge of luxurious living. Writing to Benjamin Vaughan, he put the case for enterprise and reward: "Is not the hope of one day being able to purchase and enjoy luxuries a great spur to labour and industry?" He remembered how, long ago, his wife had once made a present of "a new-fashioned cap" to a country girl at Cape May. All the girls in May resolved to have caps like it, and to earn money to buy them took to knitting worsted mittens for sale in Philadelphia. "I was more reconciled to this little piece of luxury, since not only the girls were made happier by having fine caps, but the Philadelphians by the supply of warm mittens." Yet he never fully abandoned the Puritan preachings. When his daughter wrote from America begging, amid the financial stresses of the war, for vanities like black pins, lace, and feathers, she got no such parcels, but only irony in answer: "If you wear your cambric ruffles as I do, and take care not to mend the holes, they will come in time to be lace; and feathers, my dear girl, may be had in America from every cock's tail." [13]

To his sister Jane, however, he contrived to sound becomingly modest:

I enjoy here an exceeding good State of Health, I live in a fine airy House upon a Hill, which has a large Garden with fine Walks in it, about ½ an hours Drive from the City of Paris. I walk a little every Day in the Garden, have a good Appetite and sleep well. I think the French Cookery agrees with me better than the English; I suppose because there is little or no Butter in their Sauces; for I have never once had the Heartburn since my being here tho' I eat heartily, which shows that my Digestion is good. I have got into a good Neighborhood, of very agreeable People who appear very fond of me; at least they are pleasingly civil: so that upon the whole I live as comfortably as a Man can well do so far from his Home and his Family.[14]

He stirred outside as little as possible. He hardly needed to. Ferdinand Grand, the banker for the American cause, also lived at Passy. Nearby were the ladies of the salons. Franklin's standing depended in part on his remoteness and his reticence, and on maintaining the myth of rustic and reserved philosopher. He suffered badly from gout, and by 1784 from the stone, and movement was in any case not easy. When Vergennes rebuked him for not attending *levées,* he responded, "I am hardly able to keep pace with the ministers who walk fast."[15] His uniform for outdoors was a familiar unembroidered brown coat, with a fur collar in winter, and a crabtree stick. There was a carriage and pair, which Adams thought extravagant. The household included Temple Franklin, William's illegitimate son, who served as secretary, assisted by a French clerk, and there were streams of visitors. At intervals his other grandson, Benjamin Bache, was there, when on holiday from his school in Geneva, where he was being raised as "a Presbyterian and a Republican." John Adams and John Jay and their families came for months at a time, and Polly Hewson and her family stayed one whole winter. The household was augmented by American ambassadors who could not gain admission to their own accredited countries, like William Lee, nominally commissioner to Prussia, and Ralph Izard, to Tuscany—neither of whom was free from envy.

Certainly there was much here to envy, for in Passy Franklin could do no wrong. His French, no more than passable, seemed charming. He had a good reading knowledge of the language but could not speak it with any facility. As a result he was often silent in company, especially so on his first appearances, before France became an open ally of the United States. Indeed his reputation in his own time was not only for affability but paradoxically for taciturnity—which, both in Scotland and in France, could have been due to difficulty in understanding these strong tongues and accents. Despite this, his remarks and observations became household words in both countries.

A few people, however, did raise suspicious voices. Was he a *poseur,* a *cameleon octogenaire, le doyen de tous les charlatans?* Americans in Paris or Passy in their letters home pictured him, at the center of a crowded circle, as a very old spider weaving a thickly textured web of intrigue. The French, in fact, tended to think of him as in a sort of diplomatic retirement, moving among the *savants,* his confreres, but royalist Jean-Baptiste Capefigue was openly hostile: Franklin was a charlatan; he showed himself little, "like all men who choose to exercise a mysterious influence." John Adams as usual was caustic:

The Life of Dr. Franklin was a Scene of continual discipation. I could never obtain the favour of his Company in a Morning before Breakfast which would have been the most convenient time to read over the Letters and papers, deliberate on their contents, and decide upon the Substance of the Answers. It was late when he breakfasted, and as soon as Breakfast was over, a crowd of Carriges came to his Levee or if you like the term better to his Lodgings, with all Sorts of People; some Philosophers, Accademicians and Economists; some of his small tribe of humble friends in the literary Way whom he employed to translate some of his ancient Compositions, such as his Bonhomme Richard and for what I know his Polly Baker &c.; but by far the greater part were Women and Children come to have the honour to see the great Franklin . . . These Visitors occupied all the time, commonly, till it was time to dress to go to Dinner. He was invited to dine abroad every day and never declined unless when We had invited Company to dine with Us . . . It was the Custom in France to dine between one and two O Clock; so that when the time came to dress, it was time for the Voiture to be ready to carry him to dinner. Mr. Lee came daily to my Appartment to attend to Business, but we could rarely obtain the Company of Dr. Franklin for a few minutes, and often when I had drawn the Papers and had them fairly copied for Signature, and Mr. Lee and I had signed them I was frequently obliged to wait several days, before I could procure the Signature of Dr. Franklin to them. He went according to his Invitation to his Dinner and after that went sometimes to the Play, sometimes to the Philosophers but most commonly to visit those Ladies who were complaisant enough to depart from the custom of France so far as to procure Setts of Tea Geer as it is called and make Tea for him . . . After Tea the Evening was spent, in hearing the Ladies sing and play upon their Piano Fortes and other instruments of Musick, and in various Games as Cards, Chess, Backgammon, &c. Mr. Franklin I believe however never play'd at any Thing but Chess or Chequers. In these Agreable and important Occupations and Amusements, the Afternoon and Evening was spent, and he came home at all hours from nine to twelve O Clock at night. This Course of Life contributed to his Pleasure and I believe to his health and Longevity. He was now between Seventy and Eighty and I had so much respect and compassion for his Age, that I could have been happy to have done all the Business or rather all the Drudgery, if I could have been favoured with a few moments in a day to receive his Advise concerning the manner in which it ought to be done. But this condescention was not attainable. All that could be had was his Signature after it was done, and this it is true he very rarely refused though he sometimes delayed.[16]

Franklin sat for portraits or busts by a distinguished group of artists: Duplessis, Greuze, Houdon and Jean-Jacques Caffieri. The small private press he had set up at Passy produced not only propaganda, passports, and reprints but what he called his "Bagatelles." He became the fashionable rage: there was even a *coiffure à la Franklin*. His portrait appeared on medallions and more utilitarian objects, "some to be set in the lids of snuffboxes and some so small as to be worn in rings," and, he wrote to his daughter, "the numbers sold are incredible. These, with the pictures, busts and prints (of which copies upon copies are spread everywhere), have made your father's face as well known as that of the moon, so that he durst not do anything that would oblige him to run away, as his phiz would discover him wherever he should venture to show it." Louis XVI, not exactly pleased with the homage paid to this hero of democracy—and possibly of republicanism—but not prepared openly to discountenance it, made his own comment by presenting to the Comtesse Diane de Polignac a handsome Sèvres chamber-pot with Franklin's physiognomy on the inner side of its base. When Franklin went to a session of the Parliament of Paris, the crowd gathered outside to applaud. His meeting and embrace with Voltaire at the Academy in 1778 were seen as a high point in the Enlightenment. How enchanting, it was said, "to see Solon and Sophocles embracing." Turgot coined the famous tag in 1778: *Eripuit caelo fulmen sceptrumque tyrannis*, "He seized the lightning from the sky and the scepter from tyrants." In an ultrasophisticated society Franklin's lack of pretence and pretentiousness proved captivating. To all, he was a symbol of republican simplicity and virtue; he was the American, a New Man, an Aristotle who was also both a Newton and a Rochefoucauld, but in frontier garb, and in bifocals, which were his own invention. Cast in the role of wise and simple philosopher, of *le bon Quaker, le bonhomme Richard,* he played the part, and with genial enthusiasm.[17]

Hilliard d'Auberteuil, a historian and a fellow member with Franklin of the Masonic Lodge of the Nine Sisters, described Franklin:

Everything in him announced the simplicity and the innocence of primitive morals . . . He showed to the astonished multitude a head worthy of the brush of Guide (a painter of old men) on an erect and vigorous body, clad in the simplest of garments. His eyes were shadowed by large glasses and in his hand he carried a white cane. He spoke little. He knew how to be impolite without being rude, and his pride seemed to be that of nature. Such a person was made to excite the curiosity of Paris. The people clustered around as he passed and asked, "Who is this old peasant who has such a noble air?"[18]

Hilliard also translated into French for his *Histoire de l'administration de Lord North* (1784) a tribute that had appeared two years earlier in an anonymous English work, *A View of the History of Great-Britain during the Administration of Lord North:*

This man (who formerly for many years carried on the business of a printer at Philadelphia) may be considered as the first fruits of American genius: and perhaps no man ever owed more to the time and place of his birth: had he been a native of London instead of Boston, and born into the same rank of society, the world would probably never have heard his name either as a philosopher or politician . . . He might have distinguished himself as an ingenious artist, but he would neither have formed an hypothesis to account for the phenomenon of the *Aurora Borealis,* nor have traced out the principles and operations of the electrical fluid; and what is much more important, he would never have become a powerful engine to shake a great empire, and to erect a congeries of republics from its dismembered parts; nor would he have had the appropriated distinction of being the principal agent to introduce a new aera in the history of mankind, which may prove as important as any which have yet elapsed, by procuring a legislative power to the western hemisphere. In this view he may be considered as a greater enemy to England than even Philip II or Louis XIV.[19]

John Adams, who, as we have seen, was not Franklin's warmest admirer, gave in retrospect, in 1811, what can be assumed to be an accurate description of his public role:

His reputation was more universal than that of Leibnitz or Newton, Frederick or Voltaire, and his character more esteemed than any or all of them . . . His name was familiar to government and people . . . to such a degree that there was scarcely a peasant or a citizen, a *valet de chambre,* coachman or footman, a lady's chambermaid or a scullion in a kitchen who was not familiar with it, and who did not consider him a friend to human kind. When they spoke of him, they seemed to think he was to restore the Golden Age.[20]

*   *   *

The French government had hesitated to support the American cause. A large part of the political nation, some conservative nobles and some *célébraux* doubted the wisdom of supporting *insurgents* against the monarchy. Louis XVI himself echoed the sentiments of Count Falkenstein (the Emperor Joseph II of Austria incognito), who on a visit to Paris was asked his view of the American *insurgents* and replied, "None, it is my profession to be a royalist." The finance minister Turgot, and the mathematician and philosopher D'Alembert thought that the Americans would ultimately win their freedom but need not be aided to it. Necker, who replaced Turgot as finance minister in 1776, preached the unwisdom of intervention on the grounds of economy. The Prince de Montbarey, the War Minister from September 1777 to December 1780 and a protégé of Maurepas, was anti-American. Not all Frenchmen who had visited America were happy about what they had seen. Many volunteers returned with Lafayette in 1779; and even after Saratoga, in December 1777, du Portail, one of the earliest and most distinguished of the volunteers, said of the colonists:

Americans have been used to idleness, to drinking tea and rum, to smoking etc., they will not hold out in such a war. It will not do to think of sending a French force to act in concert with them. They have a violent antipathy to the French; they would sooner go over to the British Army than to fight with the French . . . There is a hundred times more enthusiasm for the revolution in any cafe in Paris than there is in all the United States together.[21]

The American cause, however, had very influential supporters: Mirabeau, Lafayette, De Kalb, who had toured the colonies in 1768 as a secret agent of Choiseul, Beaumarchais, Liancourt, and the future Duke of Orléans, head of the Masonic Order which provided an intellectual and fashionable "underground." "The cry of the nation," Franklin wrote to the Congress on his arrival, "is for us, but the Court views an approaching war with reluctance." He wrote to Samuel Cooper in May 1777:

All Europe is on our Side of the Question, as far as Applause and good Wishes can carry them. Those who live under arbitrary Power do nevertheless approve of Liberty, and wish for it; they almost despair of recovering it in Europe; they read the Translations of our separate Colony Constitutions with Rapture; and there are such Numbers everywhere, who talk of Removing to America, with their Families and Fortunes, as soon as Peace and our Independence shall be established, that 'tis generally believed we shall have a prodigious Addition of Strength, Wealth, and Arts, from the Emigrations of Europe; and 'tis thought that, to lessen or prevent such Emigrations, the Tyrannies established there must relax, and allow more Liberty to their People. Hence, 'tis a Common Observation here, that our Cause is the Cause of all Mankind, and that we are fighting for their Liberty in defending our own.[22]

The king had two major advisers. One was Maurepas, of the Phélypeaux dynasty, president of the Council of State, an accomplished courtier seventy-five years old, with little interest in America, but influenced by Beaumarchais and favoring secret support for the American cause. The other was the foreign minister, Vergennes, dedicated, immensely hardworking, and a shrewd professional, who had served as ambassador in Constantinople and Stockholm. He deplored Britain's conquest of Canada and dominance in the North Atlantic. He was gravely concerned about the partition of Poland in 1772 and worried by the weakness of the Ottoman Empire. He believed profoundly in the maintenance of the balance of power in Europe, and saw as his goals those of Fleury, who had been first minister forty years before: peace and the status quo. If Britain was at war, he would try to weaken, but not to destroy her. His watchwords were balance and dexterity. He did not want an independent republic controlling the North Atlantic fisheries—the nursery of seamen—or any part of the mainland that was not already at war. He insisted to the end that Britain should retain Canada; he wanted his ally Spain to remain a power on the Mississippi; the new republic should not enter into separate negotiations with Britain or take any action that might alienate Spain. Indeed, if America should conquer all Florida, then Pensacola should be ceded to Spain. There should be no new or great power emerging across the Atlantic. His expectation was that a number of small republics would be the outcome. This was the wiliest and most patient operator of them all. "Je cause avec M. de Maurepas, je négocie avec M. de Vergennes" ("I chat with M. de Maurepas; Vergennes is the man I bargain with"), was the *mot* of Spanish Ambassador Aranda. Vergennes thought an open American alliance unwise, and the court reflected his views.

This statecraft was the legacy of Choiseul, who had directed French foreign policy from 1758 to 1770, and whose policy Vergennes inherited. The balance of power in Europe required possessions in America; the lands on the Gulf of St. Lawrence might be regained. It was in the colonies that Britain should be blocked; and Britain was the enemy. Choiseul had foreseen the American Revolution as early as 1764. A memo he left in the archives in 1770, "Means for France to employ in order to reduce England to the position it ought to occupy in the Balance of Europe," repeated mercantilist but also Franklinian arguments: British credit should be wrecked, trade between the French islands and British America encouraged, and American independence promoted. The key to Britain's power, he believed, lay in her economic monopoly of the American colonies and their trade; without them, her seamen would be untrained, and on them her West Indian colonies depended. To ensure the permanent separation of Britain and America was clearly in the French interest. Vergennes sent a memo to Louis XVI in July 1776 that echoed these views.[23]

It was a coherent, consistent and—as events after 1783 were to demonstrate—quite inaccurate view of the British Empire. It was this strategy that Vergennes followed, seeing in Chatham's efforts to avoid separation in 1775 the hand of the Old Imperialist about to launch destructive attacks on French and Spanish colonies, and seeing a need also for a close alliance with Spain. An open alliance with colonists in revolt was not welcome to either France or Spain, but any devices that would weaken Britain and commit its manpower to North America were to be tacitly encouraged. In Spain, Charles III, the uncle of Louis XVI, believed too in *divide et impera:* money went from Spain's governor of Louisiana, Bernardo de Galvez, to George Rogers Clark in the Northwest; and Spain proposed a joint attack on British-held Pensacola. But the aid went by legerdemain: Spain had colonies of its own at risk, and had no wish to give open support to rebellion. In this situation Franklin might be a useful tool to use against the old enemy. His popularity, however, with Freemasons and Philosophes, who saw in him a conspicuous ally in the battle for the Enlightenment, and his acceptance by the world of trade, who welcomed orders for supplies, military stores, and privateers, compelled discreet handling in the early years of his mission.

Despite these cautions, the French government was already aiding the colonies. Through the fictitious company Hortalez et Cie, set up by Beaumarchais, one million livres' worth of munitions (30,000 rifles, 30 mortars, 1,000 tents, and clothing for 30,000 men) were being sent from France, and Spain was promising similar aid. Alongside this secretly subsidized operation, Beaumarchais was aware that Silas Deane was seeking to purchase military supplies, on terms that involved payment in cash or in American produce. Thus Hortalez was supplying goods to the Congress on credit many times the value of the original grant, and other French companies were doing likewise. There was vast uncertainty over who would pay for this aid, and to whom the payments or goods in kind would go; in part this uncertainty was deliberately contrived in order to hide the transactions. Deane went through the form of signing commercial contracts promising to repay; Lee assured the Congress that this was form only, and that the supplies were in fact gifts. Beaumarchais expected tobacco in exchange; Lee, whose middle name was suspicion, later saw in these demands efforts by Beaumarchais and Deane to enrich themselves at the expense of the Congress—which they well may have been. But in the spring of 1777, Beaumarchais's secret ships, the *Mercure* and the *Amphitrite,* did reach American shores, conveying 20,000 muskets and urgently needed stocks of powder, balls, and lead. With the *Mercure* from St. Nazaire went also the first volunteer, twenty-four-year-old Thomas-Antoine de Maudit du Plessis, who was later to be Rochambeau's artillery major, to win membership of the Order of the Cincinnati, and to be killed in 1789 suppressing the troubles in Santo Domingo. With him, contentious and arrogant, was Tronson du Coudray, who in July would be drowned crossing the Schuylkill. French supplies also came in from Haiti and Martinique, where they were transshipped, and a little later Lafayette and his eleven companions from the *Victoire* made their way to Philadelphia over poor roads from Charleston: the beginnings of a gallant, sometimes rascally, and rarely selfless company.

These prewar years of the French intervention cannot be fully assessed without reference to Beaumarchais. Voltaire called him "a brilliant scatterbrain," and he had much of Franklin's range and ability: author and dramatist, controversialist and publisher, inventor and political adventurer, part confidant and part irritant to Louis XVI, and—it was rumored—blackmailer, forger, and murderer. He was prolific in the roles he played, and in noms-de-plume. His early letters to Arthur Lee were signed "Mary Johnston." Franklin was apt to call him "Figaro." Beaumarchais believed in making a noise in the world, and he invited enemies; the heraldic device he adopted was all too appropriate: a drum with the motto *Non sonat nisi percussus:* "It does not sound unless I bang it." "If I had been King," said Napoleon of him, "a man such as he would have been locked up." In fact he was incarcerated from time to time, and in the end was fortunate to escape the guillotine. He, like many others, lost most of his fortune backing the American cause.

The headquarters of Hortalez et Cie was in Paris, at the Hôtel des Ambassadeurs de Hollande, but Beaumarchais's main operating base was at Nantes. He acted there through the agents John-Joseph Carie de Montieu and Jean Peltier-Dudoyer. By the date of the French declaration of war, he had equipped eleven ships; by July 1778, Penet and the Dacosta brothers sent ten ships to America; and in 1782, the worst year of the war, thirty ships were equipped at Nantes for the American cause. Between 1776 and 1778 the Department of Marine also built the Indret arsenal at Nantes to provide cannon for ships.

In the American Congress there were two distinct policies, as viewed by two distinct factions. One group, represented by Richard Henry Lee and Samuel Adams, believed in what came to be called "militia diplomacy"; this position prevailed in October 1776. It involved, over and beyond making commercial agreements, sending commissioners to various European countries, seeking to persuade them to recognize American independence. This was what Franklin called "suitoring for alliances." Franklin and his supporters in the Congress, by contrast, thought America should wait and have the various powers come of their own accord. America should play the role, he thought, of the courted virgin—a role that demanded infinite patience, and assumed infinite desirability. Franklin wrote to John Adams, who thought that the prospect of American trade would be enough to win aid from France, in October 1780: "I have long been humiliated with the Idea of our running about from Court to Court begging for Money and Friendship, which are the more witheld the more eagerly they are solicited, and would perhaps have been offerred if they had not been ask'd. The suppos'd necessity is our only Excuse. The proverb says: *God helps them that helps themselves*. And the world too in this Sense is very Godly." [24]

The radical group won a victory when their committee reported on a plan for getting assistance, and on December 30, 1776, the Congress resolved to appoint commissioners to the courts of Vienna, Spain, Prussia, and Tuscany. Franklin preferred the patient cultivation of France by securing a treaty, working via France on Spain, and following active policies at sea, some of them even ambitious and daring. Ideally, he would have preferred America to win her independence by her own efforts. He knew, however, how dependent she was on foreign munitions, especially gunpowder.

The American plan for a treaty, approved by the Congress in September 1776, was for one of "Amity and Commerce," and not for a political or military alliance. Adams and Franklin had been its principal draftsmen in the Congress; the document Franklin showed to Deane and Lee on his arrival in France was in some measure his own handiwork. Nor was it to be in theory a relationship exclusively with France; the commissioners were charged also to approach Prussia, Spain, Tuscany, Holland, and even Russia. The plan left little to improvisation, and it became the "Model Treaty," the "Plan of 1776."

Articles 1 and 2 of the congressionally planned treaty provided for equal treatment at the countries' respective ports. Article 3 dealt with fishery rights and confirmed to the king of France the same rights that the British had granted to him in the Treaty of Paris in 1763; 4 and 5 dealt with measures of protection for each other's vessels and persons in their respective dominions. Article 6 promised joint action against pirates. In article 7 the king would accept responsibility for action against the Barbary pirates in the Mediterranean, where the French had a strong fleet. Article 8 was the major concession that America was ready to offer to France: "If, in consequence of this treaty the King of Great Britain should declare war against the Most Christian King, the said United States shall not assist Great Britain in such a war, with men, money, ships or any of the articles in this treaty denominated contraband." This was an important offer, and it implied that if France did not conclude this treaty, then America might well throw her forces and materials behind the British. The next article, 9, grew out of Franklin's strong convictions about the future expansion of continental America, and reveals how consistent and insistent he was on this. It bound the king of France never to invade New Britain, Nova Scotia, Canada, Florida, Newfoundland, Cape Breton, or St. John's, stating that it was the future destiny of the United States to extend over the whole continent. The remaining articles dealt with fishing, tariffs, the rights of neutrals at sea, definitions of contraband, right of search, an agreement not to accept commissions as privateers from a third power against each other, or to allow hostile privateers to use each other's ports.[25]

The three commissioners, thus armed, first met Vergennes secretly on December 28, 1776, for formal exchanges. A week later they were clearer in their views. Their request was not only for a treaty of commerce and amity but also for eight manned ships and 20,000–30,000 muskets and ammunition; and they wanted them sent under convoy. The official memo, dated January 5, 1777, read:

The Congress, the better to defend their Coasts, protect their Trade and drive off the Enemy, have instructed us to apply to France for eight Ships of the Line, completely mann'd, the Expense of which they will undertake to pay. As other Princes of Europe are lending or hiring their troops to Britain against America, it is apprehended that France may, if she thinks fit, afford our independent States the same kind of Aid, without giving England just Cause of Complaint. But if England should on that Account declare War, we conceive that by the united Force of France, Spain and America, she will lose all her Possessions in the West Indies, much the greatest Part of that Commerce which has render'd her so opulent, and be reduced to that State of Weakness and Humiliation which she has, by her Perfidy, her Insolence and her Cruelty, both in the East and the West, so justly merited.[26]

The reply was—very properly—that rules must be obeyed, that to send ships would be an act of war, as would the sending of convoys; in any case eight ships would be impossible to equip, insufficient in number—and provocative. The commissioners were warned of the close relations between France and Spain. Vergennes found Franklin "a man of much talent," as he told Aranda, the Spanish ambassador, "intelligent but circumspect . . . cela ne m'étonne pas." "What he told me is not very interesting," he wrote to Ossun, the French ambassador in Spain. "They do not demand anything that they do not already enjoy." There would, however, be secret help, in the form of credit: 500,000 livres immediately, followed by similar amounts each quarter, to be repaid without interest when peace was won. In December a new loan of three million livres was promised, to be matched by similar aid from Spain. Ships, however, would have to be procured elsewhere.[27]

Alongside the government, almost as an *imperium in imperio*, stood the Farmers-General. They collected almost half the royal revenues, enjoyed a tobacco monopoly, and were well and efficiently— and bureaucratically—organized; and the forty Farmers at the top stood close to the throne. To France, war and privateering made tobacco even more valuable than usual; to Americans it was their major export and their major diplomatic counter. On its sale American war supplies depended; everything turned on its transportation and the condition of the cargo afterwards. Alongside the efforts of the commissioners to make deals with the Farmers, private companies were seeking to buy and transport tobacco at their own risk or to sell to the Farmers directly. To obtain not only a deal but a contract was to commit these Farmers to the American cause. In this intricate commercial as well as diplomatic world Deane and Lee, Dubourg and Franklin were soon involved. They had few weapons to use as persuaders, since the British blockade was tight. But thanks to the closeness of the Farmers to the throne, a contract was negotiated and an advance of one million livres was agreed.

Through the rest of the year the three commissioners continued to press the French government for a treaty of commerce, and for goods to be conveyed in French vessels and at the proprietors' risk. In March 1777 they undertook that if such an accord led to war between France and Britain, they would not make a separate peace. They had to step up their own terms, for Washington was, at the last news, being driven ignominiously across the Jerseys. They argued that Negro insurrections instigated by Britain threatened the tobacco crops; and there were reports that Burgoyne would lead eight thousand Hessians in an invasion of Virginia in the spring. French support was urgent: they sought joint expeditions to conquer Canada and the British Sugar Islands, with a promise that half the Newfoundland fisheries and all the conquered islands would go to France; if Spain came in, the United States would aid Spanish conquest of Portugal; and, not least, could France help to block the transportation of German mercenaries to serve against the United States? This was ambitious, and none too well timed, for in the summer of 1777 there was, under a newly appointed Spanish foreign minister, the Count of Floridablanca, a new quest for conciliation between Spain and Portugal; Floridablanca was a cautious man, with no enthusiasm for republican causes at home or abroad. But there were renewed pledges: no peace to be made but "by mutual consent." [28]

The commissioners were equally specific in their request for aid: a loan of two million pounds sterling. Negotiations were also begun with the Farmers General, and with the Dutch by way of Franklin's correspondent and agent in the Netherlands, Charles Dumas. The bargaining now was with American tobacco and rice, sugar and indigo: the requests were for gunpowder and cannon, clothing and medical supplies.[29]

*   *   *

By the summer of 1777 Philadelphia was under British control. The commissioners now sought the formal use of French ports where they could repair and refit ships and bring their prizes for sale. Given French neutrality, prizes could not legally be sold in French ports; and British agents and sympathizers were so numerous that there was no chance of Stormont remaining ignorant of any illegal transactions. The issue was not academic and emerged early. The *Reprisal* itself had brought two prizes in with it: the *George* and the *La Vigne.* The staves, tar and turpentine, linseed and cognac were estimated to be worth £4,000. The crew of the *Reprisal,* said its captain, would not go to sea again until paid for their prizes. But could American ships of war and privateers be allowed the use of French ports? Could they go out to capture prizes, bring them in and sell them, without breaking the rules of normal neutral trade? To whom should prize money go? Clearly these things were not permitted in international law, and certainly not in Stormont's view. In fact the law was frequently flouted; and the longer the time taken over charges and rebuttals, the longer the time available for ships to refit and provision. Prizes were sold at bargain rates, with purchasers changing the names of ships and altering the records of cargoes; profits grew with the confusion. These were some of Franklin's recurring and remorseless problems through the next seven years. And sometimes in talking himself out of one situation he talked himself into another.

Vergennes was in no hurry to sign any treaty or make any commitment; and to enter into overt war with Britain France would need not only evidence of potential American success but also naval support from Spain. Where ships were concerned he would deal with individual cases and protect those needing repair, but he could not openly countenance privateering. Of Beaumarchais's activity, he affected to know nothing. There could be no French prisons or guards for captured prisoners of war. The British seamen from the *Drake* brought in by John Paul Jones stayed confined on shipboard for ten months.

Playing long enough and skilfully enough, Franklin could hardly fail to embroil France so closely in the American effort that French neutrality would in the end be impossible. By December 1777 the

French had defied the neutrality laws and the Treaty of 1713: they had lent at least three million dollars to the commissioners; they had allowed volunteers to enlist; they had opened their harbors to captains like John Paul Jones and Lambert Wickes, Samuel Nicholson and Henry Johnson, and not least the Irish-born Gustavus Conyngham, who fitted out a privateer at Dunkirk and with it seized the Harwich packet *Prince of Orange*. Stormont compelled the French government to seize Conyngham's ship and to arrest him. Despite this reprimand, Conyngham, urged on by Deane, repeated the exploit and precipitated a crisis between Britain and France: Britain threatened war unless the remaining American warships were ordered out of French ports. The French government apologized, recalled the French fishing fleet from Newfoundland—and blamed Franklin.

Meanwhile, during these formal negotiations, Franklin was being endlessly badgered by requests from the Congress for more and more assistance, especially for military equipment and for clothing, and for the loans and subsidies to pay for them. The language barrier made it difficult for him to fulfill these requests; in the early days he had to send to Britain for one of each article he asked for, to use it as a display model. This was tedious and inefficient. Moreover, ships were frequently intercepted on the high seas; supplies were thus at risk, however generous France might be, and information was slow and erratic.

Franklin was kept busy not only as consul, judge of admiralty, and director of naval policy but also as abettor of John Paul Jones. The Secret Committee (renamed in April 1777 as the Committee of Foreign Affairs) gave him precise instructions in May 1777:

This letter is intended to be delivered you by John Paul Jones Esquire, an Active, and brave Commander in our Navy, who has already performed signal Services in Vessells of little Force, and, in reward for his Zeal, we have directed him to go on board the Amphitrite, a French Ship of Twenty Guns, that brought in a valuable Cargo of Stores from Monsieur Hortalez & Co. and with her repair to France. He takes with him his Commission, some Officers and Men, so that we hope he will under that Sanction, make some good Prizes with the Amphitrite; but our design of sending him is (with the approbation of Congress) that you may purchase one of those fine Frigates that Mr. Deane writes us you can get, and invest him with the Command thereof as soon as possible . . .

If you have any Plan or Service to be performed in Europe by such a Ship, that you think will be more for the Interest and Honour of these States than sending her out directly, Captain Jones is instructed to Obey your Orders . . . and whatever you do will be approved, as it will undoubtedly tend to promote the Publick service of this Country. You see by this Step how much dependence Congress place in your Advices, and you must make it a Point not to disapoint Captain Jones's wishes and our expectations on this Occasion.[30]

Of all his problems, Jones was probably in personal terms the most troublesome. He was able, arrogant, and aggressive. He made Nantes his base of operations; to it in December 1777 he brought the *Ranger;* from it in 1778 he raided the Scottish coast; there in 1779 he planned the campaign to invade England that Lafayette hoped to lead.

Long before Jones's arrival, however, or the receipt of congressional instructions, Franklin saw the war as a war in the Atlantic. He made plain to the committee in May and June 1777 his own views on naval strategy:

The British Commerce in Europe, especially in the north, is unguarded, the Greenland whale fishery and the Hudsons Bay ships in particular. Could two or three of our frigates accompanied by lesser swift sailing cruisers get into those seas in the month of August or September, a valuable part of the Commerce of our Enemies might be interrupted . . . The coast of England to the west is unguarded either by Land or Sea. The frigates capable of landing five hundred men might destroy several of their Towns, which would alarm and shake the nation to the center, whilst the ships might fly and take refuge in the ports of France or Spain; but suppose the worst, that they are intercepted in their retreat, the inevitable consequences of *so bold an attempt will be sufficiently injurious to justify the measure*.[31]

Franklin devoted much effort to attempts to secure the release of American prisoners by direct prisoner exchanges. The British authorities, however, saw prisoners of war as traitors. They therefore ignored his readiness to issue paroles to British captives, paroles to be binding unless American seamen were released in exchange. Through David Hartley, Franklin urged the easing of the lot of prisoners as a step toward reconciliation, sent small sums of money for their relief, and sought permission for an American envoy, John Thornton, to inspect the conditions in which American prisoners were kept at Forton prison in Portsmouth and the Old Mill prison at Plymouth. Thornton found that the daily food allowance for each prisoner was twelve ounces of meat, one pint of beer, and one pound of bread;

every other day they also received a half-pint of peas, and on Saturdays six ounces of cheese and four of butter. These amounts were based on British navy rations during the Seven Years' War. With the help of the Reverend Thomas Wren as Franklin's personal agent and Good Samaritan, these victuals were now supplemented, even if little could be done to alleviate prison discipline, the sadism of the guards, or the enticements of royal recruiting officers. Until France's entry into the war, many British prisoners taken by the Americans had to be set free on reaching French shores. Once France was an ally, however, such prisoners went into French prisons. Delays and difficulties marred Franklin's plans for prisoner exchange; they were never fully realized until after Yorktown.[32]

His privateers, however, were remarkably successful. His "little Cruisers," he told Congress, "insulted the Coasts of the Lords of the Ocean." They made Dunkirk, despite the presence of its British commissioners, a haunt of pirates; it was from there that Conyngham sailed in the *Surprise* and again in the *Revenge;* Franklin had agents in Francis Coffin and John Torris, and like all the rest they made rich profits for themselves as well as for the cause. The *Black Prince* took 35 prizes, the *Black Princess* 43, and the two cruising in consort took 20; the *Fearnot* took 16; in all 114 British ships were captured, ransomed, scuttled, or burned. The raids had made havoc of the coastal trade, alarmed the coastal towns, and pushed up to worrying levels the rates for marine insurance. They were made possible by Franklin's zeal to capture prisoners, by French connivance, and by Irish support—the rough crews were overwhelmingly Irish.[33]

*   *   *

Throughout these years, Franklin was plagued by hordes of requests from French and European volunteers who sought employment in the American army—often, as in the case of von Steuben, at a higher rank than their experience or their merits warranted. More than four hundred individual applications to join the American service were made to him. The number is not especially surprising, nor perhaps as burdensome as Franklin implied in his correspondence. On him, however, the requests imposed obligations of patience, courtesy—and letter writing. Deane had been much more lavish, guaranteeing rank and conditions of service, planning at one point to replace Washington as commander-in-chief by a French nobleman, and giving Du Coudray authority to recruit forty companions for the Corps of Engineers and for the Artillery. Supplicants included a French galley slave who wrote to volunteer, if only he could win his freedom. Franklin was asked to trace missing persons like Maré de Pontgibaud, assumed to have gone off to fight in America, and to help a legion of people: the husband of his niece Jenny Mecom, held prisoner in England; the Brunswick major H. E. Lutterloh, seeking to volunteer and ultimately making a mark in the New World; the French captain Jacques Boux, with his plan for building frigates for America in the Netherlands (one ship resulted, and not until 1781); Muller de la Piolotte, who wanted to open a glassworks; wine salesmen like the Chevalier O'Gorman of Tonnerre; Capuchin monks like P. Nicephore, who was keen to go over to be chaplain in the regiment in which two of his brothers were serving; or the Benedictine who, if his gaming debts were paid, would be willing to pray for the American cause. One volunteer, Rullecourt, who had raised a company, was encouraged to station himself on an island off the North African coast in a curious republican venture into imperialism. Franklin's favorite letter of the kind read "Sir, If in your America one knows the secret of how to reform a detestable subject who has been the cross of his family, I beg you to send thither the one who will bring you this recommendation. You will thus accomplish a miracle worthy of you."[34]

Franklin was fully aware of the reservations of the Congress—and of the commander-in-chief—toward French commission-seekers. Some of them came, however, with social sponsorship and with a degree of financial backing that as diplomat he could not ignore: Crozat de Crenis had the support of Turgot; D'Orset had the backing of the Comte de Clermont-Tonnerre; the Comte de Rochechouart sponsored de Bert de Majan; the Marquis de Bretigny, accompanied by nine officers, crossed the Atlantic at his own expense and took with him arms and clothing for 130 men which he had paid for himself. And Franklin's support for the Baron d'Arros was due to the pleadings of no less a personage than Madame la Marquise de Lafayette. He had to reconcile irreconcilables, and to use his discretion; he was a diplomat with a weak bargaining hand, yet hungry for supplies and aid and support in high places. His caution was always there. When he did give his support, he was always careful to point out to his volunteers that "in a new Republick" "Interest and Solicitation" were not enough.

The importunities drove him, in April 1777, to compose a model of recommendation for such applicants; presumably his role as courtier-diplomat and his natural bonhomie restrained him from ever using it:

The bearer of this who is going to America, presses me to give him a Letter of Recommendation, tho' I know nothing of him, not even his Name. This may seem extraordinary, but I assure you it is not uncommon here. Sometimes indeed one unknown person brings me another equally unknown, to recommend him; and sometimes they recommend one another! As to this Gentleman, I must refer you to himself for his Character and Merits, with which he is certainly better acquainted than I can possibly be. I recommend him however to those Civilities which every Stranger, of whom one knows no Harm, has a Right to, and I request you will do him all the good Offices and show him all the Favour that on further Acquaintance you shall find him to deserve.[35]

*   *   *

And throughout, almost as relaxation, he wrote for the press. From 1776 to 1779 the journal *Affaires de l'Angleterre et de l'Amérique,* edited in the French Ministry of Foreign Affairs by Edme-Jacques Genet, the *Journal de Paris,* and Johann Luzac's internationally famous French-language *Gazette de Leyde,* published in Holland, gave the American point of view. He had to keep up with the work of French propagandists in London like Simon Linguet, and with the curious effusions of *L'Espion Anglais,* produced by John Adamson and Matthieu de Mairobert. He reprinted the *Edict by the King of Prussia and Rules for Reducing a Great Empire,* and he may have been the author of the hoax "Sale of the Hessians," which purported to be a letter from a Hessian count lamenting the inaccurate report of the number of Hessians killed, since every death brought a cash bounty to the Hessian princes.

. . . you cannot imagine my joy on being told that, of the 1950 Hessians engaged in the fight, but 345 escaped. There were just 1605 men killed and I cannot sufficiently commend your prudence in sending an exact list of the dead to my minister in London.

I must return to Hesse. It is true grown men are becoming scarce there, but I will send you boys . . . You did right to send back to Europe that Dr. Crumerus who was so successful in curing dysentery. Don't bother with a man who is subject to looseness of the bowels. That disease makes bad soldiers . . . Besides you know that they pay me as killed for all who die from disease, and I don't get a farthing for runaways. My trip to Italy, which has cost me enormously, makes it desirable that there should be a great mortality among them.[36]

He included ironic and sometimes gruesome pieces, notably a forged letter alleging that the British were buying bales of American scalps from their Indian allies. It purported to come from a New England captain who had seized eight packages consigned by the Seneca Indians to the English governor of Canada, containing American scalps—those of 88 women, 193 boys, 211 girls, and 29 infants ripped from their mother's bellies.

Through agents like C. W. F. Dumas, his Swiss-born correspondent living in Amsterdam, Franklin sought to shape opinion in the Low Countries too. For his network was European as well as French; he was notably close to Dumas in Amsterdam, and through Dumas to Jean de Neufville, the leading Amsterdam merchant, strongly republican and pro-American—later keen to monopolize John Paul Jones and to treat him "comme une curiosité"—and to the French ambassador, the Duc de Vauguyon. Holland was important not just for its bankers: British spies and sympathizers were active there, and Sir Joseph Yorke, who had been the British ambassador since 1751, was a dangerous, experienced, and able man. It was particularly important to assure the Dutch that France's treaty with America was not a hostile act against Great Britain; France feared that the Anglo-Dutch defensive alliance, which had so long guaranteed Dutch protection against France, might be invoked. The Dutch were officially neutral, and their highly profitable neutrality implied recognition of the American rebels as belligerents. Under British pressure, the Estates-General of the United Provinces announced an embargo on all exports of arms and munitions to America, but would not go further. Through the Dutch islands in the Caribbean, notably St. Eustatius and Curaçao, the American Congress obtained intelligence, arms, and supplies. Dutch opinion was divided. There were open admirers of the American cause, like Johann Derk Van der Capellen of Zwolle; Amsterdam burgomeister Hendrik Hooft; the Mennonite vicar van der Kemp; and Jean de Neufville, who on behalf of Amsterdam made a secret treaty with William Lee.

When John Paul Jones brought the *Serapis* into the shelter of Texel island off northern Holland in 1779 he became a popular hero; there was, in the province of Holland, the largest and richest of the United Provinces, and especially in Amsterdam, a fierce and century-old commercial jealousy of Britain. But the government was still pro-British—the Stadtholder, William V, was a cousin of George III—and there was a movement in the Estates-General to increase the size of the Dutch army. To the Estates-General, addressed formally as "Their High Mightinesses," the British ambassador, Sir Joseph Yorke, called the hero by other names—"the pirate Paul Jones of Scotland, who is a rebel subject, and a criminal of the state."[37]

Holland was lacking in "magnanimity," Franklin told Dumas in August 1781. It was "no longer a Nation, but a great shop; and I begin to think it has no other Principles or Sentiments but those of a Shopkeeper." Neufville could be, he told John Adams in November 1781, "as much a Jew as any in Jerusalem," and about Neufville his language could be unusually salty. It was important, he held, to distinguish between the Estates of Holland and the Estates-General of the United Provinces. The leading officials of Holland itself, and of Amsterdam, favored the American cause.[38]

While thus engaged, Franklin contrived to up his price by discreet—but not too discreet—negotiations with British agents who were already in Paris, or who passed through it: with Paul Wentworth, the Loyalist, and William Eden, head of the British Secret Service, who visited the city in December 1777; with William Pulteney and his fellow M.P. George Dempster in March; or his old friend David Hartley, who visited in April 1778. He wrote to his old Moravian friend James Hutton, "the good Lord Hutton" he had saluted ten years before in *The Craven Street Gazette:*

You have lost by this mad War, and the Barbarity with which it has been carried on, not only the Government and Commerce of America, and the public Revenues and private Wealth arising from that Commerce, but what is more, you have lost the Esteem, Respect, Friendship and Affection of all that great and growing People, who consider you at present, and whose Posterity will consider you, as the worst and wickedest Nation upon Earth . . .

In proposing terms, you should not only grant such as the Necessity of your Affairs may evidently oblige you to grant, but such additional ones as may show your Generosity, and thereby demonstrate your good Will. For instance, perhaps you might, by your Treaty, retain all Canada, Nova Scotia and the Floridas. But if you would have a real friendly as well as able Ally in America, and avoid all occasions of future Discord, which will otherwise be continually arising on your American Frontiers, you should throw in those Countries.

He wrote to Hartley: "America has been *forc'd* and *driven* into the Arms of France. She was a dutiful and virtuous Daughter. A cruel Mother-in-Law turn'd her out of Doors, defam'd her, and sought her Life. All the World knows her Innocence, and takes her part; and her Friends hope soon to see her honourably married. They can never persuade her Return and Submission to so barbarous an Enemy. In her future Prosperity, if she forgets and forgives, 'tis all that can reasonably be expected of her." And Hartley responded on February 18, 1778, twelve days after the treaty of alliance with France was signed:

I hope in God no fatal step is yet taken between America and the Court of France which will defeat a hope of a reunion between Great Britain and America. I told you that better times would come. They are come . . . North plans to relinquish parliamentary taxation, and to send Commissioners who, it is understood, are to be plenipotentiaries . . .

In my opinion I do attribute in a great degree the present change of measure in Lord North to the effects of your wise and temperate counsels and of your friendly, I must add, your Magnanimous affection to this Country, which were conveyed to him on a late occasion . . . He gave me full assurances that I should not be interrupted in any Correspondence with you. He told me that I could not serve my country more essentially than by cultivating every intercourse that might forward peace.[39]

Franklin corresponded with, or—where possible—wined and dined, an army of old friends and new acquaintances; not only M.P.'s like David Hartley and John Sargent, but influential figures like the future orientalist Sir William Jones, who married one of the Shipley girls and almost emigrated to America, and John Paradise, the philologist, who married a Ludwell of Virginia and did emigrate. There was much subterfuge. When the Philadelphia land-speculator Samuel Wharton wrote to Edward Bancroft, Deane's secretary, in November 1778, as when he wrote to Franklin, he wrote in cipher: "I am watched, I dare not write more." When Franklin wrote to Benjamin Vaughan in September 1777 to propose a secret meeting in Paris, he suggested that it should be at Les Bains de Poitevin, naked in the steam. Hartley's and Vaughan's accounts to him of British parliamentary opinion are precise, vivid, and detailed. The American intelligence network was varied, extensive, and polyglot, but slower and less accurate than Britain's.[40]

Through James Hutton, Lord North revealed that he was ready to offer everything "except the word independence." These overtures failed, as did the Carlisle commission of the same period in the United States, because Britain continued to refuse to grant independence. Knowledge of these discussions and the fear that peace would be patched up between the colonies and the mother country in turn pushed the French government toward a commitment. On independence Franklin now never relented.

*   *   *

The situation in the Hôtel Valentinois was complex. Loyalties were elusive, and Franklin was aware of it. Three weeks after his arrival Juliana Ritchie warned him that he was surrounded by spies. He replied:

As it is impossible to discover in every case the Falsity of pretended Friends who would know our Affairs; and more so to prevent being watched by Spies when interested People may think proper to place them for that Purpose; I have long observ'd one Rule which prevents any Inconvenience from such practices. It is simply this: to be concern'd in no Affairs that I should blush to have made publick, and to do nothing but what spies may see and welcome . . . If I was sure, therefore, that my *valet de place* was a spy, as probably he is, I think I should not discharge him for that, if in other respects I lik'd him.[41]

Stormont, the British ambassador, kept an eagle eye upon him. Stormont had agents inside as well as out, and they included Dr. Edward Bancroft, who was successively secretary to Deane and to Franklin, and by 1782 the secretary of the American Commission. Bancroft was in British pay through all the seven years, and his espionage helped the British to capture many munition carriers bound for the United States. Franklin seems never to have realized this treachery; it remained unknown for another century. The one man who saw through this was—ironically—George III, who called Bancroft a "stock-jobber unfriendly to England." The king was correct; Bancroft, alias "Mr. Edwards" or "Mr. Benson," used his inside knowledge not only to inform the enemy but to play the market. The only defense possible for him is that of Francis Bacon, who claimed that he best maintained his impartiality by taking bribes from both sides. Julian Boyd has called Bancroft "one of the most remarkable spies of all time," "at the center of this motley assemblage of flexible consciences." [42]

The methods of subterfuge were dramatic, juvenile, even elementary: code-names and pseudonyms abound (one of Franklin's code names was, appropriately, "Prométhé"), with invisible ink, schoolboyish numbered codes, and messages in a bottle left weekly in the bole of a tree on the south side of the Tuileries Gardens. British intelligence was, by contrast, professional and thorough, and the British did not lose the war from ignorance of enemy plans. Its head was William Eden, later Lord Auckland. His major aide was Paul Wentworth, a man of many identities; "everything he told us has been confirmed," said North of his reports. Wentworth recruited chiefly from American-born British subjects in what was, after all, a brother's war, in which loyalties could easily change. Wentworth's major task was as coordinator of other men's reports. Of those around Franklin, Bancroft was an agent; so was Deane's secretary William Carmichael; and toward the end Deane turned traitor himself. Arthur Lee vigilantly suspected everyone, and rightly; everyone, that is, except his own secretary, John Thornton, who, needless to say, was also a spy.

The list of British agents was long, and included "George Lupton" at the French ports (one Jacobus Van Zandt of New York); Hugh Elliot, a British minister in Berlin, who had Arthur Lee's papers rifled when Lee visited that court; Joseph Hynson, a Maryland-born ship's officer, a step-brother of Wickes of the *Reprisal,* who brought useful knowledge of activities at the ports and who achieved the daring coup of stealing dispatches designed for the Congress and replacing them with blank paper; a number of Rotterdam and Amsterdam bankers; Samuel Swinton, who was in and out of Boulogne; and a professor of divinity in New York, John Vardill, the later Loyalist claimant. Indeed many Loyalists were, or claimed to be, secret agents. Some were double agents.

Embedded, and now almost lost to view, in this thicket of intrigue is the D'Artagnan-like figure of Peter Allaire, a New York merchant of French origin who was in London and France in the years 1778–1780, and who sent information to Franklin about the British fleet. In 1779 he wrote from London saying that he would like to provide medicine, "Dr. James's fever powders," for the American army and navy. In 1780 he visited France and sent Franklin a bottle of "grand old Madeira." According to his own story, he was arrested by the

French police on February 15, 1780, and held in the Bastille on suspicion of being a spy and of trying to poison Franklin. He appears to
have been confined six weeks or more there, and then released for
lack of evidence. There are reports in the Foreign Office archives for
1790–1791 that suggest that "P. Allaire" or "P. Alexander" was one
of that indeterminate and worried group who played both sides.[43]

In this confused and uncertain world, Franklin's reputation as a
magician carried its own consequences. One report on him, from
a French agent of Stormont's, invested him with almost uncanny
powers:

We now entertain no doubt that the motive of Doctor Franklin's journey
hither was entirely philosophical and that he is consulted daily by our own
Ministry. Know then, that upon the principle of Archimedes the Doctor with
the assistance of French mechanics is preparing a great number of reflecting
mirrors which will reflect so much heat from the sun as will destroy anything
by fire at a very considerable distance.

This apparatus is to be fixed at Calais on the French coast so as to command the English shore whereby they mean to burn and destroy the whole
navy of Great Britain in our harbors.

During the conflagration the Doctor proposes to have a chain carried from
Calais to Dover. He, standing at Calais, with a prodigious electrical machine
of his own invention, will convey such a shock as will entirely overturn our
whole island.[44]

*   *   *

Not only was Franklin's task complex, his aides were uncongenial.
His fellow commissioner Arthur Lee was brash, mean, ambitious, and
contentious; he was by nature suspicious of a Catholic ally that was
in his eyes still an old enemy; he was especially suspicious of Deane,
and accused him of profiteering in the contracts made with Beaumarchais before Lee's or Franklin's arrival. For his part, Deane, who never
forgot that he too was a merchant, drew the narrowest of lines between public cargoes and those for himself, and invested heavily on
the London Stock Exchange throughout the war.

Deane had arrived in France in May 1776 as a representative of the
Committee of Secret Correspondence to purchase from the French
government arms and clothing for 25,000 men, and to discover how
likely were the chances of a commercial agreement; but he went disguised as a merchant, as a representative of Alsop and Company, part

of the Willing and Morris combine in Philadelphia; it was from this source that he drew his funds, since the Congress had little money. What was designed as a cover soon became the reality; carelessness, if such it was, compounded with secrecy, and both bred confusion. He could report to the Congress as early as December 1776 that he had shipped 80,000 pounds of saltpeter and 200,000 pounds of gunpowder by way of Martinique, and 100,000 pounds of powder via Amsterdam. His instructions were imprecise, his hopes limitless, his activities complex and frenetic. He had plans for a company to sell American tobacco; he was involved with Dubourg in tobacco negotiations with the Farmers-General and with Bancroft in investing in British stocks; he sought to charter ships from Jean-Joseph Carie de Montieu; and he planned a company with Chaumont for the supply of saltpeter and gunpowder. He sent William Carmichael, his secretary, who was himself heavily involved in intrigue, to Amsterdam and Berlin to obtain military supplies. He gave military commissions to French officers like Du Coudray, and even had plans to make the Comte de Broglie the commander-in-chief of American forces. He provided money for the unbalanced pyromaniac "John the Painter" to burn British dockyards.

When Deane was recalled in November 1777, on Lee's urging, the accounts were in immense confusion. Franklin, preoccupied with a host of affairs and the only man in the mission in whom Vergennes had confidence, for his part treated its finances with a casualness that could be called careless and which some said was venal. He was dismissive, even lordly: "he wishes that if practicable he might be excus'd from any concern in matters of commerce, which he so little understands." Knowing that Vergennes had no confidence in Lee, Franklin had left commercial matters largely in Deane's hands. Lee's charges were valid enough, and a congressional enquiry into Deane's convoluted accounts began; but he had powerful friends, including Benjamin Harrison in Virginia and Robert Morris in Philadelphia.[45]

From the beginning of the mission, Lee sniped also at Franklin. The rivalry had begun when both men shared the Massachusetts agency in London in 1770. Lee's bitterness and sensitiveness grew steadily over the years. He accused Franklin of having "concurred with Mr. Deane in systems of profusion, disorder and dissipation in the conduct of public affairs." He was not "a proper person to be trusted with the management of the affairs of America . . . haughty and self-sufficient, and not guided by principles of virtue and honour." To his brother, Lee was blunt: "the old doctor is concerned in the plunder . . . in time we shall collect the proofs." When he heard that Gérard, of Vergennes's team in the Foreign Office, was to go to America as minister and that Deane would accompany him, he wrote:

That a measure of such moment as Mr. Gerard's Mission should have been taken without any communication with the Commissioners is hardly credible. That if it was communicated, you should do such violence to the authority that constituted us, together with so great an injustice and injury to me, as to conceal it from me, and act or advise without me, is equally astonishing . . . Had you studied to deceive the most distrusted and dangerous enemy of the Public, you could not have done it more effectually . . . I trust too, Sir, that you will not treat this letter as you have done many others with the indignity of not answering it. Tho' I have been silent, I have not felt the less the many affronts of this kind which you have thought proper to offer me.[46]

This got a famous reply from Franklin, and for him a sharply cold one:

It is true I have omitted answering some of your Letters. I do not like to answer angry Letters. I hate disputes. I am old, cannot have long to live, have much to do and no time for altercation. If I have often receiv'd and borne your Magisterial Snubbings and Rebukes without Reply, ascribe it to the right Causes, my concern for the honour and success of our Mission, which would be hurt by our Quarrelling, my Love of Peace, my Respect for your good Qualities, and my Pity of your sick Mind, which is forever tormenting itself with its Jealousies, Suspicions and Fancies that others mean you ill, wrong you or fail in respect for you. If you do not cure yourself of this Temper it will end in Insanity, of which it is a Symptomatic Forerunner, as I have seen in several instances. God preserve you from so terrible an evil; and for his Sake pray suffer me to live in quiet.

The next day, Franklin rebutted in staccato fashion the various points raised by Lee:

—Deane said his voyage a secret. Tell not.
—This Court a right to send him (Gerard) as and when it pleases. France was not consulted when we were sent here—we neither "acted nor advised" in it.
—As to the concealing it from you, Reasons were given by Mr. Deane that appear'd to me satisfactory, and founded entirely on Views of Public Good. I promise to communicate them to you hereafter, if you desire it, that you may have an opportunity of refuting them if you can. At present it is not proper.[47]

American Commissioners of the Preliminary Peace Negotiations with Great Britain, ca. 1783, by Benjamin West. Jay, Adams, Franklin, Laurens, and Temple Franklin. West left space for British commissioners Oswald and Whitefoord, but they never sat for him.

Terra-cotta bust of Benjamin Franklin, 1777,
by Jean Jacques Caffieri.

Benjamin Franklin and the Ladies of the Court, engraving by W. O. Geller, 1830, painted by Baron Jolly, Brussels.

View of Passy.

Au Génie de Franklin; Eripuit Coelo Fulmen, Sceptrumque Tirannis,
by Marguerite Gérard, after Fragonard.

Le Docteur Francklin Couronné par la Liberté,
aquatint by the Abbé Jean Claude Richard de St. Non.,
after Fragonard, 1778.

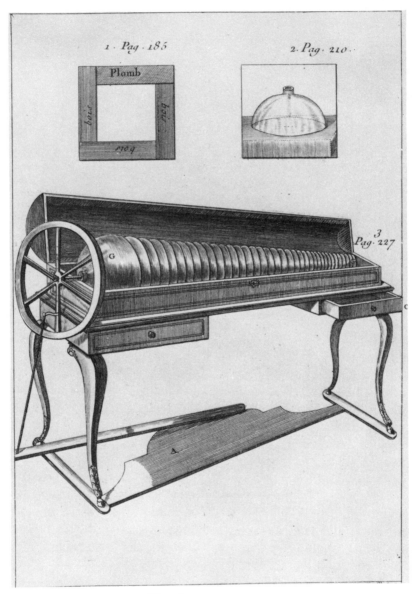

The glass armonica.

The situation had become intolerable, and Franklin looked for help to John Adams, who was named to replace Deane. He looked in vain, however, for Adams proved to be an awkward and prickly colleague. He had a New England scorn for the showy French admiration of Franklin, and thought him quite carried away by flattery. Within eight days of his arrival, he wrote in his diary: "Dr. Franklin's Knowledge of French, at least his Faculty of speaking it, may be said to have begun with his Embassy to this Court . . . He told me that when he was in France before, Sir John Pringle was with him, and did all his Conversation for him as Interpreter, and that he understood and spoke French with great Difficulty, untill he came here last, altho he read it." Adams supplied further criticisms as the months passed: Franklin had wit, he conceded, but "Beaucoup de Charlatagnerie," and he was "not a statesman." If he were recalled, "he would not return to America, but would stay in Paris." And—Adams said repeatedly—he talked too much. To Samuel Adams he wrote in December 1778 that Franklin "loves his Ease, hates to offend and seldom gives any opinion till obliged to do it . . . overwhelmed with correspondence and hospitality . . . which keeps his mind in a constant state of dissipation . . . it is his constant Policy never to say 'Yes' or 'No' decidedly but when he can avoid it." He repeated this indictment in his diary in February 1779. By 1783 he was writing of Franklin's "servility and faithless selfishness."

If, with John Adams, the attacks on Franklin's probity lapsed, the imputations of other improprieties began. The good Doctor's frank and teasing expressions of friendship for his ladies of the salons met with flinty Puritan disapproval; so did the ease and style in which he lived at Passy. Adams's qualities, however, were valuable just because they were the reverse of Franklin's. "He can't dance, drink, game, flatter, promise, dress, swear with gentlemen and small talk and flirt with the ladies," was Jonathan Sewall's comment. "In short he has none of the essential arts or ornaments which make a courtier." Franklin found it hard to have affection for Adams, but he never ceased to respect and admire his integrity and dedication.[48]

Vergennes, in the end, refused to have contact with Adams, and Adams escaped to Amsterdam to seek to raise a loan. Franklin was reduced to protesting to Vergennes that he was on terms of "civility" but not "intimacy" with his colleague, and to writing to Samuel Huntington, the president of the Congress, that "This Court is to be treated with decency and delicacy . . . and it is my intention, while I

stay here, to procure what advantages I can for our country, by endeavouring to please this court; and I wish I could prevent anything
being said by our countrymen here that may have a contrary effect."[49]

Criticisms of Deane, and indirectly of Franklin, that were made by
Lee and by Ralph Izard, in name the American minister to Tuscany
(who called Franklin "one of the most unprincipled Men upon Earth
. . . a Man of no Veracity, no Honor, no Integrity, as great a Villain as
ever breathed: as much worse than Mr. Deane as he had more experience, Art, cunning and Hypocricy"), reached Henry Laurens, the
president of the Congress. They carried weight with a Congress suspicious of France, and especially with its New England members suspicious of possible French control of North Atlantic fisheries. There
was a Boston-Virginia caucus here: in its number, alongside Lee and
Samuel Adams, were James Lovell, friend of John Adams and even
more of Abigail; William Whipple and Elbridge Gerry of New England; Thomas McKean of Delaware; Henry Laurens and Ralph
Izard of South Carolina; and General Horatio Gates. This was the
group of which Vergennes was suspicious. A rival caucus, Robert
Morris, James Wilson, John Dickinson, and secretary of Congress
Charles Thomson, listened sympathetically not to Lee but to Deane.
Both factions heard criticisms of the one John Adams called "the Old
Conjuror." There is no reason to think that Franklin was an especially
poor businessman, but his grandson and secretary Temple, a boy of
sixteen, was not efficient, and never became any more impressive dur-
ing the remaining forty-five years of his life. Jonathan Williams,
Franklin's grand-nephew serving as naval agent at Nantes, was solid
and industrious enough, but his reputation was clouded by Arthur
Lee's unproven charges against him.[50]

Not until September 1778, with Franklin's appointment as sole
plenipotentiary, did these domestic storms abate. Even then they did
not end. Lee had expected to be the sole nominee and, like Deane, felt
abused. He blackened everyone's reputation—including in consequence his own—with his vehement accusations. By mid-February
1779 even Beaumarchais was complaining to Franklin of Lee's conduct. And according to Samuel Wharton, Lee used Captain Landais
to oppose Franklin's "tool," John Paul Jones. "It is perpetually Dr.
Franklin's practice to employ his wicked tools," wrote Lee, ". . . to
accuse others of the crimes of which he is guilty." Franklin, for his
part, tried to play the role of the avuncular and benevolent chief,

above such personal maelstroms. He was aware of Lee's vanity, and probably also of Deane's intrigues. In this setting, the line between treachery and loyalty tended to be very blurred. Franklin was critical of them both, and of Ralph Izard and the Adamses. As ministers who were not recognized by the governments to which they were accredited, and therefore restless and unemployed in Paris, they lived to find fault.[51]

Arthur and William Lee (the latter in name minister to Prussia and Austria) and Ralph Izard were all recalled by the Congress in 1779. "No soul regrets their departure," Franklin wrote to William Carmichael after they had left Paris. "They separately came to take leave of me, very respectfully offering their services to carry any dispatches, etc. We parted civilly, for I have never acquainted them that I know of their writing against me to Congress. But I did not give them the trouble of my dispatches." About Arthur Lee, Franklin wrote to Joseph Reed in Philadelphia in March 1780: "I caution you to beware of him; for in sowing Suspicions and Jealousies, in creating misunderstandings and Quarrels, in Malice, Subtilty, and indefatigable industry, he has, I think, no equal."[52]

In spite of all the tensions with these quirky personalities, Franklin had few real critics. To Francis Hopkinson he wrote in September 1781: "At present I do not know of more than two such enemies that I enjoy, viz Lee and Izard. I deserved the enmity of the latter, because I might have avoided it by paying him a compliment, which I neglected. That of the former I owe to the people of France, who happened to respect me too much and him too little; which I could bear, and he could not."[53]

For Deane the story was even less happy. The news that he was in British pay became public, unhappily for him coinciding with the news of the surrender of the British at Yorktown. He planned to return to the independent United States in 1789, but he died mysteriously (perhaps a suicide, or even, if Julian Boyd is to be believed, murdered by Bancroft while they drank claret) as his ship was about to set sail. He blamed his exile, and what he called his poverty, on what he described as an error of judgment. Jefferson was more fierce—Deane's career, he said, was "a wretched monument of the consequence of a departure from right."[54]

For himself, Franklin concluded that since spies proliferated, honesty—or at least an open display of it—might be, if not wise, at least the best policy. Speaking to Cabanis, his neighbor at Auteuil, he said, "if the rascals knew the advantage of virtue they would become honest men out of rascality." He said that in dealing with politicians he took pains to speak the exact truth: "That is my only cunning." [55]

11

PLENIPOTENTIARY
FOR THE CONGRESS

$\mathcal{B}$y 1778 Franklin's major personal trials were almost over and his major task was done: France was in the war. On December 4, 1777, the news of Burgoyne's surrender at Saratoga reached Paris, brought by Jonathan Loring Austin, the secretary of the Massachusetts Board of War. Meeting Austin at Passy, Franklin asked him, "Sir, is Philadelphia taken?" "It is," replied Austin, and Franklin turned away. "But sir, I have greater news than that. General Burgoyne and his whole army are prisoners of war!" On December 6, Vergennes's undersecretary invited the commissioners to resubmit their proposals for an alliance; circumstances now were more favorable to the establishment of "a close understanding (*intelligence étroite*) between France and the United Provinces of North America." On the same day Lord North instructed Paul Wentworth to discover from the commissioners what proposals they thought "the colonies" were likely to accept. On the seventeenth Vergennes promised recognition, with or without Spanish support. Wentworth called on Franklin on January 6, to be told that propositions in writing were impossible, that even oral offers were apt to be misunderstood, and that, in any event, Franklin would listen to no offer short of independence. On January 8 Vergennes proposed an immediate alliance. From his point of view the timing was excellent. From July 1777 he had been urging action on Louis XVI, but had advised that its timing was important: it should await the return of the Newfoundland fishing fleets in the spring and the return to Spain of its annual Mexican treasure fleet, which in December was still on the high seas.[1]

Franklin did not obtain all he hoped for from France: he had hoped for a French guarantee of the conquest of the Mississippi valley as a condition of peace, but Vergennes, not wishing to alienate Spain, refused to go so far. The two treaties—a Treaty of Amity and Commerce and an agreement of alliance in case of war between Britain and France—were signed on February 6, 1778. On March 20 Louis XVI formally received the commissioners at Versailles. Franklin was not in formal dress but wigless and swordless, conspicuous in spectacles, white hat under arm, white hair flowing free. And for the occasion he put on an old coat, "to give it," or so he told Deane, "a little revenge. I wore this coat on the day Wedderburn abused me at Whitehall"—though this story has something of the apocryphal about it.[2]

In the courtly style of the epoch, the French government transmitted a copy of the first treaty to the British government. It was in fact unnecessary, because in the courtly ways of treason Dr. Bancroft had already passed to Britain copies of both. Less than two days after their signing, copies were on Lord North's desk. Vergennes had almost left it too late: news of the treaties reached the United States only just in time for the Congress to ratify the terms at York, Pennsylvania—it had been driven out of Philadelphia—just before the Carlisle Commission arrived with the British offer of a repeal of all laws passed since 1763 and a return to the status quo. It was a welcome change of climate after Valley Forge. And with it came a subsidy of three million livres.

The occasion—perhaps in part the cause—of the alliance was the American victory at Saratoga; the speed and ease of its manufacture were Franklin's doing. Through December and early January he kept Wentworth waiting, while he made sure that Vergennes knew of Wentworth's presence and mission. The purpose of that mission was a quest for peace, but it could not promise anything but a return to the status quo of 1775; Franklin now wanted nothing less than independence, and he would deal only with an accredited representative of Britain. The bluff worked. The negotiations with France were conducted almost in parallel with the much less official ones with Britain. And as further insurance, Franklin made certain that Vergennes knew that the Carlisle peace mission had already arrived in North America with the British offer of everything the Americans wanted except independence. The generous gifts of liquor sent to the Congress by the British peace commission were appropriately served to Conrad Alexandre Gérard, Vergennes's secretary and linkman to Franklin, who became the first French minister to the United States.

The first treaty, the Treaty of Amity and Commerce, embodied the most-favored-nation trading principle that had been part of Franklin's Plan of 1776. Indeed, it included provisions like respect for neutral rights and mutual protection of shipping and the suppression of piracy that came straight from the American draft. The second treaty, the "alliance eventuelle et defensive," provided that, in the event of war breaking out between Britain and France as a consequence of this first treaty, the two states would fight the war as allies; France guaranteed the United States her "liberty, sovereignty and independence, absolute and unlimited"; and the United States guaranteed France in the possession of her West Indian islands. The third and fourth articles dealt with separate and joint war tactics and strategy. The fifth article granted America the option of conquering and possessing the Northern Ports of America or the Islands of the Bermudas. In the sixth article, the King of France specifically renounced any claims to those parts of the continent of North America which had been British before the Treaty of 1763. This left the door open to possible French conquest of New Orleans and to a Spanish state in Louisiana west of the Mississippi. It also left France an opportunity to strike for inshore fishing rights, on which Vergennes insisted, and which Franklin accepted reluctantly. Neither state would make a separate peace or cease fighting until American independence was won. A secret article reserved to the king of Spain the right to join in the treaties.[3]

The importance of the French alliance can be exaggerated. American success in the field owed far more to Washington's achievement in creating and maintaining an army than to the actual entry of France. Even with that entry, Washington fought no important battle for the next three years. French aid in money, volunteers, and gunpowder had not waited on an alliance—although the amounts did now dramatically increase. In the years after Saratoga, moreover, when France deemed it safe to declare war, it intervened as a sea power. The timing was as much a result of the pace of French naval rearmament as of Saratoga, as much Sartine's doing as that of Vergennes. Vergennes's own motives were more commercial than territorial. The objectives were West Indian sugar islands rather than American independence, and France in fact gave the latter cause small

assistance. The French fleet led by Admiral the Count D'Estaing gave
no effective help in 1778, and, apart from an unsuccessful appearance
off Savannah in 1779, no French fleet operated in American waters
for the next three years. The Rhode Island operations of 1778 and
the Savannah operations of 1779 were bungled. Victory seemed far
enough away; the early hopes bred by the great news of Burgoyne's
surrender appeared premature if not totally unfounded. Indeed, this
was a period of military disasters—Savannah, Charleston, Camden;
of a great treason and a great danger—the attempted betrayal of West
Point by Benedict Arnold; of embittering military quarrels; of the defeat of General Gates at Camden in 1780; of the disgrace of Charles
Lee after the uncertainties at Monmouth Court House; and of the
increasingly rapid decline of the authority and credit of the Congress.
Bankruptcy and mutiny were internal disasters, not to be offset by the
aid of a French court with its eyes on the Channel, on Gibraltar or
Minorca, on the Antilles, on the Indian seas, and on the volatile ambitions of Emperor Joseph II. In 1781 the French admiral de Grasse
had to be persuaded by the Comte de Rochambeau, commander of
French land forces, and by Washington, at a famous parley on de
Grasse's flagship *Ville de Paris,* to stay long enough in Chesapeake
waters to allow the siege of Yorktown. He did stay long enough to be
disastrous for Britain, but it was touch and go. What Britain could
never have conquered, whether France were neutral or enemy, was
the immense territory beyond the Tidewater. As Washington knew, it
was the continent that was in the end the victor—as it was to be the
spoils. France did put some nine thousand troops into America, three
thousand of them from de Grasse's ships in 1781. Rochambeau's
force of five thousand, which arrived in 1780, was well disciplined,
well dressed, and psychologically of great importance. But the American war could still have been won without the formal intervention of
French troops.

The Bourbons had no desire to invest in revolution, and Charles III
of Spain had least desire of all. Not only was he against aid except in
a limited amount of money; the line became firmer still after 1777
when Floridablanca replaced Grimaldi as Spain's foreign minister. It
took all the best efforts of Vergennes's diplomacy to bring Spain in;
she entered the war to aid France and to recover Gibraltar and not as
an ally of the Americans. Spain allied herself with France in 1779 by
the secret Convention of Aranjuez, but not with the United States,
whose independence she persistently refused to recognize. Had she

ever been ready to do so, she might, George III permitting, have acquired Gibraltar without firing a shot, and, luck permitting, the American Southwest also.[4]

France, moreover, had assumed new obligations toward her Bourbon ally that seriously compromised the Franco-American alliance: no separate peace; and the war to continue until Spain achieved her great objective, the recovery of Gibraltar. Spain had correctly estimated the future aggressive tendencies of an independent Anglo-American republic; and her own large ambitions in the Mississippi valley put the Franco-American alliance under strain and were to be a serious obstacle to a joint French-American peace treaty. This was the most temporary and unnatural of liaisons for quite conflicting purposes.

Franklin was wiser than the Congress in disapproving of "militia diplomacy." One after another of the eager band that Adams called the "militia diplomats" (Arthur and William Lee, Ralph Izard—all three critics of Franklin—and Francis Dana) were rebuffed. "All Europe is on our side of the question," Franklin had told Cooper in May 1777, but he had added "as far as applause and good wishes can carry them." Princes and courts were not swayed by popular sentiment, or by amateur wooing, except when it coincided with state policy.[5]

For Britain, however, the entry of France was decisive. This was the long-awaited and much-feared step foreseen in Britain, particularly by Barrington at the War Office, General Lord Amherst, the Earl of Sandwich at the Admiralty, and Chatham, now ailing. It drove Britain to the Conciliatory Propositions of February 1778 and the Carlisle Commission, both unsuccessful. The American Congress now consistently refused to negotiate except on a basis of independence and a withdrawal of British forces. The arrival of the Carlisle Commission was in any event mistimed, for by April 1778 Clinton, the new British commander-in-chief, was abandoning Philadelphia, and the American treaty with France was already signed. The British commission was not aware until its arrival that Philadelphia was to be evacuated by its own army.

The entry of France into the war produced a national war effort in Britain, an effort that the war against the colonies alone had never quite aroused. It totally transformed British strategy. Until 1778 Britain could blockade American ports and attack the coast where she chose. The colonies had put tiny fleets to sea under Esek Hopkins, but they could not go beyond raiding commercial shipping. Privateering was more important; the Americans commissioned more than two thousand privateers during the war. They made many a fortune, but in doing so they attracted men out of the army, and they brought little help to the American cause as a whole. Courageous and brilliant as were the raids of John Paul Jones and Gustavus Conyngham—"le terreur des Anglais" in British cartoons—they were little more than irritants.

By 1780, however, France and Spain, Holland and the League of Armed Neutrality (Russia, Denmark, and Sweden, angered as neutrals by Britain's searching of their ships) were at war with Britain, and the British grip on the Atlantic and on the American coast was imperiled. Gibraltar was besieged, India threatened, West Indian islands lost. The troops to defend the Caribbean, as in the St. Lucia expedition, were taken from the main American theaters of war. More than this, America became a military side effort as invasion of Britain became a real threat. If invasion were to happen, there was, said Barrington, no general in the country fit to direct the army.

*   *   *

Franklin, in a task that recalled his incarnation twenty-five years before as a "general" in the frontier war, planned with the French Ministry of Marine in 1779 a joint attack on the British coast, the sea forces to be in command of John Paul Jones, the land forces to be led by Lafayette, who had proposed the scheme. "I have not enough of knowledge in such matters to presume upon advising it," Franklin wrote to Lafayette, but he proceeded to make detailed suggestions:

It is certain that the Coasts of England and Scotland are extreamly open and Defenceless; there are also many rich Towns near the Sea, which 4 or 5,000 Men, landing unexpectedly, might easily surprize and destroy, or extract from them a heavy Contribution, taking a part in ready Money and Hostages for the rest. I should suppose, for Example, that two Millions Sterling, or 48 Millions of Livres might be demanded of Bristol for the Town and Shipping; Twelve Millions of Livres from Bath; Forty-eight Millions from Liverpool; Six Millions from Lancaster; and Twelve Millions from Whitehaven . . . And if among the Troops there were a few Horsemen to make sudden incursions at some little Distance from the Coast, it would spread Terror to much greater Distances, and the whole would occasion Movements and Marches of Troops that must put the Enemy to prodigious Expence and harass them exceedingly. Their Militia will probably soon be drawn from the different

Counties to one or two Places of Encampment, so that little or no Opposition can be made to such a Force as this above mentioned in the Places where they may land . . . Much will depend on a prudent and brave Sea Commander, who knows the Coasts, and on a Leader of the Troops who has the affair at Heart, who is naturally active and quick in his Enterprizes, of a Disposition proper to conciliate the Good-will and Affection of both the Corps, and by that Means to prevent or obviate such Misunderstandings as are apt to arise between them, and which are often pernicious to joint Expeditions.[6]

A month later he gave avuncular counsel to John Paul Jones, counsel which, as events would reveal, was needed—and ignored:

The Marquis De la Fayette will be with you soon. It has been observed, that joint Expeditions of Land and Sea Forces often miscarry, thro' Jealousies and misunderstandings between the Officers of the different Corps. This must happen, where there are little Minds, actuated more by personal Views of Profit or Honour to themselves, than by the warm and sincere Desire of Good to their Country. Knowing you both as I do and your just manner of thinking on these Occasions, I am confident nothing of the kind can happen between you, and that it is unnecessary for me to recommend to either of you that Condescension, mutual Good Will and Harmony, which contribute so much to success in such Undertakings.
. . . There is Honour enough to be got for both of you, if the expedition is conducted with a prudent Unanimity. The Circumstance is indeed a little Unusual; for there is not only a Junction of Land and Sea Forces, but there is also a Junction of Frenchmen and American, which increases the Difficulty of maintaining a good Understanding. A cool, prudent Conduct in the Chiefs is, therefore, the more necessary; and I trust neither of you will in that respect be deficient.[7]

He sent specific instructions to Jones a few days later: Jones was to take French troops onto his ships, provide them with accommodations that would preserve their health, and convey them to any port or place chosen by Lafayette for their landing. He was to aid them after they landed, and to stand by to take them aboard again at the end of the expedition. Any English seamen taken prisoner were to be taken to France, later to be exchanged for Americans being held in British prisons. And retaliation against the British was forbidden:

5. As many of your Officers and People have lately escaped from English Prisons, either in Europe or America, you are to be particularly attentive to their Conduct towards the Prisoners, which the fortune of War may throw into your hands; lest resentm't of the more than Barbarous Usage by the

English in many Places towards the Americans should occasion a Retaliation, and an Imitation of what ought rather to be detested and avoided, for the Sake of Humanity and for the honour of our Country.

6. In the same view, altho' the English have wantonly burnt many defenceless Towns in America, you are not to follow this Example, unless where a Reasonable Ransom is refused; in which case, your own generous feelings, as well as this Instruction, will induce you to give timely Notice of your Intention, that sick and ancient persons, Women and Children, may be first removed.[8]

Franklin recommended a naval descent on the west coast of England, and thought that Liverpool might pay a levy of £2 million to an invader. A successful French invasion of thirty-four years before was still a vivid memory in Britain. The threat of invasion of the home islands was real, and with it came the reminder that every change of dynasty in England—in 1066, 1485, 1688—had been the result of invasion from Europe. Two French divisions, each of twenty thousand men, were assembled as the invading force.

In 1779 this Franco-Spanish armada of 64 ships with 4,774 guns, against which Admiral Sir Charles Hardy's Channel fleet had only 38 ships with 2,968 guns, was dispersed by what might seem as providential a mercy as the one in 1588. God blew not only with his winds but with sickness, in this case a coincidence of dysentery and smallpox among the sailors, with delays in the appearance of the Spanish fleet and gale-force winds in the Channel. More than seven thousand sick and dying men were landed at Brest. The plans for seizure of the Isle of Wight and a landing at Portsmouth of sixty thousand men remained paper plans only. In May the invasion plans were hastily abandoned; Vergennes had never liked them. John Paul Jones turned elsewhere, still hungry and ever-quarrelsome for fame.

Jones next created a small squadron of five ships: a cutter, *Le Cerf;* a corvette, *La Vengeance;* the frigates *La Pallas* and *L'Alliance;* and his flagship, the *Bonhomme Richard,* named in Franklin's honor. In September 1779 this fleet fought the famous battle with the *Serapis* in sight of Flamborough Head off the Yorkshire coast, one of the bloodiest naval battles of the war. When Jones sailed into the shelter of the Texel aboard the *Serapis* after the victorious *Bonhomme Richard* sank, he had 504 prisoners with him. In the course of the action the *Alliance,* commanded by the eccentric Pierre Landais, had fired a few shots, damaging the *Richard* more than the *Serapis.*

Jones, daring and successful, became the toast of many pro-

Americans in Holland, as later in Paris. With all his personal courage, however, he was also contentious, vain, and overbearing. He quarreled repeatedly with his fellow officers and his crew, and with the French authorities over what ships he should command and where he might anchor; everyone, it seemed, wrote to Franklin to complain about the licensed freebooter. Jones was, justifiably, angry with Landais. He found himself also angry with the Dutch government, which was officially neutral and which ordered him to leave Holland. In the end Jones handed over his fleet, his prizes, and his prisoners to the French ambassador to Holland, the Duc de Vauguyon; in the *Alliance,* he escaped the British ships aprowl for him and reached France in February 1780, to renew his taste for acclaim in the salons—and the boudoirs—of Paris. In his absence Landais seized command of the *Alliance* and sailed off to America.

Franklin's involvement with Jones was not ended. Jones and Conyngham had brought vigor and combativeness to the war. The combativeness continued. Jones had fought to capture men in order to hold them as hostages to exchange for American prisoners in Britain, a cause in which Franklin encouraged him. Whereas in America British soldiers were accorded the status of belligerents and therefore freely exchanged, American seamen were seen in Britain as traitors and enjoyed no such right. Jones was as anxious to take British prisoners as he was to take prizes. When he returned to Brest from his raid on the Solway in April 1778, he brought the Earl of Selkirk's silver, but it was the Earl he had first sought. The silver he honorably bought back from his crew and returned to the family. He brought also the prizes and two hundred prisoners from the British ship *Drake.* Jones was soon quarreling bitterly with Chaumont over prize money. Refusing to serve further until paid his prize money, he did not sail with Rochambeau's fleet in May 1780. Chaumont himself was ambitious and now in need of funds; although the prevailing practice was to divide proceeds from sales of prizes among the members of the crews, he saw prizes as a legitimate return on his investments. The quarrel may have also been personal: Chaumont's wife was reputed to be among Jones's conquests on land.

*   *   *

If the widening of the theater of war, and the consequent strain upon Britain's resources, was Franklin's major achievement under the Treaty, the obtaining of subsidies was his second achievement. In the end subsidies amounting to 10½ million livres (nearly 2 million dollars) and loans of 35 million livres (6½ million dollars) were received from the French government, which also guaranteed the principal and interest on the first loan for America in the Netherlands, Europe's chief financial center. This was immensely important, for, in contrast to Franklin's performance, American envoys elsewhere in Europe were finding their tasks very difficult. Arthur Lee and then John Jay in Spain, William Lee in Berlin and Vienna, Ralph Izard, posted to a Tuscany that refused to receive him, Francis Dana in St. Petersburg, all made little progress. Only in April 1782 did John Adams attain a measure of success in the Netherlands. This owed less to Adams's skill than to the British Admiral Rodney. The Dutch, more moved by cupidity than by ideology, had as traders made St. Eustatius in the West Indies the principal depot for the supply of foreign munitions. Britain trapped them into war in 1780 to put an end to their services to France and the United States as neutral carriers, and Rodney soon pounced on St. Eustatius. As a result, on the eve of the peace, John Adams at last secured Dutch recognition for the United States, a Dutch loan to restore American solvency, and a treaty of friendship and commerce.

*   *   *

In March 1781 Franklin submitted his resignation to the Congress:

I have passed my seventy-fifth year, and I find that the long and severe fit of the gout which I had the last winter has shaken me exceedingly, and I am yet far from having recovered the bodily strength I before enjoyed. I do not know that my mental faculties are impaired; perhaps I shall be the last to discover that; but I am sensible of great diminution in my activity, a quality I think perticularly necessary in your Minister for this court. I am afraid therefore that your affairs may, some time or other, suffer by my deficiency . . .

And as I can not at present undergo the fatigues of a sea voyage (the last having been almost too much for me) and would not again expose myself to the hazard of capture and imprisonment in this time of war, I purpose to remain here at least 'till the peace; perhaps may be for the remainder of my life; and if any knowledge or experience I have acquired here may be thought of use to my successor, I shall freely communicate it, and assist him with any influence I may be supposed to have, or counsel that may be desired of me.

He hinted that he would live the rest of his days in France, and asked the Congress to "take under their protection" his grandson Temple.

The request was refused, and three months later Franklin was appointed one of the five commissioners to negotiate peace with Great Britain.[9]

The plenipotentiary originally charged to negotiate the peace was John Adams, appointed in September 1779 when Spain had tendered her good offices as an intermediary. His instructions were to demand independence, the Mississippi River as a western boundary, and, to the south, the line of the thirty-first parallel. This attempt failed. When Adams then tried to reopen negotiations from Paris, Vergennes opposed him. To Adams, the French seemed to care more for their ally Spain than for their ally and client the United States; he became convinced that Franklin was the dupe of Vergennes. Franklin was in peculiar difficulties; long an intimate of Vergennes, and always badgering him for loans, he felt bound in honor to work with him. John Jay, a stiff Huguenot in background, confirmed Adams's suspicions: when he approached Spain in February 1781 and requested full alliance, he found Spain insistent on the right to navigate the Mississippi below the thirty-first parallel. Jay remained throughout firmly skeptical of Spanish intentions. The three "allies" had, he thought, three distinct purposes.

Congress thereupon revised the character and instructions of the commission. It named five men and took note of sectional interests in selecting them. The New England appointee was John Adams, charged also to negotiate with the Dutch bankers. Franklin was chosen to represent the middle states, as was John Jay, the New Yorker who was already an envoy in Spain. Two southerners were added: Jefferson of Virginia and Henry Laurens of South Carolina. Of the five, Franklin received the fewest votes, being seen as the most pro-French. As it turned out, the South was not well represented, for Jefferson refused to serve and Laurens was captured at sea by the British. He had with him plans for a treaty with the Dutch, and though he threw the plans overboard, the box stubbornly refused to sink. These plans were used by Great Britain to justify the declaration of war on the Netherlands—a declaration made primarily to end the hitherto "neutral" Dutch aid to America via St. Eustatius—and Laurens was imprisoned in the Tower of London. This left as diplomats Franklin, Jay, and Adams.

The revised instructions were simple: only a recognition of independence and of sovereignty was essential and not negotiable; on other matters the commissioners were to use their discretion. But in doing so they were to take no action without the "knowledge and concurrence" of the French government, and they were to be governed by its "advice and opinion." This instruction was a product of the mood of depression of 1780–81; the failure to gain a result in the war; the continued presence of thirty thousand British troops in America and their occupation of New York, Charleston, and Savannah; the absence from the Congress of strenuous New Englanders like Samuel Adams and Elbridge Gerry; and the dominance in Philadelphia of the Chevalier Luzerne, who in 1779 had replaced Gérard as the French minister to the United States.

If Franklin was willing to work with France, his younger colleagues were not. Jay had been snubbed and humiliated in Spain, a plaything of Floridablanca's dilatory diplomacy, and he distrusted all Bourbon agents. He was never even formally received by the Spanish government, and his letters were opened in the mail. When they were read, his chance of being received grew even smaller; they were full of complaints about the state of the roads, the extortionate charges at filthy and dusty inns, and the size and profusion of Spanish fleas, bugs, and lice. He never forgot the horrors of his family's journey from Cadiz to Madrid. A stiff-necked if admirable Puritan, he was thoroughly ill at ease in a world of mañana. Nevertheless, it is clear from Richard Morris's research that Jay was far more than the obstinate quibbler that previous estimates have made of him. He was, if not as pliant as Franklin, tougher and more single-minded, though perhaps more capable of error. But Jay's venom against Spain was dangerous. He sought the inclusion of a secret clause in the peace treaty encouraging Britain to recapture Florida from Spain. His rigidity of thinking led him to ignore the important Spanish contribution to American independence: the victories at Minorca and Pensacola, the money for Rochambeau's army raised by public subscription in Havana, the Spanish fleet that, by threatening an invasion of Britain, held back the British ships that otherwise might have reached Yorktown in October 1781 before de Grasse did. Had Jay, and not Franklin, prevailed, the North American map might look very different today.[10]

Adams, by nature suspicious, questioned French motives. To him, Vergennes and Franklin were interchangeable, neither of them in any way congenial. The Dutch were worshipers of Mammon, and on Spain he echoed Jay. He too had crossed the Pyrenees by mule train, and his memories of Spain were of people "ragged and dirty, houses universally nothing but mire, smoke, fleas and lice"; nobody was fat "but the clergy." But, whatever the suspicions, and whatever the instructions might omit, on one thing all three commissioners were obdurate. "Poor as we are," wrote Franklin, "yet, as I know we shall be rich, I would rather agree with them to buy at a great price the whole of their right on the Mississippi, than sell a drop of its waters. A neighbor might as well ask me to sell my street door." [11]

The mounting suspicion by Jay and Adams of Spain and of France was the basic reason for the method whereby the peace negotiations reached final success. They did reach success, however, only because throughout his years in Paris, Franklin had remained in touch with a number of his British friends and cronies when, in the casual manner of eighteenth-century wars, they visited the enemy capital: David Hartley, James Hutton, William Pulteney, William Alexander. The last two offered much—but short of independence. The terms included maintenance of the American government, plus a royal governor; America's right to name all judges and civil officers; no veto on the laws passed by the American Assembly; the Congress to remain in existence, but with a president named by the king; no taxes, no military forces, except with the consent of the Assemblies of the states; no Royal Customs; free trade except for existing exclusive companies; Americans to be represented in the British Parliament; mutual amnesty and compensation for wanton damage; the king to be the only supreme governor and to have the powers of war and peace and foreign alliance; all hostile resolutions to be annulled; and no British interference with the development of the colonies.

In all these discussions, however, Franklin insisted that peace now necessitated a full British recognition of American independence, and the cession to the United States of the Mississippi valley and of fishing rights off Newfoundland. He opposed the British request for recovery of debts due in 1775 and for federal compensation to the Loyalists; the Loyalists had suffered, he argued, at the hands of individual states. As a good expansionist, he hoped that a voluntary cession of Canada by Britain might allow Loyalists to be compensated by grants there. For Britain to continue to hold Canada would assuredly lead, he argued, as its retention by France in 1763 would have led, to future disputes, with the likelihood that the United States would need to lean more heavily than ever on France. He had pressed this view consistently, and in his penning it emerged less as greed than as wisdom. He had written to Hartley in October 1778: "It would be better for England to act nobly and generously on the Occasion, by granting more than she could at present be compelled to grant, make America easy on the score of old Claims; cede all that remains in North America, and thus conciliate and strengthen a young Power which she wishes to have a future and serviceable Friend." And to James Hutton in February 1778:

In propósing terms, you should not only grant such as the Necessity of your Affairs may evidently oblige you to grant, but such additional ones as may show your Generosity, and thereby demonstrate your good will. For instance, perhaps you might, by your Treaty, retain all Canada, Nova Scotia and the Floridas. But if you would have a real friendly as well as able Ally in America, and avoid all occasions of future Discord, which will otherwise be continually arising on your American Frontiers, you should throw in those Countries. And you may call it, if you please, an indemnification for the needless and cruel burning of their Towns, which Indemnification will otherwise be some time or other demanded.[12]

When Franklin was ill in the fall of 1782 and Jay, with his suspicions of the Bourbons, was in charge of negotiations, the demand for Canada was abandoned and the boundaries drawn in the Quebec Act of 1773 disappeared, to Vergennes's chagrin when he heard of it. But the terms of peace, Franklin insisted, mattered less than the spirit: Britain must show itself generous. These terms he had sedulously communicated to his ally France. And to them, as he awaited his fellow commissioners in Paris in the summer and autumn of 1781, he returned. This was the core of his agenda. When in January 1782 David Hartley, and in April Richard Oswald, arrived at Passy, these were the terms they were presented with; and they were told that America could act only with France.

The surrender at Yorktown on October 10, 1781, and the loss of Cornwallis's army, ended any remaining British hopes of victory on the American mainland. Defeats at the hands of the French in the West Indies in 1781 and early 1782 drove home to Britain the need for an end to hostilities. On February 27, 1782, the House of Commons voted against continuing the American war and authorized the government to make peace with the former colonies. The king threatened to abdicate. On March 20, North resigned and was succeeded by Rockingham, with Shelburne as the secretary of state responsible for colonial affairs, charged to open negotiations with the American peace commissioners. But British policy was gravely handicapped by Shelburne's rivalry with Charles James Fox, who, as secretary for foreign affairs, was responsible for decisions of war and peace with France and Spain. Fox wanted immediate recognition of American independence so that all negotiations would then fall to himself. Shelburne was still reluctant to face the grim facts of imperial dissolution. He wanted recognition of independence to become part of the treaty and thus made contingent on a general peace. But from April 1782 onward, Franklin was discussing the terms with Richard Oswald, an affable one-eyed Scot who had made a fortune in the slave trade, but was—otherwise—a liberal and a friend of Franklin; and with a Britain that had, it seemed, no cards left to play. Vergennes agreed that discussions should take place in parallel. Oswald, Shelburne's man, talked to Franklin; Thomas Grenville, Fox's man, talked to Vergennes. It was a dangerous tactic.

Oswald had hopes of a continuing connection: Americans could surely not be considered foreigners and would surely not want total separation. In July 1782 he wrote to Shelburne: "Upon the whole the Doctor expressed himself in a friendly way towards England and was not without hopes, that if we should settle on this occasion in the way he wished, England would not only have beneficial intercourse with the colonies, but at last it might end in a federal union between them. In the meantime we ought to take care not to force them into the hands of other people." But to Benjamin Vaughan Franklin was more explicit: "It is now intimated to me from several quarters that Lord Shelburne's plan is to retain the sovereignty for the King, giving us an otherwise independent Parliament, and a government similar to that of late intended for Ireland . . . the thing is impracticable and impossible, being inconsistent with the faith we have pledg'd, to say nothing of the General Disposition of our People." And to Robert Livingston, who in August 1781 became the American secretary of state:

However willing we might have been at the commencement of this contest, to have accepted such conditions, be assured we can have no safety in them at present. The King hates us most cordially. If he is once admitted to any degree of power and government among us, however limited, it will soon be extended by corruption, artifice and force, until we are reduced to absolute subjection, and that the more easily, as, by receiving him again for our King, we shall draw upon us the contempt of all Europe.[13]

Jay and Franklin were now aware that, while they talked to Oswald in Paris, Gérard de Rayneval, Vergennes's secretary, had gone to London on a secret mission. His suggested plan was to divide the trans-Appalachian West at the Ohio, with Britain retaining the northern areas and the south to be held by the Indians under the protection of Spain and an independent United States—an alarming curb on American expansion. Vergennes, in February 1781, had considered a Russian-Austrian mediation that would envisage a peace based upon the traditional principle of *uti possidetis*, that is, on boundaries traced by the actual possession of territories at the time of the truce. This would have left the British in possession of almost all of Georgia, most of South and North Carolina, New York City and Long Island, and forts throughout the western territories and New England. Spain would have kept West Florida, the east bank of the Mississippi up to the Arkansas River, and some posts in the Illinois and the Michigan territory. The United States would have emerged as a small, east-coast nation with no avenues open to the West. Vergennes realized that this was, in essence, to abandon the American cause, and that only the mediators could make a proposal so damaging to France's erstwhile ally. The rumors of this maneuver, and the reality of Rayneval's mission to London, presumably to discuss it, drove Jay even further toward Francophobia. He worked on his own to foil Vergennes, and to foil Franklin, who, he feared, was Vergennes's tacit ally. In particular he was afraid that all of this was confirmation that France and Spain did want to exclude the United States from the western lands beyond the mountains.[14]

In discussions with Aranda, the Spanish minister in Paris, Jay had discovered that Spain was seeking West Florida, by right of conquest, since the Spaniards had defeated the British and seized the territory, and the east bank of the Mississippi all the way north to Ohio, even to the Great Lakes. Aranda appealed to Vergennes for support under the terms of the secret treaty between France and Spain. Vergennes suggested that the Wabash might be a proper boundary for the territory north of the Ohio, and that perhaps an Indian buffer state could be created between the United States and the Mississippi. Franklin, an advocate of firmness on the Mississippi, wrote to Robert Livingston in August warning him that Spain was trying to "coop us up within the Allegheny Mountains." Franklin recommended that the Congress insist upon the Mississippi "as a boundary, and the free navigation of the river." Franklin was less suspicious of France than was Jay but he was, first and last, an expansionist. Jay, without consulting him, sent his own emissary to London—Benjamin Vaughan, who was a secret agent of Shelburne's—proposing a separate and secret treaty between Britain and the United States.[15]

In July, after Rockingham's death, Shelburne was in sole charge and Fox resigned. Franklin trusted Shelburne, the old liberal of 1763, and wrote to congratulate him, to assure him of "the continuance of my ancient respect for your talents and virtues," and to add that he found Oswald "a wise and honest man." Oswald, for his part, became Franklin's devoted admirer. Shelburne had one dominant objective: to pull America away from her continental partners. Franklin had one also: independence, if possible with French agreement, if not, then without it. But in diplomacy, if not in love, fortune favors the dilatory. In April, Rodney won a magnificent victory off the Saintes passage in the West Indies, taking three thousand French lives, destroying de Grasse's fleet, and capturing de Grasse, his tattered flagship, the *Ville de Paris,* and half a million dollars in gold and silver. Jay remained suspicious of all and sundry, and demanded British recognition of American independence as a preliminary. On September 19 Oswald was authorized to negotiate with the commission of the "Thirteen United States"—so treating them as independent from the outset. On October 5 Jay presented Oswald with the draft of a preliminary treaty, to become effective when a similar treaty was signed between Britain and France. On October 10, however, with the relief of Gibraltar and rising expectations in the West Indies, British terms were raised still more: they returned, via Henry Strachey as intermediary, to the charges of compensation for Loyalists and payment of debts in "hard money," not in worthless "Continental" paper; Canada disappeared from the discussion. Franklin countered with an American request—no doubt scornfully, for he never had much sympathy with the Loyalists—for compensation for the "carrying off of goods" by the British and the burning of towns. Secretary of State Robert Livingston, in January 1782, had reinforced his firmness on the question of the Loyalists, on the right to the fisheries as long rooted in history, and on the Mississippi boundary as a right "founded in justice."

By July 1782 Franklin had his own plans clear. To Oswald on July 10 he read a list under two heads, the necessary and the advisable. The first four points became in essence the basis of the final treaty:

1. Independence full and complete in every sense, and all troops to be withdrawn.

2. A settlement of the boundaries of the Thirteen States.

3. A confinement of the boundaries of Canada to at least what they were before the Quebec Act, if not to narrower limits.

4. A freedom of fishing on the Banks off Newfoundland and elsewhere, as well for fish as whales.

The advisable articles concerned the duty of compensation for the destruction of towns, an acknowledgment of British guilt, trading rights, and the cession of Canada. During the conversation about the terms Franklin stated that in his opinion nothing could be done in the treaty for the relief of the Loyalists, thus withdrawing his former suggestion that compensation for them might be found in the old northwest or Canada.[16]

Lord Shelburne wrote to Oswald on July 27 that he was favorably impressed with the report of Franklin's terms, that it gave "unequivocal proofs of Dr Franklin's sincerity and confidence in those with whom he treats." Again affirming his belief that the independence of the colonies must be acknowledged, he added that it should "be done decidedly so as to avoid future risks of enmity and lay the foundation of a new connexion better adapted to the present temper and interests of both countries. In this view I go further with Dr Franklin perhaps than he is aware of, and further perhaps than the professed advocates of independence are prepared to admit." In a second letter of the same date Shelburne undertook to put an end to rumors that he intended to refuse to grant independence, rumors started by Fox and his friends; he wrote that a commission would be immediately sent bearing full power to make the independence of the colonies "the basis and preliminary of the treaty," and he added that he hoped the articles Franklin called "advisable" would be dropped, and "those called necessary alone retained as the ground of discussion."[17]

On independence, Franklin had never wavered since 1775. On this George III again had shrewder insights than his ministers. He wrote to Lord North in 1778: "The many instances of the inimical conduct of Franklin towards this country, makes me aware that hatred to this Country is the constant object of his mind . . . Yet I think it so desirable to end the war with that Country, to be enabled with redoubled ardour to avenge the faithless and insolent conduct of France that I think it proper to keep open the channel of intercourse with the insidious man."[18]

*   *   *

It was the intervention of brusque and bristling John Adams that proved decisive in the negotiations. He had received his commission to negotiate peace long before the others had been named, and so was technically the senior member of the delegation. He doubted the sincerity of British overtures; he had secured a loan of half a million guilders from Dutch bankers, and was properly proud of his success at The Hague; he had hopes of a commercial treaty with the Dutch; he did not enjoy the atmosphere of Paris, or of Passy, or of Franklin. He distrusted Franklin's Francophilia, his closeness to Vergennes and to Lafayette, now the general liaison officer but in Adams's eyes a "mongrel character of French Patriot and American Patriot," "panting for glory . . . of unlimited ambition." He suspected that Franklin would pass on to Lafayette all his plans and ploys. He distrusted Vergennes, and Temple Franklin, and everyone indeed except himself.[19]

On October 26 Adams reached Paris. He and Jay agreed to keep some secrets from Franklin, as Jay was already doing over his own overtures to Shelburne via Vaughan. The three negotiators began daily meetings, but each held back some things from the others. Adams and Jay advised Franklin to proceed with Oswald without informing Vergennes. Franklin listened, and said nothing, said Adams. Adams worriedly noted in his diary in reference to Franklin and Jay: "Between two as subtle spirits as any in this World, the one malicious, the other, I think, honest, I shall have a delicate, nice, critical Part to Act. F's cunning will be to divide us. To this end, he will provoke, he will insinuate, he will intrigue, he will manoeuvre."[20]

The suspicions were mutual. Nine months later, writing to Livingston, Franklin was openly critical of Adams:

I ought not, however, to conceal from you, that one of my colleagues is of a very different Opinion from me in these Matters. He thinks the French Minister one of the greatest Enemies of our Country, that he . . . afforded us, during the War, the Assistance we receiv'd, only to keep it alive, that we might be so much the more weaken'd by it; that to think of Gratitude to France is the greatest of Follies, and that to be influenc'd by it would ruin us. He makes no secret of his having these Opinions, expresses them publicly,

sometimes in presence of the English Ministers, and speaks of hundreds of
Instances which he could produce in Proof of them. None of which however,
have yet appear'd to me . . .'[21]

But in October 1782, at the next conference with Oswald, Franklin, as Adams reported, "turned to Jay and said 'I am of your opinion
and will go on with these gentlemen in the business without consulting this Court.'" By November 5 they had agreed on a preliminary
draft; these preliminaries were signed in the Grand Hôtel Muscovite
on the rue des Petits Augustins on St. Andrew's Day, November 30,
1782, a date that pleased Oswald and his fellow Scot Caleb Whitefoord, secretary to the British commission. What was described as a
treaty of peace "proper to be concluded" enshrined all four of Franklin's "necessary" points. It included acknowledgment of the uncon-
ditional independence of the United States. The British accepted freedom of navigation and commerce on the Mississippi. Boundaries
were laid down for the United States: on the east the Atlantic and the
St. Croix River; on the north the Indian line, from the St. Lawrence
to the Lake of the Woods; on the south latitude 31° east from the
Mississippi to the Chattahoochee and then, by the northern boundary
of Florida, to the Atlantic; in the west the Mississippi. There was
agreement on fishery rights, and on the principle of reparations, but
there was no agreement on the Loyalists; any amnesty for them was
left to the discretion of the individual states.[22]

For the American negotiators, this was a remarkably successful result. They might, indeed, have erred only on one area, through Jay's
insistence on working out a secret clause with the British on Florida:
namely, that the boundary should be drawn at the thirty-first parallel
if Spain held Florida, but that if Britain retained Florida at the final
peace treaty the boundary would be drawn a degree and a half farther
north, at the Yazoo River. Jay's personal animus against the Spaniards
blurred his judgment; had Britain held Florida, and made it a Loyalist
base, it would have become a dangerous neighbor and a rival in the
ultimate opening up of the American South and West. With her strong
position also in Canada and the Northwest, Britain could have remained a formidable imperial power in North America. The result,
then, was largely due to Adams's firmness on cod and haddock, and
to Franklin's firmness, even bitterness, on Loyalists, the northern
boundary, and the Mississippi. Jay was important in speeding the pro-

cess of negotiation, but he was neither firm nor foresighted in the discussions because of his bias against Spain.

According to Franklin apocrypha, which abounded then as now, he stepped out of the room and returned wearing the same coat of Manchester Velvet he had worn in January 1774, on the occasion of his savage cross-examination by Solicitor-General Wedderburn before a committee of the Privy Council. In fact, he never left the room, never changed his coat, and wore at the signing ceremony a suit of black cloth in keeping with the period of mourning which had been decreed by the court of Versailles for the demise of a German prince. He later denied the story, as did Caleb Whitefoord. When both sides celebrated at Passy that Saturday evening, Whitefoord got the penultimate word. A French guest emphasized "the growing greatness of America," and predicted that "the Thirteen United States would form the greatest empire in the world." "Yes, sir," Caleb Whitefoord replied, "and they will all speak English, every one of 'em."[23]

The last word was Franklin's. He had defied the Congress in pursuing his negotiations without the French. The evening before the signing he informed Vergennes of the discussions, and promised to forward a copy of the articles of peace, although when he did so he omitted the separate secret article on West Florida. When he asked also, as if to add insult to injury, for a new loan of twenty million livres, Vergennes registered a formal protest at American unilateralism and reminded Franklin that in making a separate peace he had violated his instructions from the Congress. Vergennes understood the pressures Jay and Adams brought to bear on Franklin; he was bitter, however, on discovering that the British had provided a safe-conduct ship with which to convey the terms to America. This was now indeed a separate peace, regardless of the talks being held in parallel between Britain and France: "You perfectly understand what is due propriety; you have all your life performed your duties. I pray you to consider how you propose to fulfill those which are due to the King. I am not desirous of enlarging these reflections; I commit them to your own integrity. When you shall be pleased to relieve my uncertainty I will entreat the King to enable me to answer your demands." Franklin's reply to this stiff note from Vergennes was masterly. The commissioners, he agreed, had been "guilty of neglecting a point of *bienséance*," but he argued that this "indiscretion" was not a point of substance and was not from "want of respect to the King, whom we all love and honour." This was but the preliminary to the peace. "No peace is to take place between us and England till you have concluded yours." And, he added, once again playing it both ways, "The English, I just now learn, flatter themselves they have already divided us, I hope this little misunderstanding will therefore be kept a secret, and that they will find themselves totally mistaken."[24] "Full of courtesies, full of craft," as Poor Richard had said long ago (January 1735). For this was not, of course, quite the whole truth. The preliminaries included the secret clause on Florida, not shown to Vergennes and of which he might conceivably, though improbably, have been unaware.

Privately Vergennes was shocked at the liberal concessions Britain had made. He recognized also that they deprived him of an argument that he might have used to win from Britain Gibraltar, concessions in India, and other demands of the Bourbon allies. After looking over the articles, he remarked to his secretary, Rayneval, "The English buy peace rather than make it," and added "Their concessions exceed all that I could have thought possible." Rayneval in reply characterized the treaty with the Americans as a "dream." He was persuaded, he wrote, "that the English Ministers in making it have the defection of the Americans in view." "The unhappy news" of the signing, he soon pointed out, seriously weakened his position as a negotiator with Lord Shelburne. Moreover, Vergennes was most upset about the fisheries provisions, as he felt that they violated France's exclusive rights which, as he saw them, were affirmed by the Treaty of Commerce with America of 1778. What had been done, however, could not easily be undone. "Our opinion could not influence the negotiations," he later complained to La Luzerne, who had replaced Gérard as French minister in Philadelphia, "since we knew nothing of their details, and because they were completed in the most sudden, unforeseen, and, I might say, extraordinary manner." Despite his private bitterness, Vergennes did not think it prudent to insist that Franklin should withhold the preliminaries or to refuse the request for more money. The same ship that set out for Philadelphia with the American-British peace preliminaries also carried the first installment of the last French loan of six million livres.[25]

Meanwhile Alleyne Fitzherbert, who had replaced Grenville as British negotiator for peace with France, was in negotiation with Vergennes and Aranda in Paris. Gibraltar was the major source of contention here. Any rumors of readiness on Shelburne's part to surrender it—such rumors involved an exchange for a sugar island or for the return of all Spanish conquests in the war, including West Florida, a possible Loyalist refuge—produced a storm from the Opposition in the House of Commons. Gibraltar's own successful defense, and American withdrawal from the war, ended all such notions. When Britain offered to surrender to Spain Minorca and both East and West Florida on condition that it retain Gibraltar, Aranda, on Floridablanca's instructions, abandoned his hopes.

The agreements were signed at Versailles on January 20, 1783, and the final treaty on September 3, 1783. Britain recognized the former colonies as "free, sovereign and independent." It was agreed that the boundaries of the new republic would extend from the Atlantic to the Mississippi, and from the Great Lakes to the northern boundary of Florida (which Britain did now return to Spain), but without any clear definition of where the latter boundary was. The northern boundaries were similarly elusive. Had the American negotiators been a little more demanding, they might have secured the more important parts of Upper Canada; and had they done so there would, in all probability, have been in the end no Canada at all. The United States was conceded the right to fish in Canadian waters, and off the Newfoundland Banks as "heretofore," and British subjects were to share with Americans the right to navigate the Mississippi. In evacuating areas still occupied, the British armies would restore captured property; and the Americans agreed not to repudiate private obligations, such as the old debts owed to London merchants. The settlement all but ignored the claims of Britain's Indian allies and white Loyalists, although it was agreed that the Congress would "earnestly recommend" that the thirteen state legislatures treat the Tories fairly.

While deploring the independent spirit of her New World ally, France was reasonably satisfied with these arrangements. Too much can be made of Franklin's infamy. The surprising thing is the unanimity of policy until the closing weeks. Had Adams or Jay been in charge earlier, or Lee or Deane later, the outcome would have been very different, the tactics infinitely less subtle, the deep harmony most unlikely. It is doubtful that Vergennes was ever in ignorance of what Franklin was doing—or vice versa. Vergennes may even have welcomed the breakaway, which freed him from his heavy obligation to support Spain's claims in the West. If he did not lend twenty million livres, at least he lent six million. As a firm believer in the balance of power he did not wish entirely to crush Britain, or to permit a totally independent North American continent. Before the war was over, Vergennes had considered methods of obtaining British aid to support Turkey against Austrian and Russian attack. In the treaty negotiations he pressed on Britain the need for commercial agreements. His final achievement, as Jonathan Dull has noted, was not the Treaty of 1783 but the Anglo-French Treaty of 1786, made with that other believer in balance and compromise, William Eden.

The government of Louis XVI had nevertheless gained immense prestige at the expense of Britain. The Treaty of Paris of 1783 represented in fact the belated triumph of Choiseul's policy, begun thirty years earlier. Indeed, in 1760, when Franklin was urging the retention of Canada rather that Guadeloupe, the young Vergennes, then serving as ambassador to Turkey, foresaw that Britain, in freeing Canada from France, would remove the sole check on the colonies to the south. They would, he said, no longer need Britain's protection, and when asked to help shoulder her burdens would strike off all dependence. And Turgot foresaw the same destiny: America would do what Carthage did. Vergennes, who died in 1787, was fortunate not to see all the consequences. The Comte de Ségur, who had served in America, recalled later: "We walked gaily over a carpet of flowers which concealed from us an abyss." Admiral d'Estaing, who brought the first French fleet to America and hoped to lead the invasion of Britain, died on the guillotine. Pierre Penet, the trader of Nantes who absconded, Dubourg, and Chaumont were all ruined. Even the Hôtel Valentinois had to be sold in the Chaumont bankruptcy proceedings—though happily Franklin never knew it. The policy of revenge on Britain cost France one billion livres, strained Bourbon credit, and paved the way for the outbreak of the French Revolution in 1789; but few, least of all Franklin, anticipated that development in 1783.[26]

Perhaps the best assessment of the diplomacy of Franklin and his fellow negotiators in Paris in 1782–83 is that of R. B. Morris:

What was so remarkable about the achievements of the American commissioners was that where they compromised it was on inessentials and where they conceded it was to yield the trivial. From beginning to end they remained unswerving on the score of obtaining both absolute independence and a continental domain for thirteen littoral states. On the main objectives of national survival they proved uncompromising. Because the American commissioners resolutely contended for the right of a sovereign people to choose their own form of government and because they secured grudging recognition of that right from the Old Order, a free people is eternally in their debt . . .

The peacemaking began as an encounter between innocence and guile, but the Americans rapidly acquired a measure of sophistication sufficient for the task at hand. Neophytes in the arts of secret diplomacy at the start, they were the peers of their Old World counterparts at the finish.[27]

*   *   *

The two years after 1783, if years of anticlimax, were not years of leisure. "Treaties to be made with, I think, twenty powers in two years," wrote Franklin to Adams, "so that we are not likely to eat the bread of idleness." In fact, however, only Sweden and Prussia made treaties with the new country. In Britain the restrictive views of Lord Sheffield prevailed over Shelburne's liberalism. The promised dawn of 1783 was false.

Franklin sought, as before, to reveal to France and Europe what he thought was a true picture of his country. In 1783 he published his *Book of Constitutions,* containing the Articles of 1781 and of the state constitutions. The translation was the work of his friend and fellow Mason La Rochefoucauld d'Enville. By order of Congress, Franklin in 1783 gave two copies of the translation to every ambassador in Paris and dispersed copies throughout Europe. Since 1777 he had been a member of the Masonic Lodge of the Nine Sisters, and in 1779 he became Grand Master. Freemasonry in America had been social and local, with little influence in politics; in France it was freethinking and opposed to absolutism; its dream was of a constitutional monarchy for France. The Nine Sisters lodge greeted Franklin as a brother of their order who had sought to carry out its reforming aims in his own country. The members were moderate men: Bailly the astronomer; Brissot de Warville, who had been to America and who urged that France adopt a constitution like America's; Danton; Camille Desmoulins, who believed that America had revived the pure democracy of Greece; and Louis Le Veillard, Franklin's neighbor and friend, translator of his letters, and at one time mayor of Passy. Le Veillard was owner-manager of Les Nouvelles Eaux de Passy; his bottled mineral water was essential when the Seine water was unreliable, and, being essential, was a source of great profit. He helped the unfluent Franklin with his French, with his lady friends of the salons, and with some of his dinner parties. He badgered and cajoled Franklin into attempting, after the peace treaty was signed, to complete his memoirs. He was guillotined in August 1794. Condorcet died in prison, possibly poisoned, and La Rochefoucauld d'Enville was stoned to death in front of his wife and family in 1792. Liberalism was a safer indulgence in the United States than in the France of the Revolution.

Throughout his years in Paris, Franklin had kept in touch with his British friends of the 1760s, who formed an Illuminati of their own; deists, Freemasons, and radicals, to whom he was mastermind, or master Mason. Many of them saw the events of 1776 as heralding a new liberated age. They included Sir Joseph Banks, David Williams, Richard Price, Joseph Priestley, David Hartley, Benjamin Vaughan, and Sir William Jones. One of these friends, William Hodgson, took charge of the exchange of prisoners of war between America and Britain. Other members of the original Society of Thirteen or of the Club of Honest Whigs saw their own activities as near-treasonable, and as precautions used secret codes and disguises, book and number ciphers, and key words. Through Price, in February 1780 at the height of the war, Franklin sent his regards to all his old acquaintances of the Honest Whigs in his favorite haunt, the London Coffee House:

We make daily great improvements in *Natural*, there is one I wish to see in *Moral* Philosophy; the Discovery of a Plan that would induce and oblige Nations to settle their Disputes without first Cutting one another's throats. When will human Reason be sufficiently improved to see the Advantage of this! When will Men be convinc'd that even successful Wars at length become Misfortunes to those who unjustly commenc'd them, and who triumph'd blindly in their Success, not seeing all its Consequences. Your great comfort and mine in this War is that we honestly and faithfully did every thing in our Power to prevent it.[28]

This was an intellectual underground that was international, rooted in deism and liberalism—a product of Freemasonry, of the Enlightenment, and of the still-optimistic faith in reason. From these intellectual liberals came the contacts that led to the peace. They dreamed of a league of peaceful nations. On his private press at Passy, in 1782, Franklin printed Pierre André Gargaz's *Project of Perpetual Peace,* one of the first outlines of a League of Nations. He wrote warmly in praise of Gargaz, who had been for twenty years a galley slave. Gargaz was, he said, "a very honest, sensible man, and worthy of a better fortune."

The remorseless passing of the years saw the death of friends: in 1782 of Dr. Pringle, Dr. Fothergill, Lord Kames, and Lord Despencer, and in 1783 of Mrs. Stevenson. "I shall soon have no Attachment left to make me unwilling to follow," he wrote to Polly on hearing of her mother's death.[29]

*   *   *

Franklin's scientific interests continued. He wrote to Priestley in February 1780:

> The rapid progress true Science now makes occasions my regretting sometimes that I was born so soon. It is impossible to imagine the Height to which may be carried, in a thousand years, the Power of Man over Matter. We may perhaps learn to deprive large Masses of their Gravity, and give them absolute Levity, for the sake of very easy transport. Agriculture may diminish its Labour and double its Produce; all Diseases may, by sure means, be prevented or cured, not even excepting that of Old Age, and our Lives lengthened at pleasure even beyond the antediluvian Standard. O that moral Science were in as fair a way of Improvement, that Men would cease to be Wolves to one another, and that human Beings would at length learn what they now improperly call Humanity!

He echoed this letter three years later in writing to Sir Joseph Banks: "I begin to be almost sorry I was born so soon, since I cannot have the happiness of knowing what will be known 100 years hence." The French, in their admiration for Captain Cook and their regard for science, had exempted Cook's ships from molestation, and Benjamin Franklin had recommended this magnanimity to American privateers; in fact, the American Congress had been slow to follow his advice. After the war the British Admiralty showed its appreciation by presenting him with a copy of the printed *Voyage* of Captain Cook, and the Royal Society sent him one of its gold Cook memorial medals.[30]

A month later he told Sir Joseph of the current French experiments with balloons:

> Among the Pleasantries Conversation produces on this Subject, some suppose Flying to be now invented, and that since Men may be supported in the

Air, nothing is wanted but some light handy Instruments to give and direct Motion. Some think Progressive Motion on the Earth may be advanc'd by it, and that a Running Footman or a Horse slung suspended under such a Globe so as to leave no more of Weight pressing the Earth with their Feet, than perhaps 8 or 10 Pounds, might with a fair Wind run in a straight Line across Countries as fast as that Wind, and over Hedges, Ditches, and even Waters. It has been even fancied that in time People will keep such Globes anchored in the Air, to which by Pullies they may draw up Game to be preserved in the Cool, and Water to be frozen when Ice is wanted. And that to get Money, it will be contrived to give People an extensive view of the Country, by running them upon an Elbow Chair a Mile high for a Guinea, &c. &c.

The subject of balloons fascinated him and led to speculation on aerial navigation by dirigibles. Too hopefully, in a letter to Jan Ingenhousz, he assumed that one consequence would be that of "convincing Sovereigns of the Folly of Wars . . . since it will be impracticable for the most potent of them to guard his Dominions." [31]

He witnessed the first ascent in Paris, on August 27, 1783, when Jacques-Alexandre Charles raised his captive hydrogen-gas balloon from the Champ de Mars. At Passy, in November, he saw the first ascent by human passengers in a "Montgolfier." He interviewed the inventors and the aviators, and he forwarded material on them to Sir Joseph for the Royal Society. When M. Blanchard and the Loyalist Dr. John Jeffries crossed the Channel by balloon in January 1785, they brought him a letter from England, "the first through the air." By the autumn of 1783 flights lasting as long as twenty-five minutes had been made across the Seine, and to an altitude of almost ten thousand feet. There were twenty-five flights in the next two years. In Paris the talk seemed to be of little but balloons. "Don't you begin to think of taking your passage in one next spring?" Sally Jay wrote to her husband John, who had gone on a trip to England. It was thought that balloons would give their possessors military supremacy and could upset the new balance of power. Franklin was asked, "What good is this discovery that they make so much noise about it?" "What good," he replied, "is a new-born baby?" One of the pioneer aerialists, Ducarne de Blaugy, hearing of this flippant comment, wrote to Franklin in high dudgeon, maintaining in great seriousness that several successful flights had been made from Calais to Dover and that, if the balloon had been invented earlier, Gibraltar could have been taken. This rebuke did not check Franklin's levity, however; on the occasion of the flight in November 1783 of the first hydrogen balloon carrying passengers, he remarked that the earliest balloon was an infant, but the latest, a giant. Franklin detected totally different attitudes toward ballooning in Britain and France. He wrote to Banks in November 1783:

I am sorry this experiment is totally neglected in England, where mechanic genius is so strong. I wish I could see the same emulations between the two nations as I have between the two parties here. Your philosophy seems to be too bashful . . . It does not seem to me a good reason to decline prosecuting a new experiment which apparently increases the power of man over matter, till we can see to what use the power may be applied. When we have learnt to manage it, we may hope some time or other to find use for it, as men have done for magnetism and electricity, for which the first experiments were mere matters of amusement.

In France the flights were seen as scientific experiments, sanctioned by the academies of science in Paris and in the regions, and with royal support, whereas in Britain ballooning never became more than an entertainment, with a reputation for charlatanry and public disorder.[32]

Franklin was one of the members of the French Academy of Science, along with doctors Guillotin and Lavoisier, charged to investigate and report on the experiments in "animal magnetism" that Friedrich Anton Mesmer was conducting. The report was critical and discouraging:

As to the animal magnetism so much talked of, . . . I must doubt its existence till I can see or feel some effect of it. None of the cures said to have been performed by it have fallen under my observation, and there being so many disorders which cure themselves, and such a disposition in mankind to deceive themselves and one another on these occasions, and living long has given me so frequent opportunity of seeing certain remedies cried up as curing everything, and yet soon after totally laid aside as useless, I cannot but fear that the expectation of great advantage from this new method of treating diseases will prove a delusion. That delusion may, however, and in some cases, be of use while it lasts. There are in every great, rich city a number of persons who are never in health, because they are fond of medicines and always taking them, whereby they derange the natural functions and hurt their constitution. If these people can be persuaded to forbear their drugs, in expectation of being cured by only the physician's finger, or an iron rod pointing at them, they may possibly find good effects, though they mistake the cause.[33]

When Franklin's daughter Sally wrote to him in France and asked for his views on the Order of the Cincinnati, the veterans' organization open to French as well as American officers, he made plain what he saw as the ridiculousness of an hereditary aristocracy in a new republic. The notion of honor "descending to posterity is not only groundless and absurd," he wrote, "but often hurtful to that Posterity, since it is apt to make them proud, disdaining to be employ'd in useful Arts, and thence falling into Poverty." He resorted to mathematics to show that the same blood does not descend in its entirety to subsequent generations, since a man acquires only half his blood from his father's family. In nine generations—only three hundred years—the share of a distinguished ancestor's blood in a male heir would be but 1/512. The descent of titles in families he thought to be as absurd as hereditary professors of mathematics; he suggested instead "ascending honor for parents of worthy persons."[34]

The letter to Sally was private, but, as with all he wrote, he was aware of wider audiences. Mirabeau was translating into French Aedanus Burke's criticisms of the Order of Cincinnati, in what became *Considérations sur l'ordre de Cincinnatus,* published in London in 1784. Franklin gave his letter to Sally to the Abbé Morellet for translation, and it duly appeared in the notes to Mirabeau's work—against Morellet's advice. Morellet was afraid that it would lose him friends among the nobles, as it did. It certainly, also, lost him the friendship of Washington.

*   *   *

William Franklin, after two years in a Connecticut prison and four years as an ineffective president of the Board of Associated Loyalists, had moved to London. In July 1784 he wrote his father inviting himself to Passy for a reunion. Franklin made a cool reply:

Indeed nothing has ever hurt me so much and affected me with such keen Sensations, as to find my self deserted in my old Age by my only Son; and not only deserted, but to find him taking up Arms against me, in a Cause wherein my good Fame, Fortune and Life were all at Stake. You conceived, you say, that your Duty to your King and Regard for your Country requir'd this. I ought not to blame you for differing in Sentiment with me in Public Affairs. We are Men, all subject to Errors. Our Opinions are not in our own

Power; they are form'd and govern'd much by Circumstances that are often as inexplicable as they are irresistible. Your Situation was such that few would have censured your remaining Neuter, *tho' there are Natural Duties which precede political Ones, and cannot be extinguish'd by them.* This is a disagreable Subject. I drop it. And we will endeavour as you propose mutually to forget what has happened relating to it, as well as we can . . . I shall be glad to see you when convenient, but would not have you come here at present.

He countered with the suggestion that William's son Temple go to see his father in London. "You may confide to [him] the Family Affairs you wished to confer upon with me, for he is discreet. And I trust that you will prudently avoid introducing him to Company that it may be improper for him to be seen with."[35]

Franklin's grandson had another mission when he left France late in the summer of 1784: that of persuading Polly Hewson, now that her mother had died, to spend the autumn and winter with his grandfather in Passy. This outcome was happier than relations with William. Polly was impressed by Temple. "We are all pleased with our old Friend Temple changed into young Franklin. We see a strong resemblance of you, and indeed saw it when we did not think ourselves at liberty to say we did, as we pretended to be as ignorant as you supposed we were, or chose we should be. I believe you may have been handsomer than your Grandson is, but then you were never so genteel; and if he has a little less philosophy he has more polish."[36]

It was in these years also that Franklin wrote his delightful and teasing letters to Mme Helvétius, a rich and aging widow famous for her weekly dinners, to Mme Brillon to whom he was "cher papa," and to Mme le Roy, the Comtesse Golowkin, and the Comtesse d'Houdetot. Mme Helvétius was the daughter of a count and the widow of a baron; her husband had been a prominent writer, *philosophe*, and Freemason. She was no intellectual herself, but she was intelligent, generous, and openminded. She had been so beautiful that the *philosophe* Fontenelle, who lived to be a hundred years old, was said to have paid her one of the most famous compliments of the age: "Ah Madame, if I were only eighty again!" At sixty she was still so attractive that Franklin paid her another (perhaps apocryphal), which became as famous: when she accused him of having put off a visit to her, he replied, "Madame, I am waiting till the nights are longer." Her home was known as the Academy because of the quality of her entourage, one of whom, Turgot, himself had proposed marriage to her when both were young; and after his return from the Italian campaign Napoleon was to seek, unsuccessfully, to join her salon. Franklin, to whom she was "Notre Dame d'Auteuil," whether playfully or with serious intent, proposed marriage. When she declined, he wrote to her that in a dream he had met her deceased husband in the Elysian Fields and learned that he had taken a new wife there—who turned out to be Deborah Franklin! "She told me coldly, 'I have been a good wife to you for forty-nine years and four months, nearly half a century; be content with that. Here I have formed a new connection, which will endure to eternity.' Offended by this refusal of my Eurydice, I at once decided to leave these ungrateful spirits, and return to the good earth, to see again the sunshine and you. Here I am! Let us revenge ourselves."[37]

Abigail Adams's description of La Helvétius is less flattering. She was, Abigail thought, untidy and brazen. She called Dr. Franklin merely "Franklin," kissed his cheeks and forehead when she greeted him, and at dinner sometimes held his hand and sometimes carelessly threw her arms around his neck (her other arm now and then on the back of John Adams's chair).

I should have been greatly astonished at this conduct, if the good Doctor had not told me that in this lady I should see a genuine Frenchwoman, wholly free from affectation or stiffness of behavior, and one of the best women in the world. For this I must take the Doctor's word: but I should have set her down for a very bad one, although sixty years of age, and a widow. I own I was highly disgusted, and never wish for an acquaintance with ladies of this cast. After dinner she threw herself on a settee, where she showed more than her feet. She had a little lap-dog, who was, next to the Doctor, her favorite. This she kissed, and when he wet the floor she wiped it up with her chemise. This is one of the Doctor's most intimate friends, with whom he dines once every week, and she with him. She is rich, and is my near neighbour; but I have not yet visited her.[38]

The tone and conventions of French society permitted and even demanded that compliments paid should be frank and fulsome; and Franklin went to the bounds of the possible, at least as a correspondent. He had explained to his Boston stepniece Eliza Hubbard Partridge in 1779:

This is the civilest nation upon earth. Your first Acquaintances endeavour to find out what you like and they tell others. If't is understood that you like

Mutton, dine where you will you will find Mutton. Somebody, it seems, gave it out that I lov'd ladies; and then everybody presented me their ladies (or the ladies presented themselves) to be *embrac'd*—that is to have their necks kiss'd. For as to kissing of lips or cheeks, it is not the mode here; the first is reckoned rude, and the other may rub off the paint.[39]

His special favorite was Mme Brillon de Jouy, *la brillante* as he called her.

People commonly speak of *Ten* commandments. I have been taught that there are *twelve*. The *first* was *Increase* and *multiply* and replenish the Earth. The *twelfth* is, a new Commandment I give unto you *that ye love one another* . . . Pray tell me, my dear Casuist, whether my keeping religiously these two Commandments, tho' not in the Decalogue, may not be accepted in compensation for my breaking so often one of the Ten, I mean that which forbids coveting my neighbor's wife, and which I *confess* I break constantly. God forgive me, as often as I see or think of my lovely Confessor: And I am afraid I should never be able to repent of the sin, even if I had the full possession of her.

And now I am consulting you upon a case of conscience, I will mention the opinion of a certain Father of the Church, which I find myself willing to adopt, tho' I am not sure it is orthodox. It is this, that the most effectual way to get rid of a certain temptation is, as often as it returns, to comply with and satisfy it. Pray instruct me how far I may venture to practise upon this principle?

When he first met her she was thirty-six, beautiful, elegant, intelligent, marred by a marriage of convenience to a man twenty years her elder. Franklin was in his seventies. Franklin said that he spent two evenings a week with her, Wednesdays and Saturdays, for four years. She offered concerts, tea, and chess: "I call this *my Opera,* for I rarely go to the Opera in Paris." She improved his French, which seems to have needed it; on one occasion at the theater, he was chagrined to find that his most vigorous applause had been bestowed on flattering allusions to himself. When she accused him of inconstancy, he insisted that it was as plain as Euclid that whoever was constant to several persons was more constant than he who was constant to only one. He must not apologize for his French, he was told; if it was not very pure, it was at least very clear. As she said in another letter, it was "always very good French to say: 'Je vous aime.' Leave grammar to the academicians."[40]

It was for his ladies of the salons that Franklin printed the Bagatelles on his private press at Passy. These miniature essays were pieces of whimsy. They show, as Carl Becker has said, Franklin's "disposition to take life with infinite zest and yet with humorous detachment." He expressed his devotion, stronger than affection but short of passion, with playful gallantry. He had learned long ago that, in Poor Richard's words, "As charms are nonsense, nonsense is a charm" (August 1734). He had learned the fashions; here as elsewhere he was still *l'homme moyen sensuel*. The gallantries, which in all their coquetry were never free from irony, horrified Abigail Adams and shocked John, intrigued John Jay, and fascinated Jefferson. Jefferson was even led to attempt once to emulate the Master; but in this as in much else he found the task of following Franklin at the court of France "an excellent school of humility." He could not replace Dr. Franklin, he said; he was only his successor.[41]

On December 26, 1783, Franklin reminded the Congress of its promise to recall him after the peace treaty was signed. "No morning sun lasts a whole day," Poor Richard had said in November 1754. Not until May 1785, however, did the Congress accede to his request and allow him to become, as he put it, "once more a freeman." He left Passy on July 12, 1785, in style, "to ease the pain of his gout and the stone, in one of the king's Litters, carried by mules." He was seventy-nine years old, his body tormented with pain, his legs swollen. It was a sad but triumphal journey, flower-strewn, repeatedly halted for receptions in his honor: it took five days to cover 150 miles. He carried with him a royal gift: a miniature of the French king encircled by 400 diamonds. (When Sally inherited it in 1790, she and her husband would sell it to finance their own trip to Europe.) His luggage, 128 crates of it, went by barge down the Seine. He crossed to Southampton for a last cold and formal meeting with William, with whom he was never reconciled, and a warmer one with Bishop Shipley and his family.

The London Packet did not reach Philadelphia until September 14—a long voyage, but as usual it was not wasted. Franklin kept his "Maritime Observations" during those six weeks: assessing the causes and the course of the Gulf Stream, which had long fascinated him; and speculating upon methods of navigation, diets for the sailors, lifeboat drill, and the use of kayaks. He also wrote a pamphlet, "The Causes and Cure of Smoky Chimneys."

Franklin was greeted at the Market Street wharf, where he had first

landed sixty-two years before, with guns fired in tribute and the ringing of church bells. He wrote in his journal, "God be praised and
thanked for all his mercies."[42]

*   *   *

The Paris embassy is a remarkable chapter in the Franklin saga. The
only aspect of it that reflects adversely on him is not his style of living—most other ambassadors lived far more splendidly than he did—
not the Bagatelles and the piquant correspondence with the ladies of
the salons; and certainly not his crafty dealing, either with Wentworth
and Vergennes in 1778 to obtain the Treaty of Alliance or with Hartley, Oswald, and Vergennes in 1782–83 to obtain the Treaty of Peace.
Only in that aspect of an ambassador's role described as "reporting
back" to his home government did Franklin fall short. There is little
evidence that this man, hailed as the American Rousseau, as Solon to
Voltaire's Sophocles, and on arrival in Nantes, by J. Mosneron, as
"The Archimedes and Solon of his country," ever remotely glimpsed
the Revolution that was to explode in Paris in 1789. He wrote to
Benjamin Vaughan in November 1789: "The Revolution in France is
truly surprising. I sincerely wish it may end in establishing a good
constitution for that country. The mischiefs and troubles it suffers in
the operation, however, give me great concern."[43]

France seemed to him to be a benevolent monarchy with its administration in no danger of revolt from below. His view of France was
idyllic, almost Arcadian, as had long been his view of London. He
was aware, as he wrote in *The Internal State of America,* of Europe
as a place of a "few rich and haughty landlords, the multitude of poor
abject and rack'd Tenants, and the half-paid and half-starv'd ragged
labourers." He was also fully aware of its folly and extravagance, but
this awareness did not prevent his own enjoyment of the comforts of
life, in Paris as in London.[44]

He wrote in November 1789 to Jean Baptiste Le Roy: "Great part
of the news we have had from Paris, for near a year past, has been
afflicting. I sincerely wish and pray it may all end well and happy,
both for the King and the nation. The voice of Philosophy I apprehend can hardly be heard among the tumults . . . Our new Constitution is now established, and has an appearance that promises perma-
nency; but in this world nothing can be said to be certain, except
death and taxes."[45]

Franklin's criticisms of developments in France won from Brissot, in his *Le Patriote Français,* a reprimand:

We cannot keep from noticing that certain expressions reflect Dr. Franklin's long sojourn close to the court and his intimacy with the ministers. It was there, no doubt, that he learned to repeat this word *populace,* and to consider as distressing the news of a revolution which returned to a people its liberty because it was tinged with a little blood. It is doubtless not at all from this point of view that the American people regard this Revolution. They paid too dearly for their own liberty to be afflicted by the sacrifices which ours cost.[46]

It was, nevertheless, inevitable that Franklin should be seen as a forerunner of the Revolution, the "American Rousseau." But there is no evidence that he ever read Rousseau, and his taste was for science and for the observation of facts, not for abstract reasoning; he was a utilitarian, not a utopian. His Masonic friends, some of whom were, as we have seen, to die in the Terror, were fellow constitutionalists in these years, and no more prescient. He did not read the signs of a more fundamental change any more than he had read the signs in Pennsylvania in 1764–65. He was superb as a molder of public opinion, and (though not so much in London) as a political operator. He was less skilled as social analyst and, in his years at Passy, paid the price of his physical immobility, his age and isolation. Or perhaps, both in 1775–1776 and in 1789, there were fewer social causes and more pure chance at work than later historical pattern-weavers have imagined?

Sainte-Beuve's assessment of Franklin was apt:

An ideal is lacking, in his healthy, upright able frugal laborious nature . . . There was a lack of sentiment, honour, religion, chivalry . . . He brings everything down to arithmetic, and strict reality . . . The useful is always and preferably his measure . . .

We of the hasty and vivacious French race would like him to have had a little of ourselves in him . . . we feel that wings to soar are lacking . . . But he is just, judicious, firm, shrewd, immovable, seeks reconciliation as long as possible. And an inward warmth of feeling animates his prudence; a ray of sun lights up and cheers his honesty.[47]

The mission has to be assessed, however, in terms other than the personal and temperamental. As chief of mission Franklin is vulnerable to criticism: he was too casual, especially over money; too permissive toward his staff; and not the best judge of character. He admitted to Jonathan Williams that in mercantile matters he was "like a Man walking in the Dark, I stumble often, and frequently get my Shins broke." Struggling with a foreign language and unfamiliar social customs, he did not show enough firmness in many matters that came before him. Charged by the Congress to send over a few qualified engineers and artillery officers, he was overwhelmed by hundreds of requests from officers and adventurers. With his politician's wish to please and his susceptibility to flattery, he signed up many unsuitable applicants, along with a few highly talented and highly motivated ones.[48]

As ambassador, as Condorcet said in his eulogy, Franklin observed much and acted little. He held much too light a rein over rash privateer captains like Gustavus Conyngham and Lambert Wickes, whose overzealous activities imperiled American relations with France. In T. P. Abernethy's words, "he allowed vessels, money and men intended for the service of Congress to be diverted into privateering on account of individuals." He was especially lax with John Paul Jones, whose plans to capture British seamen in order to offer them in exchange for American prisoners he encouraged before any exchange plan was firmly made with his British contacts. He found Captain Landais all but impossible to handle. Franklin was aware of his own limitations in commercial and maritime affairs, however, and requested to be relieved of such responsibilities. For example, he wrote to Samuel Huntington in March 1780: "As Vessels of War under my Care create me a vast deal of Business of a kind too that I am unexperienced in and by my Distance from the Coast is very difficult to be well executed, I must repeat my earnest Request, that some Person of Skill in such Affairs may be appointed in the Character of Consul, to take Charge of them." And again to Huntington in May 1780: "The Trouble and Vexation these Maritime Affairs give me is inconceivable. I have often express'd to Congress my Wish to be reliev'd from them, and that some Person better acquainted with them, and better situated, might be appointed to manage them: Much Money as well as Time would, I am sure, be saved by such an Appointment."[49]

His age, as well as the difficulties of handling maritime and commercial affairs, and the love of tranquillity that both Vergennes and John Adams had noticed, made him a poor correspondent. Age and apathy often became silence and reserve—or what others would salute as an admirable foresight and caution.

It remains difficult to assess whether Franklin had any precise effect

on French foreign policy. French intellectual opinion appears to have
been broadly sympathetic to the American cause and to have appreciated his presence and his talents; but there is no proof that this
seriously influenced Vergennes or Maurepas. The line of French foreign policy from Fleury through Choiseul to Vergennes was a line of
self-interest and of a cool appreciation of the balance of power in
Europe. French naval rearmament had been proceeding steadily. The
policy owed nothing, except its timing, to Saratoga. Yet a man of
Franklin's talents, endlessly active in the public prints, notably in the
Journal des Affaires de l'Angleterre et de l'Amerique, shrewd, wise,
and congenial, gave Vergennes support, and—in his dealings with
Spain—reinforcement. Vergennes appreciated the American military
successes, and he needed the Spanish fleet. In all likelihood each man
was well aware that he was manipulating and being manipulated by
the other; but since it was in the interests of both of their countries at
the time, and since they liked each other, the situation suited them
well.

Franklin's French embassy did reveal that he had learned much
from his early flawed experience as a diplomat both in Philadelphia
and in London. The patience was always there, and the timing, and
the faith in America and its future. America should be firm; she
should not solicit favors but grant them, and they should be the favors of future commerce and markets. The faith rested on the vast
political and material resources of a great continent. The land, in its
wealth, was a diplomatic counter of incalculable weight. It gave
strength in argument, and it counseled patience.

Acting now as a principal and no longer as an agent, treated now
by the great men as one of themselves, he moved across the checker-
board with easy dexterity. This was especially evident in the handling
of Vergennes in 1777; and the fact that Vergennes's spies confirmed
that Franklin was doing precisely what he said he was doing gave
Vergennes confidence in him. Part of the strength here was Franklin's
firmness and consistency toward Britain. He would accept nothing
short of independence, even though the otherwise generous terms offered by the Carlisle Commission in America in 1778, and by Wentworth in Paris, were for Britain a humiliating surrender. His language
toward Britain was undeviatingly hostile, however much he stayed in
warm friendship with individuals. And the confidence thus built up
through those anguished fourteen months before February 1778 held

through the next four years. Franklin's secret weapon lay in his threat that America could in the end always make its own peace with Britain. When, in 1782, he did bring about just that, he did so in part because he had a trust in Shelburne that he had in no other British politician. There was still no deviation on any other item; not on the Loyalists, on fisheries, on boundaries, on the fur posts, or on debts. Indeed, had Franklin, Jay, and Adams made some concessions of their own, they might have strengthened Shelburne's far from stable position in the House of Commons and made the years after 1783 a smoother chapter in Anglo-American relations.

The central factor in any assessment of Franklin's role, is that he was 3,500 miles from home, with instructions always too slow and too vague to be helpful in the constantly changing diplomatic scene and amid the increasing momentum of events. His country was federal in its political system and all but disunited, with inexperienced executives, a weak army, no navy except for a few unreliable privateers, and no credit. On occasion he waited twelve months for replies and instructions.

He was constantly being instructed to ask for more and more aid, fully aware that he and the Congress had little with which to guarantee repayment, embarrassing as it was to play the role of beggar. He not only got much of what he asked for but persuaded Vergennes that France had as much to gain as had the United Colonies in securing American independence. When there was a delay in the purchase of a new ship from Holland, he helped to persuade Chaumont to buy for John Paul Jones the *Bonhomme Richard*. In this tortuous world he moved with the adroitness of the professional. Only Franklin among leading American men of affairs could have played this part— at once supple and sober, serious yet amused, and with a reputation not just as savant but as sage. It was no easy and automatic task, as Jay found in Spain and Adams at The Hague. His international standing as scientist and *philosophe*—and no other American could rival him here—won him acceptance and popularity in France, that allowed him to correspond with Turgot about his stove and with Marat about the nature of fire, to employ his diplomatic skills to extract more and more money, to recruit officers for the army, and to equip French-based privateers like the *Lexington, Dolphin,* and *Reprisal* to harass British trade.

Franklin obtained at least 45 million francs of loans and gifts; some estimates go much higher: Jonathan Dull puts the figure at 80 million dollars in today's terms. Without this, America might not have been able to maintain her independence after 1778. All the financial aid from 1776 to 1781 came by and through France; 90 percent of the powder used by Americans in the first two and a half years of war came from France. And most of the credit for this French assistance must go to Franklin. Vergennes refused to have anything more to do with John Adams in 1780. John Jay, whom Franklin wanted as his successor in Paris, had been embittered by his experiences in Spain. Dana, Izard, William Lee, and Silas Deane met with little success as fundraisers in any of their posts; none of them made Franklin's task easier, in Paris or elsewhere. Franklin's services are therefore all but incalculable. The United States might in the very long run have won the war on land without French troops. It was, however, the arrival off Yorktown of a French fleet that was decisive in 1781; and the British ships that might have been there were guarding the home islands against the prospect of an invasion from Europe that Franklin's skill had helped to manufacture. When the news of Yorktown came through, Franklin was right to thank Vergennes and to give his thanks to Louis XVI, "le plus grand faiseur d'heureux that this world affords."[50]

Franklin gives us insights into his diplomacy in an indirect way in his "Morals of Chess" (June 1779):

The Game of Chess is not merely an idle Amusement. Several very valuable qualities of the Mind, useful in the course of human Life, are to be acquir'd or strengthened by it, so as to become habits, ready on all occasions . . .

1st *Foresight,* which looks a little into futurity, and considers the Consequence that may attend an action; for it is continually occurring to the Player, "If I move this piece, what will be the advantages or disadvantages of my new situation?" . . .

2nd *Circumspection,* which surveys the whole Chessboard, or scene of action; the relations of the several pieces and their situations; the Dangers they are repeatedly exposed to; the several possibilities of their aiding each other; the probabilities that the Adversary may make this or that move, and attack this or that Piece; and what different Means can be used to avoid his stroke, or turn its consequences against him.

3rd *Caution,* not to make our moves too hastily. This habit is best acquired, by observing strictly the laws of the Game; such as, *If you touch a Piece, you must move it somewhere; if you set it down, you must let it stand.*

Therefore, it would be the better way to observe these rules, as the Game becomes thereby more the image of human Life, and particularly of War . . .

And *lastly*, we learn by Chess the habit of not being discouraged by present appearances in the state of our affairs; the habit of hoping for a favourable Change, and that of persevering in the search of resources . . . one so frequently, after contemplation, discovers the means of extricating one's self from a supposed insurmountable Difficulty, that one is encouraged to continue the Contest to the last, in hopes of Victory from our skill; or at least from the Negligence of our Adversary.[51]

Perhaps the best assessment of Franklin's services in Paris comes in fact from his foremost enemy, Arthur Lee. For all his jealousy of Franklin, Lee was struck by Franklin's unquestioning confidence in the future, and his vision of America. He reported a conversation with Franklin on October 25, 1777, at a time—just before the news of Saratoga—when all Franklin's pleas to the Congress were being left unanswered, when British armies occupied both New York and Philadelphia, and when British fleets controlled the seas:

They left us to work out our own salvation; which the efforts we had hitherto made, and the resources we had opened, gave us the fairest reason to hope we should be able to do.

He told me the manner in which the whole of this business had been conducted was such a miracle in human affairs that, if he had not been in the midst of it and seen all the movements, he could not have comprehended how it was effected. To comprehend it, we must view a whole people for some months without any laws or government at all. In this state their civil governments were to be formed, an army and navy were to be provided for those who had neither a ship of war, a company of soldiers, nor magazines, arms, artillery, or ammunition. Alliances were to be formed, for they had none. All this was to be done, not at leisure nor in a time of tranquility and communication with other nations, but in the face of a most formidable invasion, by the most powerful nation, full provided with armies, fleets, and all the instruments of destruction, powerfully allied and aided, the commerce with other nations in a great measure stopped up.

The greatest revolution the world ever saw is likely to be effected in a few years; and the power that has for centuries made all Europe tremble, assisted by twenty thousand German mercenaries . . . will be effectually humbled by those whom she insulted and injured . . .[52]

No other of Franklin's colleagues in Paris was as generous. In the years of tension and trial after 1776, what was striking in Franklin was his total faith in America and its ultimate victory, and his patience. Although each of his fellow commissioners Adams and Jay called himself the Washington of the treaty-making of 1782–1783, it was Franklin who was firm and steadfast. He was smoother, now, than in Philadelphia in 1764, more urbane and relaxed than in London in 1774–1775. Short of adequate information from home, surrounded by critics, plotters, and spies, with few weapons except his own public fame and his verbal dexterity, he was the true architect of the alliance with France of 1778, and the major engineer of the peace settlement of 1782–1783.

12

PATRIARCH OF FREE MEN

*N*o sooner was Franklin back in Philadelphia, aged seventy-nine, than he was approached by all political groups to serve on the Supreme Executive Council of Pennsylvania. He was chosen president and served for three years; his role was that of an impartial and, be it said, inactive and somewhat anecdotal chairman. He would regale the members with reminiscences until noon, when the chair, carried by four prison "trusties," would come to take him home. "Come, Gentlemen," the vice-president would then say good-naturedly, "let us come to order; it is time to proceed to business now that the president is gone." When the Assembly met he was chosen president of the Commonwealth with but two dissenting voices—one of them his own.

He had faith in the new society he found. Nowhere in the world, he said, were "the labouring poor so well fed, well clothed, well lodged and well paid as in the United States of America." He gave eloquent and characteristic expression to this faith in his *Information to Those Who Would Remove to America,* published as a pamphlet in 1784:

The Truth is that though there are in that Country few People so miserable as the Poor of Europe, there are also very few that in Europe would be called rich; it is rather a general happy Mediocrity that prevails . . . people do not inquire concerning a Stranger, "What is he?" but "What can he do?" If he has any useful Art, he is welcome; and if he exercises it and behaves well, he will be respected by all that know him; but a mere Man of Quality, who on that Account wants to live upon the Public by some Office or Salary, will be despised and disregarded.[1]

He repeated the argument in 1786 in *The Internal State of America,* a reworking of various letters he had written to British friends in recent years. In spite of the accounts in the British press of "hard times, deadness of trade and scarcity of money," property values in America in fact were climbing; those of town houses had increased fourfold; crops were plentiful, import prices low. America was a land for "Hearty young Labouring Men" willing to carve a farm from the wilderness, "tolerably good workmen in any of the Mechanic Arts," and even "Persons of Moderate Fortunes and Capitals" who sought a country where their children would have abundant opportunity. "Multitudes of poor people from England, Ireland, Scotland, and Germany," Franklin pointed out, had "in a few years become wealthy Farmers, who in their own countries . . . could never have emerged from the poor Condition wherein they were born." Apprenticeships were readily obtainable even by ignorant immigrants just off the ship. "If they are proof," he noted, expressing what he hoped would be-come the "meaning" of America in the world, "they begin first as Servants or Journeymen; and if they are sober, industrious, and fru-gal, they soon become Masters, establish themselves in Business, marry, raise Families, and become respectable Citizens."[2]

He had faith too in his country's future. By 1785 he even had faith in the Germans, whom earlier he had been prompt to criticize. He took a firm stand against the Test Act, passed by the Assembly while he was in France, which stipulated that no person could vote or hold public office who would not take an oath of allegiance to the Penn-sylvania constitution of 1776. Franklin objected to it not only on constitutional principles but also because, by requiring an oath, it excluded both the Quakers and the "sect Germans" from any partic-ipation in the government. The Assembly modified the Act to require merely an oath or an affirmation that the individual had renounced allegiance to the king of England, was loyal to the Commonwealth, and had not, since the Declaration of Independence, given aid to the British.

*   *   *

Franklin was chosen to be a member of the Constitutional Conven-tion but doubted whether he would be fit enough to attend. In fact, he never missed a session. He was no speaker, and now in any event too weak for oratory. But his presence, with his great prestige and his bland humor, was important in the crises of debate. So was his obvious openness of mind. When it appeared that the debate over representation would become acrimonious, he called for calm tempers:

We are sent here to *consult,* not to *contend,* with each other; and declarations of a fixed opinion, and of determined resolution, never to change it, neither enlighten nor convince us. Positiveness and warmth on one side, naturally beget their like on the other; and tend to create and augment discord and division in a great concern, wherein harmony and Union are extremely necessary to give weight to our Councils, and render them effectual in promoting and securing the common good.[3]

When the quarrel reached an especially partisan acrimony his intervention was pacificatory and, for him, unusual: not only did he plead for tolerance, he also asked for prayer.

The small progress we have made after four or five weeks close attendance and continual reasonings with each other . . . is methinks a melancholy proof of the imperfection of the Human Understanding. We indeed seem to feel our own want of political wisdom, since we have been running about in search of it. We have gone back to ancient history for models of Government, and examined the different forms of those Republics which having been formed with the seeds of their own dissolution now no longer exist. And we have viewed Modern States all round Europe, but find none of their Constitutions suitable to our circumstances . . . In the beginning of the Contest with G. Britain, when we were sensible of danger we had daily prayer in this room for the divine protection—Our prayers, Sir, were heard, and they were graciously answered. All of us who were engaged in the struggle must have observed frequent instances of a Superintending providence in our favor. To that kind providence we owe this happy opportunity of consulting in peace on the means of establishing our future national felicity. And have we now forgotten that powerful friend? or do we imagine that we no longer need His assistance? I have lived, Sir, a long time, and the longer I live the more convincing proofs I see of this truth—that God governs in the affairs of men . . .[4]

Franklin spoke in favor of voluntary public service. He gave examples of corruption caused by profit-seekers in government, and cited cases where good and honorable men had served in public stations without pay: "the pleasure of doing good and serving their Country and the respect such conduct entitles them to, are sufficient motives with some minds to give up a great portion of their time to the Public, without the mean inducement of pecuniary satisfaction." Alexander Hamilton seconded his proposal to bring the issue of reward before the Convention, but no debate ensued and the motion was postponed. James Madison recorded that "it was treated with great respect, but rather for the author of it, than from any apparent conviction of its expediency or practicality."[5]

Franklin opposed giving the executive an absolute veto, citing abuses of that power by the proprietary governors of Pennsylvania and the Stadtholders in the Netherlands; and he sought to prohibit reelection of the president as a protection against tyranny.

He also opposed a provision that would have limited the suffrage in national elections to freeholders. To do this, he contended, would "depress the virtue and public spirit of our common people." It was left in the end to each state to determine its own rule for the suffrage, a prerogative that was not disturbed until the adoption of the Fifteenth Amendment, eighty years later.[6]

Along with James Madison and James Wilson, Franklin opposed the insertion of a long residence requirement preliminary to naturalization. He was not, he said, "against a reasonable time, but should be very sorry to see anything like illiberality inserted in the Constitution. The people in Europe are friendly to this Country . . . We found in the Course of the Revolution, that many strangers served us faithfully—and that many natives took part against their Country. When foreigners after looking about for some other Country in which they can obtain more happiness, give a preference to ours, it is a proof of attachment which ought to excite our confidence and affection."[7] The length of the period of residence that should precede naturalization was left in the end for Congress to determine, a concession the effect of which was not materially modified by the provision that nobody but a natural born citizen, or a citizen of the United States at the time of the Constitution's adoption, who had been fourteen years a resident of the United States, should be eligible for the presidency; while similarly, senators must have resided in the United States for nine years and representatives for seven.

The Congress was split on the question of representation. Franklin himself had always favored a representation in both houses—if there must be two—based on population. It was from him that the Great Compromise came: the Senate to represent the states; the House to represent the people. And as he put it, inimitably: "If a property representation takes place, the small states contend that their liberties will be in danger. If an equality of votes is to be put in its place, the large states say their money will be in danger. When a broad table is to be made, and the edges of the planks do not fit, the artist takes a little from both and makes a good joint."[8]

Some of the political nostrums that were Franklin's special favorites, and which were features of the 1776 Pennsylvania Constitution, were thus conspicuously missing from the federal Constitution; a unicameral legislature, a plural executive, unsalaried officials. These were now, however, the core of his creed. Just as his faith in an independent America had been stimulated by his long sojourn in Britain, so his years in France, with its autocratic but inefficient government, left him decidedly a liberal. He grew with age steadily more radical in political ideas. He believed in private enterprise but recognized that private property was society's servant, not its master. When it was suggested that the Pennsylvania Constitution should have an upper chamber to represent property, he had queried whether wisdom was the necessary concomitant of riches. "The possession of property increases the desire for more property." Some of the greatest rogues he was ever acquainted with were "the richest rogues." Yet he was realistic and experienced enough to know that a strong and centralized government was needed for the new republic: "mixed" government and "balance of power" reminded him too much of the proprietary constitution.[9]

His final speech to the Convention was carefully written out the day before its delivery—and in fact he did not deliver it himself; it was read for him by James Wilson. Like most of his writings, it was addressed to a particular audience for a particular purpose. There were no passionate phrases here, no visions or ideals, no summons to battle or sacrifice, but a sense of a long experience and a political faith only in the next short step. He appealed to the Convention to adopt the Constitution unanimously.

I confess, that there are several parts of this Constitution which I do not at present approve; but, Sir, I am not sure I shall never approve them; for, having lived long, I have experienced many instances of being obliged, by better information or fuller consideration, to change opinions, even on important subjects, which I once thought right, but found to be otherwise . . . Thus I consent, Sir, to this Constitution, because I expect no better, and because I am not sure that it is not the best. The opinions I have had of its *errors* I sacrifice to the public good. I have never whispered a syllable of them abroad. Within these walls they were born, and here they shall die. I hope, therefore, for our own sakes, as a part of the people, and for the sake of our posterity, that we shall act heartily and unanimously in recommending this Constitution, wherever our influence may extend, and turn our future thoughts and endeavors to the means of having it *well administered.*

On the whole, Sir, I cannot help expressing a wish, that every member of the Convention who may still have objections to it, would with me on this occasion doubt a little of his own infallibility, and, to make *manifest* our *unanimity,* put his name to this Instrument.[10]

*   *   *

To the great debates over ratification of the Constitution, Franklin contributed only one newspaper essay, a defense of the Federalists. He was still writing letters to the papers in 1789 and 1790: an essay on the freedom of the press and its abuses; another on the slave trade. Once on a small scale a slaveowner himself, he had grown sensitive to the anomaly of slavery in a society proclaiming inalienable human rights, and in the early 1770s he had begun to collaborate with anti-slavery reformers, Granville Sharp in England and Anthony Benezet in Pennsylvania. He had used slavery then in order to attack Britain, arguing that probably not one American family in a hundred held slaves, that Britain had imposed slavery on America, and that Britons had no right to point a finger while they enslaved their own laboring poor: "All the wretches that dig coal for you, in those dark caverns under ground, unblessed by sunshine, are absolute slaves by your law, and their children after them, from the time they first carry a basket to the end of their days." Now he moved on to attack slavery as an outrage against humanity: "Can sweetening our tea, etc with sugar, be a circumstance of such absolute necessity? Can the petty pleasure thence arising to the taste, compensate for so much misery produced among our fellow creatures, and such a constant butchery of the human species by this pestilential, detestable traffic in the bodies and souls of men?" He was now president of the recently revived Pennsylvania Society for Promoting the Abolition of Slavery, and in February 1790, he signed its memorial to the first Congress. This was his last public act. His letter to the *Federal Gazette* of March 23, parodying Congressman Jackson's speech defending slavery by putting similar words into the mouth of a fictitious Algerian prince to justify the enslaving of Christians—was his last political essay. Journalism was one career he had never abandoned.[11]

During his last years he was still full of invention: a rocking chair that fanned as it rocked; a long arm for moving books on high shelves; and a combination footstool-ladder. But he finally withdrew from public office, in October 1788, at the age of eighty-two and after more than fifty eventful years in the service of province, empire, and republic. His weariness was visible to his fellow delegate William Pierce of Georgia:

Dr. Franklin is well known to be the greatest phylosopher of the present age;—all the operations of nature he seems to understand,—the very heavens obey him, and the Clouds yield up their Lightning to be imprisoned in his rod. But what claim he has to the politician, posterity must determine. It is certain that he does not shine much in public council,—he is no speaker, nor does he seem to let politics engage his attention. He is, however, a most extraordinary Man, and tells a story in a style more engaging than anything I ever heard. Let his Biographer finish his character.[12]

He lived with his daughter, "a very gross and rather homely lady," as Manasseh Cutler described her, in the house he had had built behind Market Street, surrounded by her children and the neighbors and friends who came to salute him.[13] He felt the house to be too small for comfort and, notwithstanding his age, set about planning and building some additions. In September 1786, he wrote to his sister about the project:

I had begun to build two good houses next the street, instead of three old ones which I pulled down, but my neighbor disputing my bounds, I have been obliged to postpone till that dispute is settled by law. In the meantime, the workmen and materials being ready, I have ordered an addition to the house I live in, it being too small for our growing family . . . I propose to have in it a long room for my library and instruments, with two good bed-chambers and two garrets . . . I hardly know how to justify building a library at an age that will so soon oblige me to quit it; but we are apt to forget that we are grown old, and building is an amusement.[14]

His health was now a preoccupation. In May 1785, in one of his last letters from Passy, to George Whatley, he had quoted a song called "The Old Man's Wish," "wherein, after wishing for a warm House in a country Town, an easy Horse, some good old authors, ingenious and cheerful Companions, a Pudding on Sundays, with stout Ale, and a bottle of Burgundy, etc., etc.," each stanza ends with the following lines: "May I govern my Passions with an absolute sway,/Grow wiser and better as my Strength wears away,/Without Gout or Stone, by a gentle Decay."

But what signifies our Wishing? Things happen, after all, as they will happen. I have sung that wishing Song a thousand times, when I was young, and now find, at Fourscore, that the three Contraries have befallen me, being subject to the Gout and the Stone, and not being yet Master of all my Passions. Like the proud Girl in my Country, who wished and resolv'd not to marry a Parson, nor a Presbyterian, nor an Irishman; and at length found herself married to an Irish Presbyterian Parson.

To Jonathan Shipley he wrote in February 1786:

My Health and Spirits continue, Thanks to God, as when you saw me. The only complaint I then had does not grow worse, and is tolerable. I still have Enjoyment in the Company of my Friends; and, being easy in my Circumstances, have many Reasons to like living. But the Course of Nature must soon put a period to my present Mode of Existence. This I shall submit to with less Regret, as, having seen during a long life a good deal of this world, I feel a growing curiosity to be acquainted with some other; and can cheerfully, with filial Confidence, resign my Spirit to the conduct of that great and good Parent of Mankind, who created it, and who has so graciously protected and prospered me from my Birth to the present Hour.[15]

In May 1786 he described his daily life to Polly Hewson:

I have found my family here in health, good circumstances, and well respected by their fellow citizens. The companions of my youth are indeed almost all departed, but I find an agreeable society among their children and grandchildren. I have public business enough to preserve me from *ennui*, and private amusement besides in conversation, books, my garden, and *cribbage*. Considering our well-furnished, plentiful market as the best of gardens, I am turning mine, in the midst of which my house stands, into grass plots and gravel walks, with trees and flowering shrubs. Cards we some-times play here, in long winter evenings . . . I have indeed now and then a little compunction in reflecting that I spend time so idly; but another reflection comes to relieve me, whispering: "You know that the soul is immortal; why then should you be such a niggard of a little time when you have a whole eternity before you?" So, being easily convinced, and, like other reasonable creatures, satisfied with a small reason, when it is in favor of doing what I have a mind to, I shuffle the cards again, and begin another game.

As to public amusements, we have neither plays nor operas, but we had yesterday a kind of oratorio . . . and we have assemblies, balls, besides little parties at one another's houses, in which there is some-times dancing, and frequently good music; so that we jog on in life as pleasantly as you do in England; anywhere but in London, for there you have plays performed by good actors. That, however, is, I think, the only advantage London has over Philadelphia.[16]

Later that year, Polly, whose husband had died twelve years before, moved with her three children from London to Philadelphia to be near her old friend. She lived there until her death in 1795.

In January 1788 Franklin suffered a severe fall on the stone steps in the garden, badly spraining his wrist and arm. Walking was now difficult. At about the same time, the stone became so excruciatingly painful that he was forced to take opium, which provided relief but also exhausted him. Sensing that the end was near, he revised his will. Though providing well for the other members of his family, he left only a small bequest to William, explaining that: "The part he acted against me in the late war, which is of public notoriety, will account for my leaving him no more of an estate he endeavored to deprive me of." [17] In the last year of his life he never left his bedroom. The meetings of the American Philosophical Society were now held in his home. He was still writing to friends across the world and at home and trying to complete his memoirs—but he brought the story down only to 1757.

On April 10, 1790, his final illness attacked him. His physician, Dr. John Jones, prepared an account of it.

About sixteen days before his death, he was seized with a feverish disposition ... In this frame of body and mind, he continued until five days before his death when the pain and difficulty of breathing entirely left him, and his family were flattering themselves with hopes of his recovery; but an imposthume [abscess] which had formed in his lungs, suddenly burst, and discharged a quantity of matter, which he continued to throw up while he had power; but as that failed, the organs of respiration became gradually oppressed; a calm, lethargic state succeeded; and on the 17th instant [April 1790] about eleven o'clock at night, he quietly expired, closing a long and useful life of eighty four years and three months.[18]

He was laid to rest in Christ Church Burial Ground, attended by a crowd of some twenty thousand, the largest ever to assemble in Philadelphia. The tomb has his own simple wording, as his will directed: "Benjamin and Deborah Franklin 1790."

There were many tributes. The official obituary was delivered by

William Smith, friend turned enemy. The French remembrances were more lyrical, from Mirabeau's purple prose to the simple words of Franklin's close friend Félix Vicq d'Azyr: "Un homme est mort, et deux mondes sont en deuil" (A man is dead, and two worlds mourn). But the epitaph by which he is remembered is the one he himself had written sixty-two years before his death.[19]

> The body of
> B Franklin Printer
> (Like the Cover of an Old Book
> Its Contents torn out
> And stript of its Lettering & Gilding)
> Lies here, Food for Worms.
> But the Work shall not be lost;
> For it will, (as he believ'd) appear once more,
> In a new and more elegant Edition
> Revised and corrected
> *By the Author.*

13

FATHER OF ALL THE YANKEES?

Despite the vast literature on Franklin and all that he wrote himself, there remain in the Franklin saga several problems that baffle the historian. These are not merely the personal mysteries like that of the identity of his son's mother, but far more intractable questions. Who was the real author of the Albany Plan, Franklin or Hutchinson? To what extent did Franklin miscalculate in 1764? What were his real hopes for Britain and America in 1768–1774? How sincere was he in his own judgment of himself in the affair of the Hutchinson letters? And in the years in Paris how responsible was he for the financial difficulties of the mission, for the tensions with Lee and Deane, for the recurrent leaks of information? In all the range of his activities and all the publicity in which he lived, Franklin could often remain curiously uninvolved, never quite committing the whole man to the cause of the moment, quizzically looking in on himself from outside, and (one suspects) shaking with quiet laughter at the oddity of his own career. He made his first reputation by his journalism. Yet throughout his life he was always the master of the great rule phrased not by Poor Richard but by Edward Everett: If you want your secret kept, keep it.

One must add to this his singular longevity. His career links not only three worlds—Philadelphia, London, and Paris—but three ages. That the verdicts upon him have been various should therefore occasion little surprise. Many of his contemporaries, not only the flinty Puritan spirits John and Abigail Adams, were savagely critical. William Cobbett saw him as atheist, fornicator, and hypocrite. The Lees, rallying to defend Arthur's name, did so in part by denigrating Franklin. And even in Paris, a voice or two were raised in criticism of the *caméléon octogenaire*.[1]

His modern critics have seized on other features. His early religion was at best a calculus ("that wisdom which had made all things by weight and measure"), his later no more than deism and decorum. His morality was only a sense of civic and social obligation. His realism has been seen as cynicism and his diplomatic deftness as deceit ("the Grand Incendiary," said William Allen, "the Crafty-Fellow, the Disturber of Peace"); his bland and straightforward manner was designed to hide his lack of imagination; his limpid prose is praiseworthy, but, it is stressed, he has no poetry at all. To his critics Franklin is thus a cool, complacent, compromising figure in a pre-Romantic world; his modesty of manner is part of the trickery of the first of the boosters; he is the pioneer image-maker of our age of persuasion; he is, in William Carlos Williams's phrase, "our wise prophet of chicanery."[2]

The length of his life, the range of his interests and experience, the comments of friends and foes during and since, all make a simple estimate difficult. For central to the "problems" posed to the historian by Franklin's career is the estimate of the man himself, half jester, half sage. His contemporaries referred again and again to his half-quizzical smile and to his easy laughter; son-in-law Richard Bache's abiding memory of him was that life seemed always—at least on the surface—to be a great joke; for Boswell he was "all jollity and pleasantry." His jests, always couched in universal terms, and his wisdom, rarely lacking a humorous twist, were usually too gentle and droll for cynicism, too cutting and deflating ever to permit eulogy; and there was always the remarkably even and consistent urbanity of style and manner. His manner is not, perhaps, to twentieth-century taste. His apparent immorality as a young man and his enjoyment in revealing it; the frankness and salacity of his public letters on what we would deem private subjects; his poses and his evident delight in the hoodwinking of people, especially politicians; the sense in his career that it was clever to cross forbidden zones provided you got away with it; the dionysian depths below the apollonian surface; his combination of shamelessness and success; the preachment of morality and thrift by a confessedly immoral, at times ribald and salty, and at times extravagant, old reprobate; these things could hardly meet with approval in a public figure today. The tone of his correspondence with Mme Helvétius, which appealed to the salons, would now appeal only to readers of the more lurid press. The modest, deferential manner (and cultivated obsequiousness) did not preclude a mellow enjoyment of his own success; as his correspondence with Arthur Lee shows, he felt—when pushed to the limit—that no Alexander should stand between oneself and the sun.

Nor were his services to his country's cause of the sort that are easy to describe. He was no orator—his most important speech at the Continental Congress was read for him, and it probably had more effect than any he ever delivered himself. Despite the title of "General," won—too easily—in Braddock's war, he was no soldier; though he was not the first or last general to make a reputation around the conference table and by careful organization of the supply column. Nor was he, in the first revolutionary age in modern history, in any sense a revolutionary. He abhorred violence and war. He found mobs anathema, John Wilkes and even Thomas Paine uncongenial. As he explained to William in 1768, he preferred "sober and serious men" to the "Madness of English mobs." He was distrustful of "causes," of movements, of talk of "rights." There are few paragraphs in Franklin's writing evocative of *Common Sense* or of the moving second paragraph of the Declaration of Independence. He had little time for metaphysics or the life of the imagination. His interest was not that of the radical (or of the true philosopher) in doctrine, or even in constitutions, but that of the businessman, the man of affairs, and the politician, in getting things done and in getting problems—specific and immediate problems—solved. For him, problems were for solving by reason and compromise, not raw material for crusades. He preferred the corridors of power to the parade ground, the boudoir to the barricades. Neither in America in 1776 nor in Paris after 1776 did he see the issue as one of justice; his concern was not with ends but with means. His forte was compromise, not confrontation; diplomacy, not altercation. The student of politics will learn from him how to operate, but not what to operate for. He is thus at worst a man of expedients, but at best a man for all ages, not least for ages labeled revolutionary.[3]

There was, running through the prose, a black streak. In part it was teasing, as when he wrote to his physician and friend Dr. John Fothergill about his function as a saver of lives: "Do you please yourself with the Fancy that you are doing Good? You are mistaken. Half the Lives you save are not worth saving, as being useless; and almost the other Half ought not to be sav'd, as being mischievous." But he struck a darker note in a letter to his sister Jane: "this world is the true Hell, or place of punishment for the spirits who had transgress'd in a better state." And to Joseph Priestley, in June 1782, with victory in sight but not yet won, he wrote:

Men I find to be a Sort of Beings very badly constructed, as they are generally more easily provok'd than reconcil'd, more disposed to do Mischief to each other than to make Reparation, much more easily deceiv'd than undeceiv'd, and having more Pride and even Pleasure in killing than in begetting one another; for without a Blush they assemble in great armies at Noon Day to destroy, and when they have kill'd as many as they can, they exaggerate the Number to augment the fancied Glory; but they creep into Corners, or cover themselves with the Darkness of night, when they mean to beget, as being asham'd of a virtuous Action. A virtuous Action it would be, and a vicious one the killing of them, if the Species were really worth producing or preserving; but of this I begin to doubt.[4]

*   *   *

The public man must inevitably be judged by public standards, and Franklin has, equally inevitably, been judged from the standpoint of other ages than his own. By writing so much, and by repeatedly, but unsuccessfully, seeking to complete an autobiography that was much concerned with his own reputation, he has become the prisoner of what others care to make of his career. But in the assessment of the public man attention has to be paid to the warmth and the style, the vigor and the gusto of the private, as well as the public, correspondent. The balance sheet must include tribute to the affection and depth of his lifelong relationship with his sister Jane and of his long and happy marriage to Deborah.

When he sent Jane a few small presents and she wrote to thank him, he replied: "I received here your letter of extravagant thanks, which put me in mind of the Story of the Member of Parliament, who began one of his Speeches with saying, he thank'd God he was born and bred a Presbyterian, on which another took leave to observe, that the Gentleman must needs be of a most grateful Disposition, since he was thankful for such very small Matters." And when Jane was harassed with the care of their impoverished seventy-nine-year-old sister (for whom Franklin furnished a house rent-free), he wrote:

As *having their own Way,* is one of the greatest Comforts of Life, to old People, I think their Friends should endeavour to accommodate them in that, as well as in any thing else. When they have long liv'd in a House, it becomes natural to them, they are almost as closely connected with it as the Tortoise with his Shell, they die if you remove them, 'tis ten to one that you kill them. So let our good old Sister be no more importun'd on that head. We are growing old fast ourselves, and shall expect the same kind of Indulgencies. If we give them, we shall have a Right to receive them in our Turn . . .[5]

Clearly his Debby did not belong in his sophisticated world and showed no wish to share it; had she done so she would have joined him in London—and their story, and perhaps America's, might have been very different. But he recognized that his public role rested on, and probably required, his "domestic felicity"; perhaps his remarkable ease and adaptability in the world of statecraft depended on the undemanding tranquillity and happiness of his base, even if he was long absent from it. His letters to Debby show real warmth and fondness. Take the tone of his letter of November 1756 from the Pennsylvania Indian frontier:

I wrote you a few days since, by a special messenger . . . expecting to hear from you by his return . . . but he is just now returned without a scrap for poor us. So I had a good mind not to write you by this opportunity; but I never can be ill-natured enough, even when there is the most occasion . . . I think I won't tell you that we are well, nor that we expect to return about the middle of the week, nor will I send you a scrap of news; that's poz . . . I am, Your *loving* husband, B. Franklin.
PS I have *scratched out the loving words,* being writ in haste by mistake, when I *forgot I was angry.*[6]

Another of his long and devoted friendships was with Polly Hewson, the daughter of his London landlady, whom he treated like a daughter, and who eventually settled in Philadelphia with her children to be near him. He wrote her from Passy in 1783, seeking to persuade her and her family to come over to France to stay with him, as they did:

In looking forward, Twenty-five Years seems a long Period, but, in looking back, how short! Could you imagine that 'tis now full a Quarter of a Century since we were first acquainted? It was in 1757. During the greatest Part of the Time, I lived in the same House with my dear deceased Friend, your Mother; of course you and I saw and convers'd with each other much and often. It is to all our Honours, that in all that time we never had among us the smallest Misunderstanding. Our Friendship has been all clear Sunshine, without the least Cloud in its Hemisphere. Let me conclude by saying to you, what I have had too frequent Occasions to say to my other remaining old Friends, "The fewer we become, the more let us love one another."[7]

The traits in him that seem warm, human, and impeccable in the family situation were the same traits that Franklin revealed on the public stage to those he liked, or to those whom he thought it politic to attract. His charm was his most potent weapon.

In our own century, the verdict on the private Franklin has been well rendered by Verner Crane, who summed up his personality and character as "friendly, humorous, gay, even frivolous at times, but frequently silent and reserved; shrewd, worldly-wise, genially skeptical; vain, but not conceited; ambitious, but never avid of power; often amazingly candid, but secretive when it served his turn; honestly sensuous, though not luxurious; moral by conviction and dint of practice. These traits added up to a charm which few could resist, the charm that beguiles us still in all that he said and wrote."[8]

*   *   *

Why then, in the twentieth century, do we honor Benjamin Franklin?

We do so, first, as we do George Washington, because he was so successful—not only for himself but for his country and his cause. He was indeed described, in 1764, as "the First American," a term later transferred to Washington. We have no choice but to salute a career as successful in every way as was Franklin's. From lowly origins and with no advantages except his own native talent, he achieved unusual material prosperity so that he could, as he thought, retire at the age of forty-two. He went on to a public career of great distinction, as scientist, statesman, and diplomat, honored abroad and at home. He was successful as a colonial agent, as part author of the Declaration of Independence, as writer and molder of opinion, as Founding Father. Even more than Washington's, Franklin's career was self-made; conspicuously more than Washington, he was familiar with two worlds. He passed the active years of his life almost equally in the Old World and the New. He was honored in Europe as no American had been until then and as, indeed, no American has been since. He was abused, in 1766 and still more in 1774, but that was part of the game—and part of the impact. He was idolized and lionized in Paris. He was honored in part for his very homely qualities, for his apparent scorn of pretension, for his fur cap and Quaker drab. The honor was not merely for his material success but for the nature of that success.

To his success must be added his services. Of these, three were decisive. First, he advocated colonial union long before it became politically possible, a union that should be not only political but economic, built on a sound federal basis of postal roads, corresponding philosophical societies, and a strong central government, inside or outside the Empire. Secondly, he grew steadily if reluctantly more critical of Britain and of "that fine and noble china vase, the British Empire." He did not plan independence as did Cavour; he was not the prisoner of ideas like Mazzini. Unlucky in many of his English political contacts, however, and excluded from the closed English society, in the end he became a reluctant rebel, a Founding Father of an enemy nation. As Balzac put it, he was the inventor of the lightning rod, the hoax, and the republic.

One interpretation attributes Franklin's radicalism after 1776 to his frustration when British officials thwarted his plans for a western colony. This is too simple a view. Franklin lived for almost eighteen years in London, and they were years of obvious happiness, domestic and political. By 1770 he was not only agent of four colonies but was doing well out of the Establishment, as deputy postmaster general, and with his son, William, a royal governor. He was the closest there could be to an American ambassador. It was more than patronage, opportunism, and mercenary calculation. Franklin's first intervention in continental politics was as a Federalist: at Albany in 1754, he pleaded with the colonies to form a federation, giving to a central government all powers needed for defense against French and Indians. He was ignored, locally and in London. Had he been listened to, the crises of the 1760s would not have arisen. Long afterward he could write: "The colonies so united would have been sufficiently strong to have defended themselves; there would have been no need of troops from England and, of course, the subsequent pretence for taxing America and the bloody contest it occasioned would have been avoided." He wanted Pennsylvania removed from the control of the Penns and made a royal colony. He sensed the growth of "the Empire on this side," in terms of population increase and expansion. He saw a Dominion solution—a sophisticated view of empire as a confederation of all-but-sovereign states—almost a century before Lord Durham rediscovered it. Had he been listened to—had there been only a few British figures as reasonable, as intelligent, and as patient as Franklin in the 1760s and 1770s—not only Anglo-American history but world history would have been transformed.[9]

His third decisive service was the French alliance. It is probable, indeed, that without the formal entry of France into the war, the United States would still have won. After Saratoga, it was unlikely that Britain, with only the sea as base and dependent on uncertain toeholds on land, could ever have regained control of a largely hostile and unmapped continent. Insofar as America needed assistance, it needed naval aid, and France was a land power. It is true that French troops, money, arms, and commercial privileges were of value to America, but these were being offered, in secret but in abundance, before the treaty was signed. Franklin must, moreover, share the credit for the treaty with his fellow emissaries, Lee and Deane. Franklin's belief that to await the alliance passively was more dignified than to seek it actively—a belief that, according to Lee's somewhat untrustworthy evidence, he still held as late as November 1777—and his negotiations with the British representative even as the treaty of 1778 was being discussed with France, suggest that his share in the credit must be relatively small. In any case, Vergennes had, from the beginning of the Revolution, seen in it an opportunity for revenge against Britain. Only the news of Washington's defeat on Long Island and the loss of New York checked his determination to intervene as early as the summer of 1776. The fact that the treaty was signed shortly after the American victory at Saratoga indicates that Vergennes was waiting only for the right moment, that he was influenced by events rather than by emissaries. Thus it could be argued that Franklin's services to the diplomacy of the Revolution, consisting of a small share in negotiating a treaty that was not in any case vital to the success of the cause and which would probably have come about anyway, were of negligible value. But it was the extent of the formal aid, immensely reinforced by Franklin's efforts and in the end by the public mood that he created in France, that transformed aid into alliance. The aid was valuable; behind France came Spain and Holland with their navies. Franklin was the leading emissary, and he won over many influential people, not least the king, who was very reluctant to support a revolution.

His services outside politics are a roll-call of modern inventions and innovations: the first use of cartoons, and questions and answers, in journalism; the identification of lightning as electricity; the lightning rod and the stove; bifocal spectacles; the use of oil to still unquiet water; the library chair convertible into a ladder; the copying press;

the one-arm desk chair and the artificial arm for reaching high objects; the Leyden jar and the armonica. He observed that the Gulf Stream had higher temperatures than surrounding waters and could be charted; that storms often travel in an opposite direction to the winds; that white apparel does not attract heat, while black does. He suggested, advocated, or initiated the ideas of the punishment of aggressor nations through an international organization of nations; the teaching of modern foreign languages; watertight compartments for ships; up-to-date instruction in agricultural and technical subjects; crop insurance; the study of invertebrate paleontology; the importance of frequent bathing, of fresh air bathing, and of good ventilation in hospitals and homes. He proposed daylight saving time. Mentally alert and questioning to the end, he had theories on subjects as diverse as the origin of colds, earthquakes, and the Aurora Borealis. And when the gout and gallstones laid him low, he played with the idea of "a balloon sufficiently large to raise me from the ground . . . being led by a string held by a man walking on the ground."[10]

He invented a universal language of symbols that would promote the dissemination of knowledge. He devised methods of putting Indian languages into print even though the Indians had no written symbols, and he had views on the extinction of the Pictish language in early Britain. He campaigned for language reform, anticipating Noah Webster (with whom he corresponded). He thought that six letters in the alphabet could be dropped altogether: *c, j, q, w, x* and *y.* He added, however, six new letters to represent the sounds of *a* as in *ball,* of *o* as in *folly,* of *th* as in *thy,* of *sh* as in *ship,* of *ng* as in *repeating,* and of *u* as in *unto.* As he told Polly in 1768, he wanted nothing less than a new alphabet and a reformed mode of spelling; otherwise "our writing will become the same with the Chinese as to the difficulty of learning and using it."[11]

We honor him not only for his success and his services but also for his style. Both in prose style and in personal style, he was characteristically American. He made his name as a journalist. His prose heralded Mark Twain; his ribaldry and anecdotage anticipated Lincoln; in the quality of his journalism with its simplicity and verve, he parallels H. L. Mencken. He could be by turns Rabelais and Poor Richard, Swift and Holy Scripture, and, however earthy or however savage, end with a joke. In prose style and in manner he was witty, salty, candid, and razor-sharp. He was a true representative of the American people, who by his death in 1790 were a united nation, thanks in large part to his work.

*   *   *

To Carlyle and many since his day, Franklin has been "the Father of all the Yankees." To many even outside the Southern states, Yankee is an opprobrious term, a badge of trade and a badge of infamy; yet it was these Yankee values that were transforming the eighteenth-century world. Both Boston and Virginia, in their different ways, were aristocratic: names and connections counted. But Franklin lived by trade, prospered by it, and was acclaimed across the world. He was completely and avowedly bourgeois, happy in the company of men and women, efficient in keeping a contract, adept at conciliation and in the affairs of towns. Virginian Jefferson was afraid of towns as threats to the rural democracy he worked for; Franklin, though he presented himself to the French as a backwoodsman, was only at ease when he was in them. He transformed Philadelphia. To him it owed the fact that it had a city police, the paved and lighted streets that were the surprise of Virginians and New Englanders. To him, too, it owed the American Philosophical Society and the University of Pennsylvania, its hospital, and the first circulating library in America. To him the country—before it had yet been born—owed the efficiency of its postal service, and its first collection of Rotarians, "seeking the promotion of our interests in business by more extensive recommendation." Versatile, businesslike, complaisant by disposition, Franklin strikes a modern note, the first of the joiners and boosters and glad-handers. Well might William Green call him the Patron Saint of Labor, in his practice and preaching of diligence, thrift, caution, his faith that good causes could be linked to self-advancement, that sweet reasonableness did not prevent a good opinion of oneself.

When in 1788 he drew up his will, he wrote: "I, Benjamin Franklin of Philadelphia, printer, late Minister Plenipotentiary from the United States of America to the Court of France, now President of the State of Pennsylvania." There is a ring of triumph here, but it is a bourgeois triumph; the success is not sublime but smug. The pride lay in his own varied experiences: he could—because in Europe he had to—walk with five kings and dine with one of them; in America he kept—because he had to—the common touch. He could write with the learned and pronounce with the vulgar.

Moreover, accepted as he was in France as a philosopher, popular as was *Poor Richard* there, Franklin was a New World phenomenon. Geneva was the only French-speaking city he thought uncorrupted and virtuous enough to be safe for his grandson's education. He admonished his daughter to be content with Pennsylvania homespun when she requested some elegant French silk and lace. He objected to making the bald eagle the national symbol of the new nation because the eagle "does not get his living honestly . . . He watches the labour of the Fishing-Hawk, and, when that diligent Bird has at length taken a Fish . . . the Bald Eagle pursues him, and takes it from him." The turkey, Franklin proposed instead, would be a better national symbol. He was "not only native to America, but as well useful, industrious, and courageous"—but not nearly as splendid or as charismatic.[12]

Of the fathers of his country, Franklin, whatever the years might have done to his reputation, was at once the most American and yet the most cosmopolitan, the most prescient for the future, the new man. The printer had made himself the first specimen Yankee. In his almanac and by his career he preached the American faith: reliance on oneself and on one's neighbors. Like Jefferson he saw no limits to the capacity of free men as citizens, as workers, or as liberal inquirers after truth in many fields. Like Jefferson again, he was a deist. During his years in England he undertook along with Sir Francis Dashwood a revision of the Prayer Book, and of the Catechism he retained only two questions: "What is your duty to God?" and "What is your duty to your neighbor?" Franklin's faith in political freedom was linked to a faith in economic freedom, and to a faith in scientific freedom too. He ranged widely and he ranged easily; there is no sense of superiority, rather the reverse, but there is certainly an effortlessness that comes not from Balliol or Boston but from a confidence in the capacity of what he called "the middling people." Franklin learned by reading and by observation, and what he learned he sought to apply. The test was empirical, and the tests were endless. Human, gregarious, worldly, and accommodating, with the lips ever half-smiling, unpompous, inquiring yet unspeculative, restless yet equable in temper, a preacher of moralities who honored them as much in the breach as in the observance, a counselor of prudence who was always ready to take a chance, a plain man who liked the graces and the comforts of life, a master of slogans who never deceived himself by them, skeptic and idealist and lover of children, he has left his mark conspicuously on the American character.

He was the father of all the Yankees, perhaps—for did not Poor

Richard say, in March 1754, "The cat in gloves catches no mice"?—
but he was also ambassador to two great kingdoms. His worldly wisdom was suited to the philosophers in Paris and in Edinburgh; it was
suited, too, to the old wives in the chimney corner, summing up a
lifetime of neighborly experience. He was at home in France. In England, he said, he was thought of as too much of an American, and
in America was deemed too much of an Englishman. He was rightly
thought of as a citizen of the world, and this too is part of his legacy
to Americans. And his characteristics have marked the Yankee mi-
grant in Europe ever since: the pride in trade, in hard work, and in
humbleness of origin. "I came up the hard way" is today the badge—
even when it has now to be carefully cultivated—of all the Yankees.
This was, indeed, the "new man" of the eighteenth-century dream.
That the image could be accepted so early in Europe was a sign that
the United States was truly independent.

NOTES

SELECTED BIBLIOGRAPHY

INDEX

NOTES

I am grateful to the editors of the *Papers of Benjamin Franklin* (Yale University Press, since 1959; hereafter cited as *Papers*) for permission to quote extensively from their edition. I draw on the *Papers* for all Franklin's quotes up to 1777—the date they have now reached. After that, I rely on A. H. Smyth's edition (Macmillan, 1905–1907; cited as *Writings*). For the aphorisms of Poor Richard I use the Yale *Papers* and give the date with each quotation.

1. A Tradesman in the Age of Reason

1. Crèvecoeur, *Letters from an American Farmer* (New York: New American History, 1965), letter 3; Henry Home, Lord Kames, *Sketches of the History of Man*, 2 vols. (Edinburgh, 1774); cf. *Papers* XXI, 523.

2. Adams to Rush, 4 April 1790, *Old Family Letters* (Philadelphia, 1892), 55; *Works of John Adams*, ed. C. F. Adams, 10 vols. (Boston: Little, Brown, 1850–1856), I, 649, IX, 485–486; Adams to Mercy Otis Warren, *Collections of the Massachusetts Historical Society* IV, 413, 431; John A. Schutz and Douglass Adair, eds., *The Spur of Fame: Dialogues of John Adams and Benjamin Rush* (San Marino, Calif.: Huntington Library, 1966), 11–19; Henry Hulton, quoted in Catherine S. Crary, *The Price of Loyalty* (New York: McGraw-Hill, 1973), 116; William Cobbett, *Porcupine's Works*, 12 vols. (London, 1801), I, 140, and IV, 32.

3. Mark Twain, "The Late Benjamin Franklin," in *Writings of Mark Twain*, National ed., 25 vols. (Hartford, Conn.: American Publishing Co., 1899–1907), XIX, 211–215; Nathaniel Hawthorne, "Benjamin Franklin, A Biographical Story," in Hawthorne, *Works* (Boston: Little, Brown, 1884), XII, 189–202; Herman Melville, *Israel Potter* (London: Constable, 1923), for a fictional portrait; D. H. Lawrence, *Studies in Classic American Literature* (New York: Viking, 1951), 19–31.

4. Charles Angoff, *A Literary History of the American People* (New York: Knopf, 1931), II, 295–310. Cf. William Carlos Williams, *In the American Grain* (New York: New Directions, 1925), 144–157.

5. C. A. Sainte-Beuve, "Franklin," in *Portraits of the Eighteenth Century*, trans. K. P. Wormeley (New York: Ungar, 1964), 321–327, 360, 371.

6. H. A. L. Fisher, *A History of Europe* (London: Arnold, 1936), v.

7. The theme of doing good to man is a constant in *Poor Richard* and through-out Franklin's correspondence. Its fullest and most filial expression is in his letter to his parents of 13 April 1738, *Papers* II, 202–204.

8. John Keats to George and Georgiana Keats, 14 Oct. 1818, in Keats, *Letters,* ed. M. B. Forman, 2 vols. (London: Oxford University Press, 1931).

9. Franklin, *Autobiography,* ed. Leonard W. Labaree et al. (New Haven: Yale University Press, 1964), 43. Cotton Mather, *Essays to Do Good* (Boston, 1710), 86–90.

10. To Samuel Mather, 12 May 1784, *Writings* IX, 208–209.

11. To Peter Collinson, 29 April 1749, *Papers* III, 364–365; Abbé Morellet, *Mémoires inédits,* 2 vols. (Paris, 1822), I, 197–204.

12. *Autobiography,* 64–65.

13. *Autobiography,* 125–126.

14. To Lord Howe, 20 July 1776, *Papers* XXII, 520.

15. Carl Van Doren, *Benjamin Franklin* (New York: Viking, 1938), 782.

16. 17 Sept. 1787, Max Farrand, *Records of the Federal Convention of 1787,* 4 vols. (New Haven: Yale University Press, 1937), III, 641–643.

17. To Hartley, 4 Dec. 1789, *Writings* X, 72–73.

2. A City upon a Hill

1. Samuel Sewall, *Diary, Collections of the Massachusetts Historical Society,* 5th ser., vol. 6, 73.

2. *Autobiography,* 54.

3. The best re-creation of the Boston of Franklin's birth is Walter Whitehill, *Boston: A Topographical History,* 2nd ed. (Cambridge, Mass.: Harvard University Press, 1968), 22–46.

4. *Autobiography,* 53.

5. Ibid.

6. Ibid., 62–63.

7. Ibid., 60.

8. *Boston News-Letter,* no. 916 (14–21 Aug. 1721); cf. Cotton Mather, *Diary,* II, 635, *Collections of the Massachusetts Historical Society,* 7th ser.; John W. Blake, "The Inoculation Controversy in Boston: 1721–1722," *N.E.Q. (New England Quarterly)* 25 (1952):489–506; Perry Miller, *The New England Mind: From Colony to Province* (Cambridge, Mass.: Harvard University Press, 1953), 333–334.

9. *New-England Courant,* 18 Feb. 1723; *Papers* I, 52.

10. *Autobiography,* 59.

11. *Dogood Essay* no. 12, *Papers* I, 40. Cf. George F. Horner, "Franklin's Dogood Papers Re-examined," *Studies in Philology* 37 (1940):501–523.

12. Frankliniana Collection, American Philosophical Society.

13. *Busy-body* 3, 18 Feb. 1729, *Papers* I, 119, II, 19.

14. Defoe published more than 250 books and tracts in his lifetime; *An Essay upon Projects* was first published in 1696. He advocated tax and banking reform,

friendly societies, cooperatives, and women's rights. Cf. *Dogood Essays* 5 and 10; *Autobiography,* 60.

15. Cotton quoted in A. B. Tourtellot, *Benjamin Franklin: The Shaping of a Genius, The Boston Years* (Garden City, N.Y.: Doubleday, 1977), 57; J. N. Figgis, *Studies in Political Thought from Gerson to Grotius* (London: Cambridge University Press, 1967), 6, 131; Winthrop quoted in Samuel Eliot Morison, *Builders of the Bay Colony* (Boston: Houghton Mifflin, 1958), 95; cf. Edmund Morgan, *The Puritan Dilemma* (Boston: Little, Brown, 1958).

3. Journeyman Printer

1. *Autobiography,* 75–76.

2. Gottlieb Mittelberger, *Journey to Pennsylvania,* ed. and trans. Oscar Handlin and John Clive (Cambridge, Mass.: Harvard University Press, 1960), 47; cf. Isaac Sharpless, *Political Leaders of Provincial Pennsylvania* (New York: Macmillan, 1919), 217. Philadelphia's first house census in 1749 gave a population of 13,000, and John Alexander of the University of Cincinnati estimates the number of houses in 1774 at 1,500; certainly by the 1750s Philadelphia outstripped New York in numbers. This is an area of some controversy. See David R. Boldt and Willard S. Randall, *The Founding City* (Philadelphia: The Philadelphia Inquirer, 1975), 29; Carl Bridenbaugh, *Rebels and Gentlemen* (New York: Oxford University Press, 1942), ch. 1; idem, ed., *Gentleman's Progress* (Chapel Hill: University of North Carolina Press, 1948); Robert F. Oaks, "Big Wheels in Philadelphia: du Simitière's List of Carriage Owners," *P.M.H.B. (Pennsylvania Magazine of History and Biography)* 95 (July 1971):351–363; Martin P. Snyder, *City of Independence* (New York: Praeger, 1975). Some cautions to Bridenbaugh's picture of the city's growth are offered by Gary Nash and Billy G. Smith, "The Population of Eighteenth-Century Philadelphia," *P.M.H.B.* 99 (July 1975): 362–368; Gary Nash, *The Urban Crucible* (Cambridge, Mass.: Harvard University Press, 1979); and John K. Alexander, "The Philadelphia Numbers Game: An Analysis of Philadelphia's Eighteenth-Century Population," *P.M.H.B.* 98 (1974):314–334. S. B. Warner, *A Private City: Philadelphia in Three Periods of Its Growth* (Philadelphia: University of Pennsylvania Press, 1968), 410–411, calculated the population in 1776 at 23,000, not the 40,000 formerly assumed.

3. Albert C. Myers, ed., *Narratives of Early Pennsylvania, West New Jersey and Delaware: 1630–1707* (New York: Scribners, 1912), 395 and passim; cf. Carl Bridenbaugh, *Cities in the Wilderness* (New York: Knopf, 1955), and Marian D. Learned, *Francis Daniel Pastorius* (Philadelphia: Campbell, 1908).

4. Bridenbaugh, ed., *Gentleman's Progress,* 22.

5. James Logan is well described in F. R. Tolles's biography, *James Logan and the Culture of Provincial America* (Boston: Little, Brown, 1957). He was a very generous patron of Franklin and his friends. He may well have been more loyal to Franklin than Franklin to him, if, as seems probable, Franklin had any hand in writing *An Historical Review of the Constitution and Government of Pennsylvania* (1758). Logan foresaw many of the imperial problems ahead and urged the creation of a colonial union—a plan the only existing copy of which is in

Franklin's hand and on which Franklin may well have drawn. Cf. Joseph E. Johnson, ed., "A Quaker Imperialist's View of the British Colonies in America, 1732," *P.M.H.B.* 60 (1936):97–130, which includes Logan's "State of the British Plantations"; Roy N. Lokken, "The Social Thought of James Logan," *W.M.Q. (William and Mary Quarterly)* 27, no. 1 (1970):68–69; Gary B. Nash, *Quakers and Politics: Pennsylvania, 1681–1726* (Princeton: Princeton University Press, 1968); and Joseph B. Illick, *Colonial Pennsylvania* (New York: Scribner's, 1976).

6. For Bradford see Ann Janney de Armond, *Andrew Bradford, Colonial Journalist* (Newark: University of Delaware Press, 1949). On Keimer see Stephen Bloore, "Samuel Keimer: A Footnote to the Life of Franklin," *P.M.H.B.* 54 (1930):255–287; C. Lennart Carlson, "Samuel Keimer: A Study in the Transit of English Culture to Colonial Pennsylvania," *P.M.H.B.* 61 (Oct. 1937):357–386; and Chester E. Jorgenson, "A Brand Flung at Colonial Orthodoxy," *Journalism Quarterly* 12 (1935):272–277.

7. *Autobiography,* 81.

8. See two contrasting articles, Charles P. Keith's favorable "Sir William Keith," *P.M.H.B.* 12 (April 1888):1–33, and the extract from the Penn Papers, "The Case of the Proprietor of Pennsylvania, etc., about the Appointing of a New Deputy-Governor," *P.M.H.B.* 39 (1915):201–205. Cf. Tom Wendel, "The Life and Writings of Sir William Keith, Lieutenant-Governor of Pennsylvania and the Three Lower Counties, 1717–26" (Ph.D. diss., University of Washington, 1964); and Burton A. Konkle, *The Life of Andrew Hamilton, 1676–1741* (Philadelphia: National Publishing Co., 1941), 41. Sir William, an ex-Jacobite turned King's man, identified himself with the colony and the Assembly. He proposed a stamp act to finance colonial defense. When dismissed by the Proprietors in 1726, he won a seat in the Assembly. He died in London, penniless, at the age of 70. America was not a land of opportunity for all, especially if they were egotistical and feckless.

9. *Autobiography,* 95.

10. Ibid., 99, 106. See Robert W. Kenny, "James Ralph: An Eighteenth-Century Philadelphian in Grub Street," *P.M.H.B.* 64 (April 1940):218–242; and Elizabeth R. McKinsey, "James Ralph," *P.A.P.S. (Proceedings of the American Philosophical Society)* 117, no. 1 (1973):59–78.

11. *Autobiography,* 120. Franklin's debt to his friends among the Quaker merchants, not least the little-known Thomas Denham, is explored in F. B. Tolles, "Benjamin Franklin's Business Mentors: The Philadelphia Quaker Merchants," *W.M.Q.* 4 (Jan. 1947):60–69; cf. Richard B. Schlatter, *The Social Ideas of Religious Leaders, 1660–1688* (London: Oxford University Press, 1940), 239.

12. *Papers* I, 139–157; *Autobiography,* 124.

13. *Autobiography,* 116–118.

14. Edwin Wolf II, "Franklin and His Friends Choose Their Books," *P.M.H.B.* 80 (Jan. 1956):30; also see George S. Eddy, "Dr. Benjamin Franklin's Library," *American Antiquarian Society Proceedings* 34 (Oct. 1924):206–226; William E. Lingelbach, "The Library of the American Philosophical Society," *W.M.Q.,* 3rd ser., 3 (Jan. 1946):48–69; Edwin Wolf II, "A Key to the Identification of Franklin's Books," *P.M.H.B.* 80 (Oct. 1956):407–409; and idem, "The Romance of

James Logan's Books," *W.M.Q.*, new ser., 13 (July 1956):342–353; Margaret G. Korty, "Benjamin Franklin and Eighteenth-Century American Libraries," *American Philosophical Society Transactions* 55, pt. 9 (Dec. 1965); and Leonard W. Labaree, "The Bookish Mr. Franklin," *Bucknell Review* 10 (May 1961):46–56. Cf. George M. Abbott, *A Short History of the Library Company of Philadelphia* (Philadelphia Library Company, 1913) and Austin K. Gray, *The First American Library* (Philadelphia Library Company, 1936).

15. *Papers* III, 397–420.

16. *Autobiography*, 129.

17. *Papers* VII, 384.

18. Daniel Fisher, "Diary," *P.M.H.B.* 17 (1893):263–278; and *Papers* III, 474–475n1.

19. *Papers* III, 145.

20. *Papers* II, 352–354; cf. VI, 184.

21. *Papers* I, 57–71; *Autobiography*, 114.

22. *Autobiography*, 149.

23. *Papers* I, 101–109.

24. *Autobiography*, pt. 3, 178; cf. *Papers* II, 202–204.

25. *Papers* I, 109.

26. *Autobiography*, pt. 2, 153; Gibbon, *The Decline and Fall of the Roman Empire*, ch. 2; Addison, "Ode to the Creation," *Spectator* no. 465, 23 Aug. 1712; idem, *Cato, A Tragedy* V.i.15–18.

27. 3 July 1786, *Writings* IX, 552; March 9, 1790, *Writings* X, 84.

28. To Strahan, 12 Feb. 1744/5, *Papers* III, 13.

29. *Papers* II, 236.

30. Carl Becker, *D.A.B. (Dictionary of American Biography)* VI, 587; separately published as *Benjamin Franklin* (Ithaca, N.Y.: Cornell University Press, 1946).

31. *Papers* I, 288.

32. Ibid. The most perceptive analysis of Poor Richard occurs in John F. Ross, "The Character of Poor Richard: Its Source and Alteration," *P.M.L.A. (Proceedings of the Modern Language Association of America)* 55 (Sept. 1940):785–794. Ross emphasizes that there were two Richards: the poor and talkative astrologer of each year's almanac, and the final Yankee soothsayer, whose voice is clearly the same as that of the *Autobiography*. Franklin, ever adaptable, spoke with both voices. Ross emphasizes also the indebtedness to Jonathan Swift's Isaac Bickerstaff. Equally useful are Robert Newcomb's articles "Poor Richard's Debt to Lord Halifax," *P.M.L.A.* 70 (1955):535–539; "Franklin Our Richardson," *Journal of English-German Philology* 57 (1958):27–35; and "Benjamin Franklin and Montaigne," *Modern Language Notes* 72 (1957):439–491. Cf. *Papers* I, 280–282, VII, 326–355; and A. O. Aldridge, "Benjamin Franklin and the Pennsylvania Gazette," *P.A.P.S.* 106 (Feb. 1962):77–81. The complete *Poor Richard's Almanacks* have been reproduced with illustrations by Norman Rockwell and an introduction by Van Wyck Brooks (New York: Ballantine, 1977), and in facsimile (Boston: Massachusetts Imprint Society, 1970), with an introduction by Whitfield Bell. Also relevant here are Harold A. Larrabee, "Poor Richard in an Age of

Plenty," *Harpers Magazine* 212 (Jan. 1956):64–68; and Irvin G. Wiley, *The Self-Made Man in America: The Myth of Rags to Riches* (New Brunswick, N.J.: Rutgers University Press, 1954). C. William Miller, "Benjamin Franklin's Philadelphia Printing 1728–1766: A Descriptive Bibliography," *P.A.P.S.* 102 (1974) is a superb guide. Lawrence Wroth, "Benjamin Franklin: The Printer at Work," in *Meet Dr. Franklin* (Philadelphia: Franklin Institute, 1943) is an excellent summary.

4. We, the Middling People

1. To Cadwallader Colden, 29 Sept. 1748, *Papers* III, 318. To his mother, 12 April 1750, *Papers* III, 475.

2. To Cadwallader Colden, *Papers* III, 67.

3. To David Le Roy, Aug. 1785, *Writings* IX, 394–396, 406; cf. Lloyd A. Brown, "The River in the Ocean," in *Essays Honoring Lawrence C. Wroth* (Portland, Me.: Anthoensen Press, 1951), 71–75.

4. Cf. to Sir John Pringle, 6 Jan. 1758, *Papers* VII, 357, and to the Abbé Soulavie, 22 Sept. 1782, *Writings* VIII, 597–601. To Jared Elliot, 16 July 1747, *Papers* III, 149.

5. To Jared Elliot, 13 Feb. 1749–50, *Papers* III, 464; cf. letter to Alexander Small, 12 May 1760, *Papers* IX 110–112.

6. To Mary Stevenson, 20 Sept. 1761, *Writings* IV, 115.

7. *Papers* II, 419–445; cf. *Papers* VIII, 195–196nn.

8. *American Philosophical Society Transactions*, old ser., 2 (1786):57; first draft, *Writings* IX, 443–462.

9. To Jan Ingenhousz, 28 Aug. 1783, *Writings* IX, 413–443.

10. To Susanna Wright, 21 Nov. 1751, *Papers* IV, 211.

11. To Collinson, 29 July 1750, *Papers* IV, 19–20; cf. 28 July 1747, *Papers* III, 156–165; and headnote, *Papers* III, 115.

12. To Collinson, 25 May 1747, *Papers* III, 127.

13. To Collinson, 29 April 1749, *Papers* III, 364.

14. To John Lining, 18 March 1755, *Papers* V, 524; cf. Carl Van Doren, ed., *Benjamin Franklin's Autobiographical Writings* (New York: Viking, 1945), 56.

15. To Collinson, Sept. 1753, *Papers* V, 79.

16. Carl Van Doren, *Benjamin Franklin* (New York: Viking, 1938), 171.

17. To Collinson, 19 Oct. 1752, *Papers* IV, 367.

18. To Collinson, 29 July 1750, *Papers* IV, 19.

19. To Colden, 12 April 1753, *Papers* IV, 463; Jean Torlais, *Un Physicien du Siècle des Lumières: L'Abbé Nollet, 1700–1770* (Paris: University of Paris, 1954); for Nollet's letters, see *Papers* IV, 423–428.

20. I. Bernard Cohen, "Prejudice against the Introduction of Lightning Rods," *Journal of the Franklin Institute* 253 (May 1952):396n9.

21. John Lining to Franklin, *Papers* V, 524; cf. Franklin C. Bing, "John Lining: An Early American Scientist," *Scientific Monthly* 26 (March 1928):249–252; Bernard Fay, *Franklin: The Apostle of Modern Times* (Boston: Little, Brown, 1929), 227; cf. I. B. Cohen, *Benjamin Franklin's Experiments* (Cambridge, Mass.: Harvard University Press, 1941).

22. Quoted in Cohen, "Prejudice," 436n99: "Les Arts et les Sciences sont le plus riche présent que le Ciel ait fait aux hommes; par quelle fatalité ont-ils donc trouvé tant d'obstacles pour s'établir sur la terre? . . . Croyons-nous donc que le Tout-Puissant ait besoin de ce météore que nous épouvante? . . . bénissons cette Providence bienfaisante qui, après nous avoir donné les *simples* pour quérir nos maladies, nous présente aujourd'hui des conducteurs électriques."

23. *Autobiography,* 243–244.

24. Quoted in *Writings* I, 107–108.

25. Prince quoted in Cohen, "Prejudice," 426; cf. Theodore Hornberger, "The Science of Thomas Prince," *N.E.Q.* 9 (1936):24–42; Eleanor Tilton, "Lightning-Rods and the Earthquake of 1755," *N.E.Q.* 13 (1940):85–97.

26. Quoted in Cohen, "Prejudice," 430.

27. To Jared Eliot, 12 April 1753, *Papers* III, 466.

28. To John Perkins, 4 Feb. 1753, *Papers* IV, 442 and notes.

29. Quoted in William Cabell Bruce, *Benjamin Franklin Self-Revealed,* 2 vols. (New York: Putnam's, 1917), II, 362.

30. *Papers* IV, 150.

31. *Autobiography,* 201.

32. *Autobiography,* 160.

33. 6 July 1749, *Papers* III, 383.

34. 14 Oct. 1751, *Papers* IV, 199.

35. 18 Nov. 1755, *Papers* VI, 251; cf. VI, 159, 194.

36. *Papers* I, 161.

37. *Plain Truth, Papers* III, 201.

38. *Papers* III, 180–204.

39. *Autobiography,* 184.

40. *Autobiography,* 186.

41. Quoted in Hubertis Cummings, *Richard Peters: Provincial Secretary and Cleric, 1704–1776* (Philadelphia: University of Pennsylvania Press, 1944), 133; *Papers* III, 185–186.

42. *Papers* IV, 224–234. For Franklin as demographer, see Paul W. Connor, *Poor Richard's Politics: Benjamin Franklin and the New American Order* (New York: Oxford University Press, 1965), 69–95; William Appleman Williams, *The Contours of American History* (Cleveland: World Publishing Company, 1961), 93; idem, "The Age of Mercantilism: An Interpretation of the American Political Economy," *W.M.Q.* 15 (Oct. 1958):421; A. O. Aldridge, "Franklin as Demographer," *Journal of Economic History* 9 (May 1949):25–44; Norman E. Himes, "Benjamin Franklin on Population: A Re-Examination with Special Reference to the Influence of Franklin on Francis Place," *Economic History Review* 3 (1934–1937):388–398.

43. *Papers* I, 213–214.

44. *Papers* IV, 234.

45. *Papers* V, 159, 204–205.

46. 21 May 1751, *Papers* IV, 134–136.

47. Oct. 1761, *Papers* IX, 378.

48. *Papers* VI, 487. On the Indians, see Howard Peckham, *Pontiac and the Indian Uprising* (Chicago: University of Chicago Press, 1961); Arthur Pound,

Johnson of the Mohawks (New York: Macmillan, 1930); James Flexner, *Mohawk Baronet: William Johnson of New York* (New York: Harper and Row, 1959); John R. Alden, *John Stuart and the Southern Colonial Frontier . . . 1754–75* (Ann Arbor: University of Michigan, 1944); Nicholas B. Wainwright, *George Croghan: Wilderness Diplomat* (Chapel Hill: University of North Carolina Press, 1959). Paul Wallace, *Conrad Weiser, 1696–1760: Friend of Colonist and Mohawk* (Philadelphia: University of Pennsylvania, 1945); Francis Jennings, *The Invasion of America: Indians, Colonialism and the Cant of Conquest* (Chapel Hill: University of North Carolina Press, 1975). Cf. idem, "The Vanishing Indian: Francis Parkman *versus* His Sources," *P.M.H.B.* 87 (July 1963):306–323; A. O. Aldridge, "Franklin's Deistical Indians," *P.A.P.S.* 94, no. 4 (1950):398–410.

49. To Peter Collinson, 9 May 1753, *Papers* IV, 481–482; V, 65, 107; cf. *Writings* X, 98.

50. 20 March 1750, *Papers* IV, 118.

51. *Autobiography*, 210.

52. On the Albany conference and Plan there is voluminous literature. See as basic studies Robert Newbold, *The Albany Congress and Plan of Union of 1754* (New York: Vantage, 1955), esp. 96–105; Lawrence H. Gipson, *The British Empire before the American Revolution,* 15 vols., V (New York: Knopf, 1952), 126–138; and *Papers* V, 344–392. Among the major articles are: Roger D. Trask, "Pennsylvania and the Albany Congress, 1754," *Pennsylvania History* 27 (1960):273–290; Malcolm Freiberg, "Thomas Hutchinson: The First Fifty Years (1711–1761)," *W.M.Q.* 15 (1958):51–52; Beverly McAnear, ed., "Personal Accounts of the Albany Congress of 1754," *Mississippi Valley Historical Review* 39 (1952–53):727–746; Alison G. Olson, "The British Government and Colonial Union, 1754," *W.M.Q.,* 3rd. ser., 17 (1960):22–32; Lois K. Mathews, "Benjamin Franklin's Plans for a Colonial Union, 1750–1775," *American Political Science Review* 8 (1914):393–412; Lawrence H. Gipson, "Thomas Hutchinson and the Framing of the Albany Plan of Union, 1754," *P.M.H.B.* 74 (Jan. 1950):5–35; idem, "Massachusetts Bay and American Colonial Union, 1754," *American Antiquarian Society Proceedings* 71 (1961):63–92; idem, "The Drafting of the Albany Plan of Union: A Problem in Semantics," *Pennsylvania History* 26 (Oct. 1959):291–316; and Letters to the Editor by Verner W. Crane and Lawrence H. Gipson, *Pennsylvania History* 27 (Jan. 1960):126–136.

There is an equally daunting literature on the West in Franklin's day. Basic material is provided by the *Johnson Papers,* ed. J. Sullivan, A. C. Flick, and M. W. Hamilton, 11 vols. (Albany: New York State Library, 1921–1953). K. P. Bailey, *The Ohio Company Papers, 1753–1817* (Ann Arbor: University of Michigan, 1947) is especially useful for the "suffering traders" of Pennsylvania. Cf. idem, *Christopher Gist* (Norwalk, Conn.: Archon Books, 1976); Louis Mulkearn, comp., *Papers Relating to the Ohio Company of Virginia* (Pittsburgh, 1954); George E. Lewis, *The Indiana Company, 1763–98* (Glendale, Calif., 1941); Fernand Grenier, *Papiers contrecoeur et autres documents concernant le conflit anglo-français sur l'Ohio de 1745 à 1756* (Quebec, 1952); Jack M. Sosin, *Whitehall and the Wilderness* (Lincoln: University of Nebraska Press, 1961); idem, *The Revolutionary Frontier, 1763–83* (New York: Holt, Rinehart and

Winston, 1967); and A. P. James, "Benjamin Franklin's Ohio Valley Lands," *P.A.P.S.* 98 (Aug. 1954):255–265.

Older studies still worth using are Albert T. Volwiler, *George Croghan and the Westward Movement, 1741–1782* (Cleveland: A. H. Clark, 1926); Clarence W. Alvord, *The Mississippi Valley in British Politics,* 2 vols. (Cleveland: A. H. Clark, 1917); and idem, *The Illinois Company* (Springfield, Ill.: Centennial Commission, 1920); but they need checking against the critical views about Franklin's role held by T. P. Abernethy, *Western Lands and the American Revolution* (New York: Appleton Century, 1937).

53. *Autobiography,* 211.

54. *Papers* V, 444–446, 449.

55. *Papers* VI, 468–469.

56. *Papers* V, 456, V, 332.

57. Braddock to Sir Thomas Robinson, 5 June 1755, *P.M.H.B.* 38 (1914):5; cf. *Papers* VI, 14n.

58. *Autobiography,* 223.

59. To Deborah, 25 Jan. 1756, *Papers* VI, 364–365.

60. To James Read, 2 Nov. 1755, *Papers* VI, 235.

61. 12 Jan. 1756, *Papers* VI, 352.

62. *Autobiography,* 237.

63. 16 Oct. 1755, *Papers* VI, 225.

64. *Papers* VI, 251, 264–265.

65. *Papers* VII, 10, n. 4.

66. Nicholas D. Wainwright, "Governor William Denny of Pennsylvania," *P.M.H.B.* 81 (Oct. 1957):170–198; *Papers* VI, 489.

67. 26 Jan. 1757, *Papers* VII, 108–109.

68. Kearsley to Robert Hunter Morris, 8 Feb. 1757, *Papers* VII, 110; Lloyd, Peters, and Penn from *Papers* VI, 269, VII, 5, 110–111.

69. To Isaac Norris, 14 Jan. 1758, *Papers* VII, 361.

70. *Papers* VII, 14–15.

71. Penn to Peters, 3 July 1755, Penn Papers, Historical Society of Pennsylvania; *Papers* VII, 14.

72. *Papers* VII, 350.

73. *Papers* VII, 243.

74. *Papers* VII, 73.

5. The Old England Man

1. *Papers* VII, 297.

2. To Deborah, *Papers* VII, 274.

3. 13 Sept. 1759, *Papers* IX, 216.

4. To Lord Kames, 28 Feb. 1768, *Papers* XV, 61; George S. Eddy, "Account Book of Benjamin Franklin," *P.M.H.B.* 55, no. 2 (1931).

5. Pierre Jean Grosley, *A Tour to London,* 2 vols. (London: Lockyer Davis, 1772), I, 150.

6. *The Journal of Samuel Curwen, Loyalist,* ed. Andrew Oliver, 2 vols. (Cambridge, Mass.: Harvard University Press, 1972), I, 95.

7. *Writings* X, 198. See also R. J. Allen, *The Clubs of Augustan London* (Cambridge, Mass.: Harvard University Press, 1933); Bryant Lillywhite, *London Coffeehouses* (London: Allen and Unwin, 1963); and Aytoun Ellis, *The Penny Universities: A History of the Coffee Houses* (London: Secker and Warburg, 1956).

8. J. B. Nolan, *Benjamin Franklin in Scotland and Ireland* (Philadelphia: University of Pennsylvania, 1938), 22; Henry B. Wheatley, *London Past and Present* (London, 1891), I, 135, 472.

9. *Papers* VII, 373–377.

10. *Papers* VIII, 100n2.

11. *Papers* VII, 14, 374, VIII, 89, cf. VIII, 361–362.

12. *Papers* VIII, 167; Verner W. Crane, *Benjamin Franklin's Letters to the Press, 1758–1775* (Chapel Hill: University of North Carolina Press, 1950).

13. *Papers* VIII, 293.

14. *Papers* VIII, 295.

15. *Papers* VII, 449–452.

16. *Papers* IX, 70–71.

17. *Papers* IV, 228–229; IX, 90–91.

18. *Papers* IX, 74–75.

19. *Papers* IX, 7–8.

20. *Papers* X, 200, 236, 261.

21. *Papers* X, 146–147n; William A. Duer, "The Life of William Alexander, Earl of Stirling," *New Jersey Historical Society Collections,* II (1847), 70; Thomas Bridges to Jared Ingersoll, 30 Sept. 1762, New Haven Colonial History Society Papers, IX, 278; *Diary and Autobiography of John Adams,* ed. L. H. Butterfield, 4 vols. (Cambridge, Mass.: Harvard University Press, 1961), IV, 1.

22. *Papers* IX, 124.

23. *Papers* X, 148.

24. *Papers* IX, 9.

25. *Papers* VIII, 196.

26. *Papers* VII, 210, VIII, 216.

27. *Papers* VIII, 281–286, IX, 271, 294.

28. Evans to Giambatista Beccaria, 10 July 1762, *Papers* X, 116–130; cf. Kenneth Silverman, *Cultural History of the American Revolution* (New York: Crowell, 1976), 35, 639.

29. *Papers* X, 113.

30. *Papers* VII, 383.

31. *Papers* X, 149, 147.

32. *Papers* X, 169.

6. The Prime Mover

1. To Collinson, 7 Dec. 1762, *Papers* X, 165. To Jackson, 8 March 1763, *Papers* X, 209; cf. William Franklin to Board of Trade, 10 May 1763, *Papers* X, 209; Anne Bezanson, Robert D. Gray, and Miriam Hussey, *Prices in Colonial Pennsylvania* (Philadelphia: University of Pennsylvania Press, 1935), 306–307, 433.

2. To James Bowdoin, 11 Oct. 1763, *Papers* X, 352.

3. To Jackson, 8 March 1763, *Papers* X, 208–211, 362.

4. 27 June 1763, *Papers* X, 295–296. Howard Peckham, *Pontiac and the Indian Uprising* (Chicago: University of Chicago Press, 1961), 101–107; Jackson to Franklin, 27 Dec. 1763, *Papers* XI, 411–416.

5. To Fothergill, 14 March 1764, *Papers* XI, 327; *Narrative of the Late Massacres, Papers* XI, 42–68.

6. Brooke Hindle, "The March of the Paxton Boys," *W.M.Q.* 3 (1946):476; Theodore G. Tappert and John W. Doberstein, eds., *The Journals of Henry Melchior Muhlenberg* (Philadelphia: University of Pennsylvania Press, 1945), II, 18–24; Theodore Thayer, *Israel Pemberton, King of the Quakers* (Philadelphia: University of Pennsylvania Press, 1943), 189.

7. To Jackson, 1 Sept. 1764, *Papers* XI, 327.

8. *Papers* XI, 82; Charles H. Lincoln, *The Revolutionary Movement in Pennsylvania, 1760–1766* (Philadelphia, 1901), 45–48; Theodore Thayer, "The Quaker Party of Pennsylvania, 1765–1775," *P.M.B.H.* 71 (1947):28–31.

9. *Papers* XI, 119, 129 for taxation; XI, 76, 130 for militia bill.

10. To Fothergill, 14 March 1764, *Papers* XI, 104.

11. *Papers* XI, 126–131.

12. *Papers* XI, 294–295.

13. William Smith, *Brief State of the Province of Pennsylvania* (London, 1755), 39–43; *Papers* VI, 52n.

14. "Cool Thoughts," *Papers* XI, 153; preface to Galloway, *Papers* XI, 290; note Richard Jackson's warning of the probable imminence of a stamp tax, 26 Jan. 1764, *Papers* XI, 33.

15. To Jackson, 1 May 1764, *Papers* XI, 186.

16. *Papers* XI, 192–200. For the *Plain Dealer* (usually attributed to Hugh Williamson, a professor of mathematics in the College of Pennsylvania), see *Papers* XI, 102, 154.

17. Penn Papers, Historical Society of Pennsylvania, 5 May 1764, quoted in *Papers* XI, 173n7.

18. *Papers* XI, 200.

19. *Papers* XI, 381–384; cf. Thayer, "The Quaker Party of Pennsylvania," 29–38; J. Philip Gleason, "A Scurrilous Colonial Election and Franklin's Reputation," *W.M.Q.* 18 (1961):68–84.

20. To Jared Ingersoll, 8 July 1762, *Papers* X, 113.

21. Pettit to Reed, 3 Nov. 1764, in W. B. Reed, ed., *Life and Correspondence of Joseph Reed,* 2 vols. (Philadelphia, 1847), I, 36; *Papers* XI, 390–391.

22. *Papers* XI, 213–214n.

23. *Papers* XI, 329.

24. Allen quoted in *Papers* XI, 404n3; *Answer to Remarks,* 7 Dec. 1764, *Papers* XI, 512–516; Remonstrance, 26 Oct. 1764, *Papers* XI, 405–406.

25. *Papers* XI, 429–441.

26. Penn to Benjamin Chew, 8 June 1764, *Papers* XI, 328n1.

27. *Papers* XI, 447–448.

7. Two Views of Empire

1. For the British administration's view of its American responsibilities see K. G. Davies, ed., *Documents of the American Revolution,* 21 vols. (London: Colonial Office Services, 1972–1978), and Davies's Sarah Tryphena Phillips lecture to the British Academy in 1975, "The End of British Administration in the North American Colonies." See also John Shy, "The Spectrum of Imperial Possibilities: Henry Ellis and Thomas Pownall, 1763–1775," in Shy, *A People Numerous and Armed* (New York: Oxford University Press, 1976), 35–72.

2. See O. M. Dickerson, *The Navigation Acts and the American Revolution* (Philadelphia: University of Pennsylvania Press, 1951); and Lawrence Harper, *The English Navigation Laws* (New York: Columbia University Press, 1939). Cf. Thomas C. Barrow, *Trade and Empire: the British Customs Service in Colonial America, 1660–1775* (Cambridge, Mass.: Harvard University Press, 1967); Carl Ubbelohde, *Vice-Admiralty Courts and the American Revolution* (Chapel Hill: University of North Carolina Press, 1960); James F. Shepherd and Gary M. Walton, *Shipping, Maritime Trade and the Economic Development of Colonial North America* (New York: Cambridge University Press, 1972); and Dora M. Clark, "The American Board of Customs, 1767–83," *A.H.R. (American Historical Review)* 45, no. 4 (1940):777.

3. *Works of Edmund Burke,* 6 vols. (London: Bell, 1893), I, 403.

4. George Washington, *Writings,* ed. John C. Fitzpatrick, 39 vols. (Washington, D.C.: Government Printing Office), II, 512; III, 229.

5. The revenue arising from customs duties in America and the West Indies was not "sufficient to defray a fourth part of the expence necessary for collecting it"; Order in Council, 14 Oct. 1763, in Jack P. Greene, ed., *Colonies to Nation: 1761–1789* (New York: Norton, 1967), 14; *Papers* XVIII, 102–103; cf. Joseph A. Ernst, *Money and Politics in America, 1755–1775* (Williamsburg, Va.: Institute of Early American History and Culture, 1974), and Lawrence H. Gipson, *The British Empire before the American Revolution,* 15 vols. (New York: Knopf), XI, 119–120.

6. To Collinson, 30 April 1764, *Papers* XI, 181–182.

7. Burke, *Works* I, 205; Margaret Spector, *The American Department of the British Government, 1768–1782* (New York: Columbia University Press, 1940).

8. For the mood of high imperialism in Britain in 1763 see, in addition to the writings of Galloway, Franklin, Pownall, and Bernard, two studies by Richard Van Alstyne, *Empire and Independence* (New York: Wiley, 1965); and *The Rising American Empire* (New York: Norton, 1965), esp. chs. 1–3; Max Savelle, *The Seeds of Liberty* (Seattle: University of Washington Press, 1965); Louis B. Wright, ed., *An Essay upon the Government of the English Plantations on the Continent of America* (San Marino, Calif.: Huntington Library, 1945); Gipson, *The British Empire before the American Revolution;* idem, "The View of the Thirteen Colonies at the Close of the Great War for the Empire, 1763," *New York History* 40 (1959):327–357; idem, "The American Revolution as an Aftermath of the Great War for the Empire," *Political Science Quarterly* 65 (1950):86–104; Jack Greene, "Martin Blander's Blueprint for a Colonial

Union," *W.M.Q.* 18 (1960):516–530; idem, "William Knox's Explanation for the American Revolution," *W.M.Q.* 30 (1973):293–306; Charles Mullett, "English Imperial Thinking, 1764–1783," *Political Science Quarterly* 45 (1930): 550–558; and G. H. Guttridge, "Thomas Pownall: The Administration of the Colonies: The Six Editions," *W.M.Q.* 26 (1969):31–46.

9. William Blackstone, *Commentaries on the Laws of England,* 9th ed., 4 vols. (Oxford, 1783), I, 78.

10. Burke, *Works* I, 265.

11. 4 Dec. 1754, *Papers* V, 443; Thomas Pownall, *The Administration of the British Colonies,* 5th ed., 2 vols. (London, 1774), II, 234; *The Barrington-Bernard Correspondence and Illustrative Matter, 1760–1770,* ed. Edward Channing and Archibald Cary Coolidge (Cambridge, Mass.: Harvard University Press, 1912), 97; Burke, *Works* I, 488–489; to Cushing, 10 June 1771, *Papers* XVIII, 123.

12. Lady Osborn quoted in Gerrit P. Judd, *Members of Parliament, 1734–1832* (New Haven: Yale University Press, 1955), 73; John Gay, "An Epistle to a Lady" (1714), in *Poetical Works,* ed. G. C. Faber (London: Oxford University Press, 1926), 151; Lewis B. Namier, *England in the Age of the American Revolution,* 2nd ed. (London: Macmillan, 1961), 229–273.

13. Stanley Pargellis, "Braddock's Defeat," *A.H.R.* 41 (1936):253; idem, *Military Affairs in North America: Documents from the Cumberland Papers in Windsor Castle* (London: H.M.S.O., 1936); Report of House of Commons Debates, 10 May 1768 to 13 June 1774, partly written by Sir Henry Cavendish (Egerton MSS. 253–262, British Library).

14. Clarence E. Carter, ed., *The Correspondence of General Thomas Gage,* 2 vols. (New Haven: Yale University Press, 1931–1933), I, 355, 368; Colonial Office series 5/769 f. 82, 5/763 ff. 453–456 (P.R.O.) and War Office series W.O. 1/2 and W.O. 1/9 (P.R.O.); E. R. Hughes, "Lord North's Correspondence, 1766–1783," *E.H.R. (English Historical Review)* 62 (1947):218–238; *Barrington-Bernard Correspondence,* 167, 177. Cf. John R. Alden, *General Gage in America* (Baton Rouge: Louisiana State University, 1948).

15. William Cobbett and T. C. Hansard, eds., *The Parliamentary History of England,* 36 vols. (London, 1813), XVII, 82, XVIII, 149; J. Debrett, ed., *The History, Debate and Proceedings of Both Houses of Parliament . . . 1743 . . . to 1774,* 7 vols. (London, 1792), VII, 41; J. Wright, ed., *Debates of the House of Commons in the Year 1774* (London: Longman's, 1839), I, 13.

16. Burke, *Works* II, 241; W. B. Reed, ed., *Life and Correspondence of Joseph Reed,* 2 vols. (Philadelphia, 1847), II, 206.

17. Carter, ed., *Gage's Correspondence,* II, 142; Sir John Fortescue, ed., *The Correspondence of King George III,* 6 vols. (London: Macmillan, 1927–1928), I, 216.

18. T. P. Abernethy, *Western Lands and the American Revolution* (New York: Appleton Century, 1937), 44; *Papers* XV, 74–80; see also K. P. Bailey, *The Ohio Company of Virginia and the Westward Movement 1748–92* (Glendale, Calif., 1939); Bernard Donoughue, *British Politics and the American Revolution: The Path to War, 1773–1775* (London: Macmillan, 1965); and Nicholas B. Wain-

wright, *George Croghan, Wilderness Diplomat* (Chapel Hill: University of North Carolina Press, 1959).

19. *Papers* XVII, 214, 311, XIV, 69.

20. *Papers* XXI, 417.

21. Knox to Grenville, 15 Dec. 1768, Additional MS. 42086 f. 167, British Library; De Berdt to Thomas Cushing, 2 Jan. 1769, *Letters of Dennys De Berdt* (Cambridge, Mass.: John Wilson, 1911), 350–351.

22. Benevolus, "On the Propriety of Taxing America," 11 April 1767, *Papers* XIV, 110–116. Franklin's imperial views are, of course, scattered through his writings. In 1770 he told Samuel Cooper he was writing a paper on what we would now call "dominion status"; it seems to have been entitled "Every Lady of Genoa Is Not a Queen of Corsica"; see Verner W. Crane, "Franklin's Marginalia and the Lost 'Treatise' on Empire," *Papers of the Michigan Academy of Sciences, Arts and Letters* 42 (1957):163–176; idem, "Dr. Franklin's Plan for America," *Michigan Alumnus Quarterly Review* 44 (1958):322–333.

23. *Observations, Papers* IV, 225; to Lord Kames, 3 Jan. 1760, *Papers* IX, 7.

24. *Papers* IV, 74; *Writings* X, 107.

25. To Lord Kames, 25 Feb. 1767, *Papers* XIV, 69–70.

26. 2 Feb. 1774, *Papers* XXI, 75; 2 Mar. 1789, *Writings* X, 3; cf. *Papers* XVI, 108, XXI, 75.

27. 4 Apr. 1769, *Papers* XVI, 109.

28. *Autobiography*, 124.

29. To Thomas Percival, 15 Oct. 1773, *Papers* XX, 443.

30. To Cooper, 22 Apr. 1779, *Writings* VII, 293–294; cf. to Cushing, 10 June 1771, *Papers* XVIII, 122, 126.

31. To Hume, 27 Sept. 1760, *Papers* IX, 229; *Papers* XXI, 175—it should be noted that he reached this view at least two years before the publication of Adam Smith's *Wealth of Nations*.

32. Paul W. Conner describes Franklin's view as "free trade mercantilism," since it was a blend of contradictions: *Poor Richard's Politics* (New York: Oxford University Press, 1965), 74.

33. *Papers* XXI, 166; to Shirley, 22 Dec. 1754, *Papers* V, 449.

34. To Lord Kames, 25 Feb. 1767, *Papers* XIV, 65.

35. *Papers*, XIII, 220, XXI, 417; to William, 13 Mar. 1768, *Papers* XV, 74; *Causes of the American Discontents before 1768, Papers* XV, 12. Cf. Crane, "Franklin's Marginalia," 169.

8. One Community with One Interest

1. *Acts of the Privy Council, Colonial* (P.R.O.), IV, 741.

2. To Jackson, 16 Jan. 1764, *Papers* XI, 19; to Collinson, 30 April 1764, *Papers* XI, 181.

3. To Jackson, 25 June 1764, *Papers* XI, 237.

4. To Evans, 9 May 1766, *Papers* XIII, 268–269; Edmund S. Morgan, ed., *Prologue to Revolution: Sources and Documents on the Stamp Act Crisis, 1764–*

1766 (Chapel Hill: University of North Carolina Press, 1959), 62–69; *Papers* V, 449, XIII, 63.

5. Horace Walpole, *Memoirs of the Reign of George III*, 2 vols. (London, 1894), I, 172, II, 183.

6. To Thomson, 11 July 1765, *Papers* XII, 207; from Thomson, 24 Sept. 1765, *Papers* XII, 279.

7. To Hughes, 9 Aug. 1765, *Papers* XII, 235.

8. From Jane Mecom, 30 Dec. 1765, *Papers* XII, 418; from Hutchinson, 18 Nov. 1765, XII, 381; to Hall, 8 June 1765, XII, 171; from Hall, 6 Sept. 1765, XII, 256; from Hughes, 8–17 Sept. 1765, XII, 264.

9. *Papers* XII, 270, 299.

10. "Correspondence between William Strahan and David Hall," *P.M.H.B.* 10 (1886):96, 220.

11. Walpole, *Memoirs*, II, 140.

12. From William, 13 Nov. 1765, *Papers* XII, 369.

13. Verner W. Crane, *Benjamin Franklin's Letters to the Press, 1758–1775* (Chapel Hill: University of North Carolina Press, 1950), 30; *Papers* XII, 123, 132, 135, 413, XIII, 7–10, 118.

14. *Papers* XIII, 135–137. D. H. Watson, "Barlow Trecothick and Other Associates of Lord Rockingham during the Stamp Act Crisis" (M.A. thesis, Sheffield University, 1958); cf. Lawrence H. Gipson, "The Great Debate in the Whole House of Commons on the Stamp Act, 1766, as Reported by Nathaniel Ryder," *P.M.H.B.* 86 (1962):10, 41; W. T. Laprade, "The Stamp Act in British Politics," *A.H.R.* 35 (1930):735–757; and P. D. G. Thomas, ed., "Parliamentary Diaries of Nathaniel Ryder, 1764–67," *Camden Miscellany* 23, 4th ser., 7 (1969): 229–351.

15. To Thomson, 27 Sept. 1766, *Papers* XIII, 428.

16. To Debby, 6 April 1766, *Papers* XIII, 233.

17. 28 Nov. 1768, *Papers* XV, 273; to William, *Papers* XV, 15, 159; to John Ross, 14 May 1768, *Papers* XV, 129.

18. To Lord Kames, 25 Feb. 1767, *Papers* XIV, 65; to Galloway, 11 Oct. 1766, *Papers* XIII, 449.

19. *Papers* V, 441, 455; XIII, 136–139, 278n.

20. Garth to Committee of Correspondence, 6 June 1766, *South Carolina Historical and Genealogical Magazine* 29 (1927):233; *Papers* XIV, 117; P. Langford, *The First Rockingham Administration, 1765–1766* (London: Oxford University Press, 1973), 210.

21. 22 Feb. 1767, *Papers* XIV, 22.

22. To William, 13 March 1768, *Papers* XV, 75–76.

23. *Papers* XV, 75–76n8; cf. XIII, 156.

24. Verner W. Crane, "Certain Writings of Benjamin Franklin on the British Empire and the American Colonies," *Papers of the Bibliographical Society of America* 28, pt. 1 (1934): 14; *London Chronicle*, 5–7 Jan. 1768, *Papers* XV, 5–13; *Papers* XVI, 325.

25. To Galloway, 9 Jan. 1768, *Papers* XVI, 18.

26. To William, 2 July 1768, *Papers* XV, 160.

27. To George Whitefield, 1769, *Papers* XVI, 192.

28. To Charles Thomson, 18 March 1770, *Papers* XVII, 111.

29. *Papers* XIII, 220, XIII, 153, XV, 36–37, XVI, 277.

30. Marginalia, 1766, *Papers* XIII, 215, 1769, XVI, 276; Verner W. Crane, "Franklin's Marginalia, and the Lost 'Treatise' on Empire," *Papers of the Michigan Academy of Sciences, Arts and Letters* 42 (1957):163–176.

31. To Lord Kames, 25 Feb. 1767, *Papers* XIV, 65, 69; to Evans, 9 May 1766, *Papers* XIII, 269.

32. To Cooper, 8 June 1770, *Papers* XVII, 162–164.

33. Ibid.

34. *Public Advertiser,* 2 Jan. 1770, *Papers* XVII, 3–4.

35. *Papers* XIII, 424–425.

36. To William, 9 Oct. 1767, *Papers* XIV, 275.

37. To Samuel Cooper, 5 Feb. 1771, *Papers* XVIII, 24.

38. Additional MSS. 32861, f. 275, British Museum; T. P. Abernethy, *Western Lands and the American Revolution* (New York: Appleton Century, 1937), 111.

39. To William, 30 Jan. 1772, *Papers* XIX, 49; to Cushing, ibid., 21.

40. To William, 19 Aug. 1772, *Papers* XIX, 258–259.

41. To Mary Stevenson, 22 Sept. 1770, *Papers* XVII, 220–226.

42. To Debby, 14 Aug. 1772, *Papers* XVIII, 204–205.

43. James Boswell, *Private Papers,* ed. F. A. Pottle and G. Scott, 18 vols. (New Haven: Yale University Press, 1928–1934), VII, 193–194.

44. See note 7 to Chapter 5 and Verner W. Crane, "The Club of Honest Whigs," *W.M.Q.* 23 (1966):210–213. Eighteen pence in 1986 terms is about 30 cents.

45. To Benjamin Rush, 14 July 1773, *Papers* XX, 314.

46. To John Bartram, 9 July 1769, *Papers* XVI, 172; cf. *Papers* XX, 506; to Joshua Babcock, 13 Jan. 1772, *Papers* XIX, 7.

47. To Sally Bache, 29 Jan. 1772, *Papers* XIX, 46.

48. To Mary Stevenson, 14 Sept. 1767, *Papers* XIV, 253; to Cooper, 27 April and 30 Sept. 1769, *Papers* XVI, 118, 211.

49. 15 May 1771, *Papers* XVIII, 102–103.

50. To Cushing, 7 July 1773, *Papers* XX, 273.

51. To Cushing, 5 Jan. 1773, *Papers* XX, 10; 9 March 1773, ibid., 99.

52. To Cushing, 6 May 1773, *Papers* XX, 201.

53. *Papers* XX, 389–399.

54. Ibid., 413–418.

55. To William, 6 Oct. 1773, *Papers* XX, 438.

56. *Public Advertiser,* 16 March 1773, *Papers* XX, 121.

57. To Cushing, 2 Dec. 1772, *Papers* XIX, 412.

58. To Lord Howe, 20 July 1776, *Papers* XXII, 520.

59. *Papers* XXI, 37–70; Burke to General Charles Lee, *Letters and Papers of General Charles Lee* (New York: New York Historical Society Collections, 1874), I, 119–121.

60. To Cushing, 6 Oct. 1774, *Papers* XXI, 327–328.

61. To Galloway, 18 Feb. 1774, *Papers* XXI, 468, 507–508.

62. Ibid.

63. To William, 14 July 1773, *Papers* XX, 308.

64. Continental Congress to Franklin and others, 26 Oct. 1774, *Papers* XXI, 337; 5 Feb. 1775, *Papers* XXI, 477–478; Journal of Negotiations, 22 March 1775, *Papers* XXI, 583. Cf. to Lord Kames, 3 Jan. 1760 and 11 April 1767; and Worthington C. Ford et al., eds., *Journals of the Continental Congress, 1774–1789,* 34 vols. (Washington: Government Printing Office, 1904–1937), I, 63, 75.

65. To Galloway, 25 Feb. 1775, *Papers* XXI, 509.

66. *Papers* XXI, 596–600.

67. David Barclay to James Pemberton, *Papers* XXI, 531; Journal of Negotiations, *Papers* XXI, 596–597.

68. *Papers* XXI, 540–599; *Works of Edmund Burke,* 6 vols. (London: Bell, 1893), III, 43.

69. To Lord Howe, 20 July 1776, *Papers* XXII, 520.

70. Walpole, *Memoirs,* II, 213; L. B. Namier and John Brooke, *The History of Parliament: The House of Commons,* 3 vols. (London: H.M.S.O., 1964), II, 658–662.

71. To Charles Thomson, 5 Feb. 1775, *Papers* XXI, 475; cf. J. W. Copeland et al., eds., *The Correspondence of Edmund Burke,* 9 vols. (Chicago: University of Chicago Press, 1958–1970), III, 197; and Dixon Wecter, "Burke, Franklin and Samuel Petrie," *Huntington Library Quarterly* 3 (1939–40):315–318.

9. The Ungrateful Incendiary

1. To Jonathan Shipley, 7 July 1775, *Papers* XXII, 94; cf. to David Hartley, 8 May 1775, *Papers* XXII, 34.

2. Adams to James Warren, 22 April 1776, *Papers of John Adams* (Cambridge, Mass.: Harvard University Press, 1977–), IV, 135; to Abigail Adams, 17 June and 24 July 1775, in L. H. Butterfield, M. Friedlaender, and M.-J. Kline, eds., *The Book of Abigail and John* (Cambridge, Mass.: Harvard University Press, 1975), 89, 105; Edmund C. Barnett, *The Continental Congress* (New York: Macmillan, 1941), 46.

3. Adams to Warren, 24 July 1775, *Papers of John Adams,* III, 89; Josiah Quincy, *Memoir of the Life of Josiah Quincy, Jr.* (Boston, 1825), 478.

4. Franklin to Williams, 28 Sept. 1774, *Papers* XXI, 323; to Priestley, 7 July 1775, *Papers* XXII, 91; Adams to Warren, 24 July 1775, *Papers of John Adams,* III, 89.

5. Warren-Adams Letters, *Massachusetts Historical Society Collections* 72 (1917):82.

6. Clarence E. Carter, ed., *The Correspondence of General Thomas Gage,* 2 vols. (New Haven: Yale University Press, 1931–1933), II, 187–189, 192–193.

7. To Priestley, 3 Oct. 1775, *Papers* XXII, 218.

8. Charles Carroll, *Journal . . . during his visit to Canada in 1776* (Baltimore, 1845), 53; Gustave Lanctot, *Canada and the American Revolution,* trans. Margaret Cameron (Cambridge, Mass.: Harvard University Press, 1967), 140; cf. *Papers* XXII, 380–386, 413–432.

9. Louise Kellogg, "A Footnote to the Quebec Act," *Canadian Historical Review* 13 (1932):147–156; *Papers* XXII, 413.

10. "Committee of Secret Correspondence: Instructions to Silas Deane," 2 March 1776, *Papers* XXII, 371.

11. *Papers* XXI, 600–604; *Diary and Autobiography of John Adams,* ed. L. H. Butterfield, 4 vols. (Cambridge, Mass.: Harvard University Press, 1961), II, 235; to Abigail, 23 July 1775, *Book of Abigail and John,* 105.

12. To William, 28 Aug. 1767, *Papers* XIV, 244.

13. Adams to Horatio Gates, 23 March 1776, *Papers of John Adams,* IV, 59.

14. *The Papers of Thomas Jefferson,* ed. Julian P. Boyd et al. (Princeton: Princeton University Press, 1950–), XVIII, 169–170.

15. Jared Sparks, ed., *Works of Benjamin Franklin,* 10 vols. (Boston, 1836–1840), I, 407.

16. To Lord Howe, 20 July 1776, *Papers* XXII, 519.

17. From William, 3 Sept. 1771, *Papers* XVIII, 217; 18 Feb. and 7 Sept. 1774, *Papers* XXI, 107, 287.

18. To William, 16 Aug. 1784, *Writings* IX, 252.

19. To Strahan, 5 July 1775, *Papers* XXII, 85.

20. To Strahan, 3 Oct. 1775, *Papers* XXII, 218.

21. John Adams, "Thoughts on Government," *Papers of John Adams,* IV, 65–92.

22. Francis N. Thorpe, ed., *The Federal and State Constitutions and Other Organic Laws,* 7 vols. (House Documents, 1909), V, 3084–92; *Works of John Adams,* ed. C. F. Adams, 10 vols. (Boston: Little, Brown, 1850–1856), IV, 193–200; Franklin to Priestley, 21 Aug. 1784, *Writings* IX, 266; cf. Anon., "The Interest of America," in Peter Force, ed., *American Archives,* 4th ser., VI, 840–843; J. Paul Selsam, *The Pennsylvania Constitution of 1776: A Study in Revolutionary Democracy* (Philadelphia: University of Pennsylvania Press, 1936); Elisha P. Douglass, *Rebels and Democrats* (Chapel Hill: University of North Carolina Press, 1955); Charles L. Lincoln, *The Revolutionary Movement in Pennsylvania, 1760–1776* (Philadelphia: University of Pennsylvania, 1901); Robert L. Brunhouse, *The Counter-Revolution in Pennsylvania, 1776–1790* (Philadelphia: University of Pennsylvania Press, 1942).

The revolutionary movement in Pennsylvania has been a favorite area for doctoral research. Relevant dissertations in recent years include James B. Hunt, "The Crowd and the American Revolution: A Study of Urban Political Violence in Boston and Philadelphia, 1763–76" (University of Washington, 1973); Glyn W. Jacobson, "Politics, Parties and Propaganda in Pennsylvania, 1776–88" (University of Wisconsin, 1976); Robert F. Oaks, "Philadelphia Merchants and the American Revolution, 1765–76" (University of Southern California, 1970); Douglas Arnold, "Political Ideology and the Internal Revolution in Pennsylvania, 1776–90" (Princeton, 1976); and Richard A. Ryerson, "Leadership in Crisis: the Radical Committees of Philadelphia and the Coming of the Revolution in Pennsylvania, 1765–76; A Study in the Revolutionary Process" (Johns Hopkins, 1972).

23. *Writings* X, 57–58.

24 *Papers* XXII, 625–632; to Arthur Lee, 21 March 1777, *Papers* XXIII, 511.

25. George W. Corner, ed., *The Autobiography of Benjamin Rush* (Princeton: Princeton University Press, 1948), 149; *Papers* XXII, 625n.

10. Bonhomme Richard

1. *Papers* XIV, 244, 251–253.
2. Arthur Young, *Travels in France* (London: Dent, 1915), 77.
3. *Papers* XIV, 251; Young, *Travels in France*, 85.
4. Young, *Travels in France*, 329.
5. To Polly Stevenson, 14 Sept. 1767, *Papers* XIV, 251.
6. To Jane Mecom, 8 Dec. 1776, *Papers* XXIII, 34; to Quincy, *Writings* VII, 290; *Mémoires secrets,* quoted in A. O. Aldridge, *Franklin and His French Contemporaries* (New York: New York University Press, 1957), 194.
7. Bertier to Franklin, 27 Feb. 1769, *Papers* XVI, 56.
8. *Public Advertiser* (London), 16 Feb. 1774, in Verner W. Crane, *Benjamin Franklin's Letters to the Press, 1758–1775* (Chapel Hill: University of North Carolina Press, 1950), xxix; Stormont to Weymouth, 11 Dec. 1776, State Papers Foreign, S.P. 78/300 f. 382/1 P.R.O. For Stormont's surveillance of Franklin and his reports on him to Weymouth, see Edward E. Hale, Sr., and Edward E. Hale, Jr., *Franklin in France,* 2 vols. (1887; rpt. New York: Burt Franklin, 1970), II, 417–439.
9. Louis-Philippe, Comte de Ségur, *Mémoires ou souvenirs et anecdotes,* 3 vols. (Paris, 1824–1826), I, 116–117.
10. *Papers* XXIII, 244–246; *Writings* VIII, 589. The terms of the agreement were later to give rise to controversy. On 28 January 1777 it was set out as follows:

> 1. M. Franklin, et M. son petit fils payeront chacun la somme de six francs pour chaque Diner qu'ils feront ensemble ou separement chez M. De Chaumont. Ce qui fera, en supposant qu'ils y dînent tous les Jours 4380 p[a]r An.
>
> 2. Ils ne payeront ces 6 francs p[a]r Dîne, qu'autant qu'ils y dînent, comme de raison.
>
> 3. M. F. payera également Six livres, pour chaque Ami qu'il pouroit amèneroit [sic] dîner chez M. De Chaumont.
>
> 4. Quand M. Franklin aura du Monde, et qu'l voudra faire Table à part, Il payera en entier le montant du Diner, qu'il lui aura été pourvu par Mlle de Chaumont.
>
> 5. M. Franklin fournira le vin et autres Liqueurs, aux Diners qui se feront à part chez lui—et M. De Chaumont fournira les mêmes pour ceux qui se feront chez lui.

11. Duc de Croy, *Journal inédit,* 4 vols. (Paris: Flammarion, 1907), IV, 169; *Diary and Autobiography of John Adams,* ed. L. H. Butterfield (Cambridge, Mass.: Harvard University Press, 1961), IV, 109.
12. *Writings* IX, 470.
13. To Vaughan, *Writings* IX, 243–244; to Mrs. Stevenson, 25 Jan. 1779, *Writings* VII, 223; to Sally, *Writings* VII, 347. For the lifestyle at Passy, see Elkanah Watson, *Memoirs,* ed. Winslow Watson (New York, 1856); and Claude-

Anne Lopez, *Mon Cher Papa: Franklin and the Ladies of Paris* (New Haven: Yale University Press, 1966), 132.

14. To Jane, 5 Oct. 1777, *Letters of Benjamin Franklin and Jane Mecom* (Princeton: Princeton University Press, 1950), 191.

15. 5 May 1783, *Writings* IX, 39.

16. Capefigue quoted in Hale and Hale, *Franklin in France* I, 141; Adams, *Diary and Autobiography*, IV, 118.

17. To Sally, 3 June 1779, *Writings* VII, 347; Mme de Campan, *Mémoires sur la vie de Marie-Antoinette* (Paris, 1858), 177; Adams, *Diary and Autobiography*, III, 147; Aldridge, *Franklin and His French Contemporaries*, 126–130.

18. Hilliard d'Auberteuil, *Essais historiques et politiques sur les Anglo-Americans*, 2 vols. (Brussels, n.d.), II, 44–47.

19. *A View of the History of Great-Britain during the Administration of Lord North* (Dublin, 1782), 269; cf. Aldridge, *Franklin and His French Contemporaries*, 43, 211.

20. *Works of John Adams*, ed. C. F. Adams, 10 vols. (Boston: Little, Brown, 1850–1856), I, 663.

21. Du Portail quoted in C. Stedman, *History of the Origin, Progress and Termination of the American War* (Dublin, 1794), I, 433.

22. To the Congress, 4 Jan. 1776, *Papers* XXIII, 114; to Cooper, 1 May 1777, *Papers* XXIV, 6–7.

23. Vergennes's *Reflexions*, April 1776, in Henri Doniol, ed., *Histoire de la participation de la France à l'établissement des Etats-Unis d'Amérique*, 5 vols. (Paris, 1884), I, 243–249; cf. Vergennes to Gérard, 29 March 1778, in William C. Stinchcombe, *The American Revolution and the French Alliance* (Syracuse: Syracuse University Press, 1969), 27; Orville T. Murphy, "Charles Gravier de Vergennes: Profile of an Old Régime Diplomat," *Political Science Quarterly* 83 (Sept. 1968):400–418; Gerald Stourzh, *Benjamin Franklin and American Foreign Policy* (Chicago: University of Chicago Press, 1956), 136–140, 291.

24. To Arthur Lee, 21 March 1777, *Writings* VII, 35; to Adams, 2 Oct. 1780, *Writings* VIII, 146; for "militia diplomacy," see S. F. Bemis, *Diplomacy of the American Revolution* (Bloomington: Indiana University Press, 1957), 114; and James H. Hutson, *John Adams and the Diplomacy of the American Revolution* (Lexington: University of Kentucky Press, 1980), 150–155.

25. *Papers* XXII, 624–630.

26. *Papers* XXIII, 122.

27. To Ossun, in Doniol, ed., *Histoire*, II, 114–115; Archives du Ministère des affaires étrangères, Paris: Correspondance politique, Angleterre, vol. 521, f. 31, Espagne 583, f. 40–42; Franklin Papers, Yale, doc. 20882.

28. 18 March 1777, *Papers* XXIII, 503.

29. 1 and 14 March 1777, *Papers* XXIII, 501, 514.

30. 9 May 1777, *Papers* XXIV, 46–47.

31. To the Committee of Secret Correspondence, 26 May and 2 June 1777, *Papers* XXIV, 80, 107.

32. Catherine M. Prelinger, "Benjamin Franklin and the American Prisoners

of War in England during the American Revolution," *W.M.Q.*, 3rd ser., 32 (April 1975):268.

33. William Clark, *Ben Franklin's Privateers* (Baton Rouge: Louisiana State University Press, 1956); Lords of the Admiralty to Weymouth, 28 June 1777, C.O. 5: 140, f. 188, P.R.O.; William Clark, *Lambert Wickes: Sea Raider and Diplomat* (New Haven: Yale University Press, 1932), 88–109.

34. Gilbert Chinard, "Recollections," *P.A.P.S.* 94 (1960):221; Catherine M. Prelinger, "Less Lucky than Lafayette: A Note on French Applicants to Benjamin Franklin for Commissions in the American Army, 1776–1785," in Joyce D. Falk, ed., *Proceedings of the Fourth Meeting of the Western Society for French History* (Santa Barbara, Calif.: University of California, 1977), 263–271.

35. *Writings* VII, 36.

36. *Writings* VII, 27; but contrast *Papers* XXIII, 480.

37. As reported in the *London Evening Post*, 30 Oct. 1779, in Don C. Seitz, *Paul Jones: Bibliography* (New York: Dutton, 1917), 122.

38. To Dumas, *Writings* VII, 292; to Adams, *Writings* VIII, 332.

39. To Hutton, *Writings* VII, 100; to Hartley, 12 Feb. 1778, *Writings* VII, 103.

40. Francis Wharton, *Revolutionary Diplomatic Correspondence of the United States*, 6 vols. (Washington: Government Printing Office, 1889), II, 555; for Wharton, *Papers* XI, 187n. and Franklin Papers, Yale, docs. 22553, 24166; to Vaughan, 18 Sept. 1777, *Papers* XXIV, 539.

41. To Juliana Ritchie, 19 Jan. 1777, *Writings* VII, 11.

42. Julian Boyd, "Silas Deane: Death by a Kindly Teacher of Treason?" *W.M.Q.*, 3rd ser., 16 (1959):165–187; Wharton, *Revolutionary Diplomatic Correspondence*, I, 640–641; and Samuel F. Bemis, "British Secret Service and the French-American Alliance," *A.H.R.* 29 (1923–24):475–495.

43. For insights into this confused world see Jonathan Dull, "Franklin the Diplomat: The French Mission," *Transactions of the American Philosophical Society* 72 (1982), pts. 1 and 4; and Claude-Anne Lopez, "The Man Who Frightened Franklin," *P.M.H.B.* 106 (October 1982).

44. *New Jersey Gazette*, 2 Oct. 1777, quoted in James Parton, *Life and Times of Benjamin Franklin* (New York, 1864), II, 252.

45. *Auckland Papers*, MS 34414 f. 380; to Arthur Lee, 17 May 1778, *Writings* VII, 154; cf. T. Balch, ed., *Papers in Relation to the Case of Silas Deane* (Philadelphia, 1855); William B. Clark, "John the Painter," *P.M.H.B.* 63 (1939): 1–23.

46. Lee to Richard Lee, 12 Sept. 1778; Richard Henry Lee, *Life of Arthur Lee*, 2 vols. (Boston, 1829), II, 148; Arthur Lee to Franklin, 2 April 1778, *Writings* VII, 130.

47. To Arthur Lee, 3 and 4 April 1778, *Writings* VII, 132–138.

48. Adams, *Diary and Autobiography*, 16 April 1778, II, 302; 27 May 1778, IV, 118; 9 Feb. 1779, II, 346; 10 May 1779, II, 367; 2 June 1779, II, 390; 2 May 1783, III, 118; William B. Evans, "John Adams's Opinion of Benjamin Franklin," *P.M.H.B.* 92 (1968):220–238.

49. *Writings* VIII, 124, 127.

50. Kenneth Bowling, "Good-by 'Charle': The Lee-Adams Imbroglio and the

Political Demise of Charles Thomson, Secretary of Congress, 1774–1789," *P.M.H.B.* 100 (July 1976):335; Fred S. Rolater, "Charles Thomson, 'P.M.' of the U.S.," *P.M.H.B.* 101 (July 1977):322–348.

51. Lee, *Life of Arthur Lee,* II, 118; Franklin Papers, Yale, docs. 3115, 13306.

52. To Carmichael, 31 March 1780, *Writings* VIII, 52; to Reed, 19 March 1780, *Writings* VIII, 44.

53. To Hopkinson, 12 Sept. 1781, *Writings* VIII, 306.

54. Jefferson to James Madison, 28 Aug. 1789, *The Papers of Thomas Jefferson,* ed. Julian P. Boyd et al. (Princeton: Princeton University Press, 1950–), XV, 368.

55. P. J. G. Cabanis, *Oeuvres complètes,* 5 vols. (Paris, 1825), V, 230, 248, 269.

11. Plenipotentiary for the Congress

1. Edward E. Hale, Sr., and Edward E. Hale, Jr., *Franklin in France,* 2 vols. (1887; rpt. New York: Burt Franklin, 1970), I, 159; Samuel F. Bemis, *The Diplomacy of the American Revolution* (Bloomington: Indiana University Press, 1957), 58–62.

2. Hale and Hale, *Franklin in France,* I, 155–164.

3. Hunter Miller, *Treaties and Other International Acts of the U.S.* (Washington, D.C., 1931), 35–40. Cf. Bemis, *Diplomacy,* ch. 5 and bibliography; Henri Doniol, *Histoire de la participation de la France à l'établissement des Etats-Unis d'Amérique,* 5 vols. (Paris, 1884), II, 432.

4. Bemis, *Diplomacy,* ch. 7.

5. To Arthur Lee, 21 March 1777, *Writings* VII, 35; to Cooper, 1 May 1777, *Writings* VII, 56.

6. To Lafayette, 22 March 1777, *Writings* VII, 269–271.

7. To Jones, 22 April 1779. For Jones see Samuel E. Morison, *John Paul Jones: A Sailor's Biography* (London: Faber and Faber, 1959); Don Seitz, *Paul Jones: His Exploits in English Seas and Bibliography* (New York: Dutton, 1917), shows how the legend grew.

8. To Jones, 28 April 1779, *Writings* VII, 299.

9. 12 March 1781, *Writings* VIII, 220.

10. H. P. Johnston, ed., *Correspondence and Public Papers of John Jay,* 4 vols. (New York, 1890–1893); R. B. Morris, *The Peacemakers* (New York: Harper and Row, 1965), ch. 13; Jonathan Dull, "Franklin the Diplomat: The French Mission," *Transactions of the American Philosophical Society* 72 (1982):58–59. Cf. Gerald S. Graham, *British Policy and Canada, 1774–1791: A Study in 18th Century Trade Policy* (London: Longman's, 1930); and Bemis, *Diplomacy,* chs. 17, 18.

11. *Diary and Autobiography of John Adams,* ed. L. H. Butterfield, 4 vols. (Cambridge, Mass.: Harvard University Press, 1961), Dec. 1779, IV, 218; to Jay, 2 Oct. 1780, *Writings* VIII, 144.

12. To Hartley, 26 Oct. 1778, *Writings* VII, 196; to Hutton, 1 Feb. 1778, *Writings* VII, 100.

13. Oswald to Shelburne, 10 July 1782, in Lord John Russell, *Memories and Correspondence of Charles James Fox,* 4 vols. (London, 1853–1857), IV, 239–241; to Vaughan, 11 July 1782, *Writings* VIII, 566; to Livingston, 28 June 1782, *Writings* VIII, 536.

14. Bemis, *Diplomacy,* chs. 8, 13; S. F. Bemis, *The Hussey-Cumberland Mission and American Independence* (Princeton: Princeton University Press, 1931), 118; Francis Wharton, *Revolutionary Diplomatic Correspondence of the United States,* 6 vols. (Washington: Government Printing Office, 1889), III, 406, 503, 814, 854, and V, 544–566; Lord Fitzmaurice, *Life of William, Earl of Shelburne,* 2nd ed., 2 vols. (London, 1912), II, 128–136; Sir John Fortescue, ed., *The Correspondence of King George III,* 6 vols. (London: Macmillan, 1927–1928), VI, 44, 45; Morris, *The Peacemakers,* ch. 9.

15. To Livingston, 12 Aug. 1782, *Writings* VIII, 580.

16. *Writings* VIII, 470–473; Hale and Hale, *Franklin in France,* II, 169; Bemis, *Diplomacy,* 230.

17. For Oswald and Shelburne, Foreign Office Papers, July 12, 1782, F.O. 95/511, 27/2; "Journal of the Negotiation for Peace with Great Britain," 9 May 1782, *Writings* VIII, 459–560; Russell, *Memories and Correspondence of Fox,* IV, 293–341; Bemis, *Diplomacy,* ch. 15; Vincent Harlow, *The Founding of the Second British Empire,* 2 vols. (London: Longman's, 1952), I, 238, 251, 268–273.

18. George III to Lord North, 26 March 1778, in Fortescue, ed., *Correspondence of King George III,* IV, 80.

19. Adams, *Diary and Autobiography,* III, 71, IV, 83.

20. Ibid., III, 38.

21. To Livingston, 22 July 1783, *Writings* IX, 61.

22. Adams, *Diary and Autobiography,* III, 82; Morris, *The Peacemakers,* 357.

23. W. A. S. Hewins, ed., *Whitefoord Papers* (Oxford, 1898), 187.

24. From Vergennes, 15 Dec. 1782; to Vergennes, 17 Dec. 1782, *Writings* VIII, 640–641.

25. Vergennes to Rayneval, 12 Dec. 1782, and to La Luzerne, 21 July 1783, in Morris, *The Peacemakers,* 383.

26. Louis-Philippe, Comte de Ségur, *Mémoires ou souvenirs et anecdotes* (Paris, 1824–1826), I, 25, quoted in Jonathan R. Dull, "France and the American Revolution Seen as Tragedy," in Ronald Hoffman and Peter J. Albert, eds., *Diplomacy and Revolution: The Franco-American Alliance of 1778* (Charlottesville: University of Virginia Press, 1981).

27. Morris, *The Peacemakers,* 459.

28. To Price, 6 Feb. 1780, *Writings* VIII, 9.

29. *Writings* IX, 46; to Polly Hewson, 27 Jan. 1783, *Writings* IX, 11.

30. To Priestley, 8 Feb. 1780, *Writings* VIII, 10; to Banks, 27 July 1783, *Writings* IX, 74–75.

31. To Banks, 30 Aug. 1783, *Writings* IX, 79–84; to Ingenhouse, 16 Jan. 1784, *Writings* IX, 155.

32. Baron von Grimm, *Correspondance littéraire, philosophique et critique,* 16 vols. (Paris, 1877–1882), XIII, 349; to Banks, *Writings* IX, 114.

33. To La Sabrière de la Condamine, 19 March 1784, *Writings* IX, 182–183; also 268, 271.

34. 26 Jan. 1784, *Writings* IX, 162–163.

35. To William, 16 Aug. 1784, *Writings* IX, 252.

36. Polly Hewson to Franklin, 25 Oct. 1784, in Whitfield J. Bell, "'All Clear Sunshine': New Letters of Franklin and Mary Stevenson," *P.A.P.S.* 100 (Dec. 1956):533.

37. *Writings* VII, 204 (the original is in French).

38. *Letters of Mrs. Adams,* ed. C. F. Adams, 2nd ed., 2 vols. (Boston: Little, Brown, 1840), II, 55–56; cf. *Writings* X, 439.

39. To Eliza Hubbard Partridge, 11 Oct. 1779, *Writings* VII, 393.

40. To Mme Brillon, 10 March 1784, *Writings* X, 437; from Mme Brillon, *Writings* X, 429.

41. See the facsimile edition of *The Bagatelles from Passy* (New York: Eakins Press, 1967); Richard Amacher, ed., *Franklin's Wit and Folly: The Bagatelles* (New Brunswick, N.J.: Rutgers University Press, 1953); A. O. Aldridge, "The Bagatelles," in *Franklin and His French Contemporaries* (New York: New York University Press, 1957), 159–187; and for a superb description of Franklin's mistresses of the salons, Claude-Anne Lopez, *Mon Cher Papa: Franklin and the Ladies of Paris* (New Haven: Yale University Press, 1966). Jefferson, *Writings,* 20 vols. (Washington, 1905 ed.), VIII, 129; Carl Becker, "Benjamin Franklin," *D.A.B.* VI, 597.

42. *Writings* X, 456–471; cf. IX, 363–372.

43. *Papers* XXIII, 102; to Vaughan, 2 Nov. 1789, *Writings* X, 50.

44. *Writings* X, 116–122.

45. To Le Roy, 13 Nov. 1789, *Writings* X, 68–69.

46. 2 Jan. 1790, in Aldridge, *Franklin and His French Contemporaries,* 91.

47. C. A. Sainte-Beuve, *Portraits of the Eighteenth Century,* trans. K. P. Wormeley (New York: Ungar, 1964), 323, 327.

48. To Jonathan Williams, 15 June 1781, *Writings* VIII, 271.

49. T. P. Abernethy, "The Franklin-Lee Imbroglio," *North Carolina Historical Review* (1938):52; to Huntington, 4 March and 31 May 1780, *Writings* VIII, 23–24, 72.

50. Jonathan R. Dull, *The French Navy and American Independence* (Princeton: Princeton University Press, 1975), 345–350; idem, "Franklin the Diplomat," 50; cf. Robert D. Harris, "French Finances and the American War, 1777–1783," *Journal of Modern History* 48 (1976):233–358; Vergennes to La Luzerne, 19 Feb. 1781, in Doniol, *Histoire,* IV, 583; to Vergennes, 20 Nov. 1781, *Writings* VIII, 328–329.

51. *Writings* VII, 357–362. Dubourg printed the "Morals of Chess" in *Le Journal de Paris;* they were also published by Richard Twiss in London in 1787; and a facsimile, with a preface by Whitfield Bell, was published in Philadelphia by the American Philosophical Society in 1974.

52. Richard Henry Lee, *Life of Arthur Lee,* 2 vols. (Boston, 1829), I, 346.

12. Patriarch of Free Men

1. *Writings* VIII, 603–606; cf. IX, 177.
2. *Writings* X, 116.
3. Arthur T. Prescott, *Drafting the Federal Constitution: A Re-arrangement of Madison's Notes* (Baton Rouge: Louisiana State University Press, 1941), 282. Besides Prescott, I have used three basic sources for the debates in the Constitutional Convention: James Madison, *Notes of Debates in the Federal Convention of 1787*, with an introduction by Adrienne Koch (Athens: Ohio University Press, 1966); Max Farrand, *Records of the Federal Convention of 1787*, 4 vols. (New Haven: Yale University Press, 1937); and Jonathan Elliot, *Debates in the State Conventions*, 5 vols. (Philadelphia: Lippincott, 1941). I cite them hereafter by author's name alone.
4. Farrand I, 450–452; Elliot V, 253.
5. Prescott, 594–596; Elliot V, 145.
6. Prescott, 216; Farrand II, 204–205; Elliot V, 152, 387.
7. Elliot V, 143, 399; Farrand II, 236–237.
8. Prescott, 311; Elliot V, 266.
9. Farrand II, 249.
10. Prescott, 784; Farrand II, 641–643.
11. Verner W. Crane, "Benjamin Franklin on Slavery and American Liberties," *P.M.H.B.* 62 (Jan. 1938):9; *Writings* X, 86–91.
12. *Writings* IX, 483; Pierce quoted in Prescott, 28.
13. W. P. Cutler and Julia Cutler, *Life, Journals and Correspondence of Rev. Manasseh Cutler*, 2 vols. (Cincinnati, 1888), I, 267.
14. To Jane Mecom, 21 Sept. 1786, *Writings* X, 494.
15. To Whatley, 23 May 1785; to Shipley, 24 Feb. 1786.
16. To Polly Hewson, 6 May 1786, *Writings* IX, 512.
17. *Writings* X, 494.
18. *Pennsylvania Gazette*, 21 April 1790; Hardwicke papers, vol. 308, Additional MS. 35656 f. 6, British Library.
19. *Papers* I, 111. See L. H. Butterfield, "Benjamin Franklin's Epitaph," *New Colophon* 3 (1950):9–30; P. L. Ford, *The Many-Sided Franklin* (New York: Century Co., 1899), 262; Charles J. Smith, *Historical and Literary Curiosities* (London: Bohn and Co., 1840), plate 18; A. O. Aldridge, *Franklin and His French Contemporaries* (New York: New York University Press, 1957), 212–234.

13. Father of All the Yankees?

1. *Works of John Adams*, ed. C. F. Adams, 10 vols. (Boston: Little, Brown, 1850–1856), I, 660–664; William Cobbett, *Porcupine's Works* (London, 1801), IV, 32–33; A. O. Aldridge, *Franklin and His French Contemporaries* (New York: New York University Press, 1957), 136.
2. Lewis B. Walker, ed., *The Burd Papers: Extracts from Chief Justice William*

Allen's Letter Book (Pottsville, Pa., 1897), 57, 62; William Carlos Williams, *In the American Grain* (New York: New Directions, 1925), 153.

3. James Boswell, *Private Papers*, ed. F. A. Pottle and G. Scott, 18 vols. (New Haven: Yale University Press, 1928–1934), VII, 193, VIII, 111; to William, 16 April 1768, *Papers* XV, 98–99.

4. To Fothergill, 14 March 1764, *Papers* XI, 101; to Jane, 30 Dec. 1770, *Papers* XVII, 315; to Priestley, 7 June 1782, *Writings* VIII, 451–452.

5. 28 June 1756, *Papers* VI, 463; 19 April 1757, *Papers* VII, 190.

6. Nov. 1756, *Papers* VII, 17. For the most vivid portrait of this aspect of the man, see Claude-Anne Lopez and Eugenia W. Herbert, *The Private Franklin* (New York: Norton, 1975).

7. To Polly Hewson, 27 Jan. 1783, *Writings* IX, 12–13.

8. Verner W. Crane, *Franklin and a Rising People* (Boston: Little, Brown, 1954), 205.

9. *Autobiography*, 211.

10. *Writings* IX, 572–573.

11. 28 Sept. 1768, *Papers* XV, 216–218.

12. To Sarah Bache, 26 Jan. 1784, *Writings* IX, 166; *Writings* X, 493.

SELECTED BIBLIOGRAPHY

Primary Sources

Bailyn, Bernard, ed. *Pamphlets of the American Revolution, 1750–1776*, vol. I: *1750–1765*. Cambridge, Mass.: Harvard University Press, 1965.

Bell, Whitfield, ed. *"All Clear Sunshine": New Letters of Franklin and Mary Stevenson Hewson. Papers of the American Philosophical Society* 100 (Dec. 1956).

Crary, Catherine, ed. *The Price of Liberty: Tory Writings from the Revolutionary Era*. New York: McGraw-Hill, 1973.

Fortescue, Sir John. *The Correspondence of George III, 1760–1783.* 6 vols. London: Macmillan, 1927–28.

Franklin, Benjamin. *The Autobiography of Benjamin Franklin.* Ed. L. W. Labaree et al. New Haven: Yale University Press, 1964.

———— *Benjamin Franklin's Autobiographical Writings.* Ed. Carl Van Doren. New York: Viking, 1945.

———— *Benjamin Franklin's Letters to the Press.* Ed. Verner W. Crane. Chapel Hill: University of North Carolina Press, 1950.

———— *Benjamin Franklin's Memoirs.* Parallel text edition, ed. Max Farrand. Berkeley: University of California Press, 1949.

———— *The Papers of Benjamin Franklin.* Ed. L. W. Labaree and Whitfield Bell et al. (to vol. 14); W. B. Willcox et al. (vol. 15–). New Haven: Yale University Press, 1959–.

———— *The Writings of Benjamin Franklin.* Ed. Albert H. Smyth. 10 vols. New York: Macmillan, 1905–1907.

Hays, I. Minis, ed. *Calendar of the Papers of Benjamin Franklin.* 5 vols. Philadelphia: American Philosophical Society, 1908.

Hyneman, Charles S., and Donald S. Lutz, eds. *American Political Writing during the Founding Era, 1760–1805.* 2 vols. Indianapolis: Liberty Press, 1983.

Madison, James. *Notes of Debates in the Federal Convention of 1787 Reported by James Madison.* With an introduction by Adrienne Koch. Athens: Ohio University Press, 1966.

Morgan, Edmund, ed. *Prologue to Revolution: Sources and Documents on the Stamp Act Crisis, 1764–1766.* Chapel Hill: University of North Carolina Press, 1959.

Namier, L. B. *Additions and Corrections to Sir John Fortescue's Correspondence of George III.* Vol. I. London: Macmillan, 1937.

Oliver, Andrew, ed. *The Journal of Samuel Curwen, Loyalist.* 2 vols. Cambridge, Mass.: Harvard University Press, 1972.

Palmer, J. Gregory. *A Bibliography of Loyalist Source Material in the United States, Canada, and Great Britain.* Westport, Conn.: Meckler, 1982.

Prescott, Arthur T. *Drafting the Federal Constitution.* Baton Rouge: Louisiana State University Press, 1941.

Roelker, William Greene, ed. *Benjamin Franklin and Catharine Ray Greene: Their Correspondence, 1755–1790.* Philadelphia: American Philosophical Society, 1949.

Sedgwick, Romney, ed. *The Letters of George III to Lord Bute.* London: Macmillan, 1939.

Stifler, J. M., ed. *"My Dear Girl."* New York: George Doran Co., 1927.

Van Doren, Carl, ed. *The Letters of Benjamin Franklin and Jane Mecom.* Princeton: Princeton University Press, 1950.

————, ed. *Letters and Papers of Benjamin Franklin and Richard Jackson, 1753–1785.* Philadelphia: American Philosophical Society, 1947.

Secondary Sources

Aldridge, A. O. *Benjamin Franklin and Nature's God.* Durham, N.C.: Duke University Press, 1967.

———— *Franklin and His French Contemporaries.* New York: New York University Press, 1957.

Andrews, Charles. *The Colonial Period of American History.* Volume IV: *England's Commercial and Colonial Policy.* New Haven: Yale University Press, 1964.

Bailyn, Bernard. *The Ideological Origins of the American Revolution.* Cambridge, Mass.: Belknap Press of Harvard University Press, 1967.

———— *The Ordeal of Thomas Hutchinson.* London: Allen Lane, 1974.

Becker, Carl. *The Heavenly City of the Eighteenth-Century Philosophers.* New Haven: Yale University Press, 1932.

Bemis, S. F. *The Diplomacy of the American Revolution.* Bloomington: Indiana University Press, 1957.

Boorstin, Daniel. *The Americans: The Colonial Experience.* New York: Random House, 1958.

Bridenbaugh, Carl, and Jessica Bridenbaugh. *Rebels and Gentlemen: Philadelphia in the Age of Franklin.* New York: Oxford University Press, 1962.

Brooke, John. *King George III.* London: Constable, 1972.

Burnett, Edmund C. *The Continental Congress.* New York: Macmillan, 1941.

Cappon, Lester. *Atlas of Early American History: The Revolutionary Era, 1760–1790.* Princeton: Princeton University Press, 1976.

Cohen, I. Bernard. *Benjamin Franklin's Experiments.* Cambridge, Mass.: Harvard University Press, 1941.

Conner, Paul. *Poor Richard's Politicks: Benjamin Franklin and His New American Order.* New York: Oxford University Press, 1965.

Crane, Verner. *Benjamin Franklin and a Rising People.* Boston: Little, Brown, 1954.

Dull, Jonathan. *Franklin the Diplomat: The French Mission. American Philosophical Society Transactions* 72, part 1 (1982).

Ferguson, E. James. *The Power of the Purse: The History of American Public Finance, 1776–1790.* Chapel Hill: University of North Carolina Press, 1961.

Gipson, Lawrence H. *The British Empire before the American Revolution.* 15 vols. New York: Knopf, 1939–1969.

Hanna, William S. *Benjamin Franklin and Pennsylvania Politics.* London: Oxford University Press, 1964.

Haraszti, Zoltan. *John Adams and the Prophets of Progress.* Cambridge, Mass.: Harvard University Press, 1952.

Hindle, Brooke. *The Pursuit of Science in Revolutionary America.* Chapel Hill: University of North Carolina Press, 1956.

Hutson, James. *John Adams and the Diplomacy of the American Revolution.* Lexington: University of Kentucky Press, 1980.

Jensen, Merrill. *The Articles of Confederation, 1774–1781.* Madison: University of Wisconsin Press, 1948.

Kammen, Michael G. *A Rope of Sand: The Colonial Agents, British Politics, and the American Revolution.* Ithaca: Cornell University Press, 1968.

Lopez, Claude-Anne. *Mon Cher Papa: Franklin and the Ladies of Paris.* New Haven: Yale University Press, 1966.

Miller, Perry. *The New England Mind: From Colony to Province.* 2 vols. Cambridge, Mass.: Harvard University Press, 1953.

Morison, Samuel E. *John Paul Jones.* Boston: Little, Brown, 1959.

Morris, Richard B. *The Peacemakers and American Independence.* New York: Harper and Row, 1965.

Namier, L. B. *The Structure of Politics at the Accession of George III.* London: Macmillan, 1929.

Nolan, J. Bennett. *Benjamin Franklin in Scotland and Ireland, 1759 and 1771.* Philadelphia: University of Pennsylvania Press, 1956.

Parton, James. *The Life and Times of Benjamin Franklin.* 2 vols. Boston: Houghton Mifflin, 1864.

Randall, Willard. *A Little Revenge.* Boston: Little, Brown, 1984.

Robbins, Caroline. *The Eighteenth Century Commonwealthman.* Cambridge, Mass.: Harvard University Press, 1959.

Sellers, Charles Coleman, ed. *Benjamin Franklin in Portraiture.* New Haven: Yale University Press, 1962.

Stourzh, Gerald. *Benjamin Franklin and American Foreign Policy.* Chicago: University of Chicago Press, 1954.

Tourtellot, Arthur Bernon. *Benjamin Franklin: The Shaping of Genius: The Boston Years.* Garden City, N.Y.: Doubleday, 1977.

Van Doren, Carl. *Benjamin Franklin.* New York: Viking Press, 1938.

Weber, Max. *The Protestant Ethic and the Spirit of Capitalism.* Trans. Talcott Parsons. London: Allen & Unwin, 1930.

Wood, Gordon. *The Creation of the American Republic.* Chapel Hill: University of North Carolina Press, 1961.

INDEX